P9-BIJ-337

ARS MEDICA

This exhibition is made possible by

SmithKline Beckman Corporation

and is supported by generous grants from

the National Endowment for the Humanities and

The Pew Memorial Trust.

ARS MEDICA
Art, Medicine, and the Human Condition

Prints, Drawings, and Photographs from
the Collection of the Philadelphia Museum of Art
Selected and Organized by Diane R. Karp

Catalogue by Diane R. Karp with contributions
by Ben Bassham, Mimi Cazort, Martha Chahroudi,
Frima Fox Hofrichter, John Ittmann, Ellen Jacobowitz,
Ann Percy, Kimerly Rorschach, Darrel Sewell,
Aaron Sheon, and Faith H. Zieske

Philadelphia Museum of Art

Distributed by the University of Pennsylvania Press

Cover: Detail of *The Sun: Tarot XIX,* by Jess (no. 20)

Designed by Katy Homans
Composition by John C. Meyer & Son, Inc., Philadelphia
Printed by Meriden-Stinehour Press, Meriden, Connecticut

Library of Congress Cataloging-in-Publication Data

Philadelphia Museum of Art.
Ars medica, art, medicine, and the human condition.

Catalogue of an exhibition to be held at Philadelphia Museum of Art, Sept.–Oct. 1985.
Bibliography: p.
Includes index.
1. Art and medicine—Exhibitions.
2. Philadelphia Museum of Art—Exhibitions.
I. Karp, Diane R., 1948– . II. Title.
N8223.P5 1985 760'.044961'074014811 85-19154
ISBN 0-8122-7953-0 (University of Pennsylvania Press)

Distributed by the
University of Pennsylvania Press
Blockley Hall, 418 Service Drive
Philadelphia, PA 19104

CONTENTS

PREFACE

The late Carl Zigrosser, former Curator of Prints at the Museum, wrote that the evolving Ars Medica Collection of his department represented "a happy conjunction of the Fine Arts with the Healing Arts." In 1980, upon the occasion of an exhibition drawn from the collection, Jean Sutherland Boggs, then Director of the Museum, noted that "art and medicine share the same patron saint, Saint Luke. They also share curiosity, the need to penetrate reality, and the desire to ameliorate the life of man." The Museum's tradition of collecting works of art related to the history of medicine has flourished over the decades, supported with extraordinary generosity by SmithKline Beckman Corporation in a sequence of grants beginning in 1948. The initiative taken by this eminent Philadelphia-based firm in funding acquisitions of important objects and exhibitions that have traveled across the United States, Europe, and Mexico is impressive, and appropriate in the context of a well-established history of interaction between the visual arts and the medical sciences in this city. Thomas Eakins's overwhelming portrait of a great surgeon in *The Gross Clinic*, painted from studies made at Jefferson Medical College, where the painting now hangs, and William Rush's ingenious anatomical models, carved in wood for the use of medical students at the University of Pennsylvania and now preserved at the Wistar Institute, testify to the intense interest on the part of Philadelphia artists in the medical advances of their day.

The present exhibition is the fourth and most ambitious of a series begun in 1952. Launched by a splendid multiyear grant from SmithKline in 1982, it reveals a scope of acquisition broadened to encompass photographs and works by contemporary artists. In the eloquent muscle figures standing against landscape backgrounds that illustrate Andreas Vesalius's sixteenth-century *De Humani Corporis Fabrica* (nos. 8b–e) and in the anatomical forms emerging from a flux of ancient and contemporary images in the monumental collage of 1960 by the California artist Jess (no. 20), the artist's sense of the innate mystery and beauty in the precise structure of human anatomy is equally vivid.

The Ars Medica Collection as it now stands reflects years of thoughtful growth guided by Carl Zigrosser and his successor Kneeland McNulty. As Assistant Curator for the Ars Medica Collection over the past three years and organizer of this exhibition, Diane R. Karp has sought out and presented for acquisition splendid works of art ranging from the elegant mid-sixteenth-century tour de force of etching *Pyramid of Six Men* (no. 9) to the powerful photographic narrative of the progress of a cancer patient by Eugene Richards (nos. 72a–d). Fifty-six of the objects in the exhibition were acquired during her tenure, and their diversity attests to her range of interests and enthusiasm. Ellen Jacobowitz, Ann Percy, and Martha Chahroudi, curators responsible respectively for prints, drawings, and photographs in the department, collaborated actively in the acquisition process and contributed to the shaping of the exhibition and to the catalogue. The staff of the Print Department as a whole and a great many colleagues within the Museum also worked hard to bring this project to realization. We are most grateful to the contributing authors and to the consultants Diana Long Hall, Christine A. Ruggere, and Charles Rosenberg, who gave us the benefit of their expertise in a variety of specialized fields.

The exhibition is accompanied in Philadelphia by a wealth of programs at the Museum and in sister institutions around the city, ably coordinated by Cheryl McClenney. A generous grant from the National Endowment for the Humanities has made it possible to bring the ideas and images in this complex project to a wide audience. The Pew Memorial Trust has contributed to the exhibition, as it has to so many of the important programs of the Museum over the past years. Above all, this exhibition proves an occasion to celebrate collaboration: between artist and physician, historian of art and historian of medicine, and the enlightened generosity of a Philadelphia company and the international interests and mission of a great museum.

Anne d'Harnoncourt
The George D. Widener Director

INTRODUCTION

Since the early 1920s the Philadelphia Museum of Art has been collecting prints, drawings, and illustrated books related to the history of medicine, but the establishment of a major collection of works of art described as "Ars Medica" was given impetus by the late Carl Zigrosser, Curator of Prints at the Museum from 1941 to 1963. In 1948 a grant from the SmithKline corporation initiated an acquisition fund for the Department of Prints and supported the first Ars Medica exhibition in 1952. During the intervening years the Museum's holdings of Ars Medica have grown in size and in quality by purchase with subsequent grants from SmithKline Beckman and by gift from various sources, reflecting the institution's ongoing interest in the complex interrelationship between the history of man, the history of medicine, and the visual arts. The Museum's collection in this field currently spans nearly six centuries, from 1400 to the present, and includes over 1,100 prints, drawings, photographs, and rare books.

The recent inclusion of photographs in the collection has added an important dimension to the exploration of ways in which the visual arts and the study and practice of medicine interrelate. The photographic process, revered from the time of its invention for its truth to nature, was used both as an art form and as a technique for scientific investigation. Dr. Hugh Welch Diamond, a nineteenth-century English physician-photographer, placed his art in the service of medicine, recording human physiognomy for documentation and as an aid in the treatment of the female patients at the Surrey County Lunatic Asylum during the 1850s. His beautiful portrait of depression (no. 81) brings together the developing art of photography and the developing science of psychiatry.

During the past three decades since the Museum's first exhibition devoted to this theme there has been a renewal of interest on the part of contemporary artists in figurative concerns and in a narrative, sometimes allegorical or moralizing approach to themes of health and sickness in the modern world. This gives an exciting immediacy to many recent additions to the collection, making it freshly relevant for a contemporary audience.

Important repositories for prints, drawings, photographs, and rare books related to the history of medicine exist in the United States and Europe primarily within university or medical libraries or as collections begun by individual physicians. Much relevant material can also be found in the print rooms and drawing collections of great museums, but the Philadelphia Museum of Art is distinguished in having such an important group of thematically related objects chosen for their aesthetic quality as well as for their content. This allows for an exhibition of works of art drawn from the Museum's collection, in which the significance of the phenomena and the concepts presented is matched by the capacity of the objects and the artists to convey that significance.

The focus of this presentation is a group of outstanding images by important artists from Master E. S. (no. 95) to Robert Rauschenberg (no. 21), which, in a vast array of mediums, explore Ars Medica subject matter from a variety of points of view. Giovanni Domenico Tiepolo's charming ink drawing records the eighteenth-century itinerant tooth puller at his work (no. 37); some one hundred and fifty years later, W. Eugene Smith photographed the everyday lives of a doctor (nos. 46a,b) and a nurse-midwife in rural America (nos. 47 and 92). Albrecht Dürer's handsome woodcut from "The Life of the Virgin" (no. 88) not only illustrates the New Testament story but also delineates for posterity a birthing scene typical of the sixteenth century. Thomas Eakins's dispassionate studies of his own posture and that of two of his students (nos. 18a–d) served as anatomical aids in his training of artists, while Francesco Clemente visually dissects his own body to present a powerful image of introspection (no. 22).

Using such remarkably varied objects as the points in an historical matrix, this exhibition draws upon aspects of two distinct disciplines (the history of art and the history of medicine) in order to gain a broader perspective on the works of art themselves and, in turn, an expanded insight into the times during which they were created. In some instances, direct collaboration between artist and physician produced masterpieces of aesthetic and scientific importance, such as the superbly illustrated anatomical treatises of Vesalius (see nos. 8a–g). In others, an artist's record of village life (see nos. 27 and 34a,b) or his vision of the sufferings of a saint (see nos. 73, 74, and 76) illuminates contemporary medical practice or attitudes toward madness and hallucination. The visual arts and medicine have other profound relationships that govern them both. The trained predisposition of our vision sometimes controls what we see by determining which details register and which go unnoticed.

No single exhibition devoted to this theme can include all the most ideal objects in the history of art or represent all crucial stages in the history of medicine, and a full chronology is not attempted here in either field. Rather the exhibition serves as a compendium of works whose collective presence and juxtaposition afford a sense of man's own understanding of the human condition in its myriad states of health and illness, from birth to death, transmuted by each individual artist's particular grasp of technical and imagistic skills. A number of these images provide a modern viewer with visual records of medical attitudes, tools, and practices that may not have survived in written form. In some cases these were simply scenes of their times recorded by artists, while in others the artist's intention was accurate documentation of current levels of knowledge in order to convey it to scientists and other artists. The more we know of the ways in which a society treated its sick and disabled, viewed the events of birth and death, and understood the structure and function of the human body, the greater is our insight into that society's view of itself and its place in the world. The works of art in the exhibition offer compelling evidence of concerns shared by artists and physicians in unraveling the mysteries of the human body and observing the vicissitudes of human life.

The exhibition and catalogue have been divided into four sections: Anatomy; Healers; Disease, Disability, and Madness; and The Cycle of Life. Within each section, the objects are considered thematically in chronological order.

ANATOMY

The gaining of knowledge about the human body, for all its ready availability for study, seems to have been a slow process, in which the artist and the physician have often collaborated to make significant advances. Medieval medicine was centered not in laboratories or hospitals but in universities and libraries, and dogma rather than observation was the teacher. Although in the fourteenth century public dissection was no longer a rare occurrence, anatomy was not a field of research or a science of discovery but a ceremony aimed at verifying and illustrating the texts and treatises of the ancient authorities or providing documentary support for forensic purposes.

In his desire to comprehend the mechanisms of the world, Renaissance man moved in two seemingly contradictory directions: He looked backward, to the authority of classical texts, and forward, to the discoveries he could make through his own observations and intellectual investigation.

Dedication to the writings of the ancients was a central element of Renaissance Humanism. The writings of the second-century A.D. Greek physician Galen, the most influential of the ancient medical authors, had been abstracted and digested by scholars of late antiquity and Islam and carried forward as the authority on medicine into the medieval era. Other early authors were also seminal to Renaissance medical practice, and each new revelation of a previously unknown classical work was hailed as a major achievement, whether it was the 1426 discovery of the encyclopedic treatise *De Medicina* by the second-century A.D. writer Celsus or the publication of Latin translations of Greek medical or anatomical texts.

The fifteenth and sixteenth centuries were also characterized by growing reliance on direct observation and a gradual move toward the understanding of experiment as a carefully planned and reproducible test, whether of the theories of the ancients or of the newly formulated theories of anatomy, medicine, and other sciences. But early texts continued to be revered and followed long after empirical knowledge was to prove them false, and the growing conflict between received wisdom from the ancient authorities and observable reality was one of the greatest difficulties that Renaissance studies of anatomy and medicine had to overcome.

As a striking demonstration of the coexistence of two influences, one might note that perceptions of the mechanisms of the human body and the universe were most affected during the Renaissance by the thought of six men, three from the sixteenth century—Copernicus, Vesalius, and Paracelsus—and three from antiquity—Archimedes, Ptolemy, and Galen. Their impact was to strike the learned world at approximately the same moment. Astoundingly, Copernicus's *De Revolutionibus Orbium Coelestium*, which revolutionized our understanding of the cosmos, Vesalius's *De Humani Corporis Fabrica*, which revolutionized our understanding of the human body, and the first major Latin translation of the works of Archimedes were all published in 1543.

A new understanding of the human body resulted from anatomical studies that were pursued with a method and intensity of curiosity previously unknown. Increasing interest in depicting the myths and heroes of classical antiquity, and reawakened admiration for Greek and Roman sculpture, led Renaissance artists to investigate anatomy for their own purposes. The need for accurate, reproducible images to illustrate new scientific findings also brought the artist into the role of partner with the scientist. Leonardo, who planned a great (unrealized) textbook on the structure and mechanisms of the human body, articulated the crucial role that visual art would play in anatomical studies: "Dispel from your mind the thought that an understanding of the human body in every aspect of its structure can be given in words; for the more thoroughly you describe, the more you will confuse: . . . I advise you not to trouble with words unless you are speaking to blind men."[1]

Although the physician's eye and hand were trained in the techniques of dissection, he was rarely capable of recording his observations with the degree of competence necessary to convey all he had found. On the other hand, while the artist who wanted to understand the mechanism of the human body to render it more accurately might be skilled in the recording of observed reality, he was often not sufficiently trained to dissect the human body properly, and therefore needed an experienced hand to expose and isolate each element or system within it. This mutual need, coupled with a shared concern for observing, understanding, and improving the human condition, made artists and physicians appropriate partners. A. Hyatt Mayor observed that "once the Renaissance artists started dissecting, they quickly discovered more than the doctors ever had about the look and functioning of the bones and muscles. . . . Artists saw what doctors had not seen because they approached anatomy with an entirely different practical purpose . . . ."[2]

The joining of the talents of a master printmaker, possibly Jan Stevensz. van Calcar, and the anatomical genius of the anatomist and physician Andreas Vesalius gave rise in the 1540s to a publication that revolutionized the study of anatomy and established it with startling suddenness as a modern observational science. Their landmark work, *De Humani Corporis Fabrica* (see nos. 8a–g), exemplifies the new Humanistic approach whereby man came to trust his own senses in assessing and exploring the world around and within him. This remarkably beautiful wedding of art and science established a model that other artists and anatomists were to emulate for more than three centuries. Refinements in anatomical detail and printing technique were to follow, but the Vesalian model was to endure.

In the sixteenth and seventeenth centuries, elaborate public dissections were held by the faculties of medicine at the principal universities when the difficulties of obtaining the Church's permission, a cadaver, and a suitable location could be overcome (see no. 12). Such events attracted members of the clergy, artists, scientists, Humanists, and physicians, whether for the opportunity of searching for the seat of the soul, proving or disproving the ancient texts, understanding the intricacies of the human structure and physiology, or simply taking part in an extraordinary event and the musical or dramatic festivities that usually followed.

Intensive study of anatomy came to be an absolute necessity for the artist who wished to portray the human body with any credibility. Hendrik Goltzius's dramatic engraving *The Large Hercules* of 1589 (no. 10), created as a work of art and not as illustration, was so legible in its rendering of external anatomy that it was hung as a reference tool in the anatomy theater of the University of Leiden. An artist of great success and fame such as the eighteenth-century Italian painter Pompeo Batoni continued to study anatomy and draw from the live human model throughout his career (see no. 16), not just as a learning method while young. Thomas Eakins's comparative anatomy photographs and drawings (see nos. 18a–d) done in the later nineteenth century demonstrate his profound belief in the training of an artist's eye and hand through analysis of the human figure. Well into the twentieth century, artists continue to explore human anatomy as a relevant subject; some have absorbed scientific methods and incorporated medical imagery into their own work, such as the x-rays of his own body that Robert Rauschenberg used as the central image of *Booster* of 1967 (no. 21). From *Zodiac Man* of 1493 (no. 1), in which the artist fused man, contemporary medical knowledge, and the powers of the cosmos into one image, we travel some five centuries to *Booster*, which conjoins the same elements in a thoroughly modern way.

HEALERS

The written history of medicine focuses primarily on great discoveries and important individuals within the discipline. A study of literature, folklore, and the visual arts, however, reveals the practices, tools, and attitudes of ordinary healers: physician, barber-surgeon, dentist, quack, and church figure. Until recent times the healers available to the population in European villages and towns were not usually the university-trained physicians (see no. 32) but rather an assortment of these practitioners (see nos. 27 and 34a,b). Some were certainly charlatans, as various images shown here suggest (see nos. 26 and 33), but other itinerant healers possessed skills and common sense, and the arrival of even a quack dentist, for example (see nos. 37 and 38), was often awaited with the justifiable expectation of the relief from pain he might provide.

Recurrent images of Christ and many Christian saints as healers demonstrate another avenue of relief for the sufferer (see no. 23). In the face of epidemics or the plague, the need to find solace and hope in the miracles of healing documented in the New Testament made the figures from the Christian liturgy powerful forces, reinforced by the active efforts of the church and numerous of its holy orders in the care of and ministering to the sick, whose plight was perceived as bringing them closer to God (see nos. 28a–c).

Artists have frequently provided enduring records of the status, tools, and practices of healers and the society of which they were a part: from the fifteenth-century image of a physician in Johannes de Ketham's *Fasciculus Medicinae* (no. 24), through Abraham Bosse's tart portrayals of seventeenth-century French medical practice (nos. 31a,b) and Henry Alken's nineteenth-century caricature of the pseudoscience of phrenology (no. 39), to the powerful photographs of mid-twentieth-century healers by W. Eugene Smith (nos. 46–48).

DISEASE, DISABILITY, AND MADNESS

Because disease has no regard for age, occupation, or status and seems to move frighteningly free from the rational mechanisms of logic or predictability, it has loomed as man's most formidable adversary, especially because it often remains invisible until too late. Since ancient times man has sought effective weapons to combat this enemy, calling upon every resource in his problem-solving armamentarium. The devastating power of epidemics has laid waste to whole populations, recorded in grim images such as Stefano della Bella's *Plague* (no. 53). It has also stimulated civilizations to develop scientific and social mechanisms to deal with such awesome forces. For example, George John Pinwell's eloquent drawing *Death's Dispensary* (no. 60) demonstrates that the development of standards of public health and sanitation was sometimes clearly in response to the impact of disease on an urban population, a situation in which experience and insight as well as social outcry led to positive change.

While some diseases move rapidly in waves of destruction, there are others whose patterns are slow and chronic, such as mental disorders, physical disabilities resulting from disease, accident, or genetic abnormalities, and drug addiction. These constitute, as William Hardy McNeill has written, the "background noise" of human life.[3] In earlier times those who had lost limbs or were blind or mad were still clearly part of the fabric of day-to-day life, as is shown in Hieronymus Cock's mid-sixteenth-century print *Beggars* (no. 51). As society's complexity increased, however, public acceptance of the disabled began to be increasingly limited, as is clearly conveyed in Théodore Géricault's lithograph *A Paraleytic Woman* of 1821 (no. 57). The theme of the Tribulations of Saint Anthony provided artists such as Martin Schongauer (no. 73), Lucas Cranach the Elder (no. 74), and Jacques Callot (no. 76) with a vehicle for externalizing and presenting in a metaphor the attitudes toward and perceptions of madness in their respective societies. Their works each differ greatly from nineteenth-century images of disturbed patients by Ambroise Tardieu (no. 80) or Hugh Welch Diamond (no. 81), as well as from the twentieth-century views of asylums by Max Beckmann (no. 83) or Raymond Depardon (nos. 86a,b).

If, as Susan Sontag has observed, each of us "holds dual citizenship, in the kingdom of the well and in the kingdom of the sick,"[4] the artist's records of the darker world of disease carry with them a universality of meaning for all viewers.

THE CYCLE OF LIFE

The universality of the themes of birth, aging, and death contributes to the remarkable freshness and accessibility of many of the images included here. No matter how much knowledge we acquire, the miracle of birth retains its aura of magic. Albrecht Dürer's woodcut *Birth of the Virgin* (no. 88), which sheds light on sixteenth-century German birthing practices, Abraham Bosse's seventeenth-century etching (no. 91), which extols the pain and joy of birth, and W. Eugene Smith's extraordinary twentieth-century photograph of a nurse-midwife in rural South Carolina (no. 92) all articulate the artist's fascination with the beginning of life, drawing the viewer into the miraculous event.

Observing and recording the transformations of the human face with the passage of time have also long attracted the interest of the artist. Guercino's delicate ink drawing of an old man from the seventeenth century (no. 93) conveys a sensitivity to the subject that is as fresh and compassionate as Nicholas Nixon's recent photographic portrait of extreme old age (no. 94).

The traditional view of death as but one aspect of the cycle of life emphasizes the connections between man, nature, and the cosmos. Responding to society's need to come to terms with death, artists have often turned to allegory, metaphor, and symbol to make their images comprehensible and potent yet approachable and not so realistic as to be overwhelming. The symbolism of death has also encompassed the passing of youth and beauty and the loss of pleasure and wealth (see nos. 100, 101, and 116).

Devastating epidemics such as the Black Death of 1348 reinforced the realities of death on a vast scale, and the *Ars Moriendi* (see no. 95) and other illustrated tracts (see nos. 96 and 98) were a response to the realization that every man, woman, and child must prepare to face an imminent and unexpected end. Similarly, the popularity of Dance of Death imagery (see no. 98), which stressed the idea that death comes to all ages and social strata, was a reaction to mass destruction by disease, as was the development of the *vanitas* (nos. 99a,b; 100; 102; and 103) and Apocalypse (no. 97) themes. However, death has not always been seen as an unwelcomed intruder. In Michel Wolgemut's *Dance of the Dead*, for example (no. 96), death is presented as a release from the toils and travails of the working world; some three-and-a-half centuries later, in Alfred Rethel's moving image (no. 108a), it is depicted as a friend arriving to escort a good soul to a much deserved afterlife.

Works in this section of the exhibition reveal the physician (no. 98), the ordinary man or woman (nos. 100 and 104), and the artist himself (nos. 105 and 110) confronted by death, a state that none can record firsthand. Each society, each artist, must find images that can convey the power, permanence, and reality of death, responding to mass extinction (see nos. 97, 99a, and 103) or individual loss (see nos. 113–15). The two seventeenth-century quarantine signs (nos. 106 and 107) are perhaps the most potent symbols in their utter simplicity.

1. Translated and quoted in Robert Herrlinger, *History of Medical Illustration from Antiquity to A.D. 1600* (Nijkerk, The Netherlands, 1970), p. 70.
2. A. Hyatt Mayor, *Artists & Anatomists* (New York, 1984), pp. 48–49.
3. William Hardy McNeill, *Plagues and Peoples* (Garden City, N.Y., 1976), p. 12.
4. Susan Sontag, *Illness as Metaphor* (New York, 1978), p. 3.

D.K.

CATALOGUE

Contributors

Ben Bassham B.B.

Mimi Cazort M.C.

Martha Chahroudi M.Ch.

Frima Fox Hofrichter F.F.H.

John Ittmann J.I.

Ellen Jacobowitz E.J.

Diane Karp D.K.

Ann Percy A.P.

Kimerly Rorschach K.R.

Darrel Sewell D.S.

Aaron Sheon A.S.

Faith H. Zieske F.H.Z.

Height precedes width in all measurements. All translations are by authors unless otherwise noted.

ANATOMY

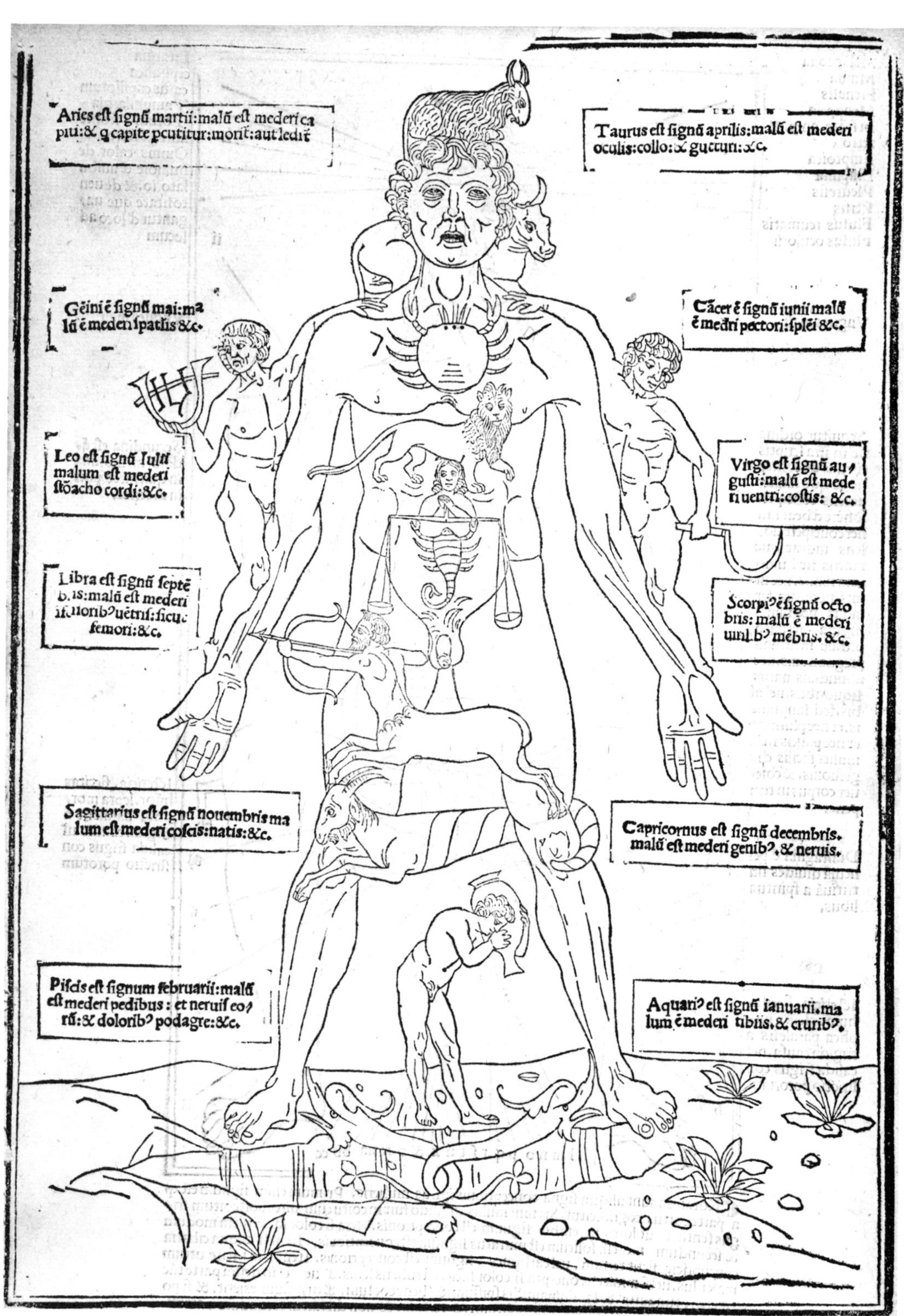

• 1 •

Anonymous (Italian, late fifteenth century)

ZODIAC MAN, 1493

From Johannes de Ketham, *Fasciculus Medicinae* (Venice: Cesarem Arrivabenum, 1522)

Woodcut, 11⁷⁄₁₆ x 8⁵⁄₁₆″ (29.1 x 21.1 cm)

Purchased: SmithKline Beckman Corporation Fund

49-97-3e

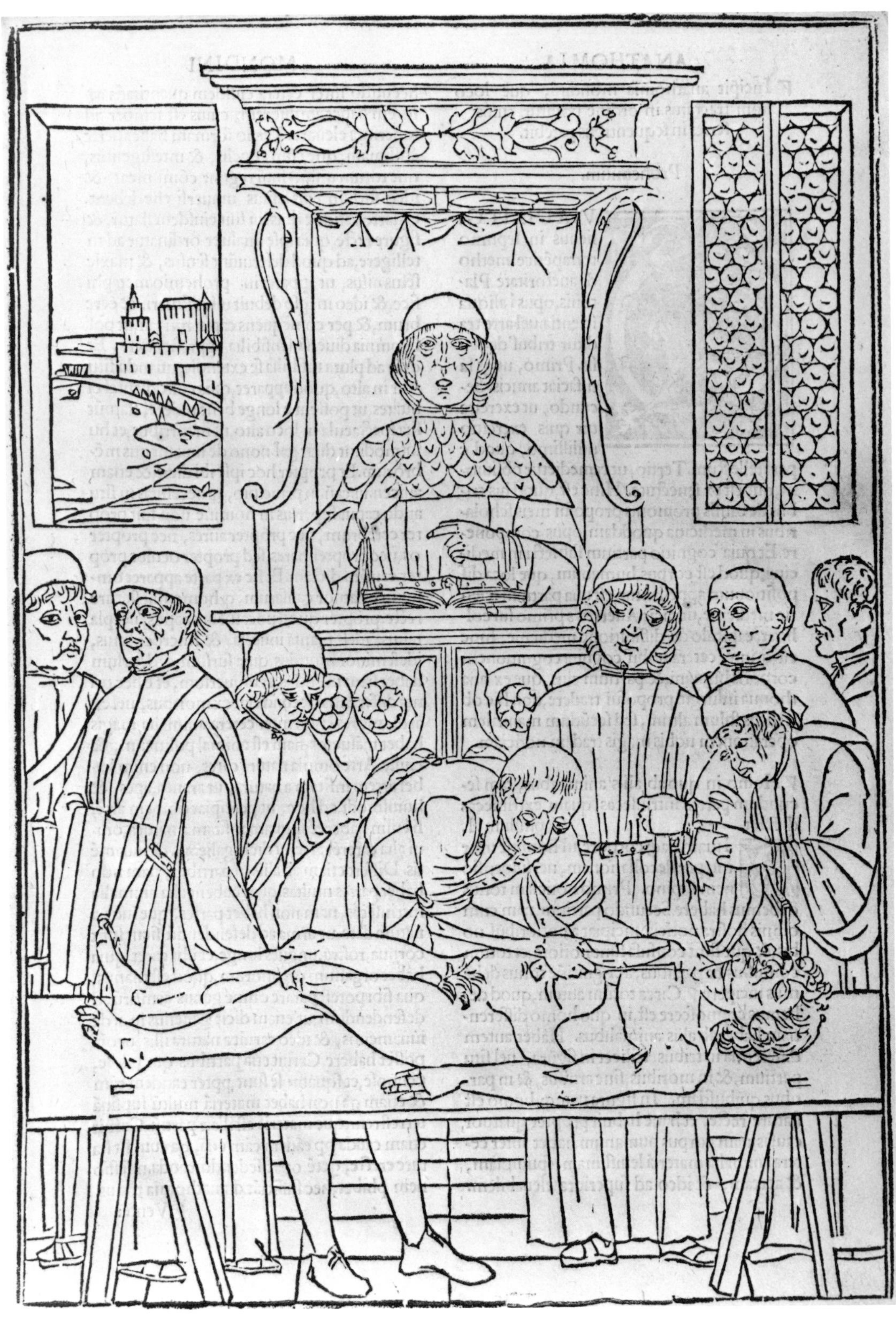

• 2 •

Anonymous (Italian, late fifteenth century)

Possibly after designs by Gentile Bellini (Italian, c. 1429–1507)

ANATOMY LESSON, 1495

From Johannes de Ketham, *Fasciculus Medicinae* (Venice: Cesarem Arrivabenum, 1522)

Woodcut, 11 7/16 x 8 1/4" (29.1 x 20.9 cm)

Purchased: SmithKline Beckman Corporation Fund

49-97-3d

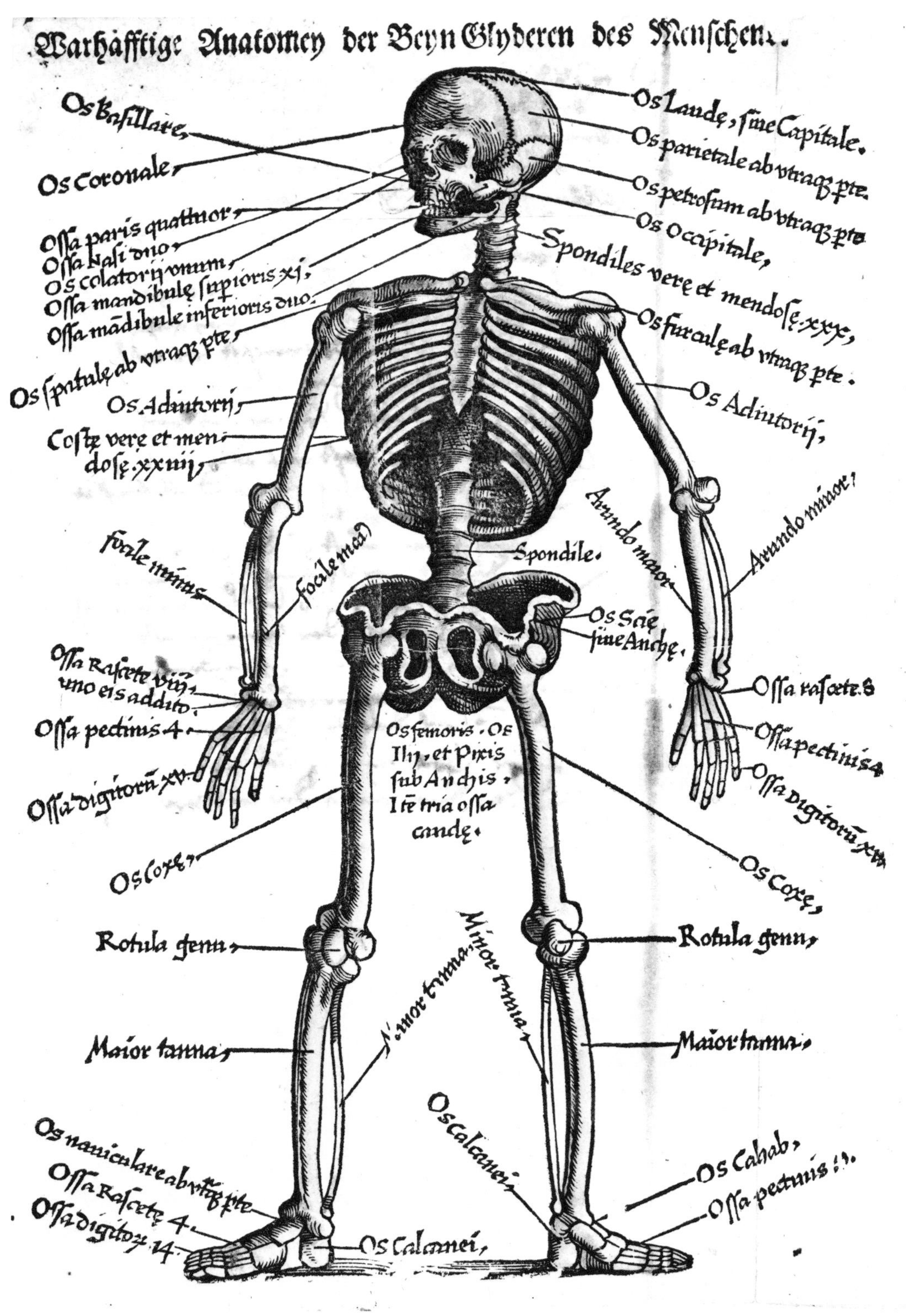

• 3 •

Anonymous (German, early sixteenth century)

EXACT ANATOMY OF THE BONE STRUCTURE OF MAN, 1517

Inserted in Hans von Gersdorff, *Feldtbuch der Wundartzney* . . . (Strasbourg: Hans Schotten, 1540)

Hand-colored woodcut, $11\frac{5}{16} \times 9\frac{1}{4}$″ (28.7 x 23.5 cm)

Purchased: SmithKline Beckman Corporation Fund

49-97-11a

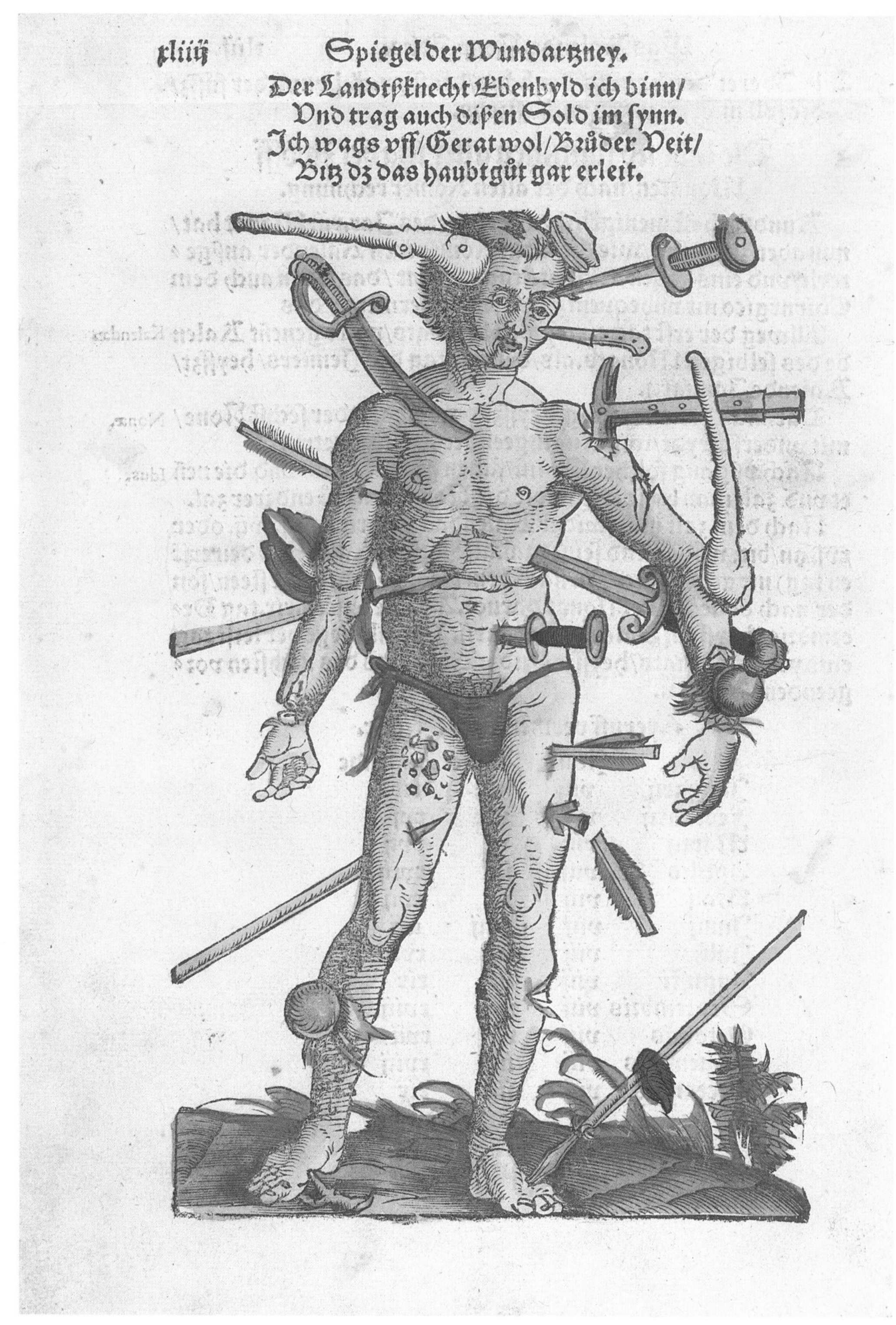
xliiij Spiegel der Wundartzney.

Der Landtßknecht Ebenbyld ich binn/
Vnd trag auch disen Sold im synn.
Ich wags vff/Gerat wol/Brůder Veit/
Bitz dz das haubtgůt gar erleit.

• 4a •

Anonymous (German, early sixteenth century)

WOUND MANIKIN, 1517

From Hans von Gersdorff, *Feldtbuch der Wundartzney* . . . (Strasbourg: Hans Schotten, 1540)

Hand-colored woodcut, 10⁵⁄₁₆ x 7³⁄₁₆" (26.2 x 18.3 cm)

Purchased: SmithKline Beckman Corporation Fund

49-97-11m

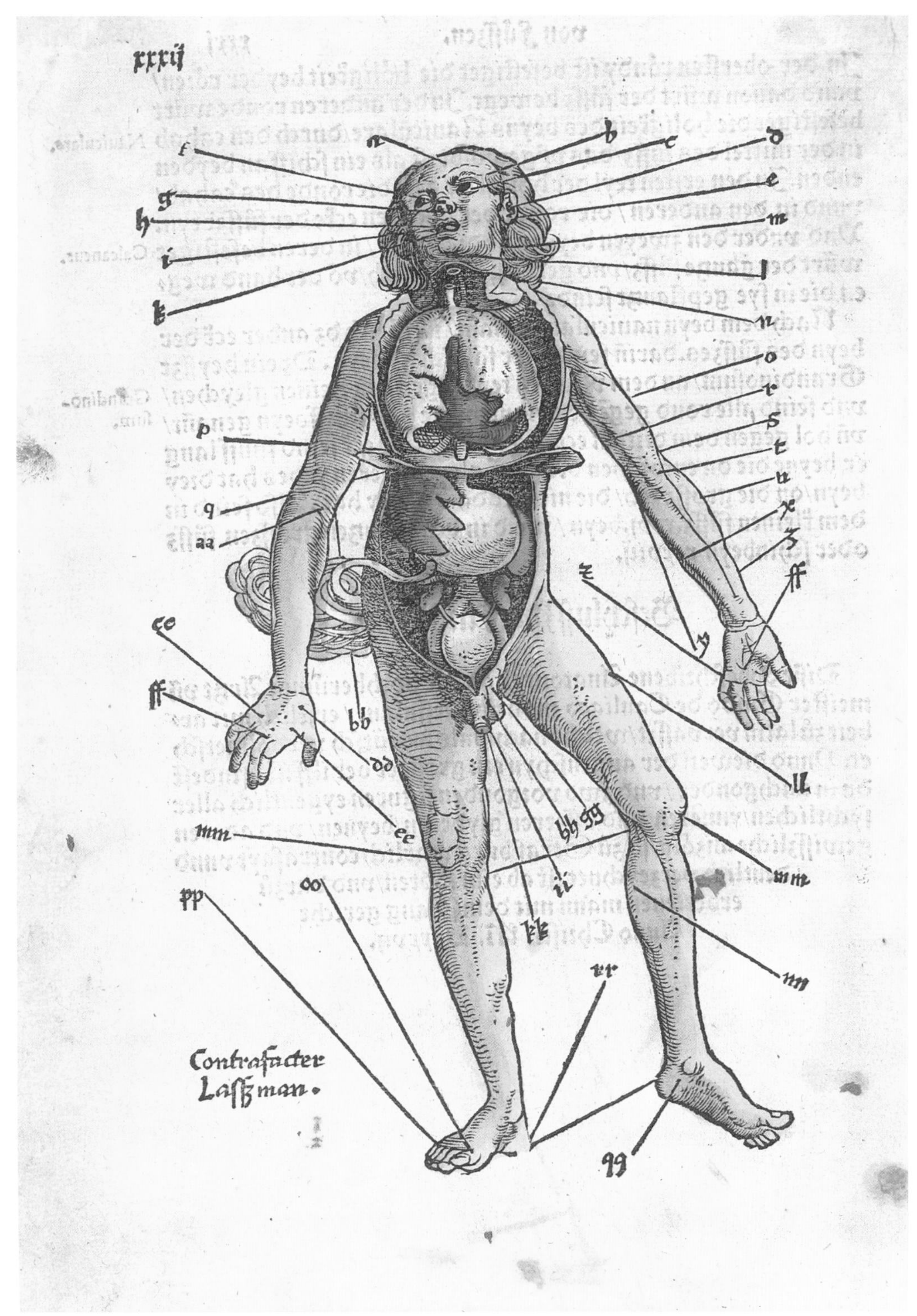

• 4b •

Anonymous (German, early sixteenth century)

BLOODLETTING MANIKIN, 1517

From Hans von Gersdorff, *Feldtbuch der Wundartzney* . . . (Strasbourg: Hans Schotten, 1540)

Hand-colored woodcut, 9 13/16 x 6 15/16" (24.9 x 17.7 cm)

Purchased: SmithKline Beckman Corporation Fund

49-97-11b

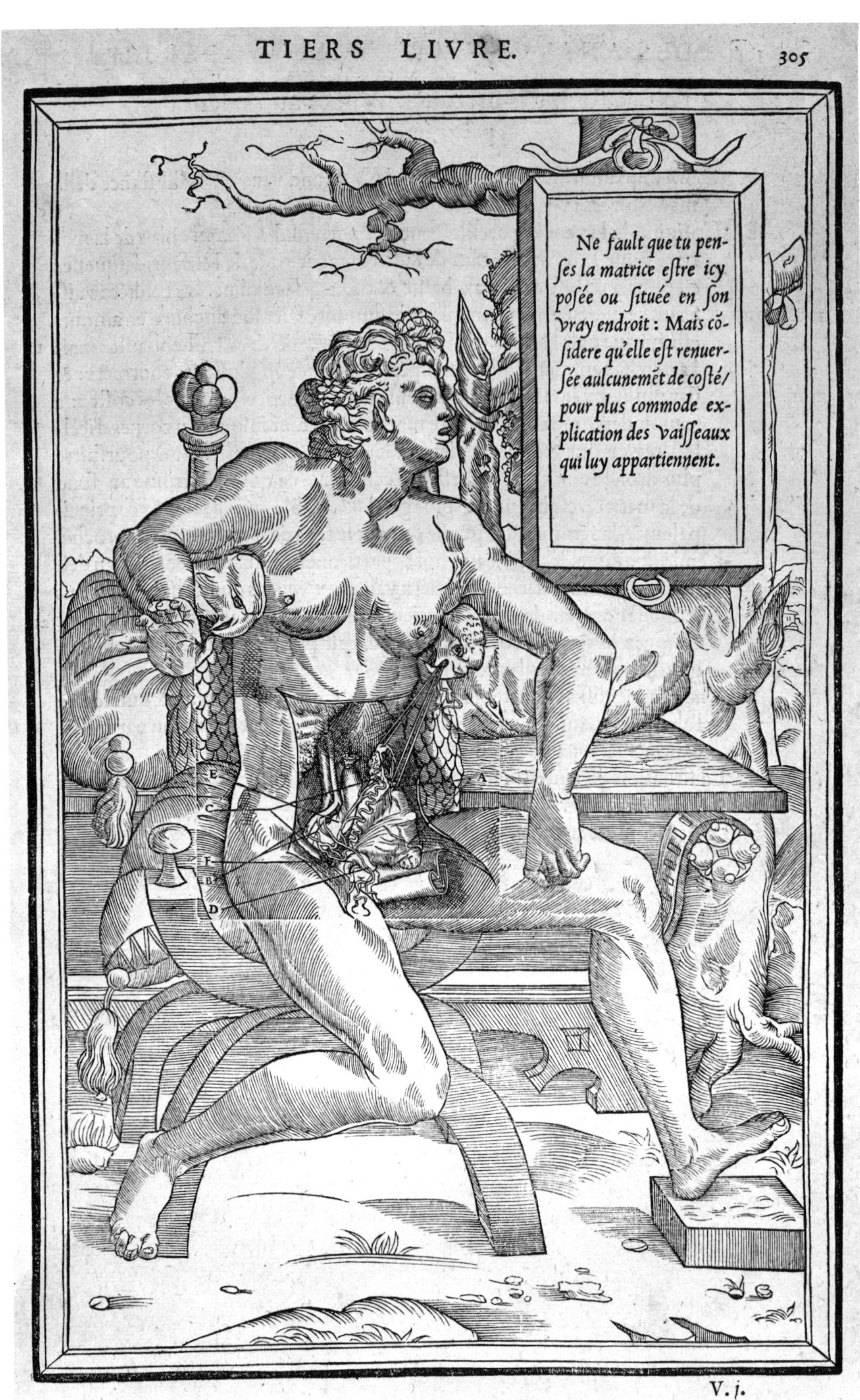

• 5a •

Anonymous, possibly by François (Jean) Jollat (French, active 1502–50)
After Perino del Vaga (Italian, 1501–1547) and possibly Etienne de la Rivière (French, died 1569)
FEMALE FIGURE, 1530–39

From Charles Estienne, *La Dissection des parties du corps humain* . . . (Paris: Simon de Colines, 1546)
Woodcut, 14⅞ x 9$\frac{5}{16}$" (37.8 x 23.7 cm)
Purchased: SmithKline Beckman Corporation Fund
1980-93-2

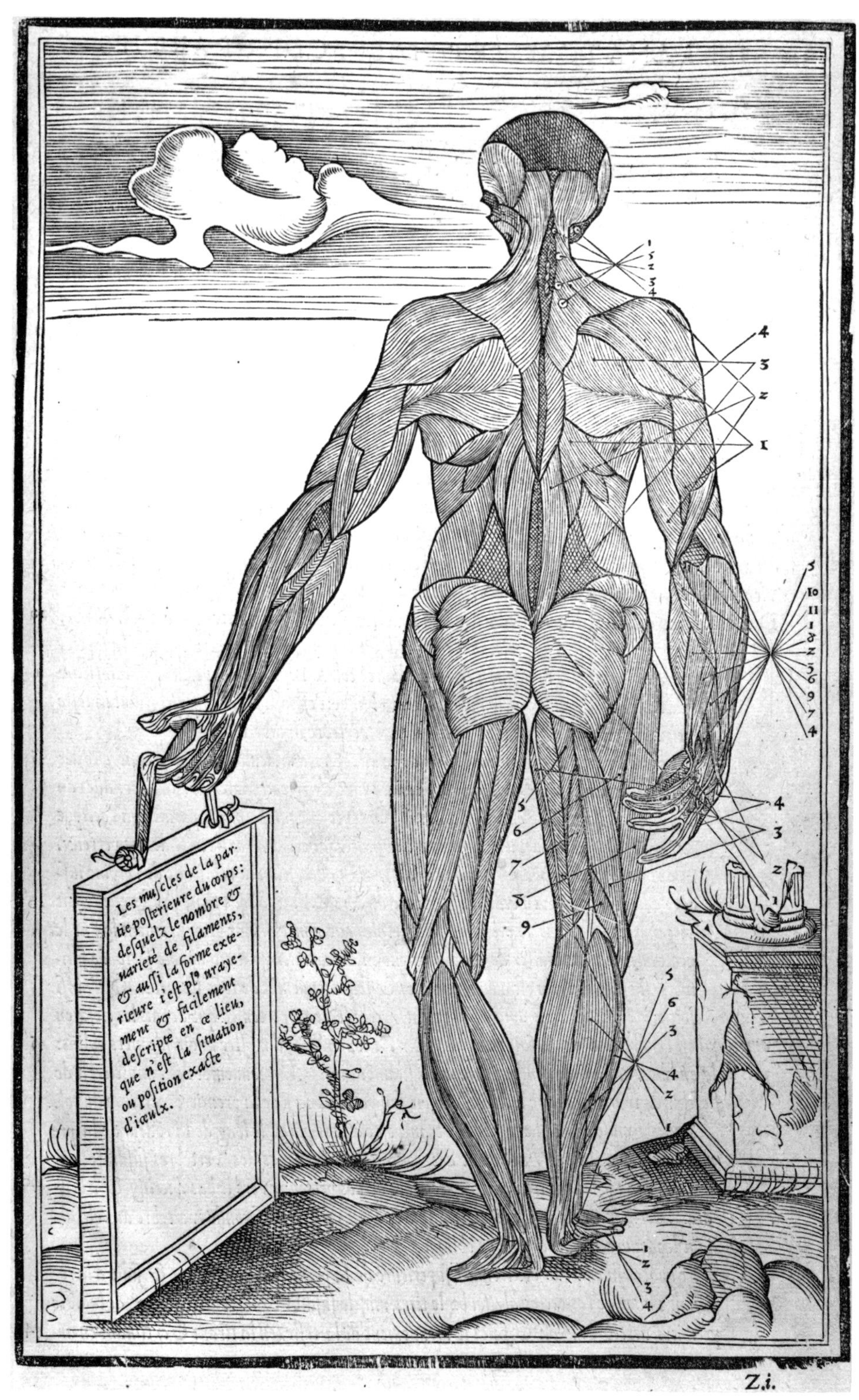

• 5b •

Anonymous, possibly by François (Jean) Jollat (French, active 1502–50)
Possibly after Etienne de la Rivière (French, died 1569)
MUSCLES OF THE BACK, 1530–39

From Charles Estienne, *La Dissection des parties du corps humain . . .* (Paris: Simon de Colines, 1546)
Woodcut, 14 15/16 x 9½" (38 x 24.1 cm)
Purchased: SmithKline Beckman Corporation Fund
1980-93-5

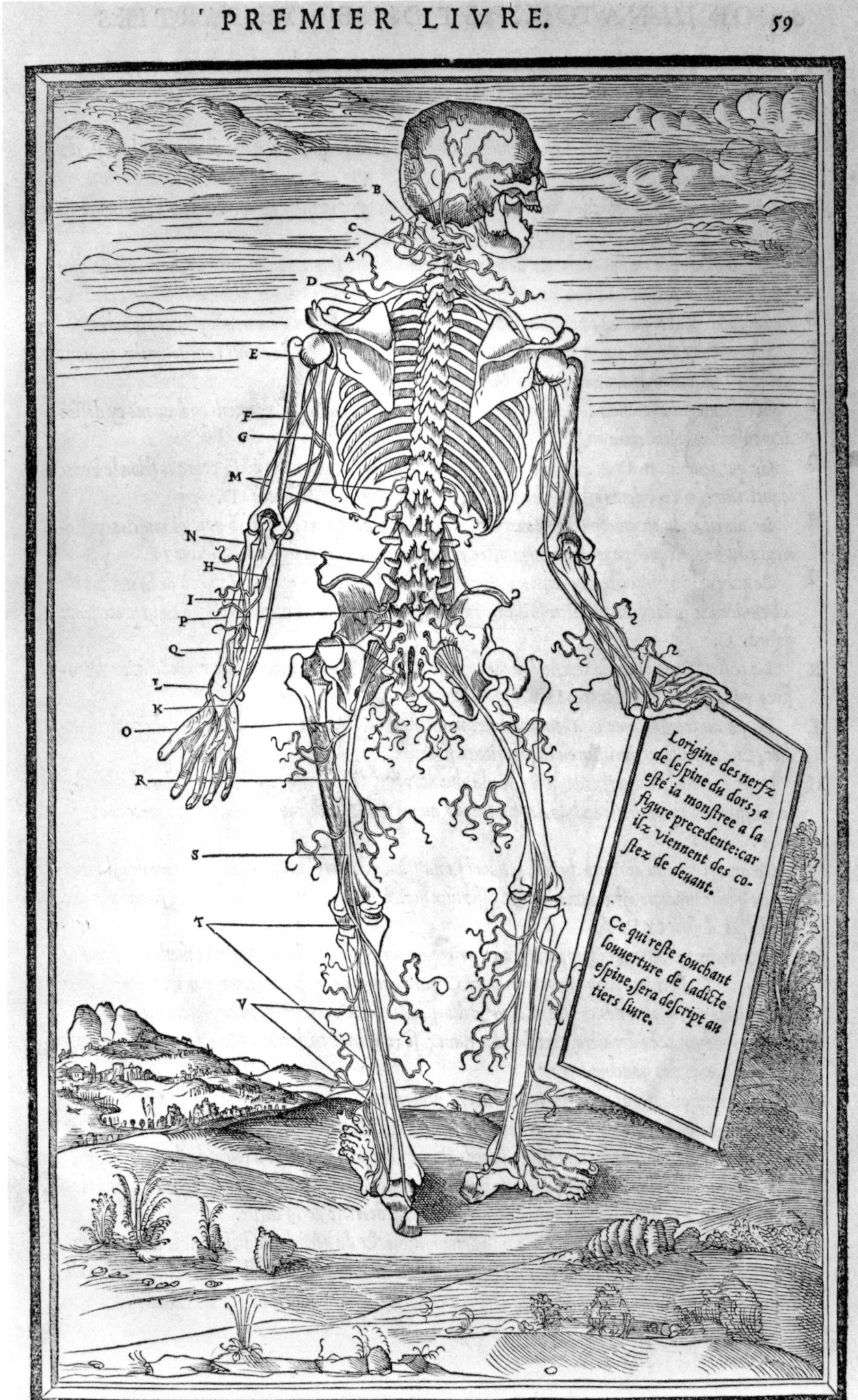

• 5c •

Anonymous, possibly by François (Jean) Jollat (French, active 1502–50)
Possibly after Etienne de la Rivière (French, died 1569)
PERIPHERAL NERVOUS SYSTEM, 1530–39

From Charles Estienne, *La Dissection des parties du corps humain* . . . (Paris: Simon de Colines, 1546)
Woodcut, 14 15/16 x 9 3/8" (38 x 23.8 cm)
Purchased: SmithKline Beckman Corporation Fund
1980-93-3

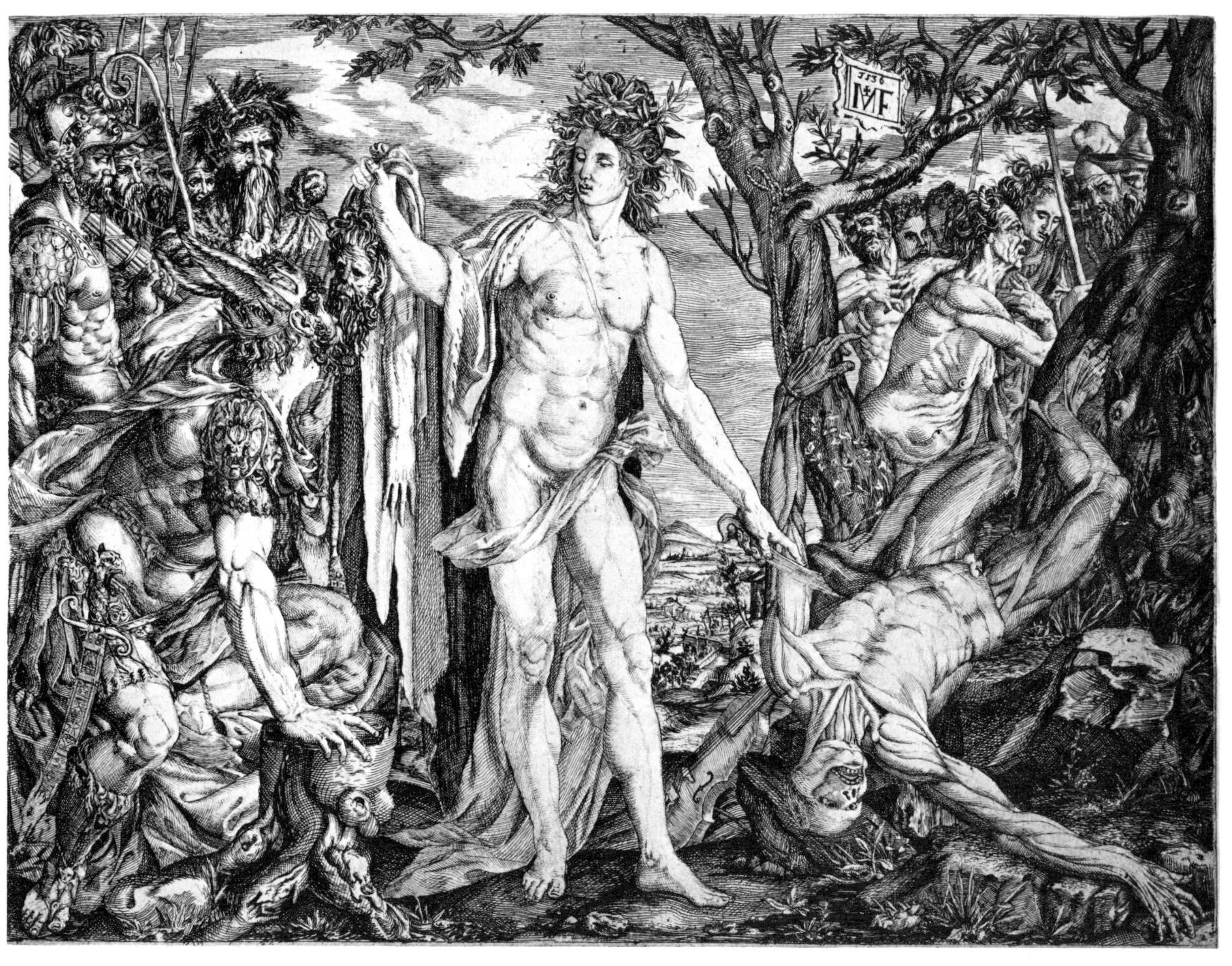

• 6 •

Monogrammist M. F.

Possibly after Melchior Meier (German/Swiss, active 1580s)

APOLLO AND MARSYAS, sixteenth century

Engraving, 9 x 12¼" (22.8 x 31.1 cm) (trimmed)

Purchased: SmithKline Beckman Corporation Fund

1982-36-1

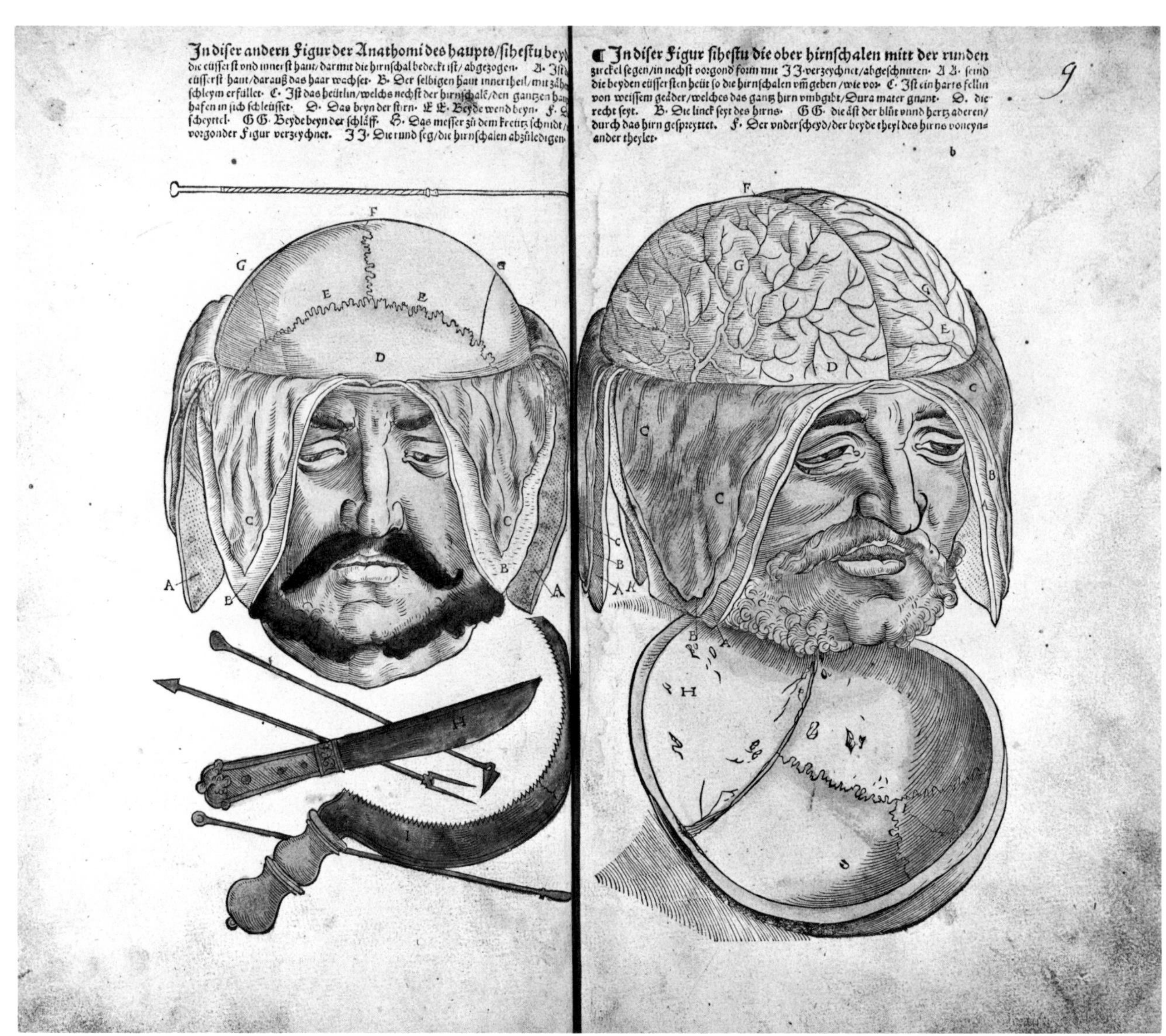

• 7a •

Hans Baldung Grien (German, 1484/85–1545)

DISSECTION OF THE SCALP AND EXPOSURE OF THE HEMISPHERES OF THE BRAIN, 1541

From Walter Hermann Ryff, *Des aller fürtrefflichsten . . . gschöpffs aller Creaturen . . . beschreibung oder Anatomi*
(Strasbourg: Balthasar Beck, 1541)
Hand-colored woodcut, 12 x 15⅛" (30.5 x 38.4 cm)
Purchased: SmithKline Beckman Corporation Fund
1982-40-1h,i

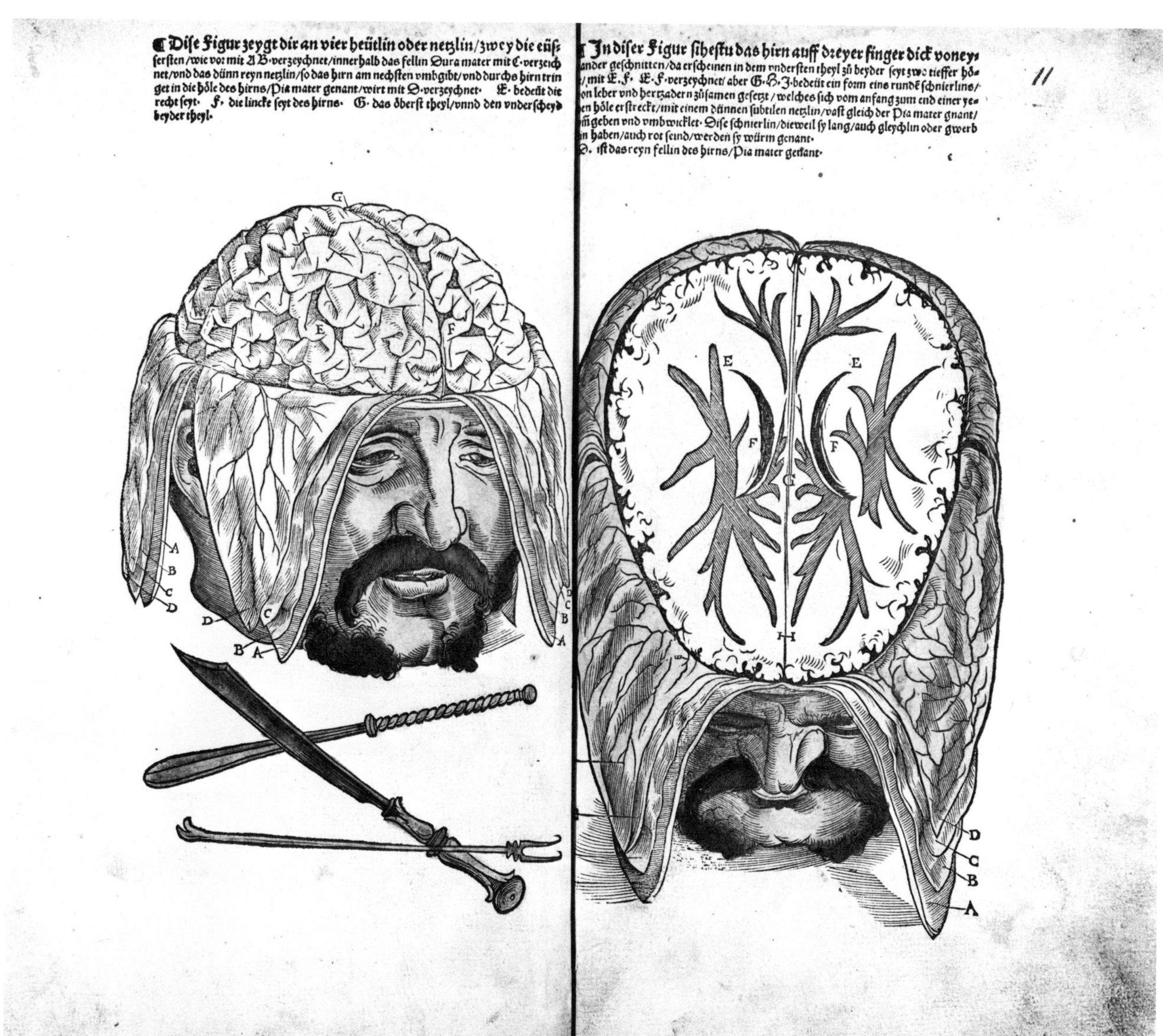
Dise Figur zeygt dir an vier heütlin oder netzlin/zwey die eüſ-
ſerſten/wie vor mit A B·verzeychnet/innerhalb das fellin Dura mater mit C·verzeich
net/vnd das dünn reyn netzlin/ſo das hirn am nechſten vmbgibt/vnd durchs hirn trin
get in die hôle des hirns/Pia mater genant/wirt mit D·verzeychnet· E· bedeüt die
recht ſeyt· F· die lincke ſeyt des hirns· G· das öberſt theyl/vnnd den vnderſcheyd
beyder theyl·

In diſer Figur ſiheſtu das hirn auff dreyer finger dick voney-
ander geſchnitten/da erſcheinen in dem vnderſten theyl zů beyder ſeyt zwo tieffer hô-
/mit E.F· E·F·verzeychnet/ aber G·H·J·bedeüt ein form eins runden ſchnierlins/
on leber vnd hertzadern zůſamen geſetzt/welches ſich vom anfang zum end einer ye-
en hôle erſtreckt/mit einem dünnen ſubtilen netzlin/vaſt gleich der Pia mater gnant/
mgeben vnd vmbwicklet· Diſe ſchnierlin/dieweil ſy lang/auch gleychlin oder gwerb
in haben/auch rot ſeind/werden ſy würm genant·
D· iſt das reyn fellin des hirns/Pia mater genant·

• 7b •

Hans Baldung Grien (German, 1484/85–1545)

REMOVAL OF THE PIA MATER AND A CROSS-SECTION OF THE BRAIN, 1541

From Walter Hermann Ryff, *Des aller fürtrefflichsten . . . gschöpffs aller Creaturen . . . beschreibung oder Anatomi*
(Strasbourg: Balthasar Beck, 1541)
Hand-colored woodcut, 12 x 15⅛" (30.5 x 38.4 cm)
Purchased: SmithKline Beckman Corporation Fund
1982-40-1j,k

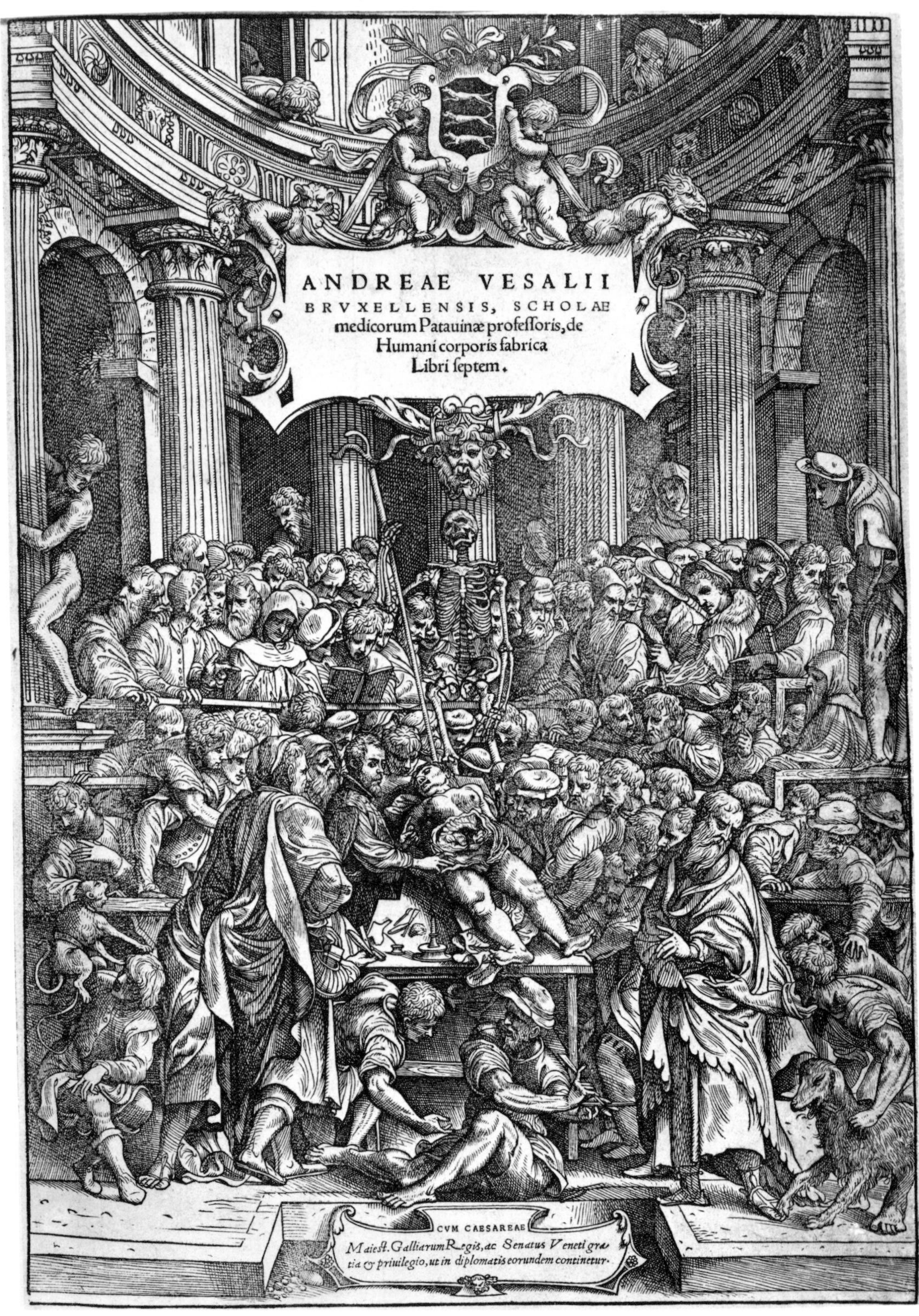

• 8a •

Anonymous, possibly by Jan Stevensz. van Calcar (Flemish, c. 1499–c. 1550)

VESALIUS CONDUCTING AN ANATOMICAL DISSECTION, 1543

From Andreas Vesalius, *De Humani Corporis Fabrica* (Basel: Johannes Oporinus, 1543)

Woodcut, $15\frac{15}{16}$ x $10\frac{5}{8}$" (40.5 x 27 cm)

Purchased: SmithKline Beckman Corporation Fund

49-97-41a

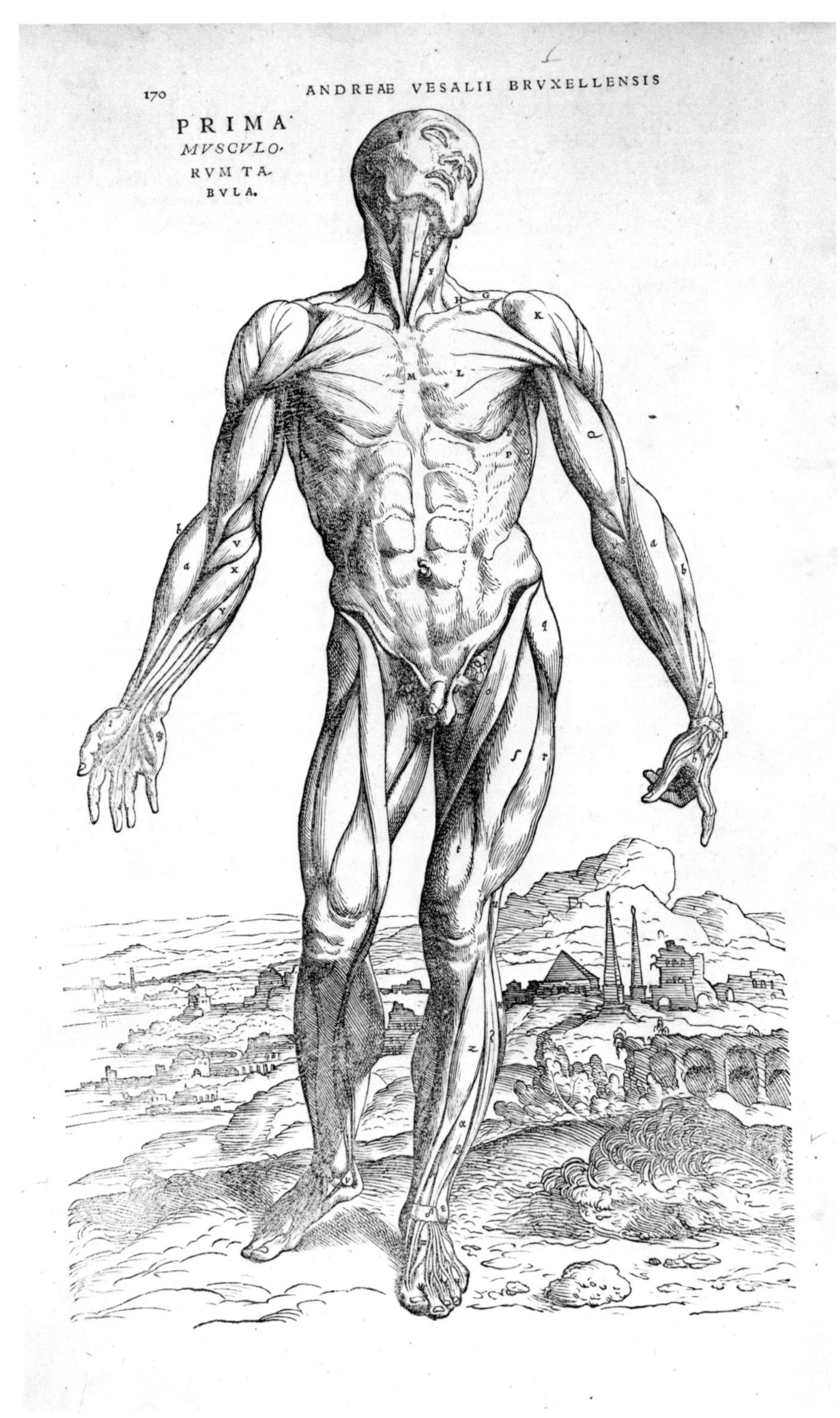

• 8b •

Anonymous, possibly by Jan Stevensz. van Calcar (Flemish, c. 1499–c. 1550)

THE FIRST PLATE OF MUSCLES, 1543

From Andreas Vesalius, *De Humani Corporis Fabrica* (Basel: Johannes Oporinus, 1543)

Woodcut, 15 15/16 x 10 5/8" (40.5 x 27 cm)

Purchased: SmithKline Beckman Corporation Fund

49-97-41f

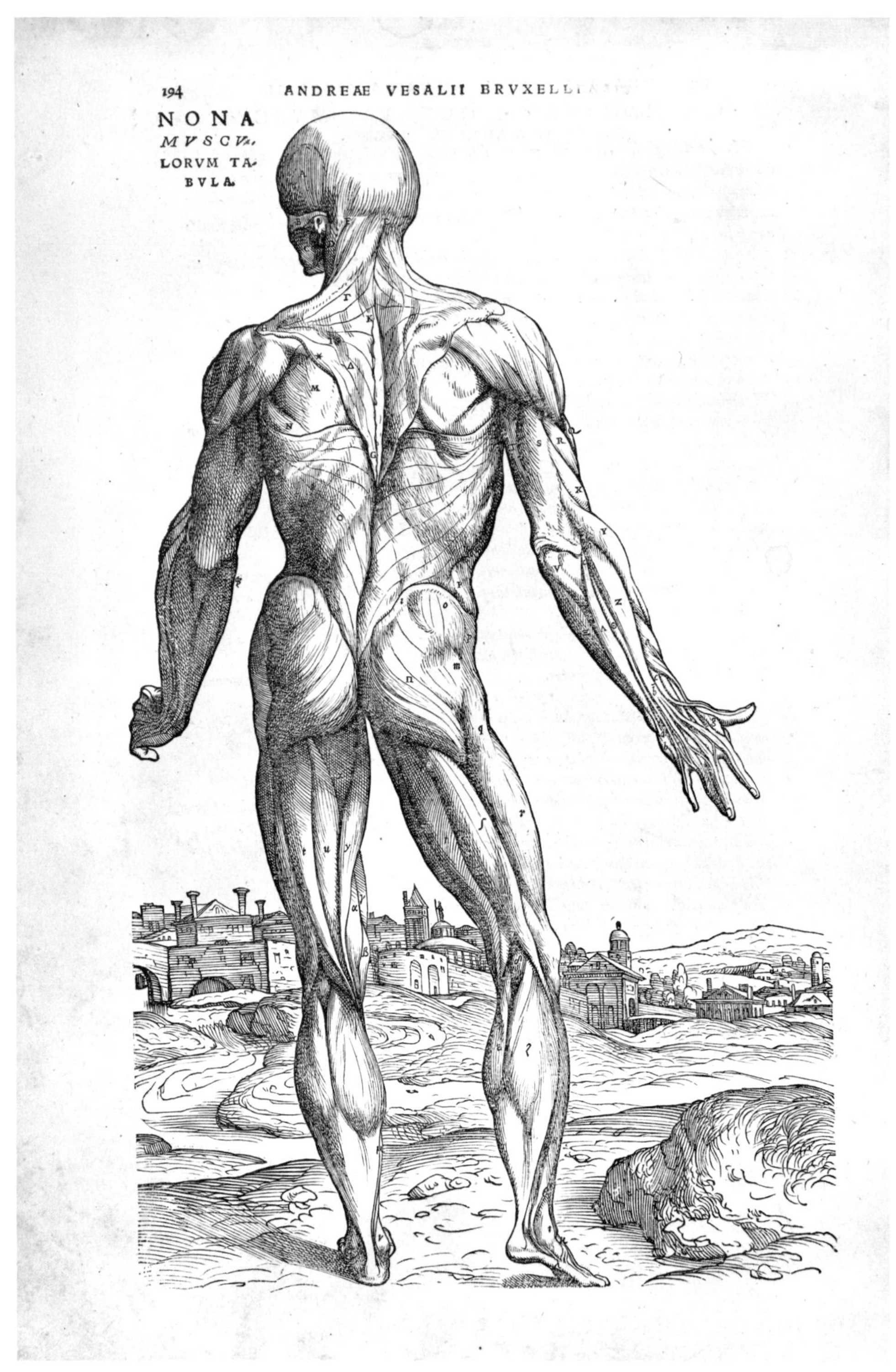

• 8c •

Anonymous, possibly by Jan Stevensz. van Calcar (Flemish, c. 1499–c. 1550)

THE NINTH PLATE OF MUSCLES, 1543

From Andreas Vesalius, *De Humani Corporis Fabrica* (Basel: Johannes Oporinus, 1543)

Woodcut, 15 15/16 x 10 5/8" (40.5 x 27 cm)

Purchased: SmithKline Beckman Corporation Fund

49-97-41d

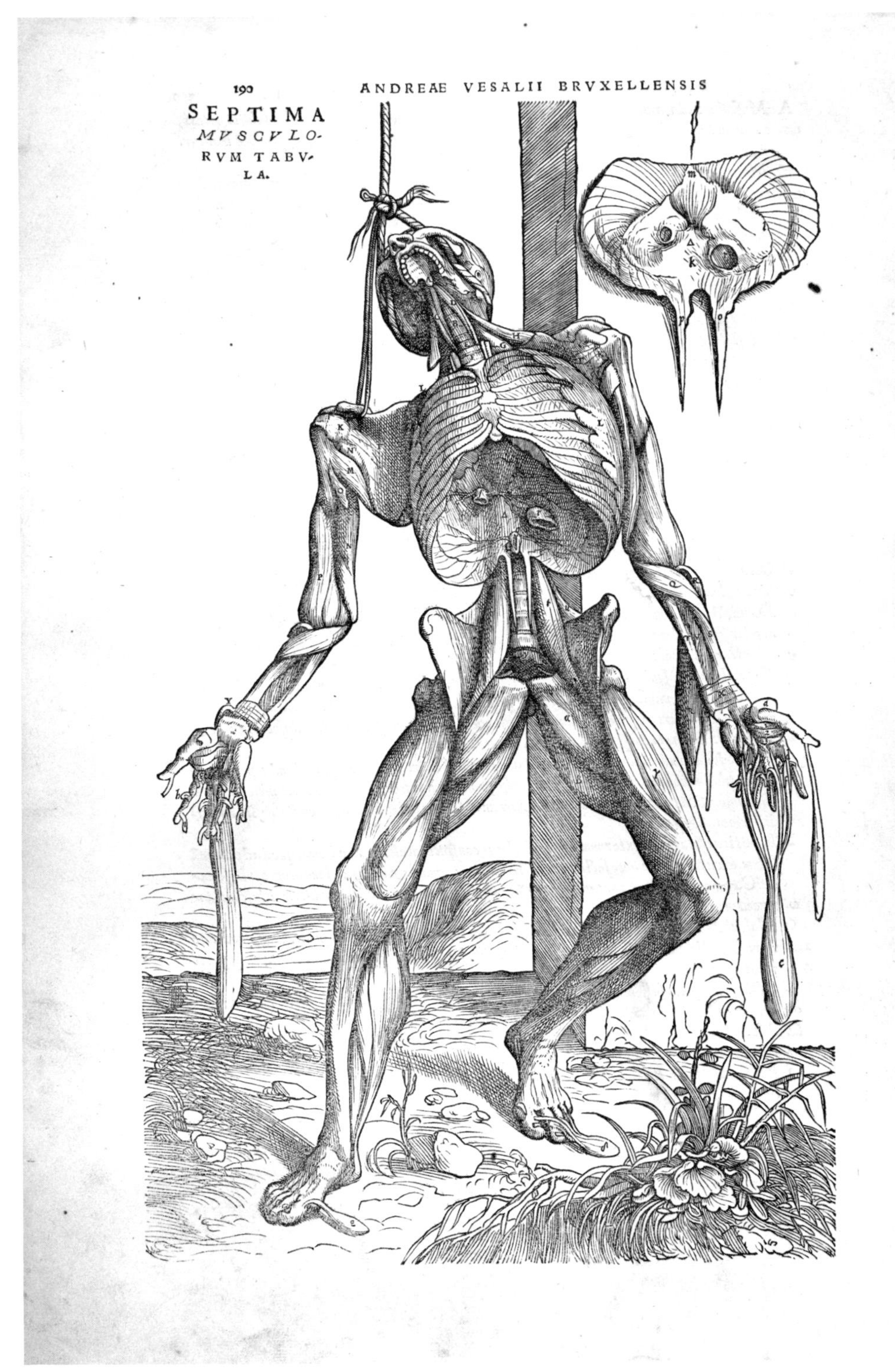

• 8d •

Anonymous, possibly by Jan Stevensz. van Calcar (Flemish, c. 1499–c. 1550)

THE SEVENTH PLATE OF MUSCLES, 1543

From Andreas Vesalius, *De Humani Corporis Fabrica* (Basel: Johannes Oporinus, 1543)

Woodcut, 15 15/16 x 10 5/8" (40.5 x 27 cm)

Purchased: SmithKline Beckman Corporation Fund

49-97-41h

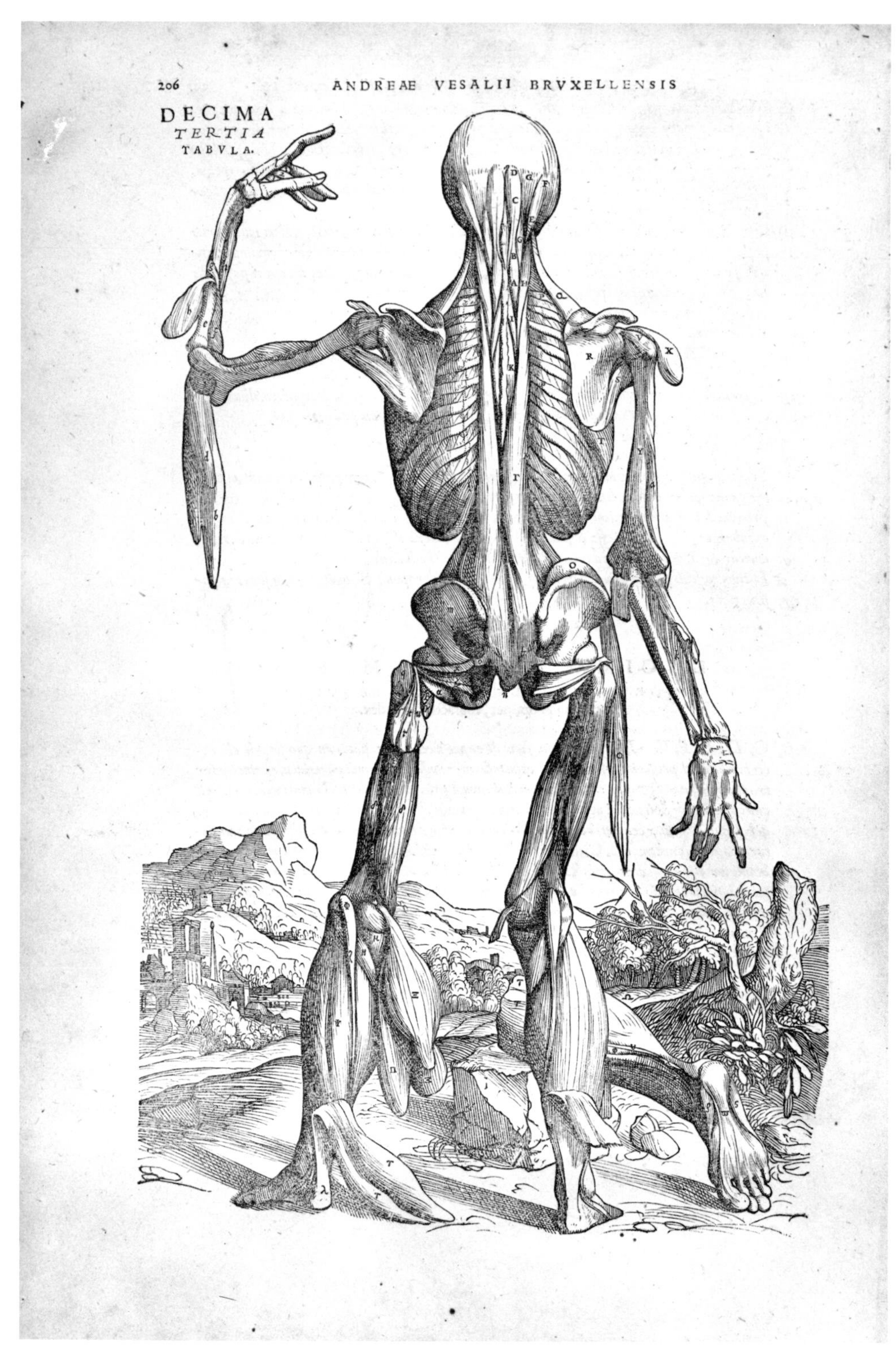

• 8e •

Anonymous, possibly by Jan Stevensz. van Calcar (Flemish, c. 1499–c. 1550)

THE THIRTEENTH PLATE OF MUSCLES, 1543

From Andreas Vesalius, *De Humani Corporis Fabrica* (Basel: Johannes Oporinus, 1543)

Woodcut, 15 15/16 x 10 5/8" (40.5 x 27 cm)

Purchased: SmithKline Beckman Corporation Fund

49-97-41i

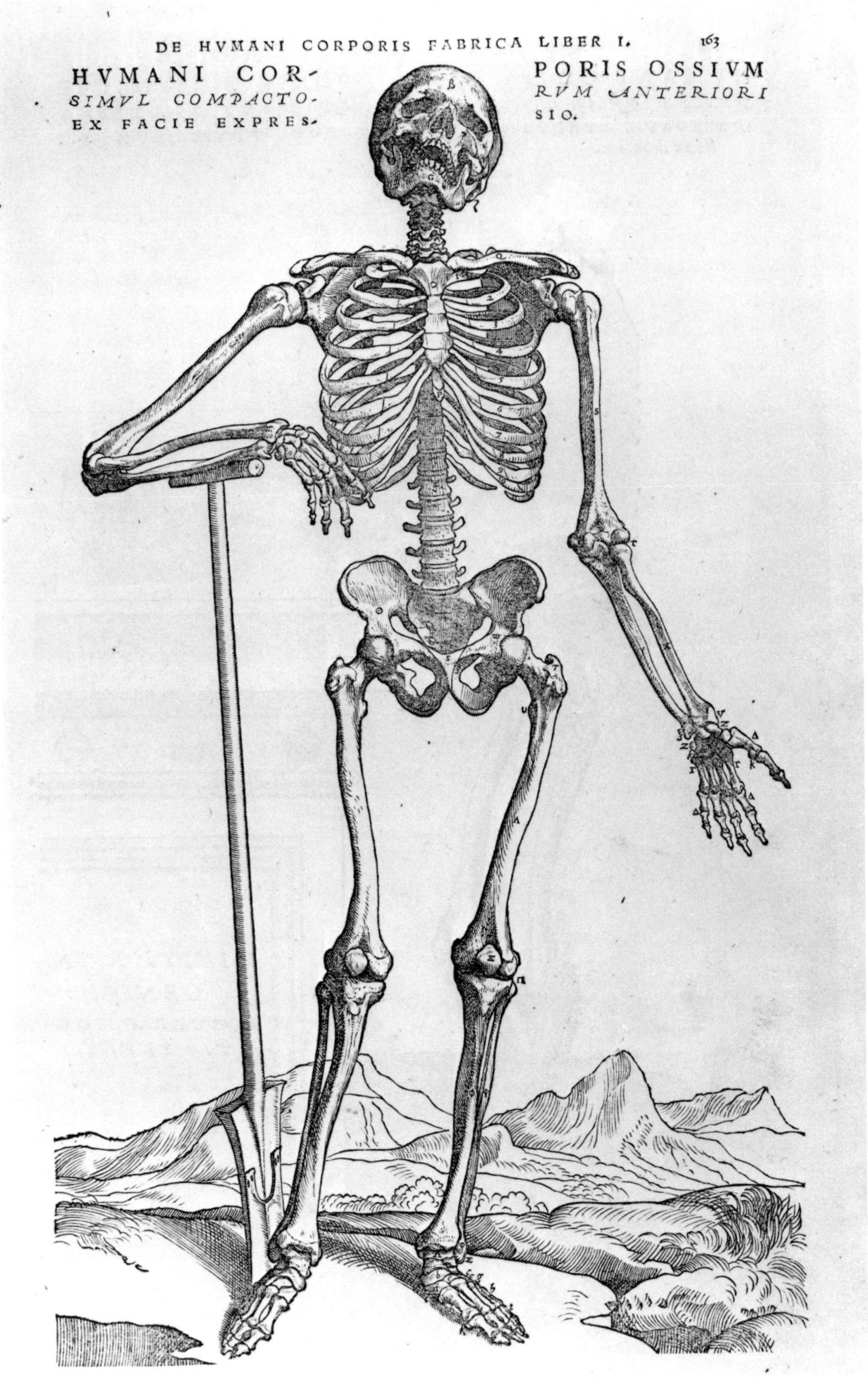

• 8f •

Anonymous, possibly by Jan Stevensz. van Calcar (Flemish, c. 1499–c. 1550)

ANTERIOR VIEW OF THE SKELETON, 1543

From Andreas Vesalius, *De Humani Corporis Fabrica* (Basel: Johannes Oporinus, 1543)

Woodcut, 15$\frac{15}{16}$ x 10$\frac{1}{2}$" (40.5 x 26.7 cm)

Purchased: SmithKline Beckman Corporation Fund

49-97-41c

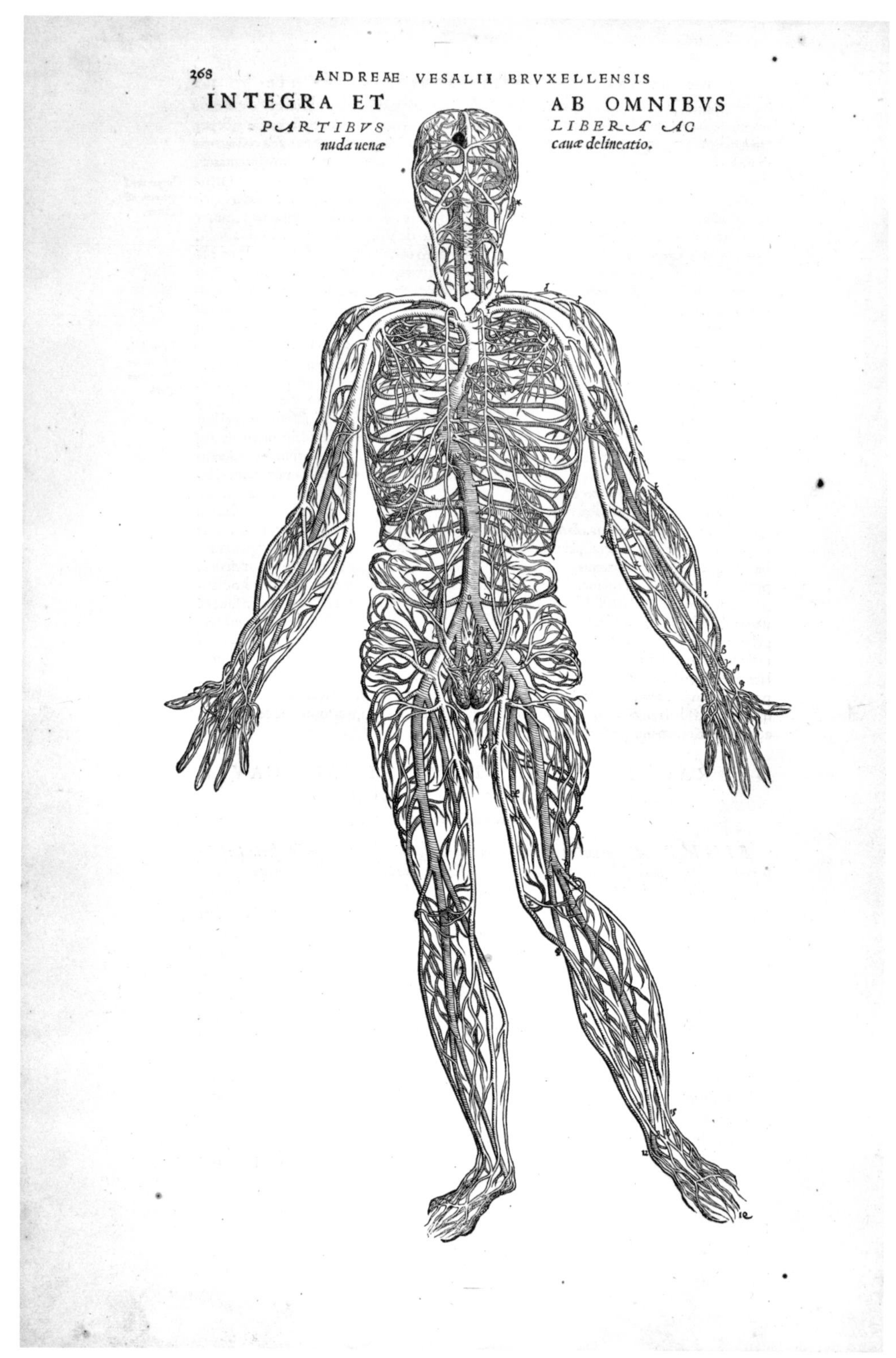

• 8g •

Anonymous, possibly by Jan Stevensz. van Calcar (Flemish, c. 1499–c. 1550)

DELINEATION OF THE VENA CAVA, 1543

From Andreas Vesalius, *De Humani Corporis Fabrica* (Basel: Johannes Oporinus, 1543)

Woodcut, 15 15/16 x 10 5/8" (40.5 x 27 cm)

Purchased: SmithKline Beckman Corporation Fund

49-97-41e

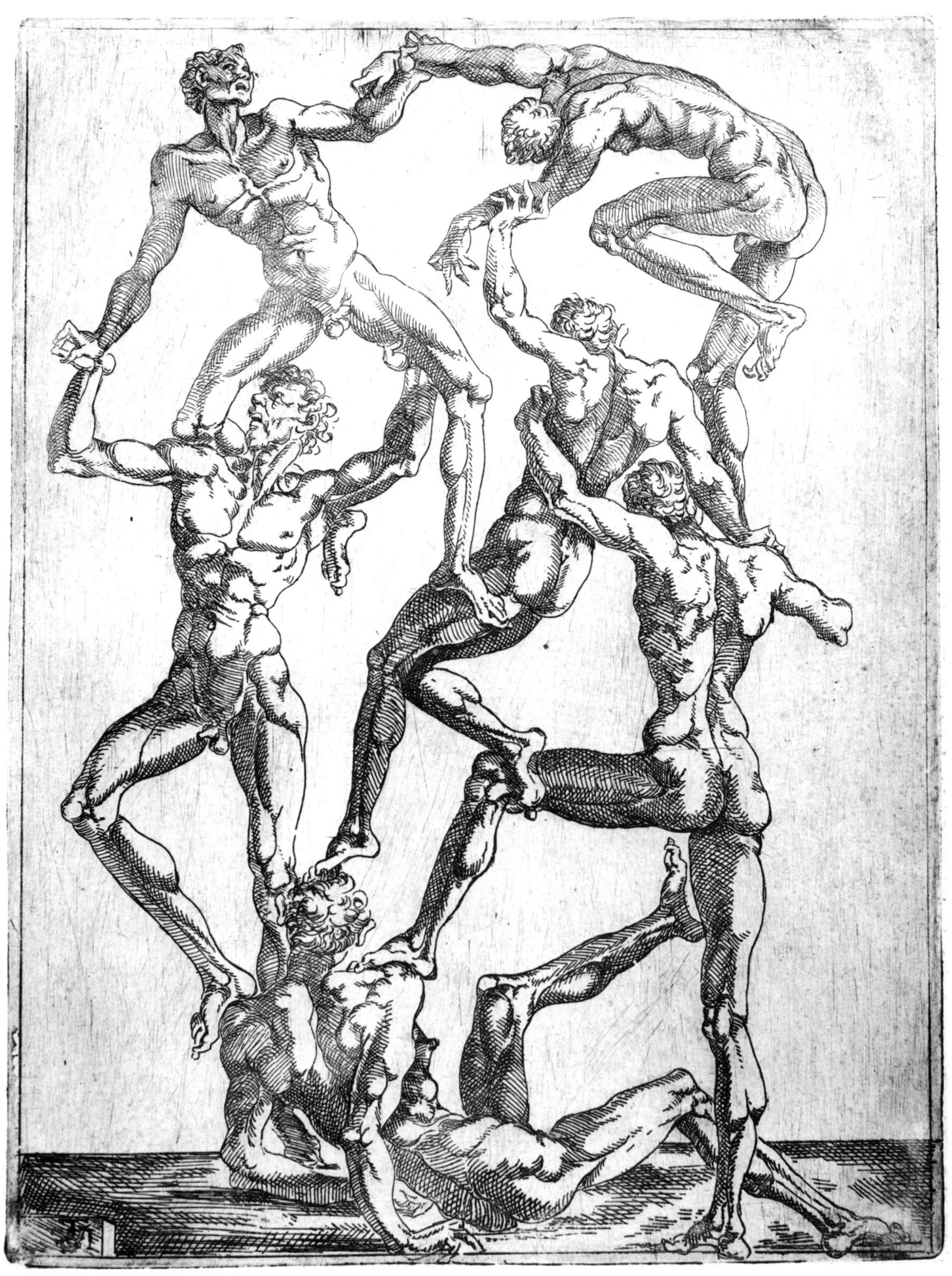

• 9 •

Anonymous, possibly by Juste de Juste (French, 1505–1559)

PYRAMID OF SIX MEN, 1542–48

Etching, 10$\frac{9}{16}$ x 8$\frac{1}{8}$" (27 x 20.6 cm)

Purchased: SmithKline Beckman Corporation Fund

1984-52-1

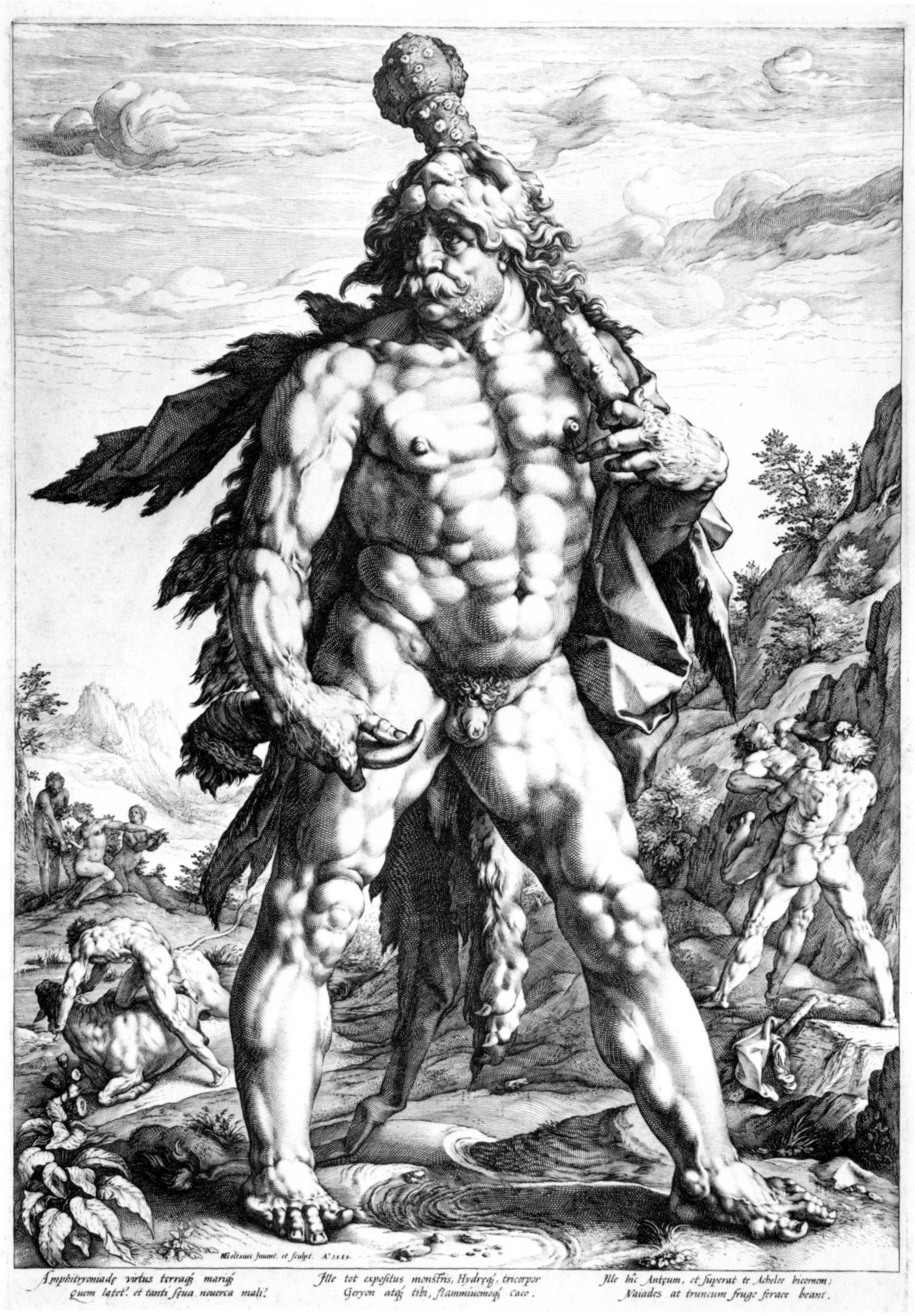

• 10 •

Hendrik Goltzius (Dutch, 1558–1617)

THE LARGE HERCULES, 1589

Engraving (i/ii), 22⅜ x 16″ (56.8 x 40.7 cm)

Charles M. Lea Collection

28-42-1596

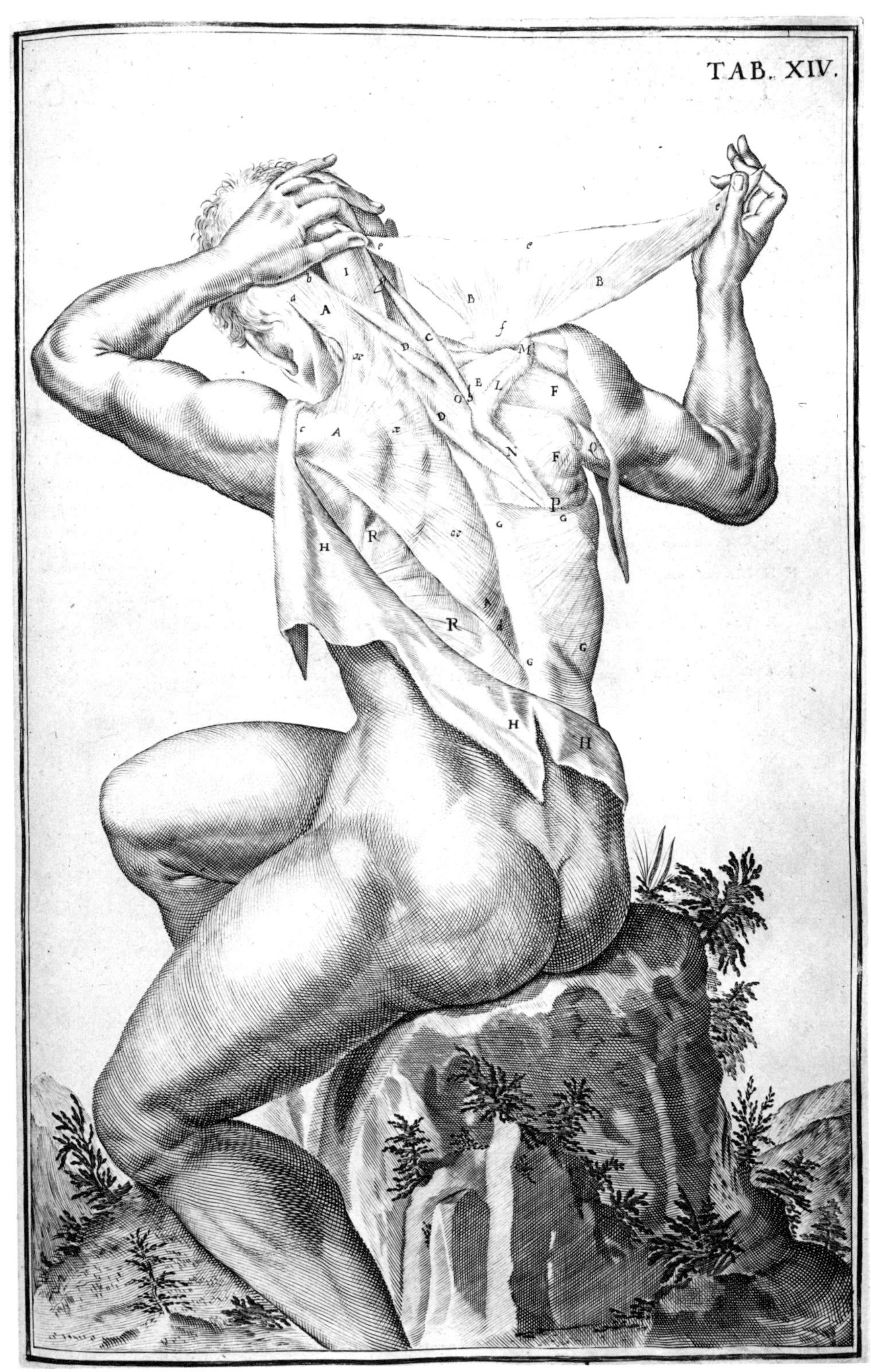

• 11 •

Anonymous (Northern, active early seventeenth century)

MUSCLES OF THE BACK, c. 1600–1616

From Adriaan van den Spieghel, *Opera Quae Extant, Omnia,* ed. Johannes Antonides van der Linden (Amsterdam: Johannem Blaeu, 1645)

Engraving, 16¾ x 10 15/16" (42.6 x 27.8 cm)

Purchased: SmithKline Beckman Corporation Fund

1982-41-1bb

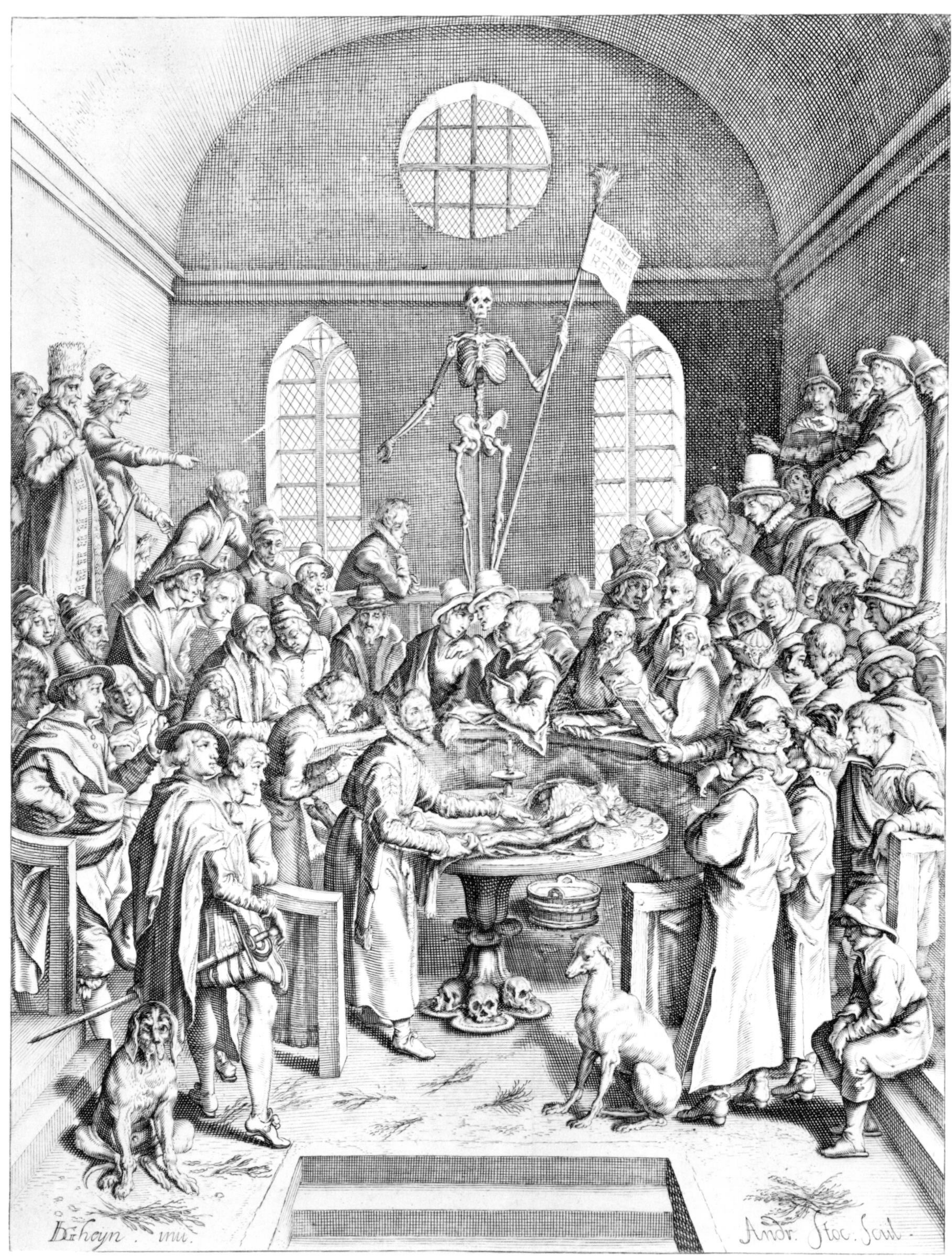

Andries Jacobsz. Stock (Dutch, c. 1580–after 1648)
After Jacques de Gheyn II (Flemish, 1565–1629)
THE ANATOMY LESSON OF DR. PIETER PAAW, 1615

First inserted in Pieter Paaw, *Primitiae Anatomicae. De Humani Corporis Ossibus* (Leiden: Justi à Colster, 1615)
Engraving, 11⅝ x 9″ (29.5 x 22.9 cm) (trimmed)
Charles M. Lea Collection
28-42-4554

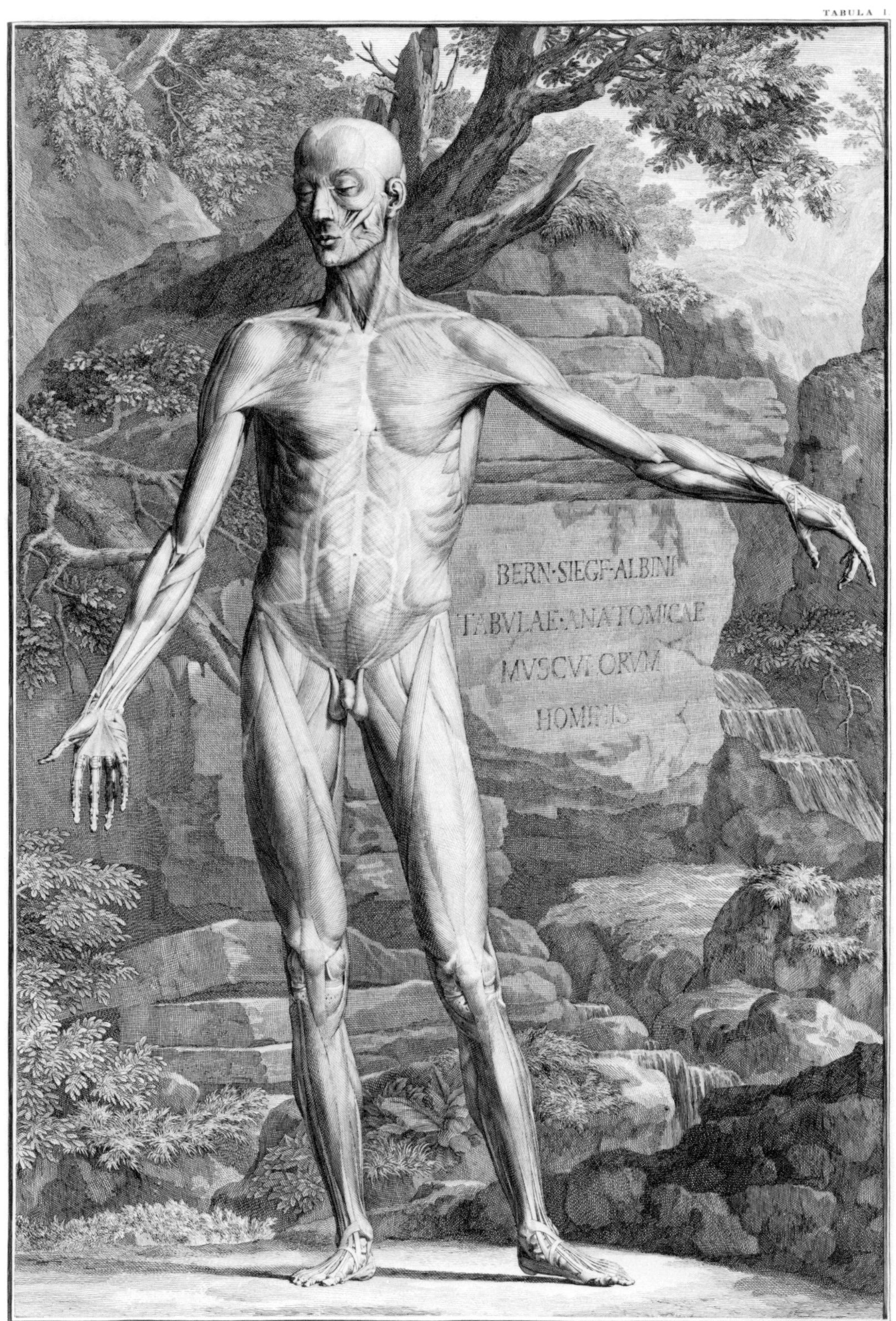

Jan Wandelaer (Dutch, 1690–1759)

MUSCLE MAN, 1739

From Bernhard Siegfried Albinus, *Tabulae Sceleti et Musculorum Corporis Humani* (Leiden: J. & H. Verbeek, 1747)
Etching and engraving, 22¾ x 16⁵⁄₁₆″ (57.8 x 41.4 cm)
Gift of Dr. Richard H. Chamberlain
73-83-1

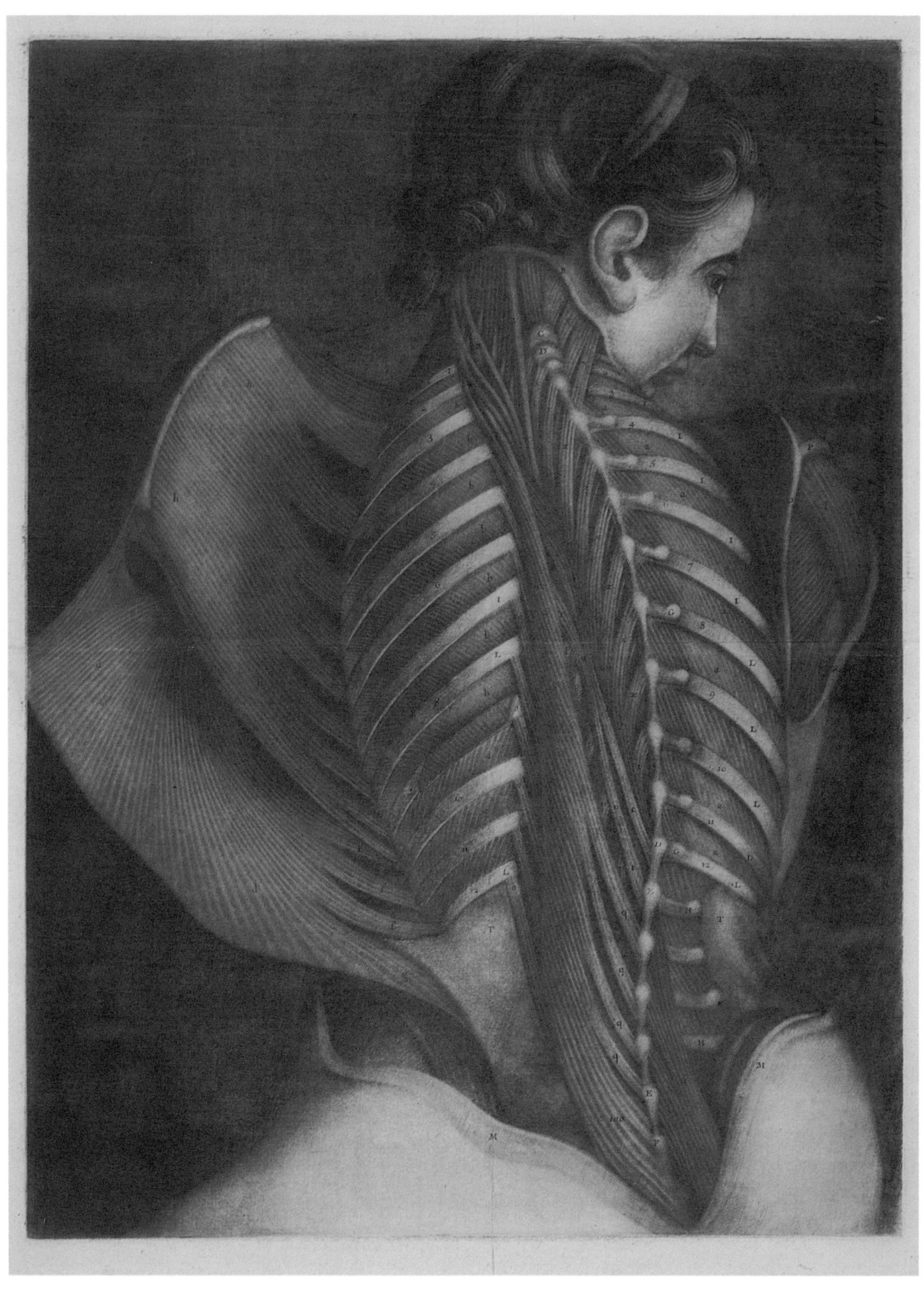

• 14 •

Jacques-Fabien Gautier-Dagoty (French, 1716–1785)

MUSCLES OF THE BACK, 1746

From Joseph Guichard Duverney, *Essai d'anatomie, en tableaux imprimés . . .* (Paris: Chez Le Sieur Gautier, 1745–48)

Color mezzotint, 23¹⁵⁄₁₆ x 18⅛" (60.8 x 46 cm)

Purchased: SmithKline Beckman Corporation Fund

68-25-79m

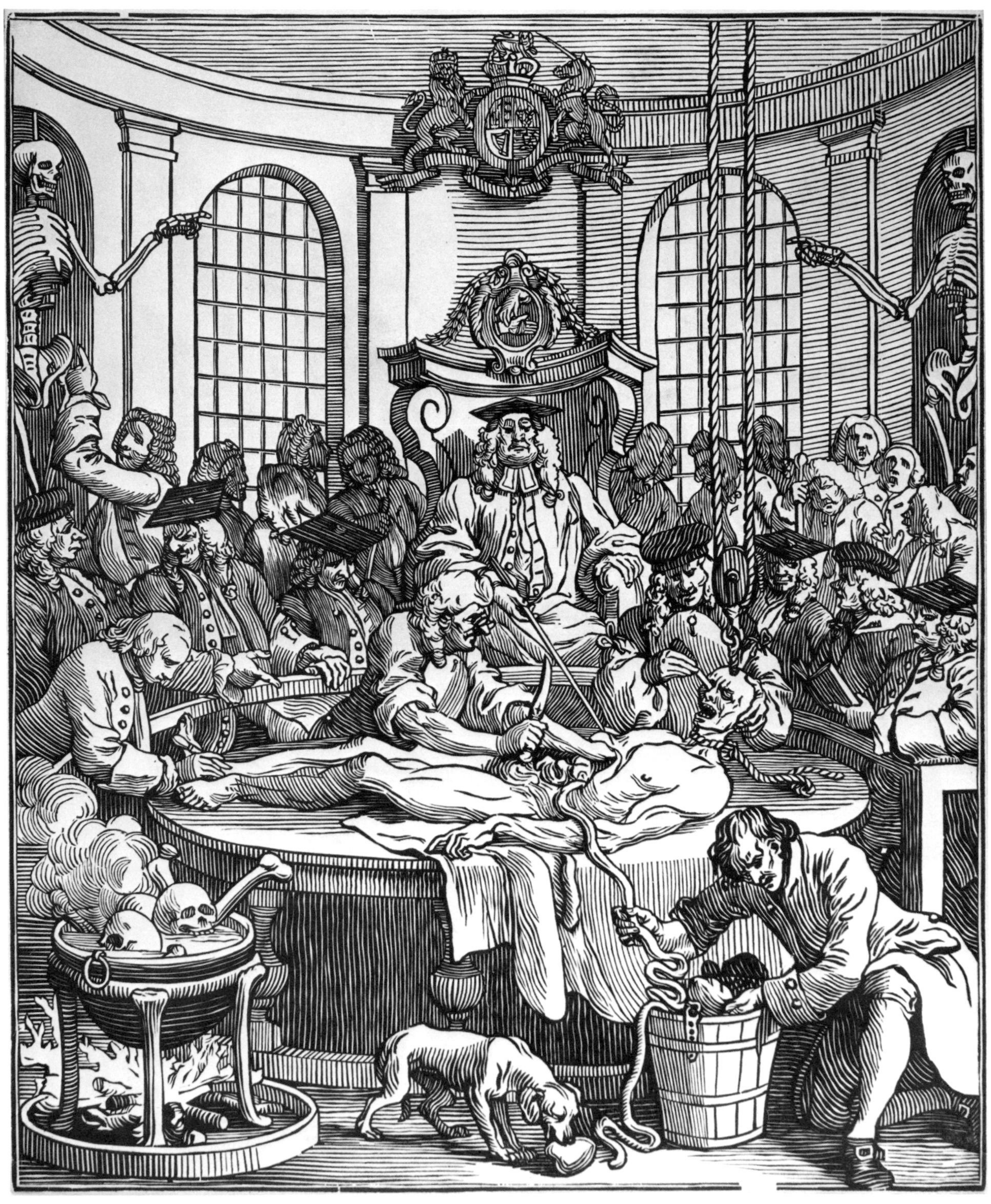

• 15 •

John Bell (English, active mid-eighteenth century)
After William Hogarth (English, 1697–1764)
THE REWARD OF CRUELTY, 1751

Woodcut, 18⅛ x 15¼" (46.1 x 38.7 cm)
Purchased: SmithKline Beckman Corporation Fund
1980-18-2

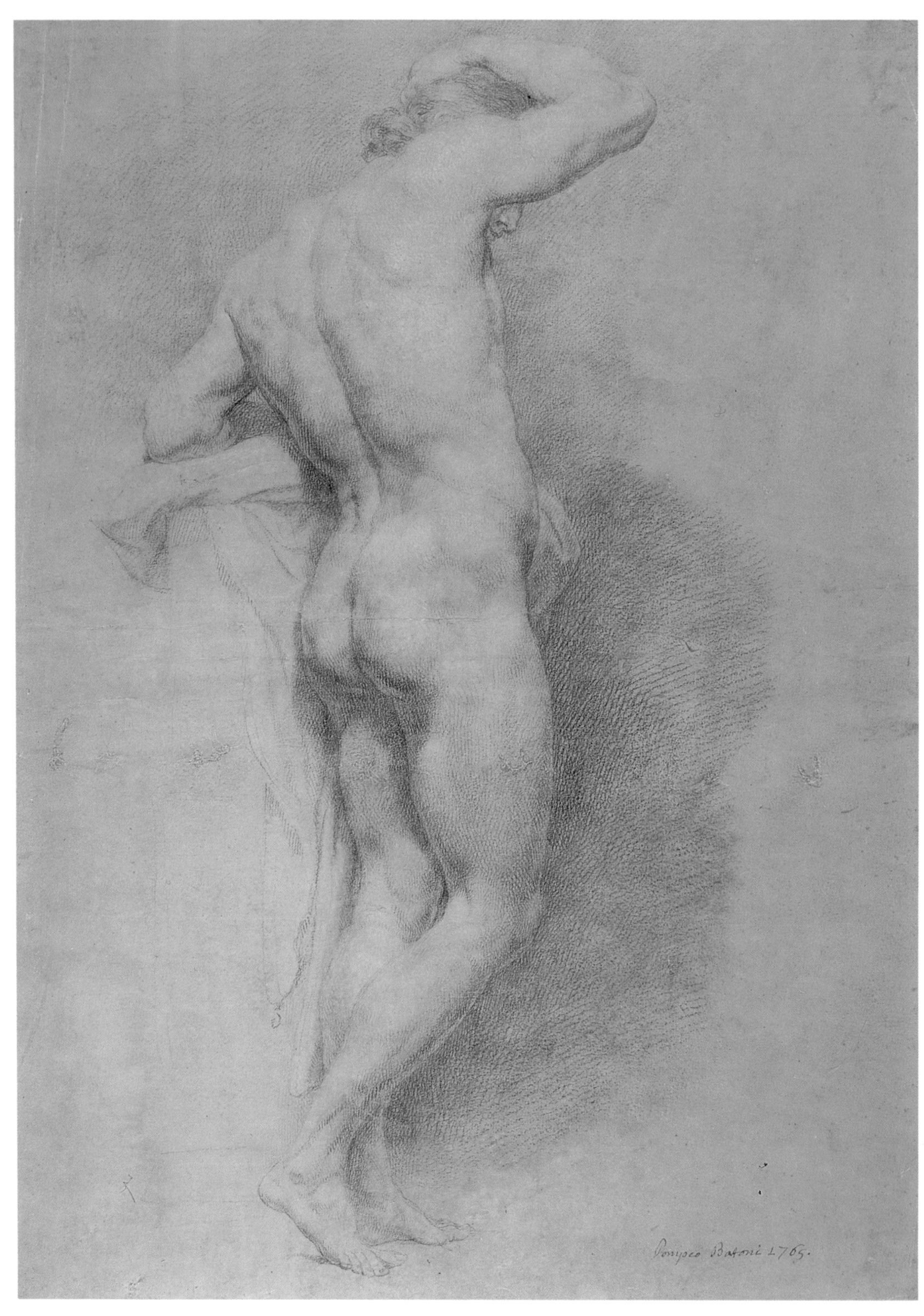

• 16 •

Pompeo Batoni (Italian, 1708–1787)

MALE NUDE LEANING ON A PEDESTAL, 1765

Black and white chalk on blue prepared paper, 20¹¹⁄₁₆ x 15¼" (52.5 x 38.7 cm)

Bequest of Anthony Morris Clark

1978-70-171

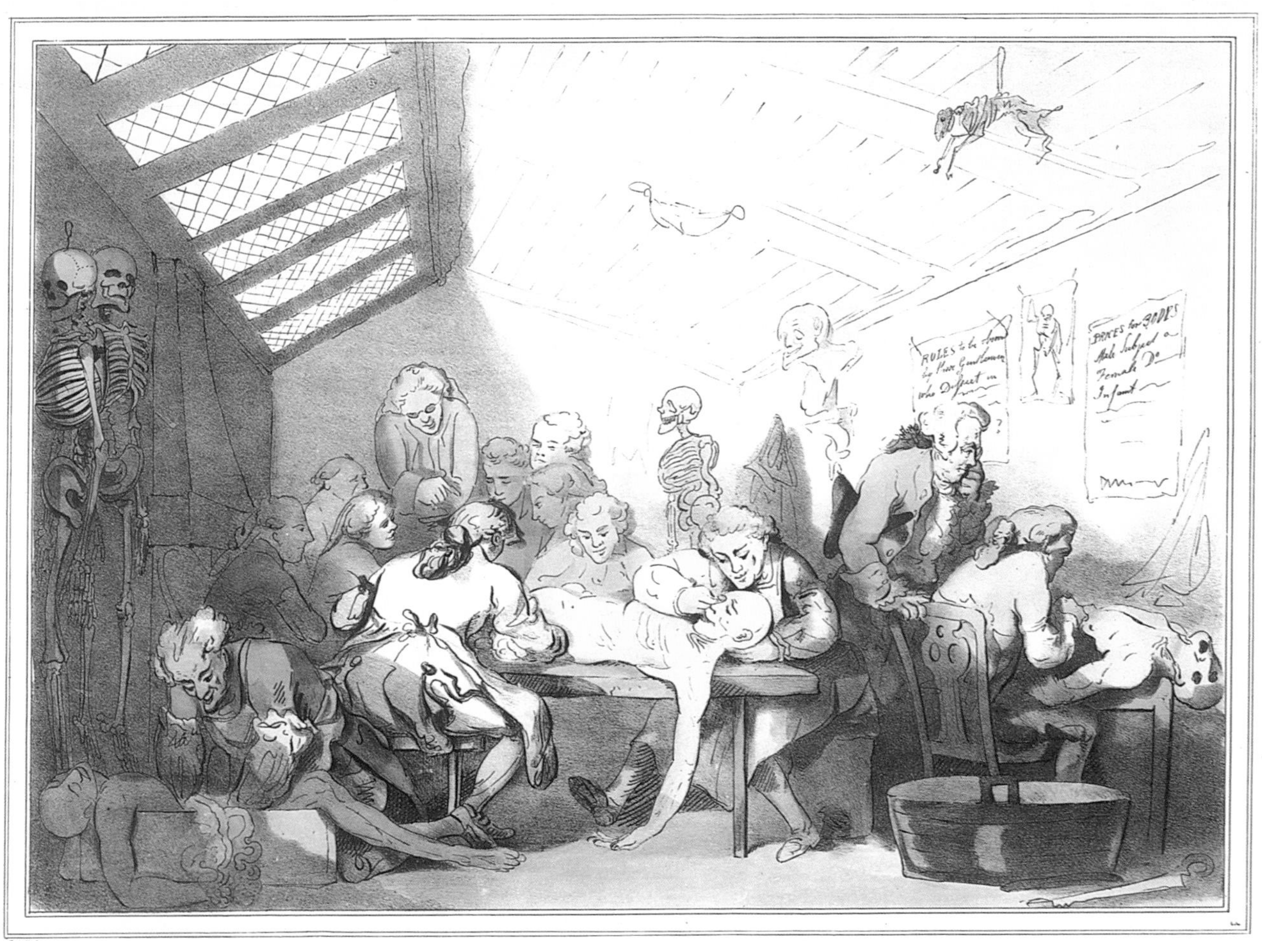

• 17 •

T. C. Wilson (English, nineteenth century)
After Thomas Rowlandson (English, 1756–1827)
THE DISSECTING ROOM, early nineteenth century

Hand-colored lithograph, 11 5/16 x 14 13/16" (28.8 x 37.6 cm) (image)
Purchased: SmithKline Beckman Corporation Fund
68-215-34

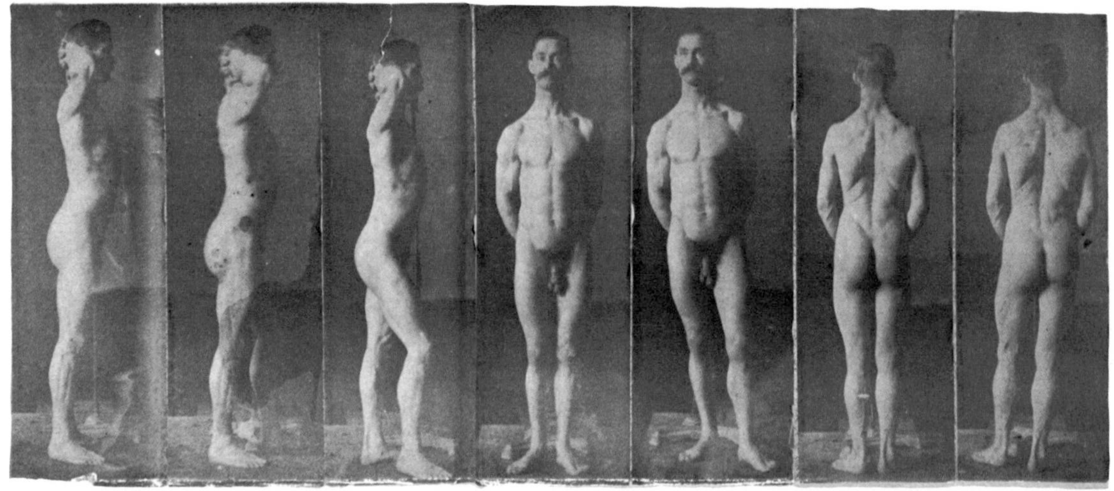

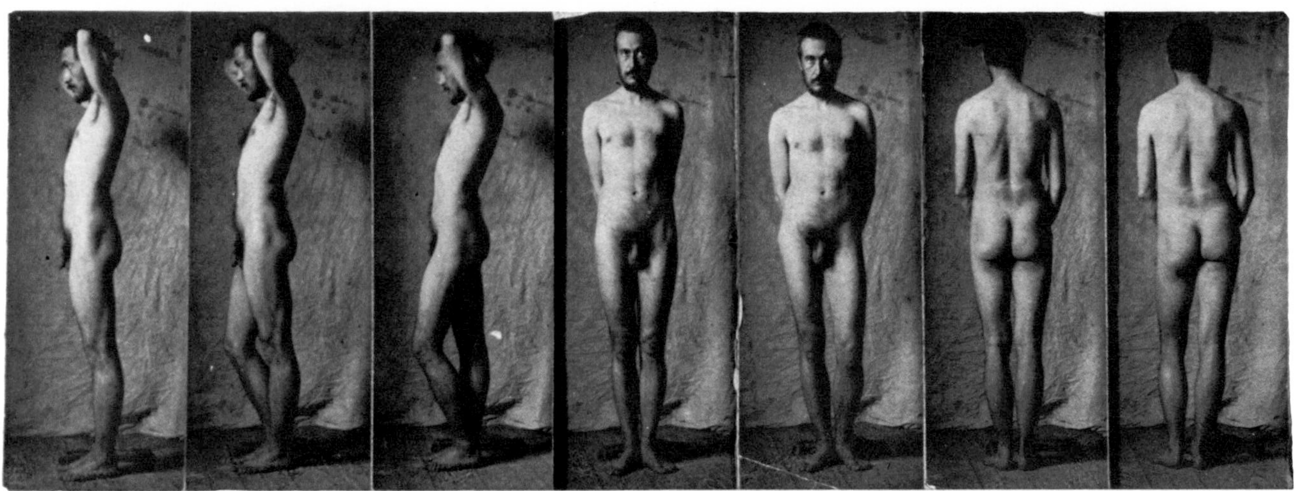

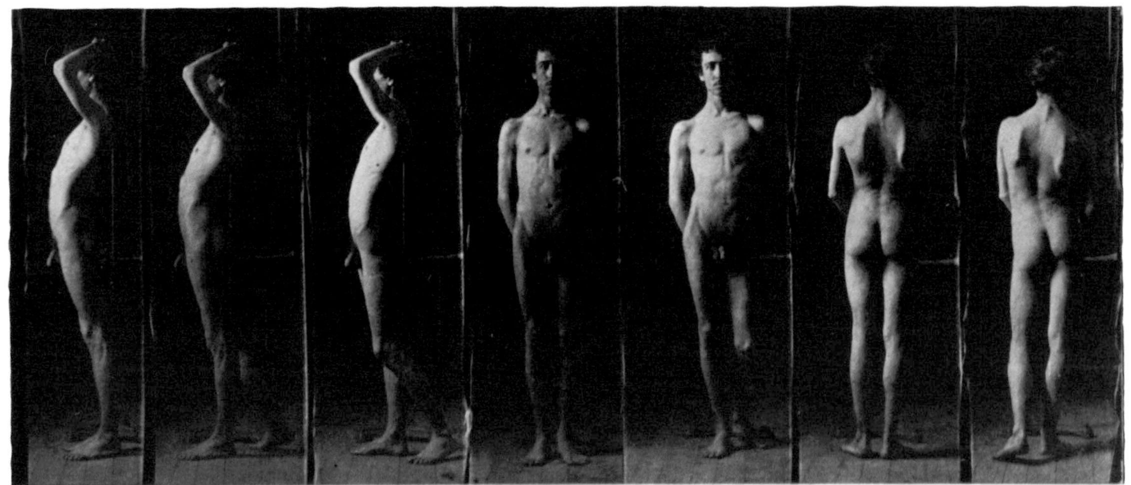

• 18a–c •

Thomas Eakins (American, 1844–1916)

a: JESSE GODLEY, b: THOMAS EAKINS,
c: JOHN LAURIE WALLACE; 1883–84

Albumen prints; a: 3⁵⁄₁₆ x 7¹¹⁄₁₆" (8.4 x 19.5 cm), b: 3¹⁄₁₆ x 8³⁄₈" (7.8 x 21.3 cm), c: 3¹⁄₈ x 7⁷⁄₁₆" (7.9 x 18.9 cm)

Purchased: SmithKline Beckman Corporation Fund

1984-89-6,3,1

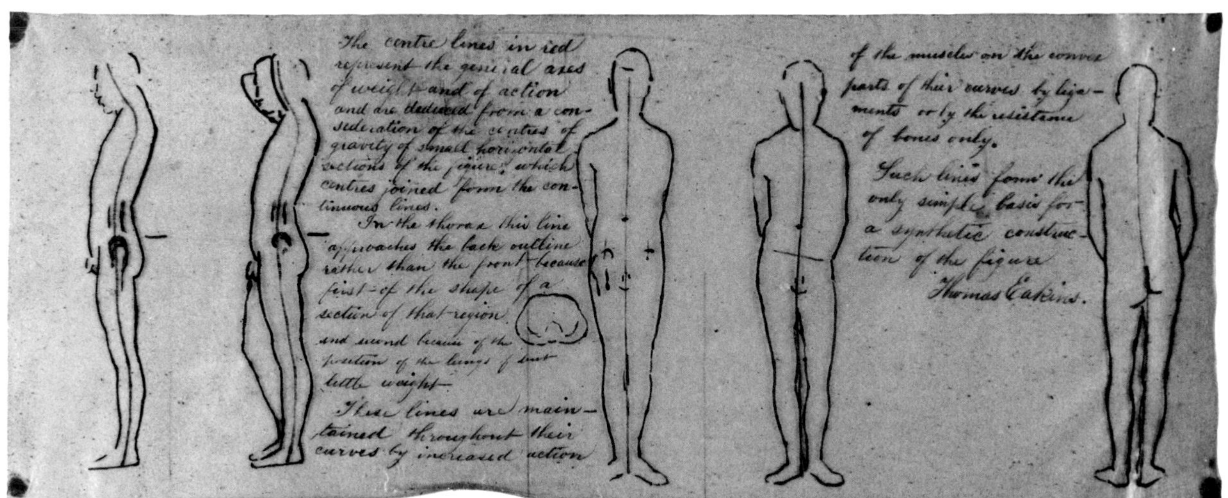

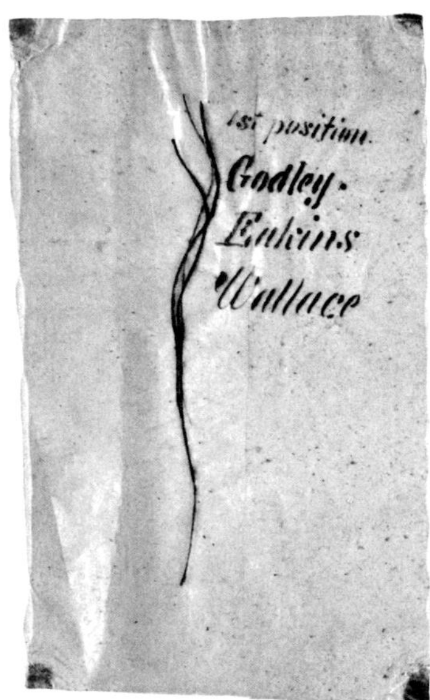

• 18d •

Thomas Eakins (American, 1844–1916)

FIRST POSITION: GODLEY, EAKINS, AND WALLACE, 1883–84

Black, red, and blue ink with traces of graphite on tracing paper; two irregular sheets: 3¼ x 8½" (8.3 x 21.6 cm), 3¹¹⁄₁₆ x 2⁵⁄₁₆" (9.4 x 5.8 cm)

Purchased: SmithKline Beckman Corporation Fund

1984-22-7,8

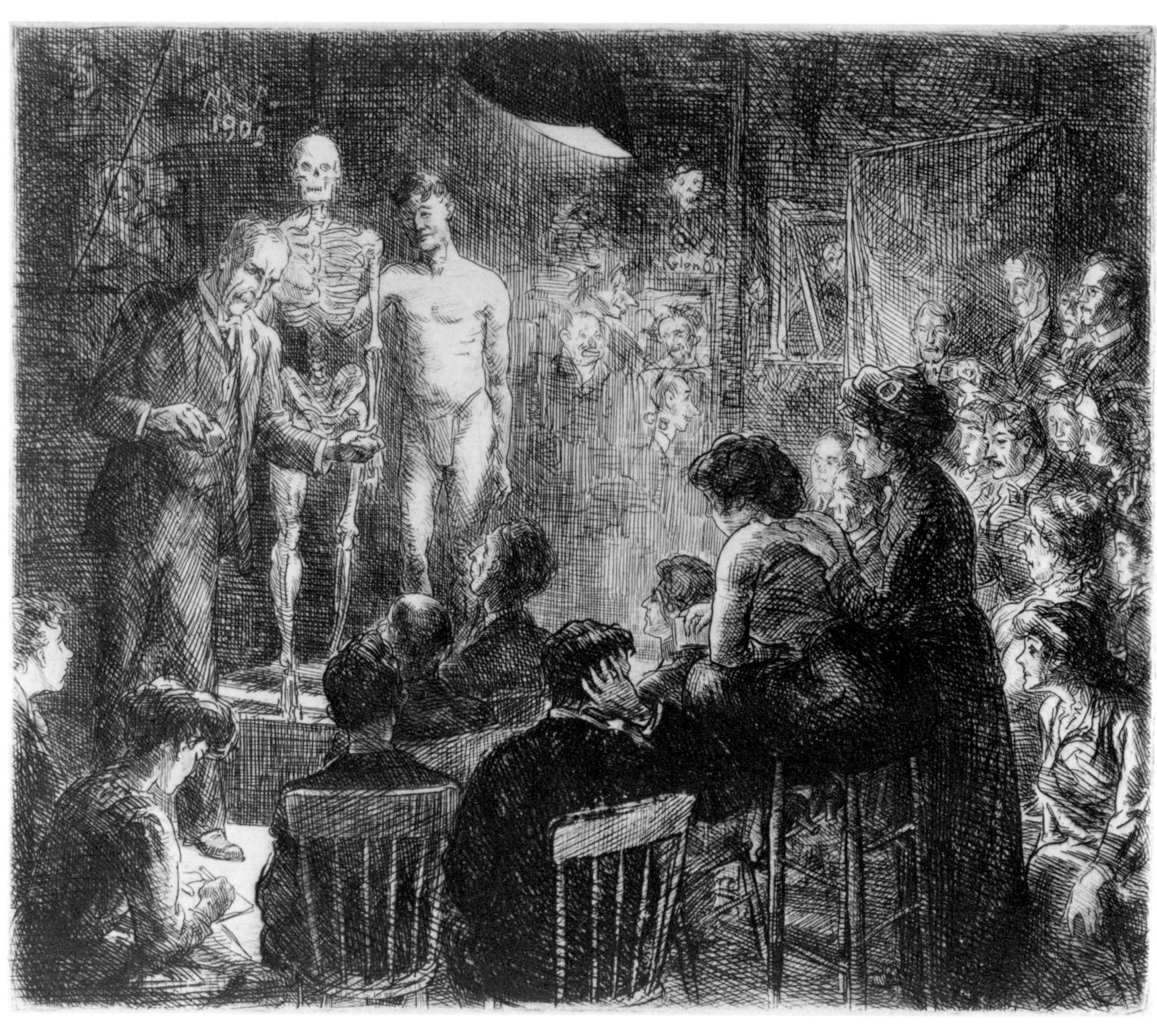

• 19 •

John Sloan (American, 1871–1951)

ANSHUTZ ON ANATOMY, 1912

Etching (vii/viii), 7⁹⁄₁₆ x 8¹⁵⁄₁₆" (19.2 x 22.7 cm)

Gift of Mrs. John Sloan

75-155-206

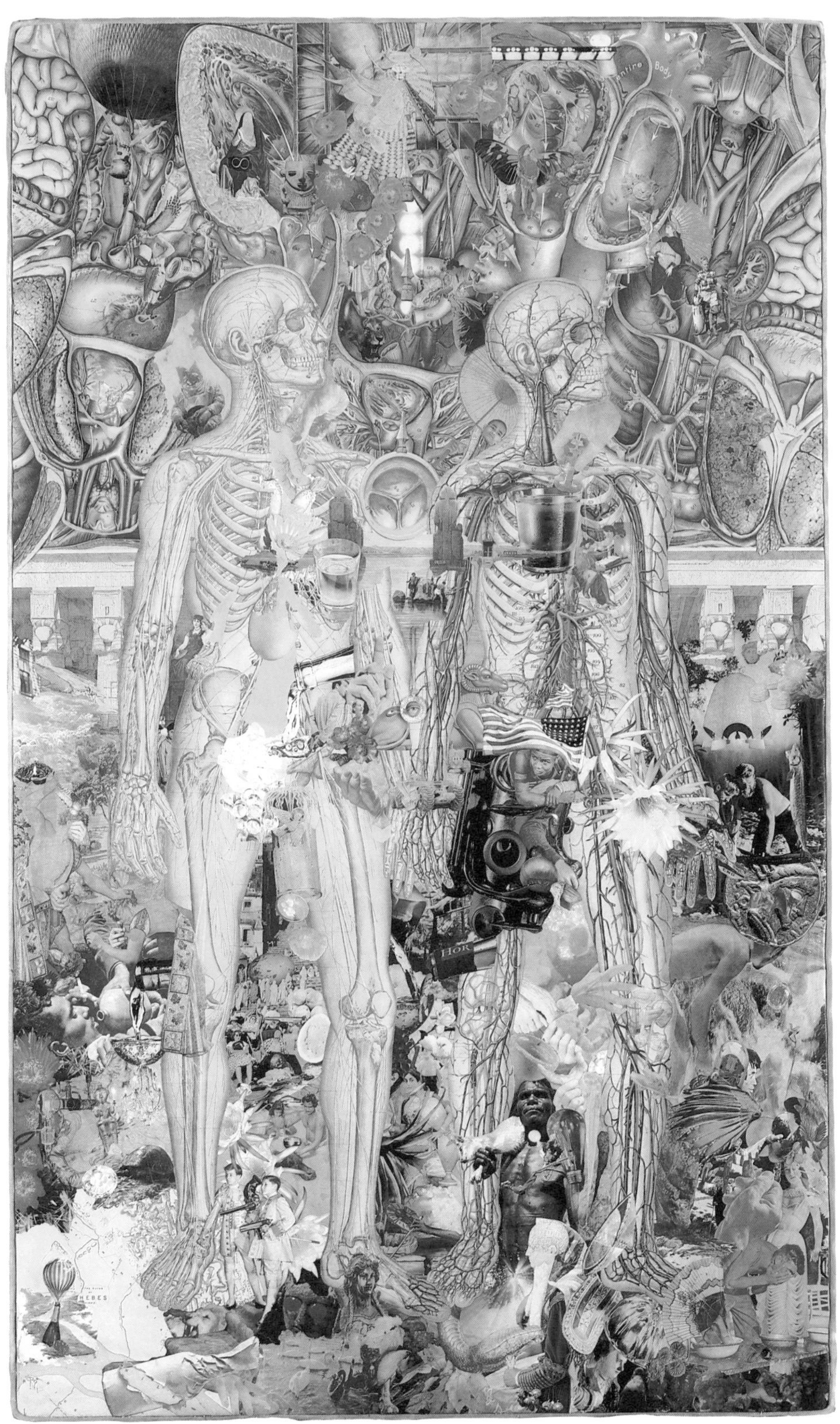

• 20 •

Jess (American, born 1923)

THE SUN: TAROT XIX, 1960

Collage of various lithographic illustrations, primarily offset, mounted on heavy wove paper, with a window-shade pull, 75½ x 45¾" (191.8 x 116.3 cm) (sight)

Purchased: SmithKline Beckman Corporation Fund

1984-78-1

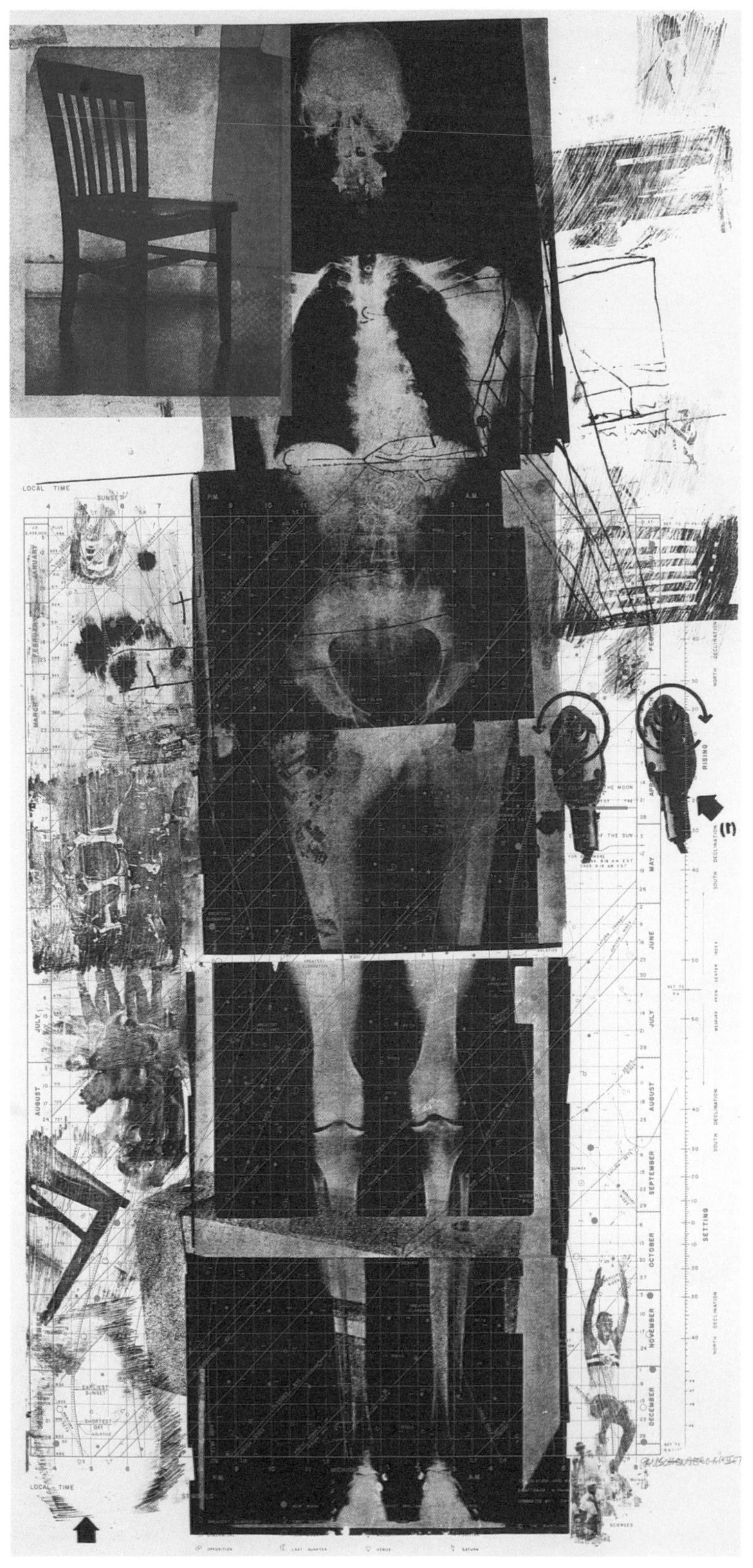

• 21 •

Robert Rauschenberg (American, born 1925)

BOOSTER, 1967

From "Booster and Seven Studies," 1967

Color lithograph and silkscreen, 72 x 35⁹⁄₁₆" (182.9 x 90.3 cm)

Purchased with funds contributed by the International Graphic Arts Society in honor of Carl Zigrosser

67-183-1

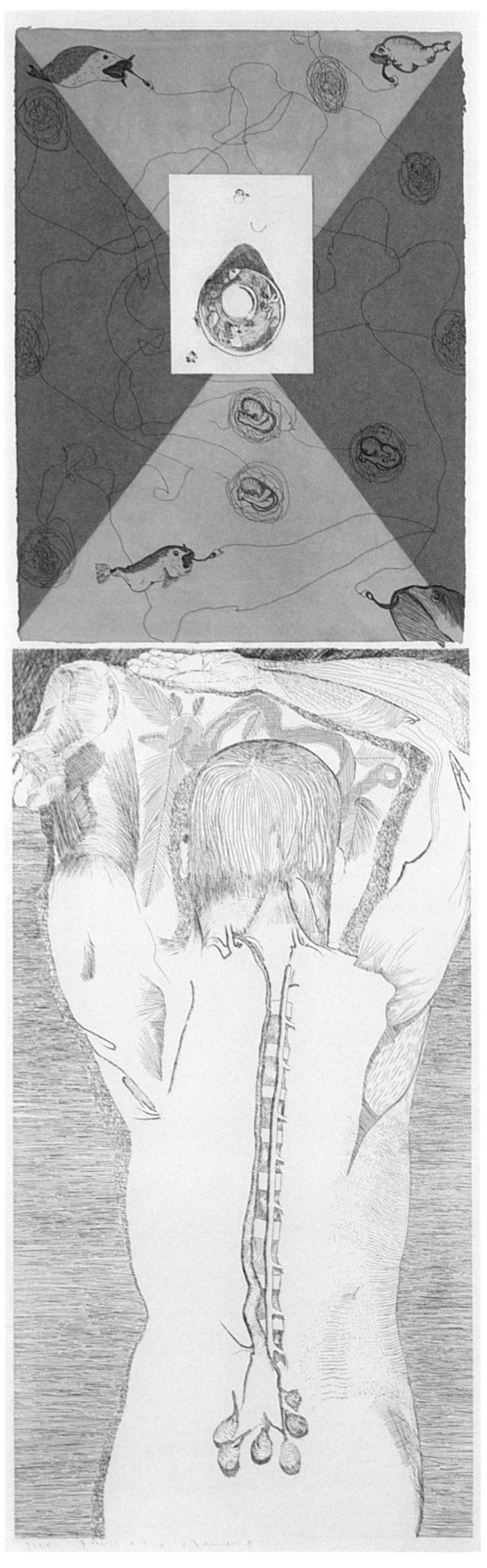

• 22 •

Francesco Clemente (Italian, born 1952)

TELAMON #1, 1981

Etching, drypoint, soft-ground etching, and aquatint, 61 1/16 x 19 1/8" (155.1 x 48.6 cm)

Purchased: SmithKline Beckman Corporation Fund

1982-80-2

HEALERS

mȳn kint ley̅t gichtich indē huy̅se eñ
wort qualy̅ck ghepinicht Eñ om die
brooschey̅t v̄ natueren. die stinckent-
hey̅t v̄ sonden. eñ menichfuldichey̅t v̄
aley̅nden en ben ic n̄z weerdich dattu
soudes comē ond̄ mȳ dack. so nauwe
so onrey̅ne eñ so v̄uallende Mer segt
alleen een woert. eñ si sal ghenesen tot
uwen ghebode Eñ wāt dit woert vā
centurio vā alsulcker cracht was dat
tet hē weerdich maecte dz cristus sȳn
herte bewoende. eñ ō tlichaem xp̄i te
ōtfaen inden hey̅ligē sacramēte n̄ye
māt weerdich en is Daerō als wȳ ter
tafelen gods gaē eñ wi ons brooschz
aenmerckē soe sellen wi hier by̅ ghe-
leert sȳnde segghē Here ic en ben n̄z
weerdich dattu comē soudes ond̄ mȳ
dack / ic en ben n̄z weerdich dat ic dinē
weerdigē lichaem ōtfae in minē mōt

Mer segt alleen een woort eñ mȳne
ziele sal ghesont werdē. ¶ Ghebet.
Here ih̄u xp̄e ic en ben n̄z weerdich
dattu incomes ond̄ dat dack mȳns
vley̅schs. wāt dz kint v̄ sinlichey̅t ley̅t
gichtich ghebrokē mits die siechey̅t v̄
sonden int huy̅s mȳns lichaems eñ
wort qualic ghepinicht met beroerin
ghen v̄ begeertē Mer comt by̅ instor
tinghen v̄ gracien. eñ segt met eenen
woerde v̄ warachtichey̅t. dat mȳ kint
ghesont worde eñ opsta vanden son
den Ontfermhertige here gheeft mi
ond̄ die macht dȳnre graciē ghestelt
sȳnde Eñ vā dȳnre gracien ond̄ mȳ
hebbende natuerlike crachten dat ic
macht hebbē moet te v̄driuē scadelȳ
ke ghedachtē eñ beruertē Eñ int goe
de te gheduerē. eñ den lichaē te beuelē
dattet ond̄danicht si den gheest Amē

q ij

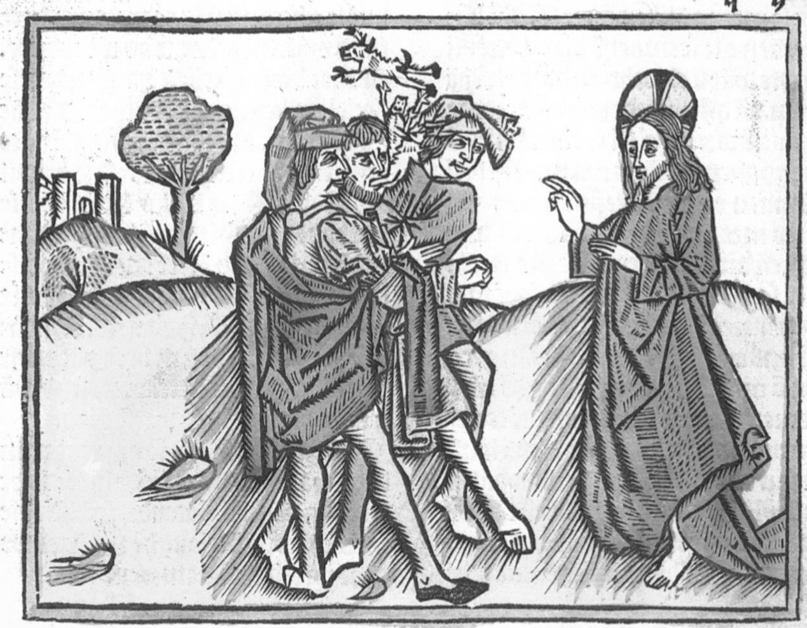

• 23 •

Attributed to the First Antwerp Woodcutter (Flemish, active 1485–91)

CHRIST CASTING OUT DEMONS, 1487

From Ludolphus of Saxony, *Tboeck vanden Leven ons Heeren Ihesu Christi* (Antwerp: Gerard Leeu, 1487)

Hand-colored woodcut, 9⅝ x 6⅞" (24.4 x 17.5 cm)

Purchased: SmithKline Beckman Corporation Fund

58-150-1

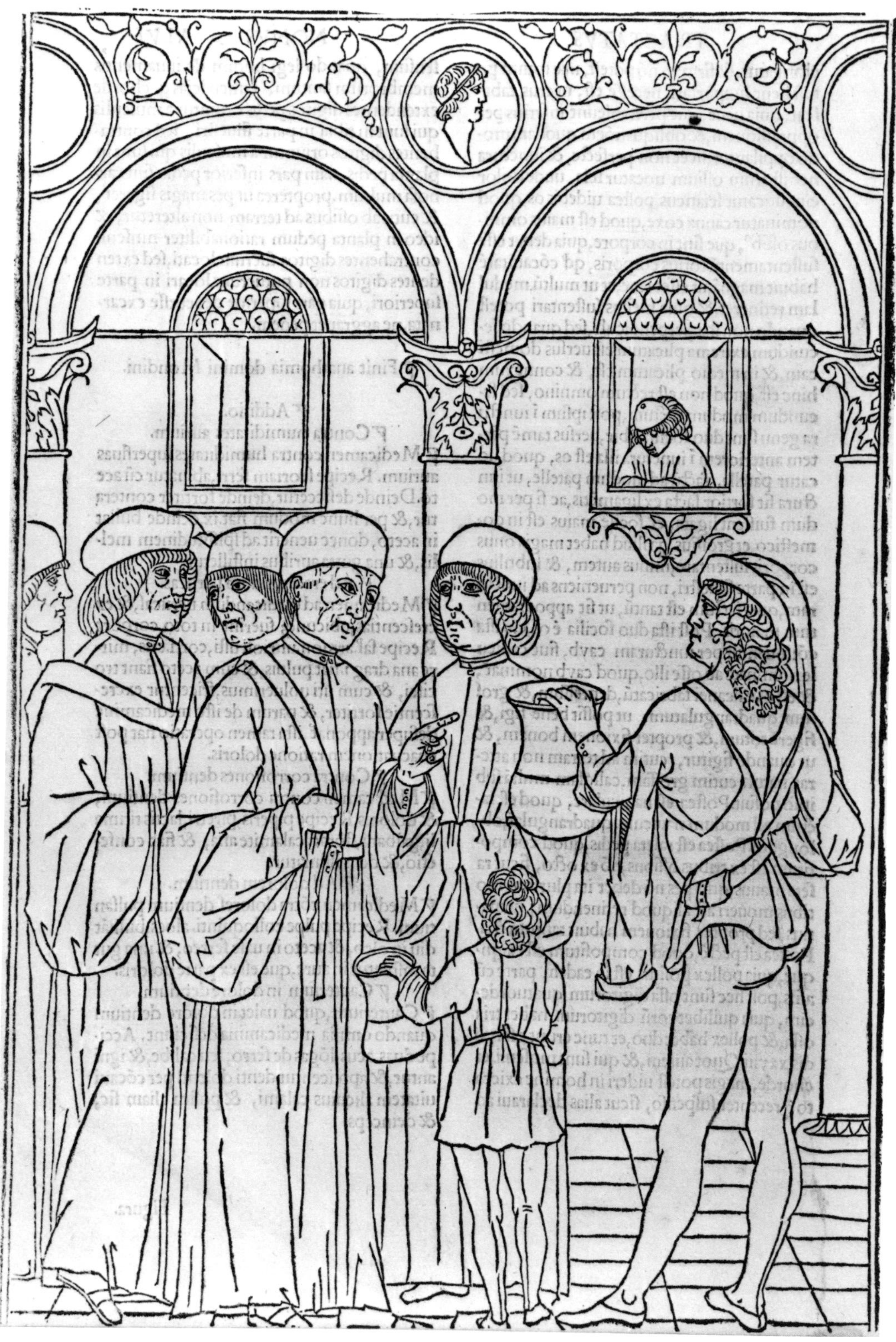

• 24 •

Anonymous (Italian, late fifteenth century)
Possibly after designs by Gentile Bellini (Italian, c. 1429–1507)
PHYSICIAN URINE GAZING, 1493

From Johannes de Ketham, *Fasciculus Medicinae* (Venice: Cesarem Arrivabenum, 1522)
Woodcut, 11⁷⁄₁₆ x 8¼" (29.1 x 21 cm)
Purchased: SmithKline Beckman Corporation Fund
49-97-3c

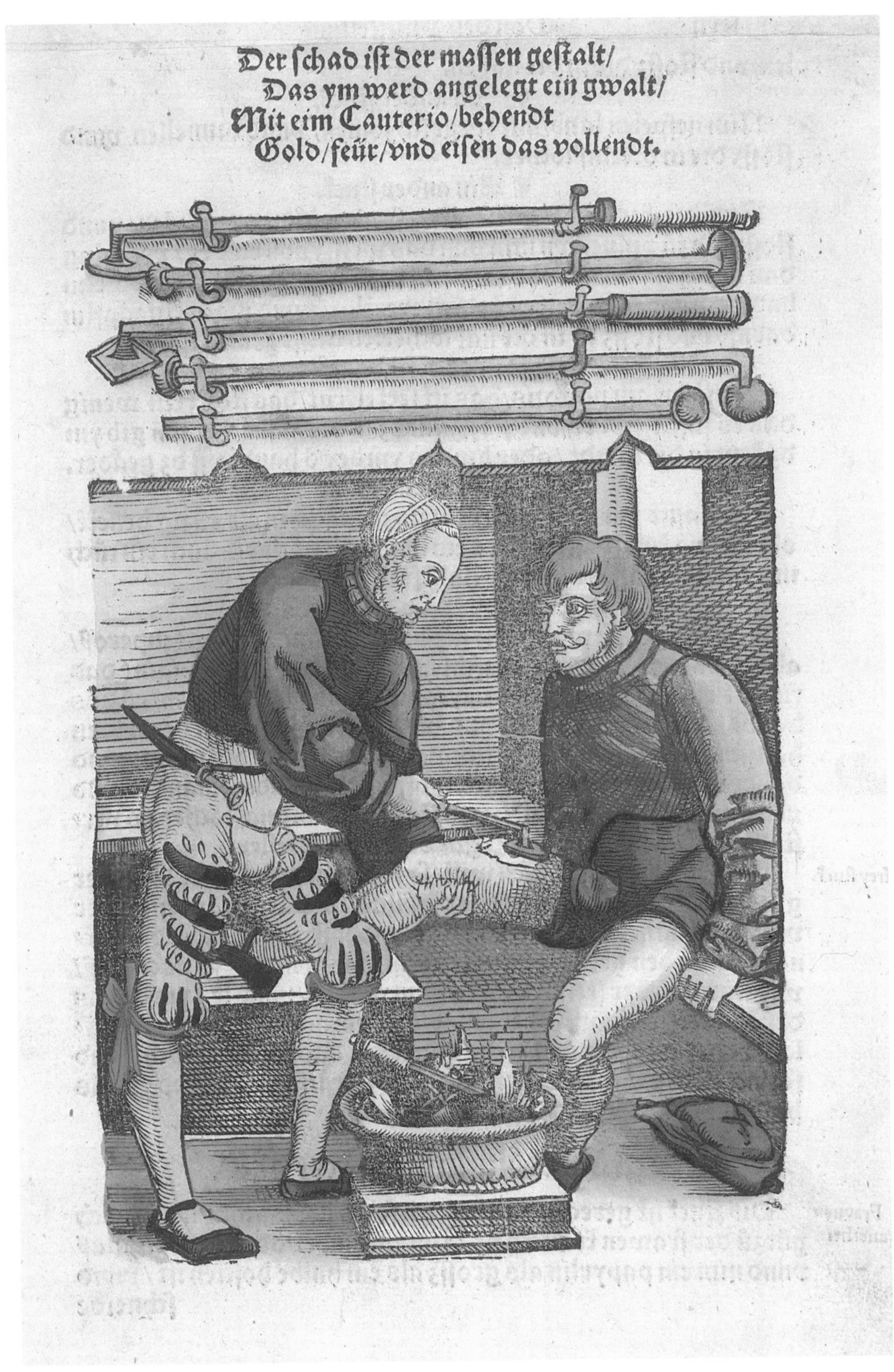

• 25a •

Anonymous (German, early sixteenth century)

CAUTERIZING A THIGH WOUND, 1517

From Hans von Gersdorff, *Feldtbuch der Wundartzney* . . . (Strasbourg: Hans Schotten, 1540)

Hand-colored woodcut, 9¾ x 6⅝" (24.8 x 16.9 cm)

Purchased: SmithKline Beckman Corporation Fund

49-97-11c

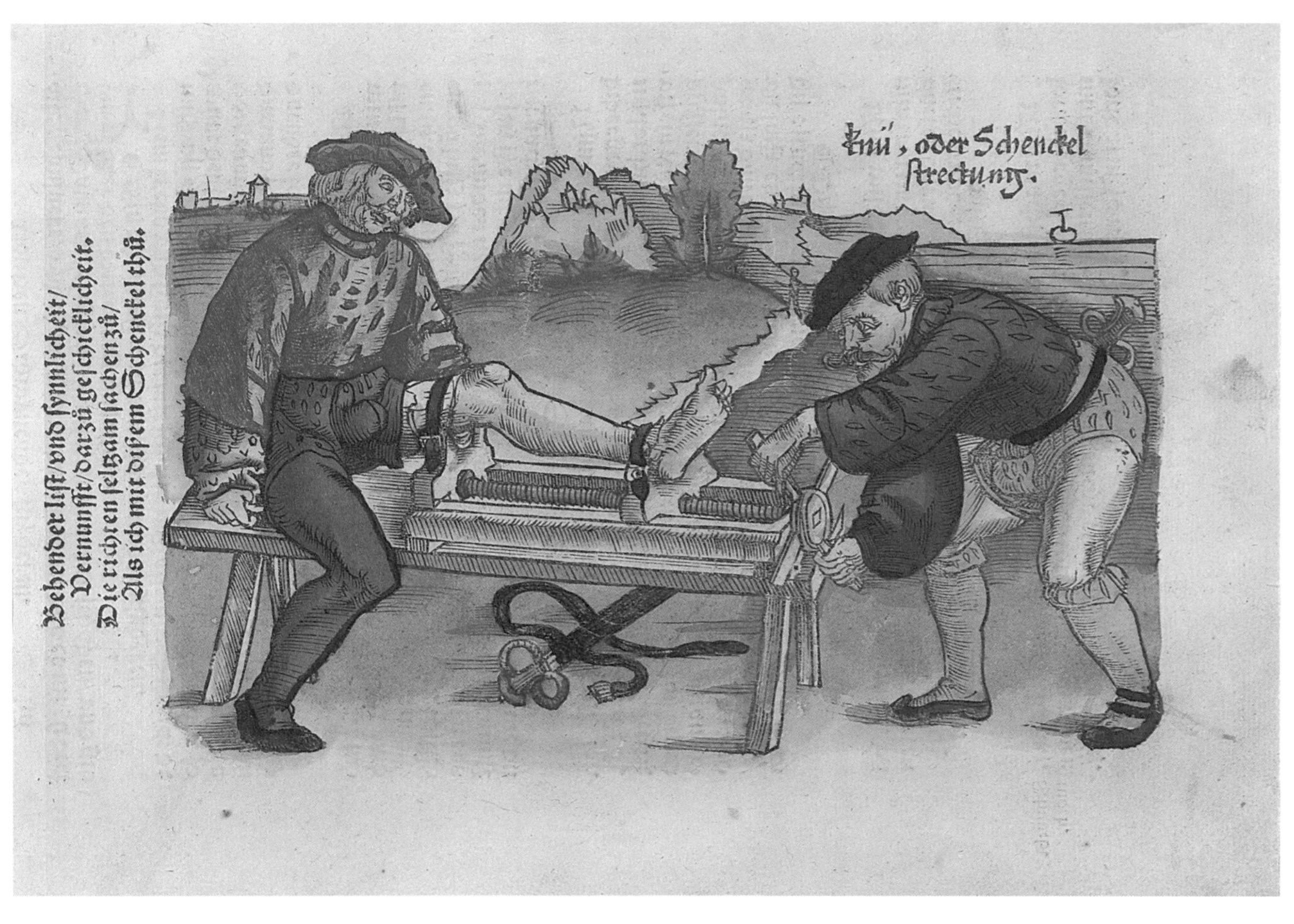

• 25b •

Anonymous (German, early sixteenth century)

EXTENSION APPARATUS, 1517

From Hans von Gersdorff, *Feldtbuch der Wundartzney* . . . (Strasbourg: Hans Schotten, 1540)

Hand-colored woodcut, 7 1/16 x 10 5/16" (18 x 26.2 cm)

Purchased: SmithKline Beckman Corporation Fund

49-97-11l

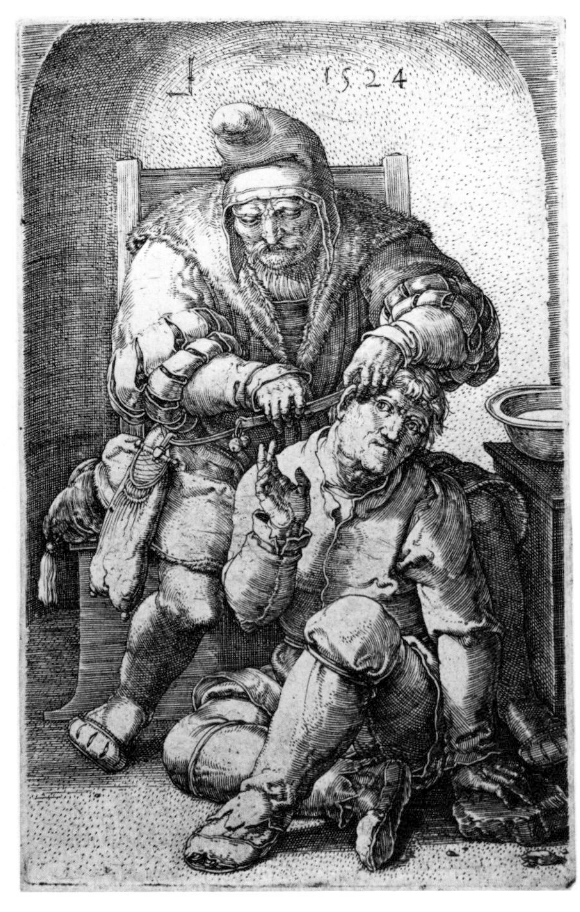

• 26 •

Lucas van Leyden (Dutch, 1489/94–1533)

THE SURGEON, 1524

Engraving, 4⁹⁄₁₆ x 2¹⁵⁄₁₆" (11.6 x 7.5 cm)

Purchased: SmithKline Beckman Corporation Fund

70-191-4

Troſtſpiegels Ander Bůch/
Von weechumb der Zene. Cap. XCIIII.

Multa premunt ſenium, ſenio ſunt multa ferenda, Si modò digna tibi grata ſenecta venit.

Darmit der menſch nit bleib gar rein/
Es můßt vns eh ein kleines bein

Vexiren/ Merckt mann wol darbei/
Wie elend vnſer leben ſei.

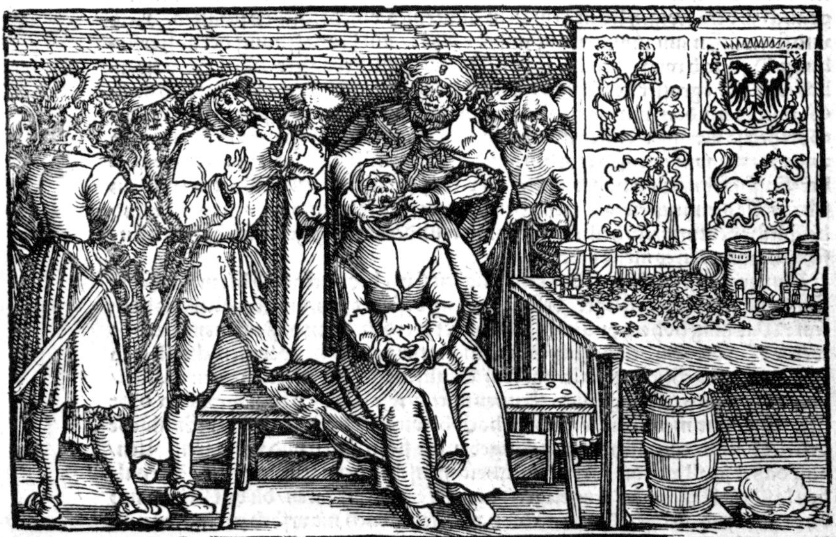

Schmertz.

JCh hab grauſam zan wee / ſie fahen mir an zu faulen / ſtincken vnnd wacken/ fallen mir auß/ bin ſchier gar zanloß.

Vernunfft.

Zanwee-chumb.

Sihe zu was für vertrawen du auff deine weiche därm vnd ingeweid ſetzeſt/ ſo dich deine harte zene ſo verlaſſen / Ein menſch iſt ein ſchwach / zerbrechlichs hinfallends ding / dañ was er vermeinet das aller feſteſt zuſein / das fellt jhm dahin/ Was jhm die natur zur ſtercke vnd ziere ſeines munds verlihen hat / kom̃t jhm zu trauren vnd ſchmertzen/ auff das er mercken ſoll/ wie menſchlicher leib ſo bald vergehe. Jetz gedenck was / vnnd wie vil du Gott ſchuldig biſt / wie vil er dir zeen vnd andere gaben geben habe / vnd wann du nur einer/ ja der geringſten gerathen ſolteſt/ wie es dir ein pein were. Ein knecht achtet wenig ſeines herren miltigkeit / wann er volauff hat gegenwertiglich / wann mann aber jm das fůter höher ſchütt / vnd jm die ſpůlen läer lauffen / als dann verſtehet er mit ſeinem ſchaden/ was er verloren hat. Haſtu keinn zan mehr / ſo haſtu ein vortheyl/ darffeſt nicht hart beiſſen / würdſt weniger lachen dann vor / ſchandt würt dich wol halten/ daß du nicht vnzůchtiglich wie ein alter narr vmb dich gaffeſt / daß mann dir nicht in hals als ein verbrandt dorff ſehe / Sage der natur fleiſſigen danck/ daß ſie dir die zeen biß in dein alter gelaſſen hat/ ſie hats manchem jungen geſellen in ſeiner beſten jugent genom̃en. Het dir dein alter deine zeen nicht genommen/ ſo het ſie doch der tod dir nit gelaſſen/ Da hilfft kein ſtercke / da iſt kein ſchöne/ da gilt nicht wie vil oder wenig jhr ſind. Die Königin Cenobia in Orient / würdt vnder andern jhrer ſchöne alſo gerůmpt / daß ſie ſo weiſſe / hůbſche zene

Hans Weiditz (German, active c. 1500–1536)
ON THE PAIN OF TEETH, 1532

From Petrarch, *Trostspiegel in Glück und Unglück* (Frankfort on the Main: Den Christian Egenolffs Erben, 1572)
Woodcut, 11¼ x 7¼" (28.5 x 18.4 cm)
Purchased: SmithKline Beckman Corporation Fund
58-150-37b

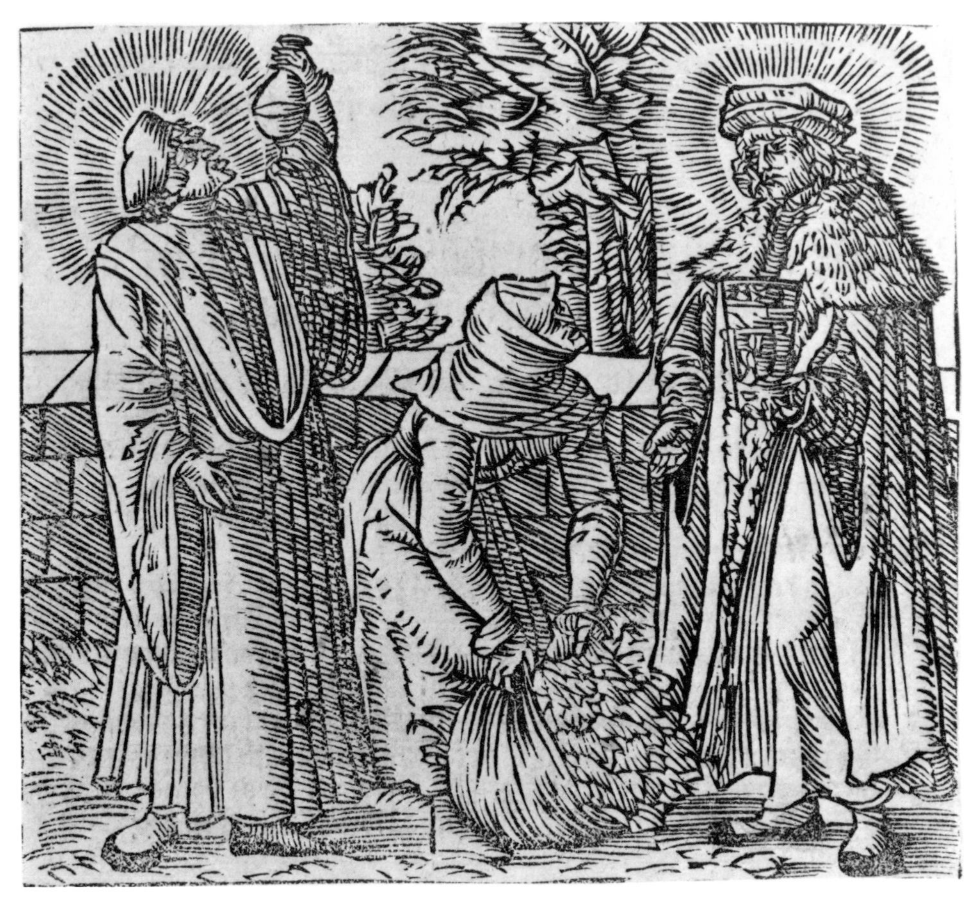

• 28a •

Anonymous (Polish, sixteenth century)

COLLECTING HERBS FOR MEDICINE, 1534

From Stefan Falimirz, *O ziołach i o moczy ich . . .* (Crakow: Florian Ungler, 1534)

Woodcut, 4⁷⁄₁₆ x 5" (11.3 x 12.7 cm) (trimmed)

Purchased: SmithKline Beckman Corporation Fund

69-190-31

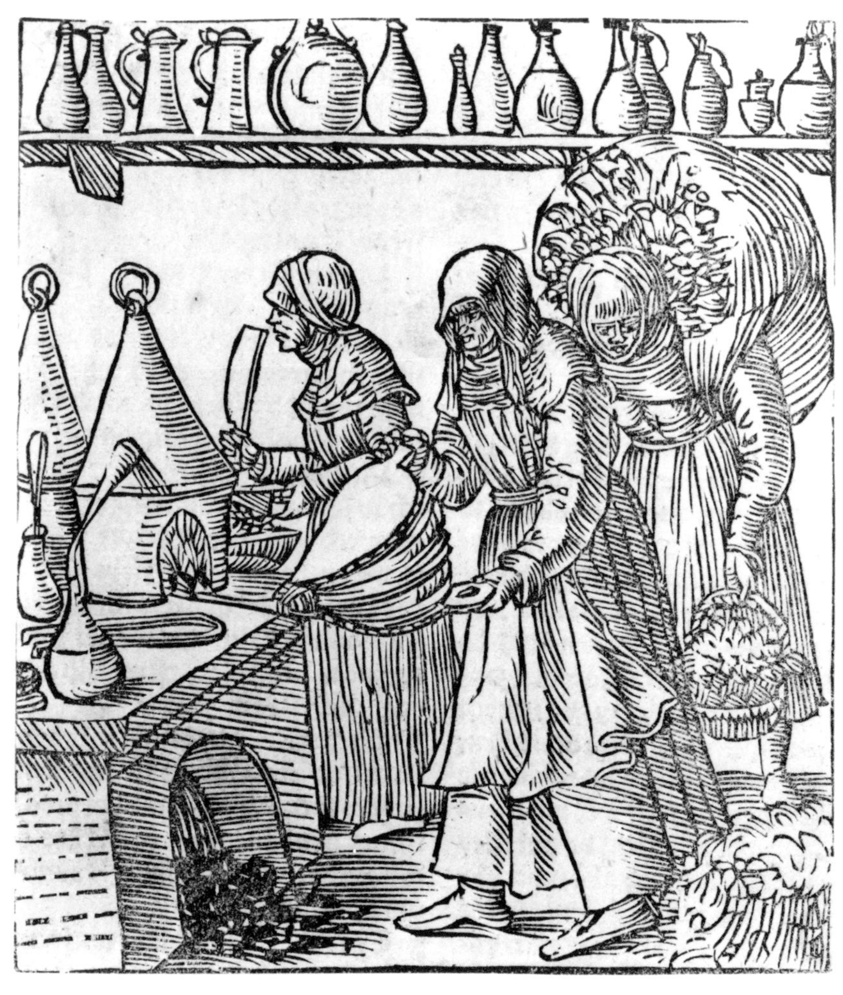

• 28b •

Anonymous (Polish, sixteenth century)

COOKING HERBS FOR MEDICINE, 1534

From Stefan Falimirz, *O ziołach i o moczy ich . . .* (Crakow: Florian Ungler, 1534)

Woodcut, 5 x 4 7/16" (12.7 x 11.3 cm) (trimmed)

Purchased: SmithKline Beckman Corporation Fund

69-190-30

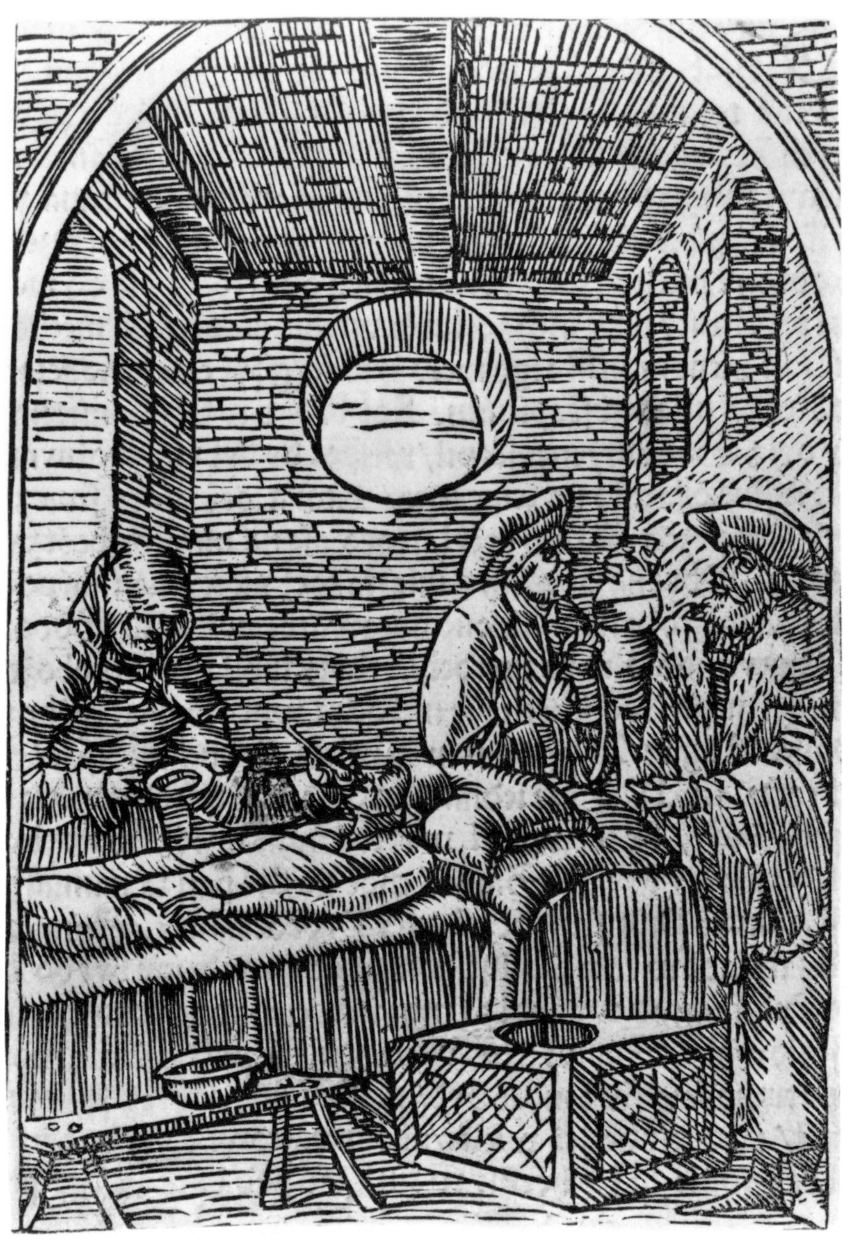

• 28c •

Anonymous (Polish, sixteenth century)

ADMINISTERING MEDICINAL HERBS, 1534

From Stefan Falimirz, *O ziołach i o moczy ich . . .* (Crakow: Florian Ungler, 1534)

Woodcut, 6³⁄₁₆ x 4⁷⁄₁₆" (15.8 x 11.3 cm) (trimmed)

Purchased: SmithKline Beckman Corporation Fund

69-190-29

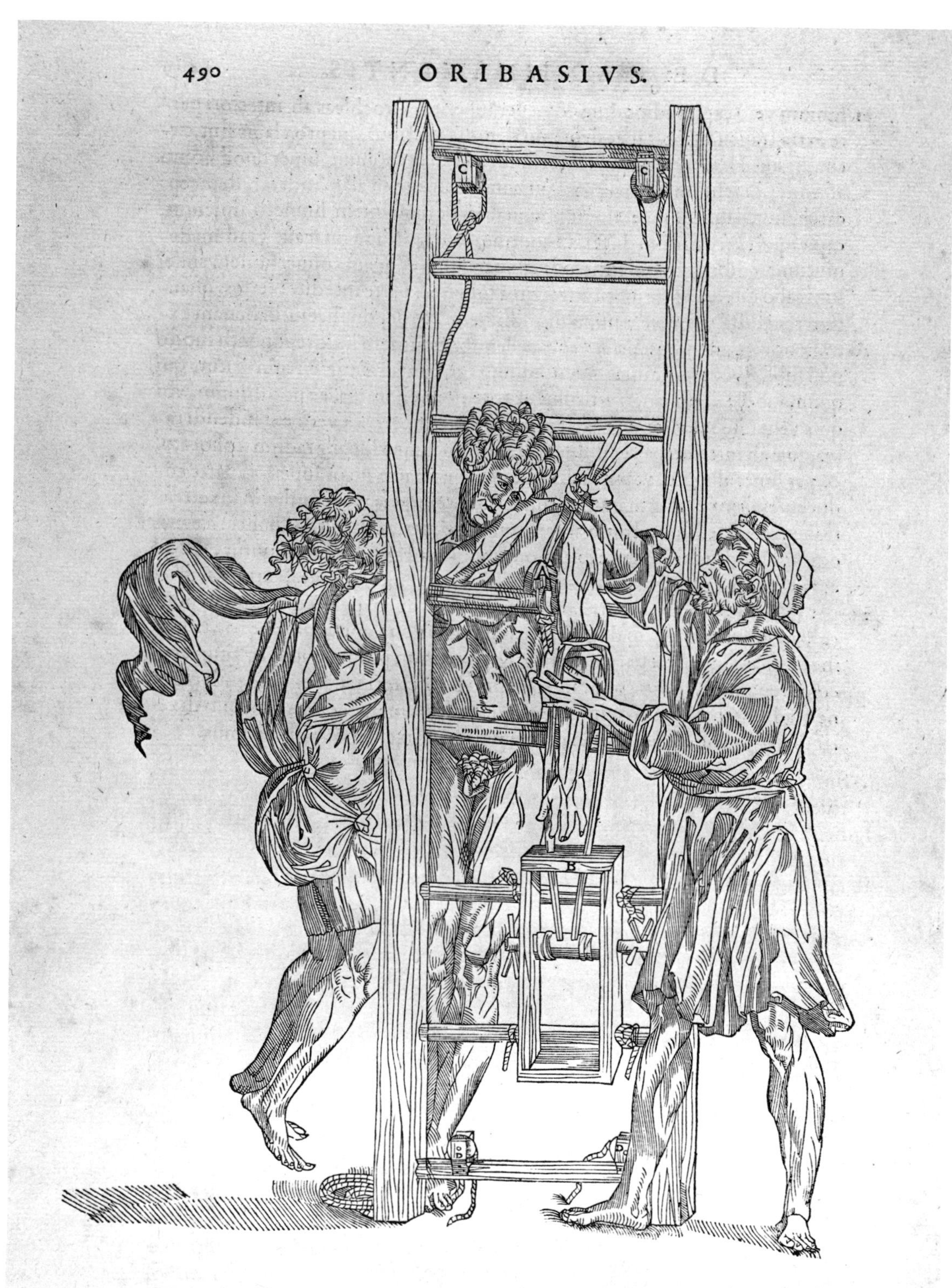

· 29 ·

Anonymous, possibly by François (Jean) Jollat (French, active 1502–50)
After Francesco de' Rossi, known as Cecco di Salviati (Italian, 1510–1563)
MANUAL REDUCTION OF A DISLOCATED SHOULDER, 1544

From Guido Guidi, *Opera Varia. Omnibus Medicinae Studiosis Utilissima* . . . (Lyons: Ioannem Veyrat, 1599), a cancel title for *Chirurgia é Graeco in Latinum Conversa* (Paris: Pierre Gaultier, 1544)
Woodcut, 13⁷⁄₁₆ x 9⅛" (34.1 x 23.2 cm)
Purchased: SmithKline Beckman Corporation Fund
68-25-80

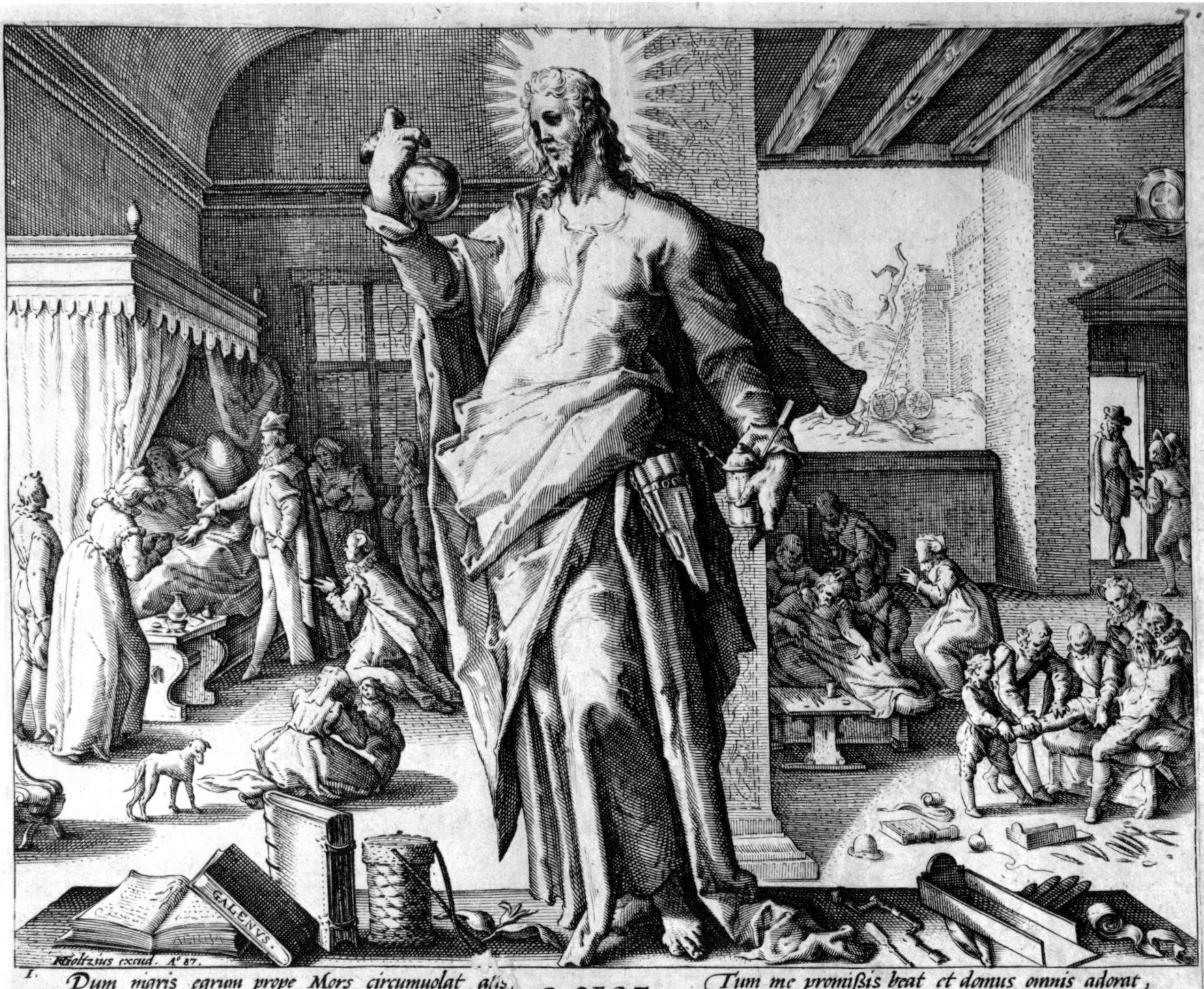

• 30a •

Anonymous (Dutch, late sixteenth century)

After Hendrik Goltzius (Dutch, 1558–1617)

THE PHYSICIAN AS GOD, 1587

From "The Medical Professions," 1587

Engraving with woodcut inscription, 7¹⁵⁄₁₆ x 8⁷⁄₈" (20.1 x 22.5 cm)

Anonymous gift

59-6-6

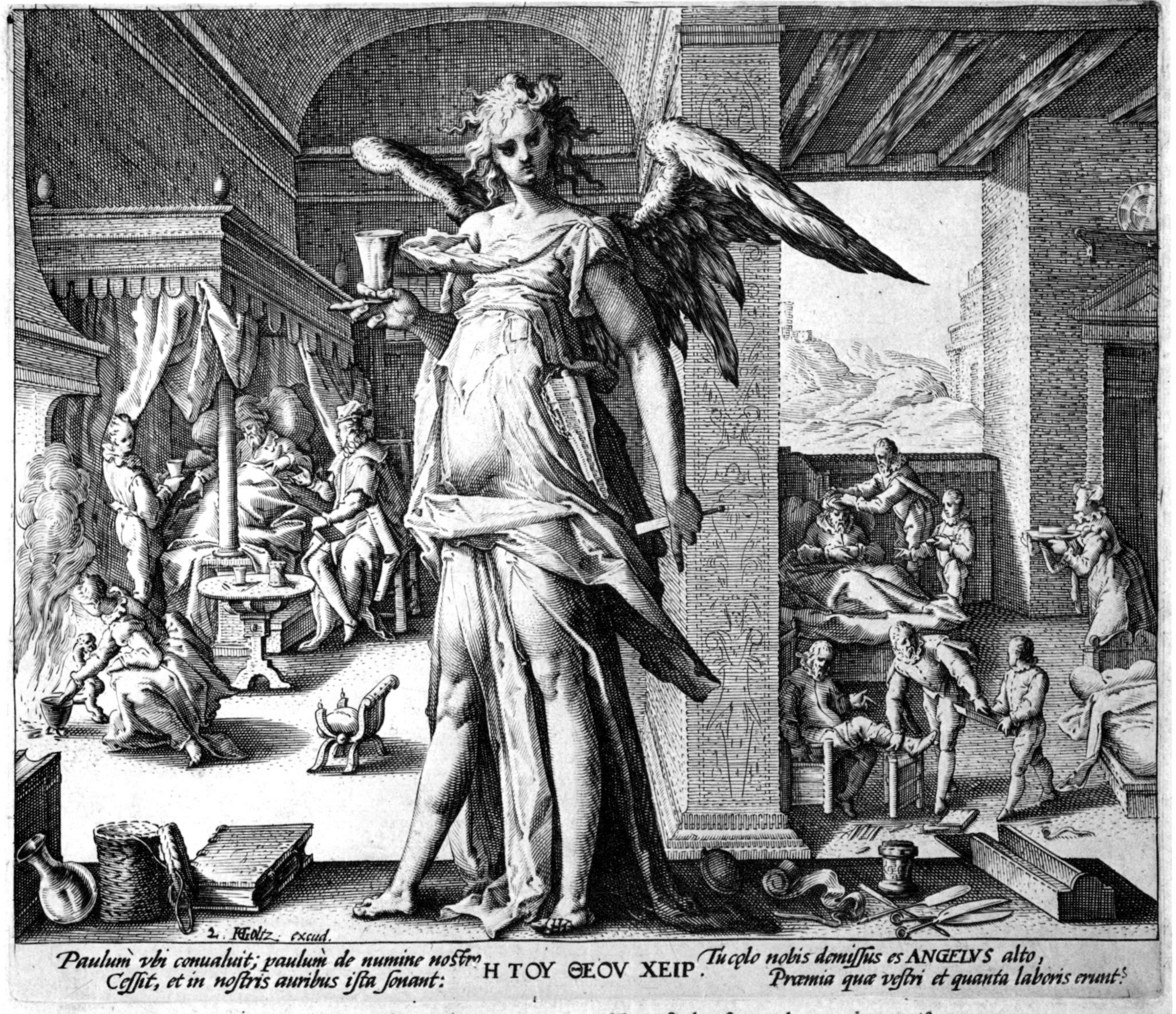

• 30b •

Anonymous (Dutch, late sixteenth century)

After Hendrik Goltzius (Dutch, 1558–1617)

THE PHYSICIAN AS ANGEL, 1587

From "The Medical Professions," 1587

Engraving with woodcut inscription, 7¹⁵⁄₁₆ x 8¹⁵⁄₁₆" (20.1 x 22.6 cm)

Anonymous gift

59-6-7

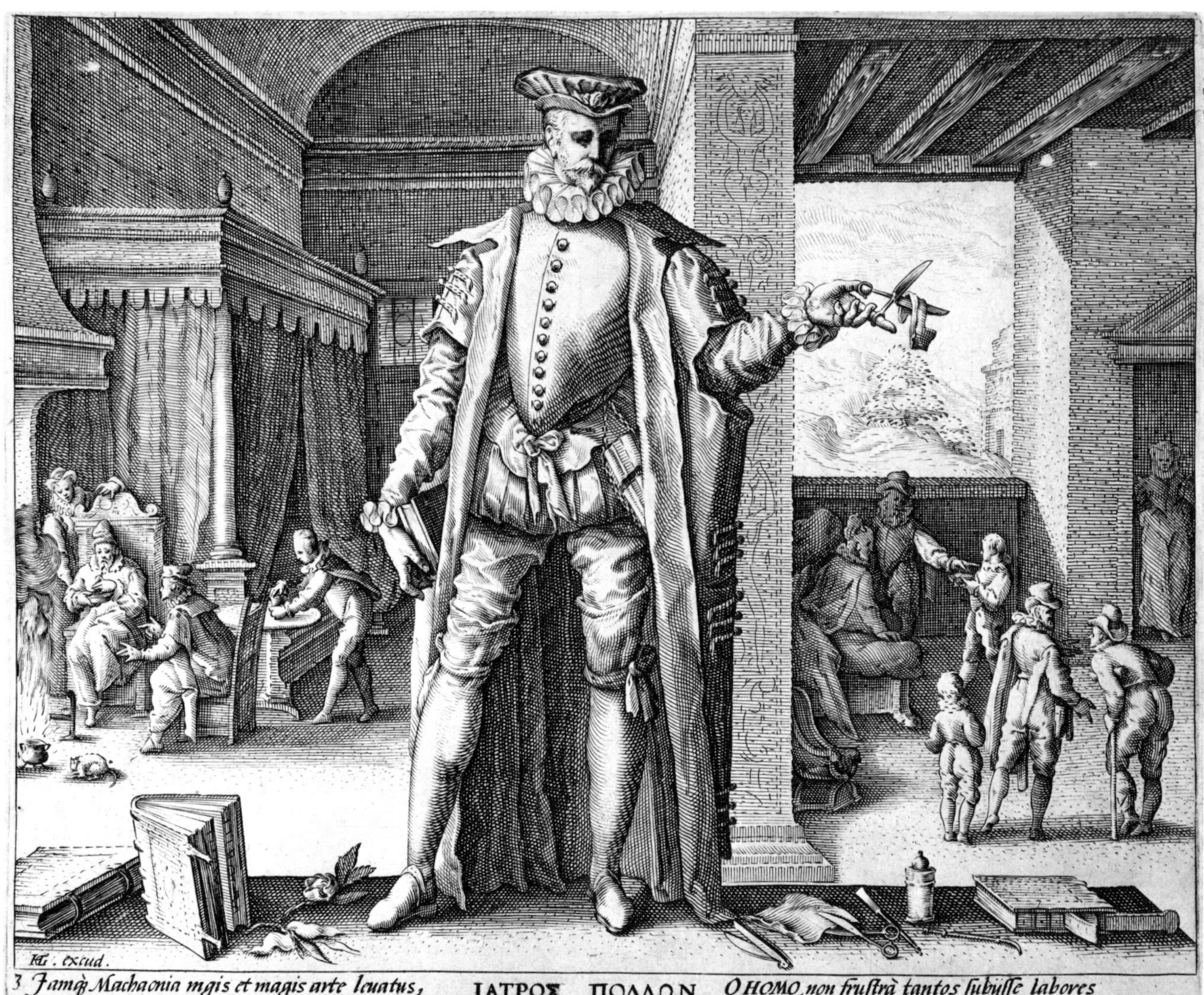

• 30c •

Anonymous (Dutch, late sixteenth century)

After Hendrik Goltzius (Dutch, 1558–1617)

THE PHYSICIAN AS MAN, 1587

From "The Medical Professions," 1587

Engraving with woodcut inscription, 8 x 9⅛" (20.3 x 23.1 cm)

Anonymous gift

59-6-8

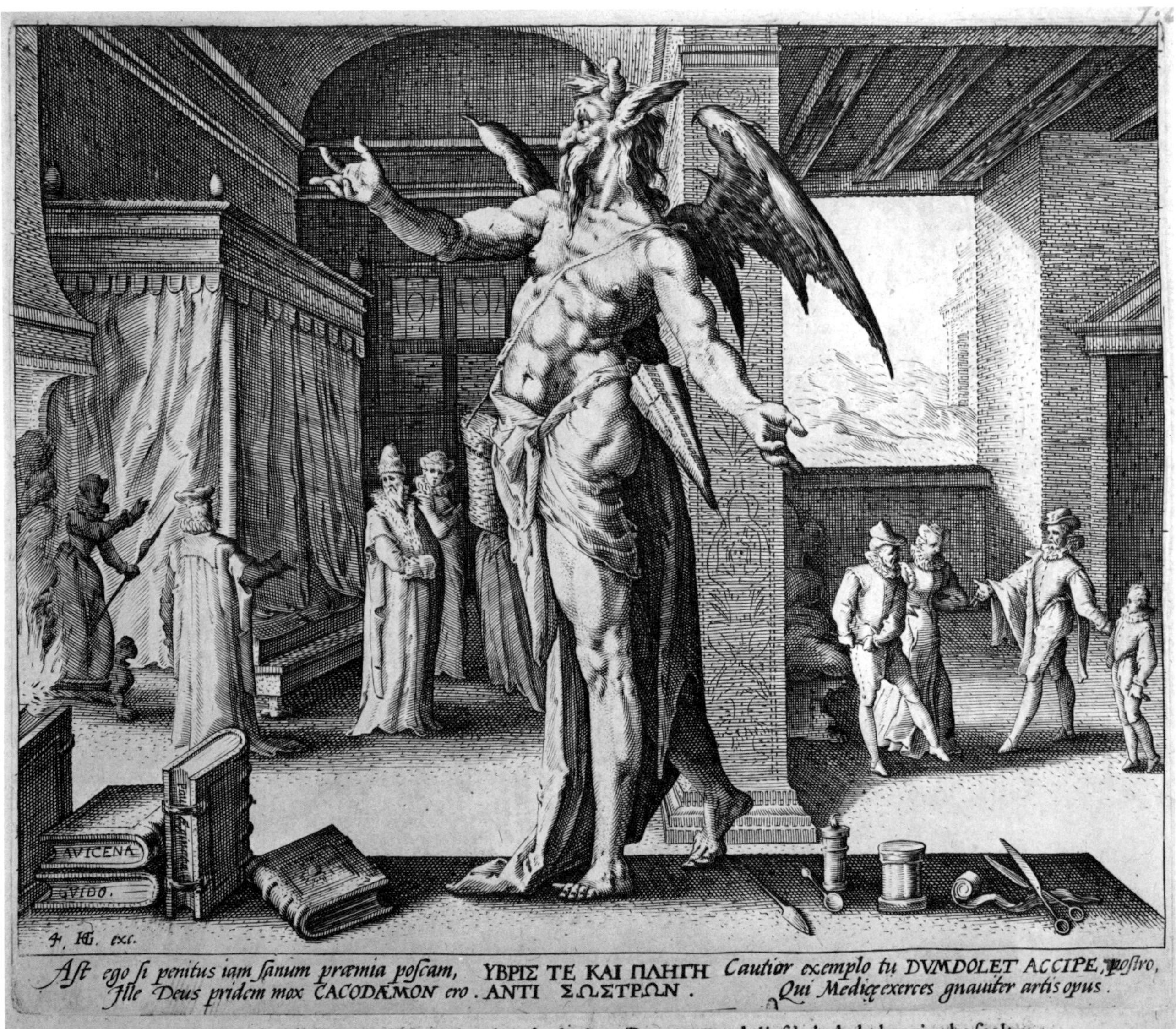

• 30d •

Anonymous (Dutch, late sixteenth century)

After Hendrik Goltzius (Dutch, 1558–1617)

THE PHYSICIAN AS DEVIL, 1587

From "The Medical Professions," 1587

Engraving with woodcut inscription, 8 x 9" (20.3 x 22.9 cm)

Anonymous gift

59-6-9

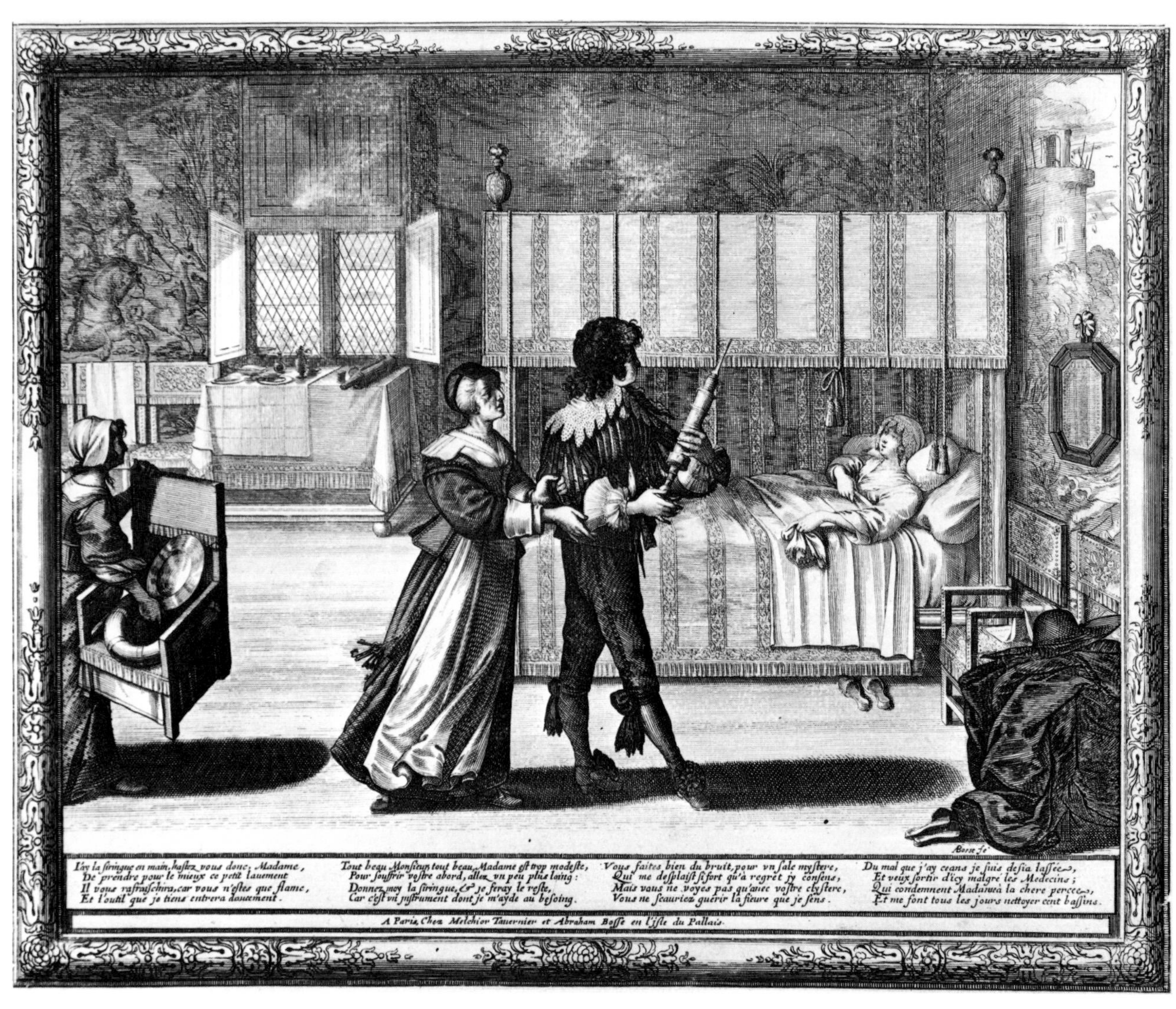

• 31a •

Abraham Bosse (French, 1602–1676)

THE PURGE, c. 1635

From "The Trades," c. 1635

Etching, 10½ x 13³⁄₁₆" (26.7 x 33.5 cm) (trimmed)

Acquired by exchange

61-191-11

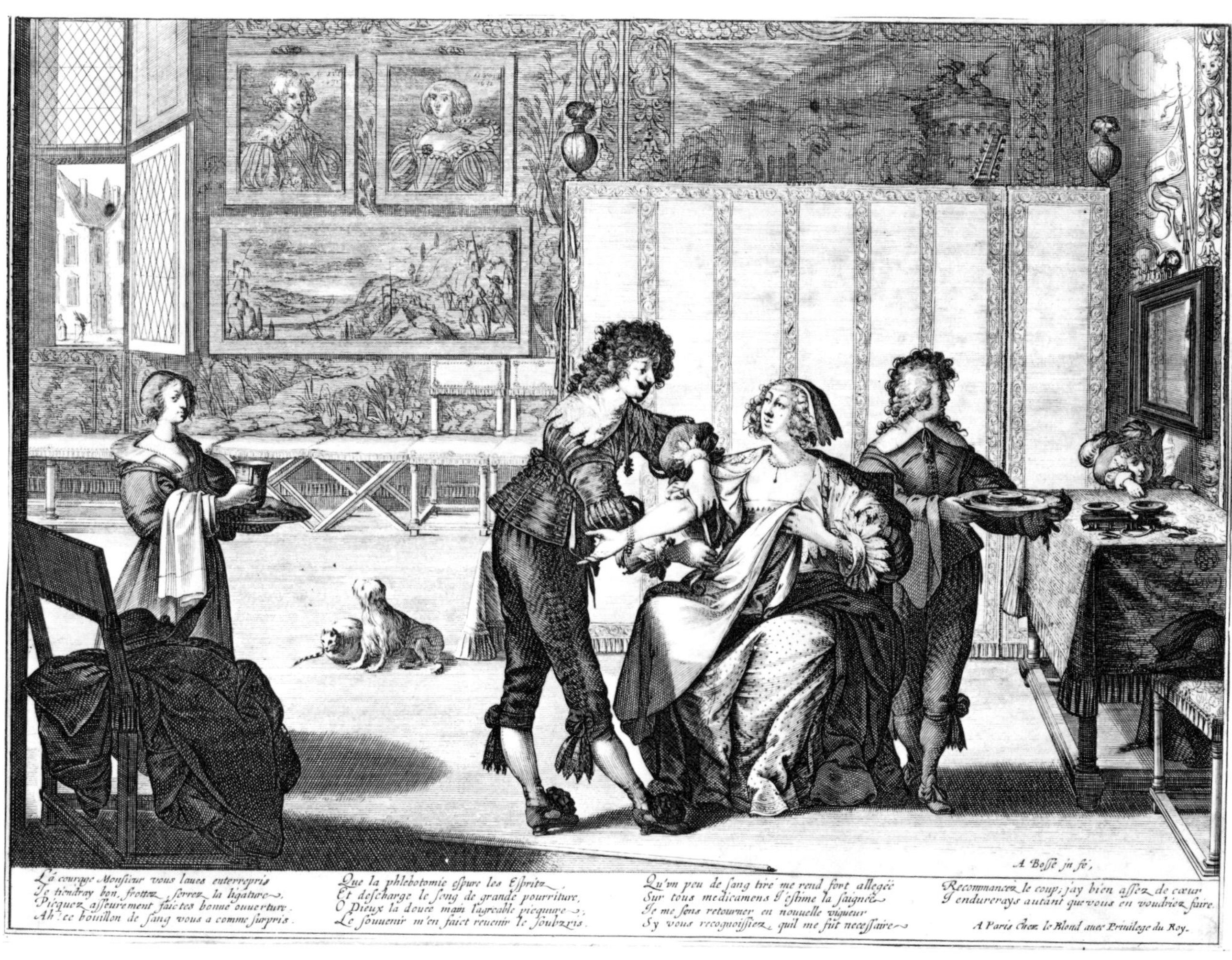

• 31b •

Abraham Bosse (French, 1602–1676)

BLOODLETTING, c. 1635

From "The Trades," c. 1635

Etching, 9⁵⁄₁₆ x 12⁷⁄₁₆" (23.7 x 31.6 cm) (trimmed)

Purchased: SmithKline Beckman Corporation Fund

49-97-18

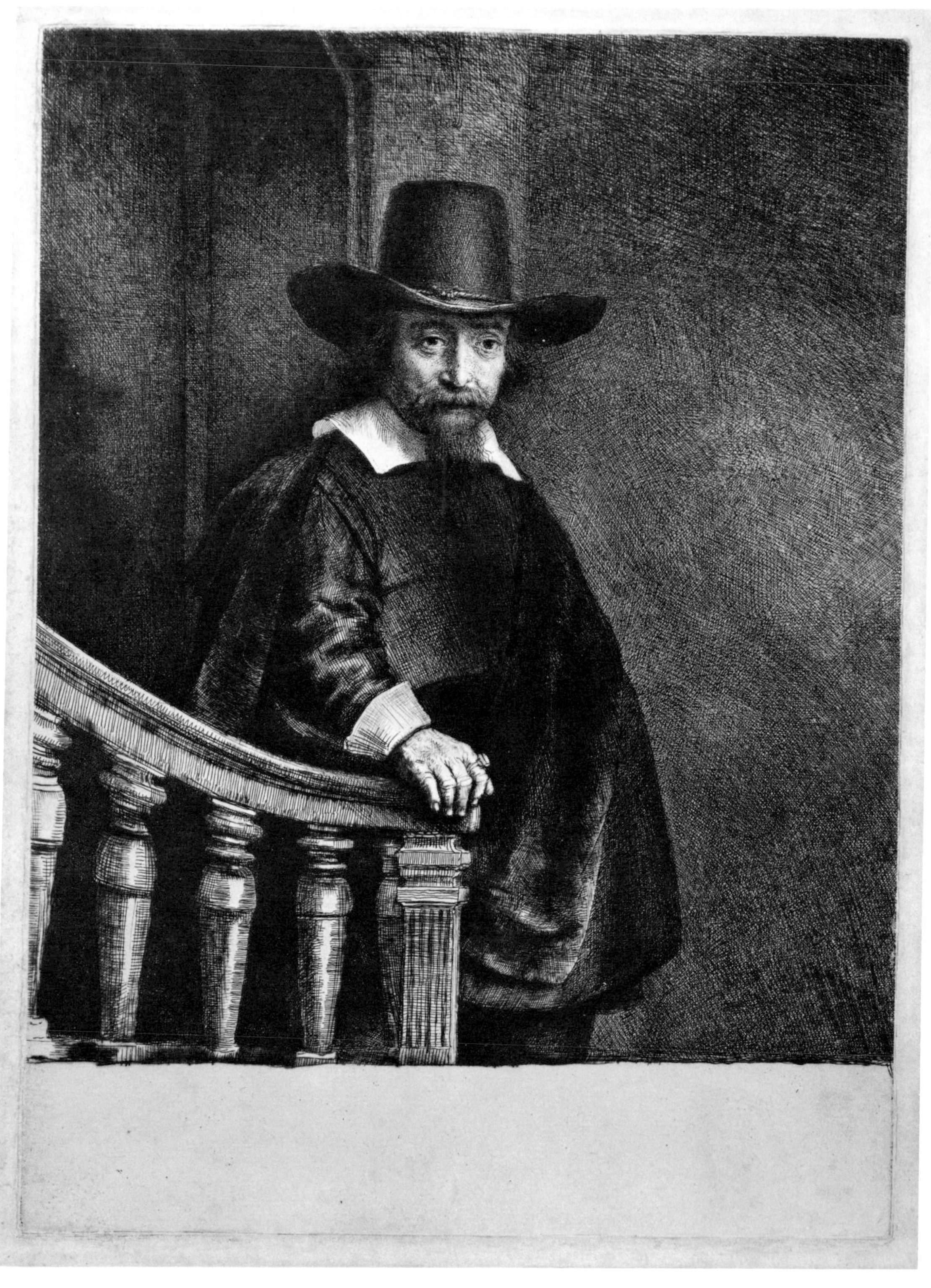

• 32 •

Rembrandt Harmensz. van Rijn (Dutch, 1606–1669)

THE JEWISH PHYSICIAN EPHRAIM BONUS, 1647

Etching, drypoint, and engraving (ii/ii), 9½ x 7″ (24.1 x 17.8 cm)

Purchased: SmithKline Beckman Corporation Fund

49-97-6

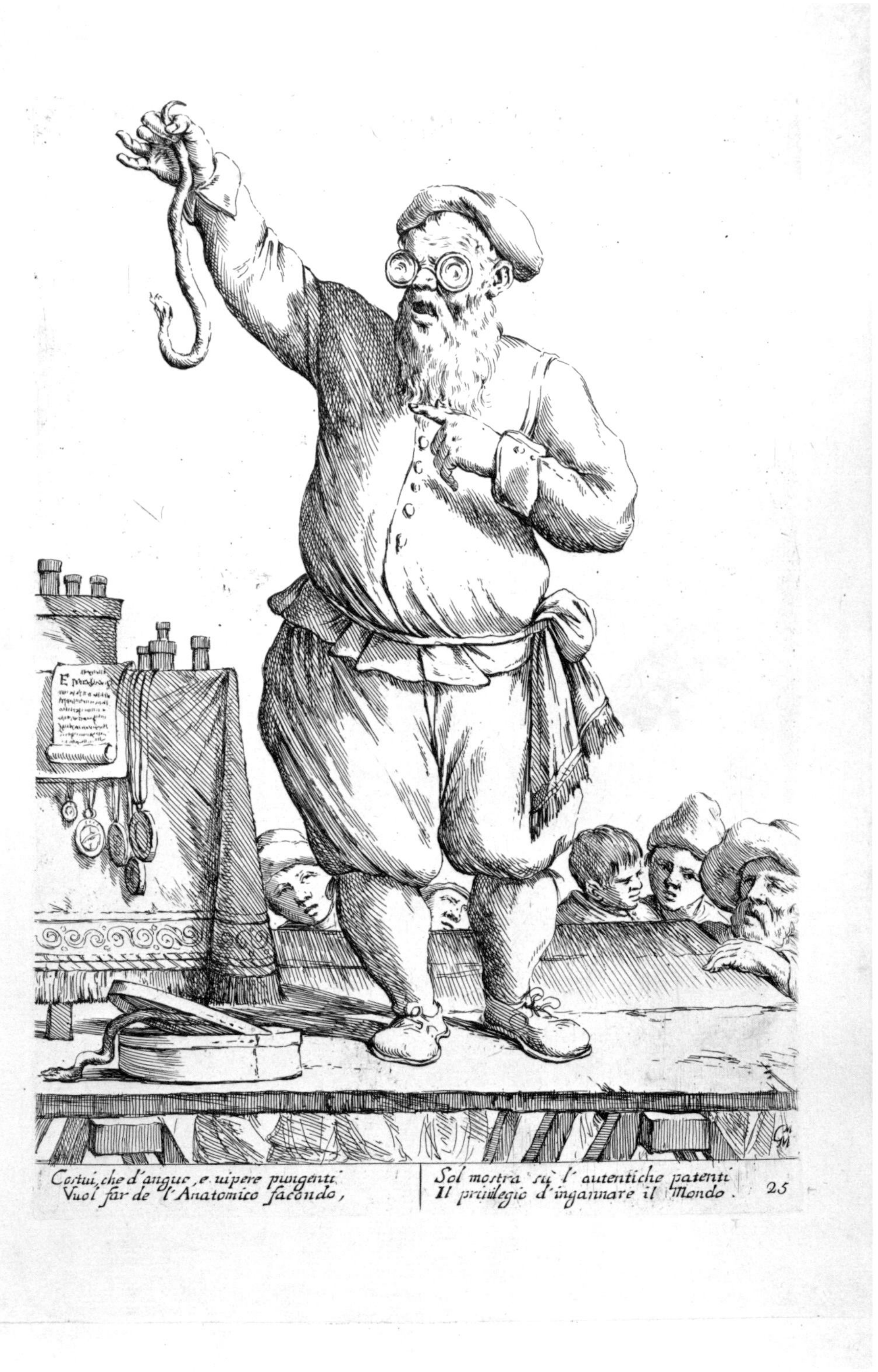

• 33 •

Giuseppe Maria Mitelli (Italian, 1634–1718)
After Annibale Carracci (Italian, 1560–1609)
CHARLATAN ON HIS STAGE, HOLDING A SNAKE, 1660

From *Di Bologna l'arti per via d'Anibal Caraci [Le Arti di Bologna]* (Rome: Gio. Iacomo Rossi, 1660)
Etching, 11³⁄₁₆ x 7¾" (28.4 x 19.7 cm)
Purchased: SmithKline Beckman Corporation Fund
58-150-33(25)

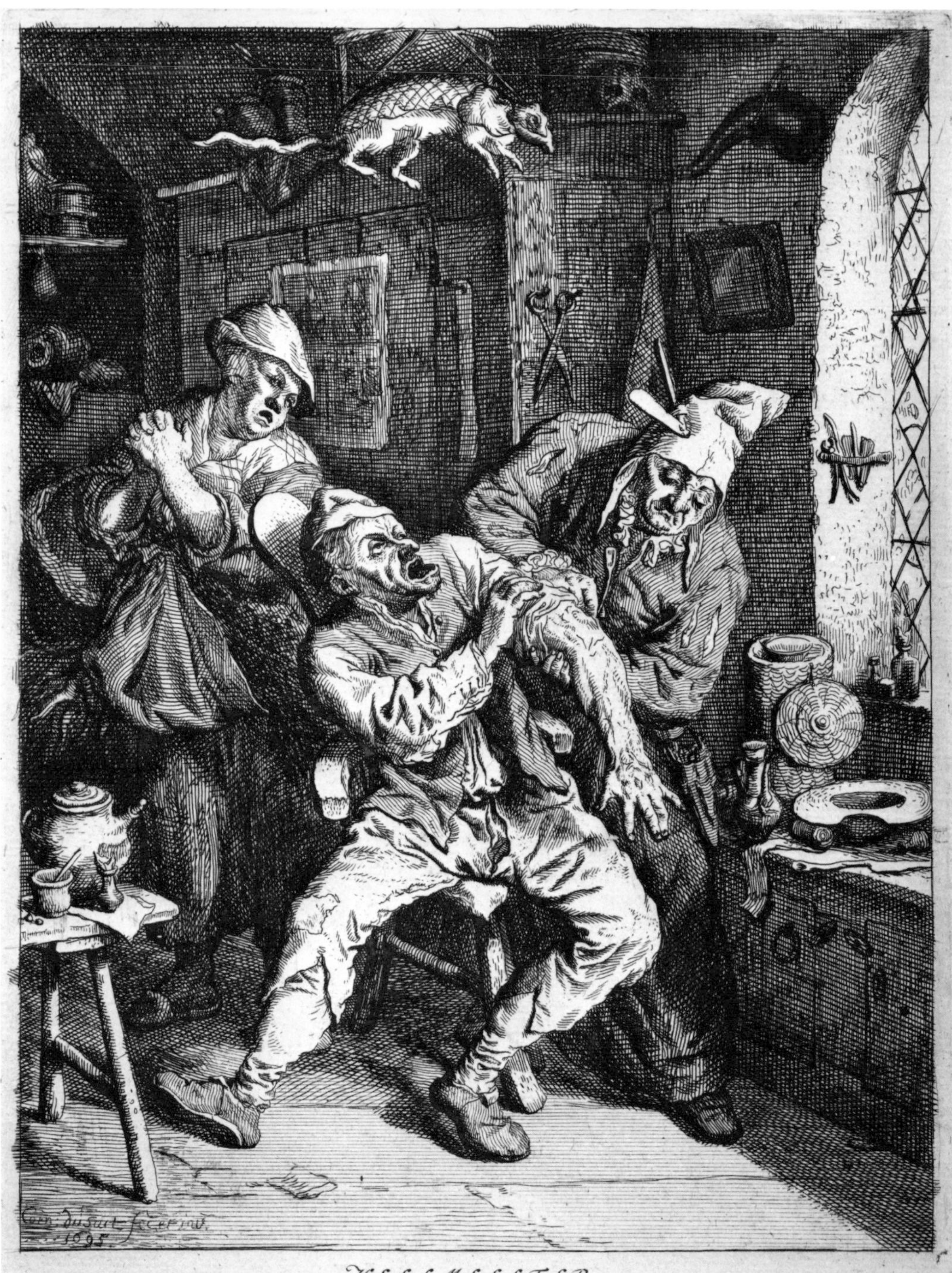

• 34a •

Cornelis Dusart (Dutch, 1660–1704)

THE VILLAGE SURGEON, 1695

Etching, 10¼ x 7⁷⁄₁₆″ (26 x 18 cm)

Charles M. Lea Collection

28-42-1270

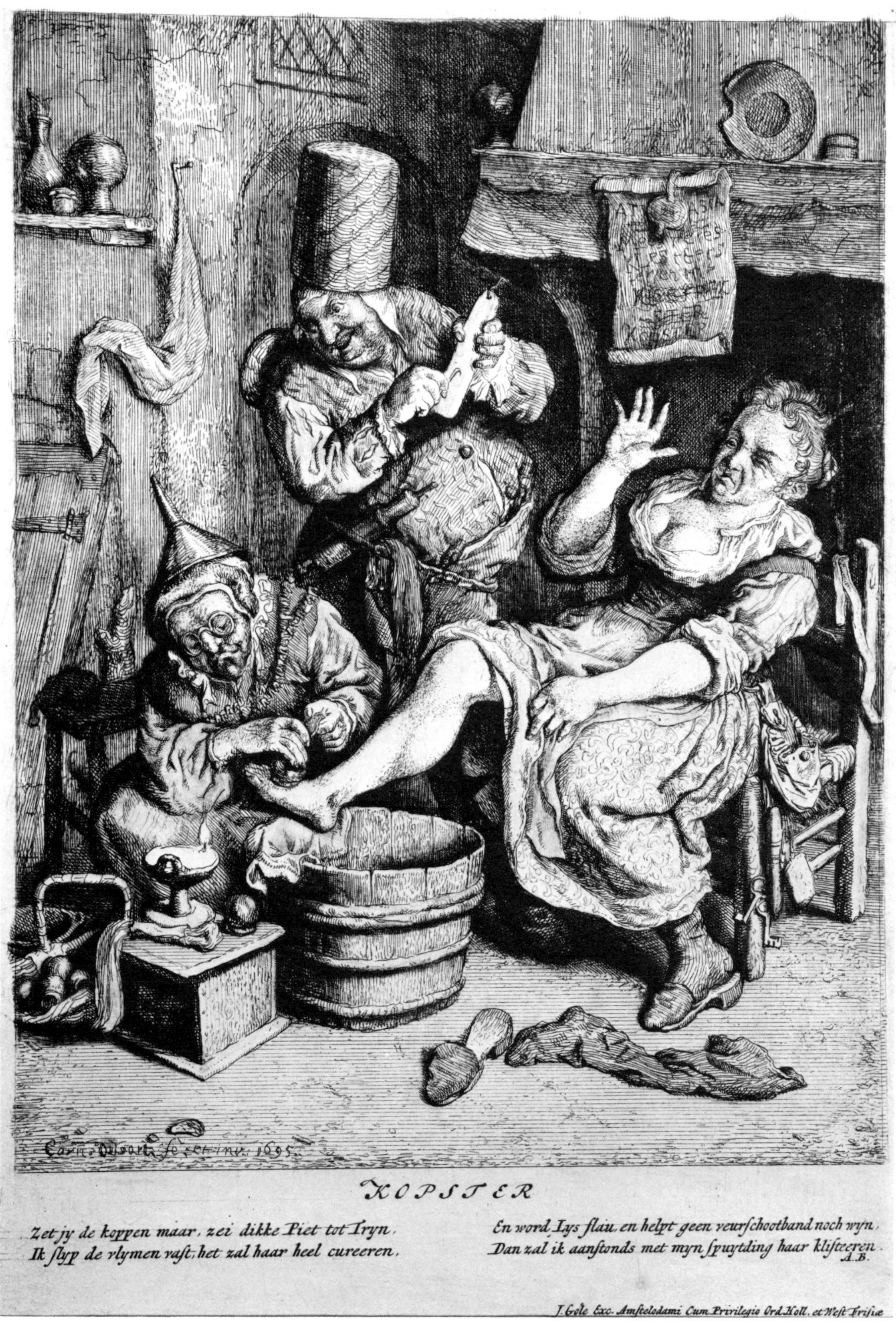

• 34b •

Cornelis Dusart (Dutch, 1660–1704)

THE CUPPER (THE LEECH WOMAN), 1695

Etching, 10³⁄₁₆ x 7¹⁄₁₆″ (25.8 x 18 cm)

Purchased: SmithKline Beckman Corporation Fund

71-116-7

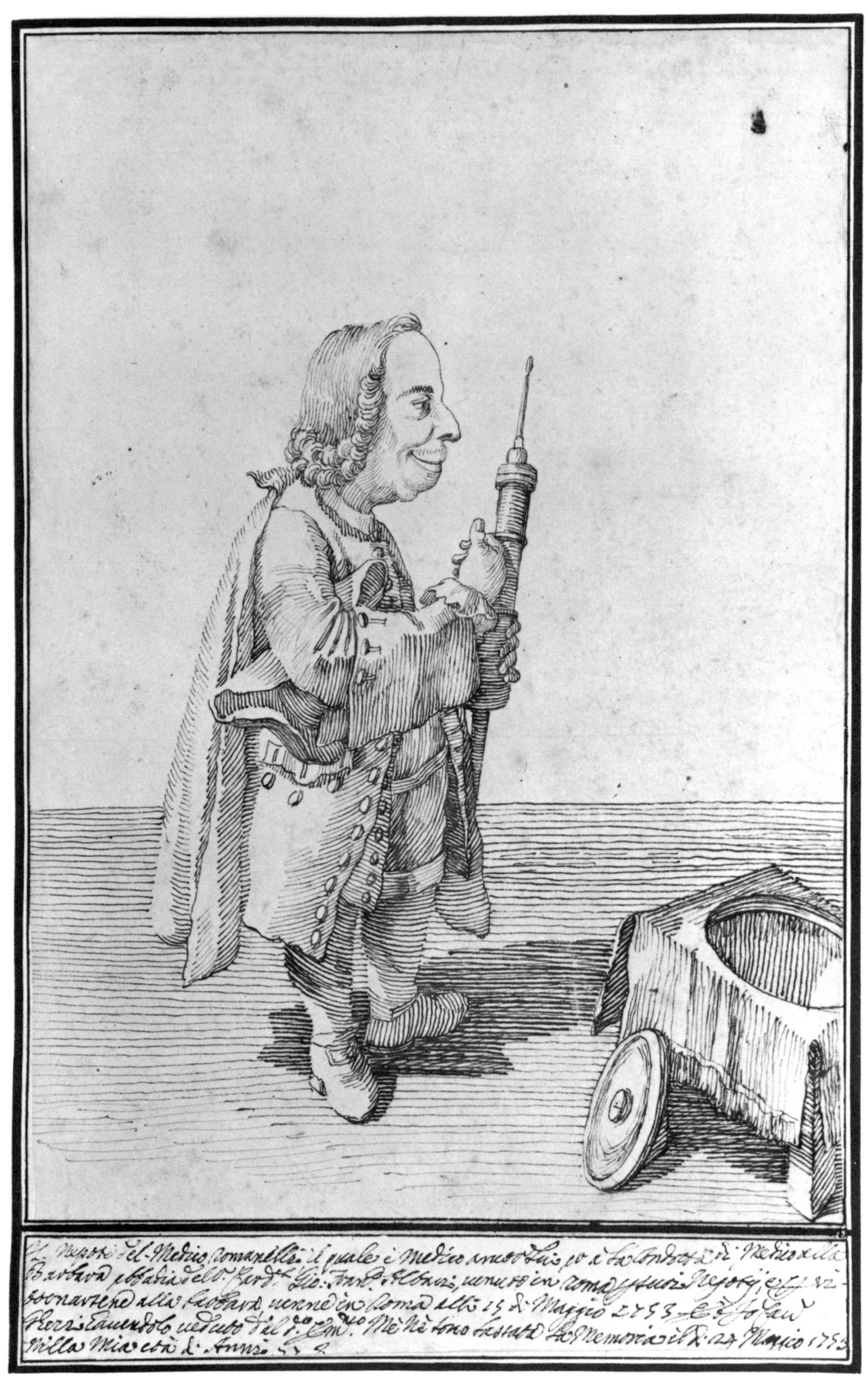

• 35 •

Pier Leone Ghezzi (Italian, 1674–1755)

CARICATURE OF A DOCTOR HOLDING AN ENEMA SYRINGE, 1753

Brown ink over traces of black chalk on light buff laid paper, 12¾ x 8¾" (32.4 x 22.2 cm)
Purchased: SmithKline Beckman Corporation Fund
1978-62-1

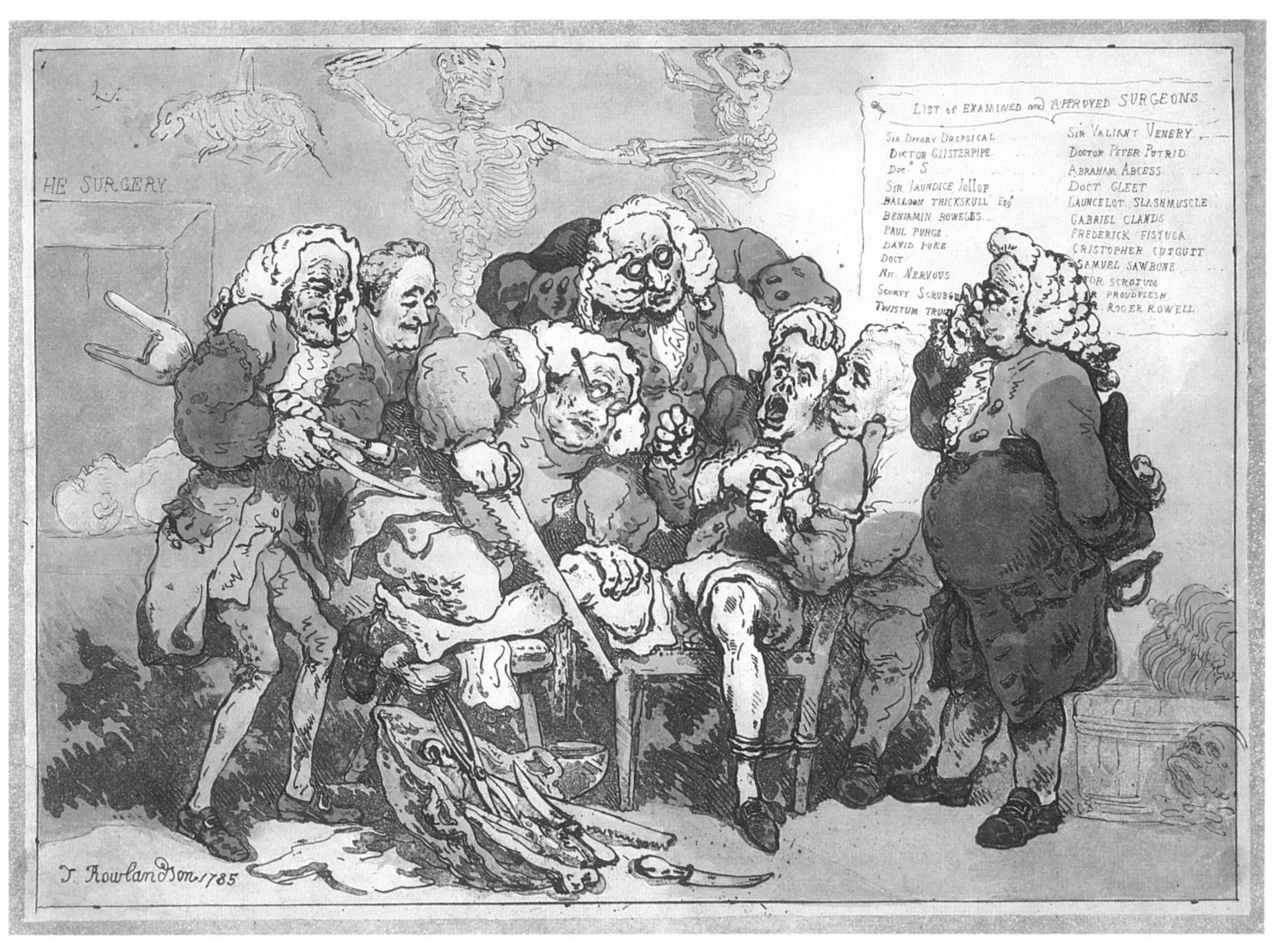

• 36 •

Thomas Rowlandson (English, 1756–1827)

THE AMPUTATION, 1785

Hand-colored etching, aquatint, and stipple etching, 10⅜ x 14⅝" (26.4 x 37.1 cm) (trimmed)

Purchased: SmithKline Beckman Corporation Fund

1982-82-1

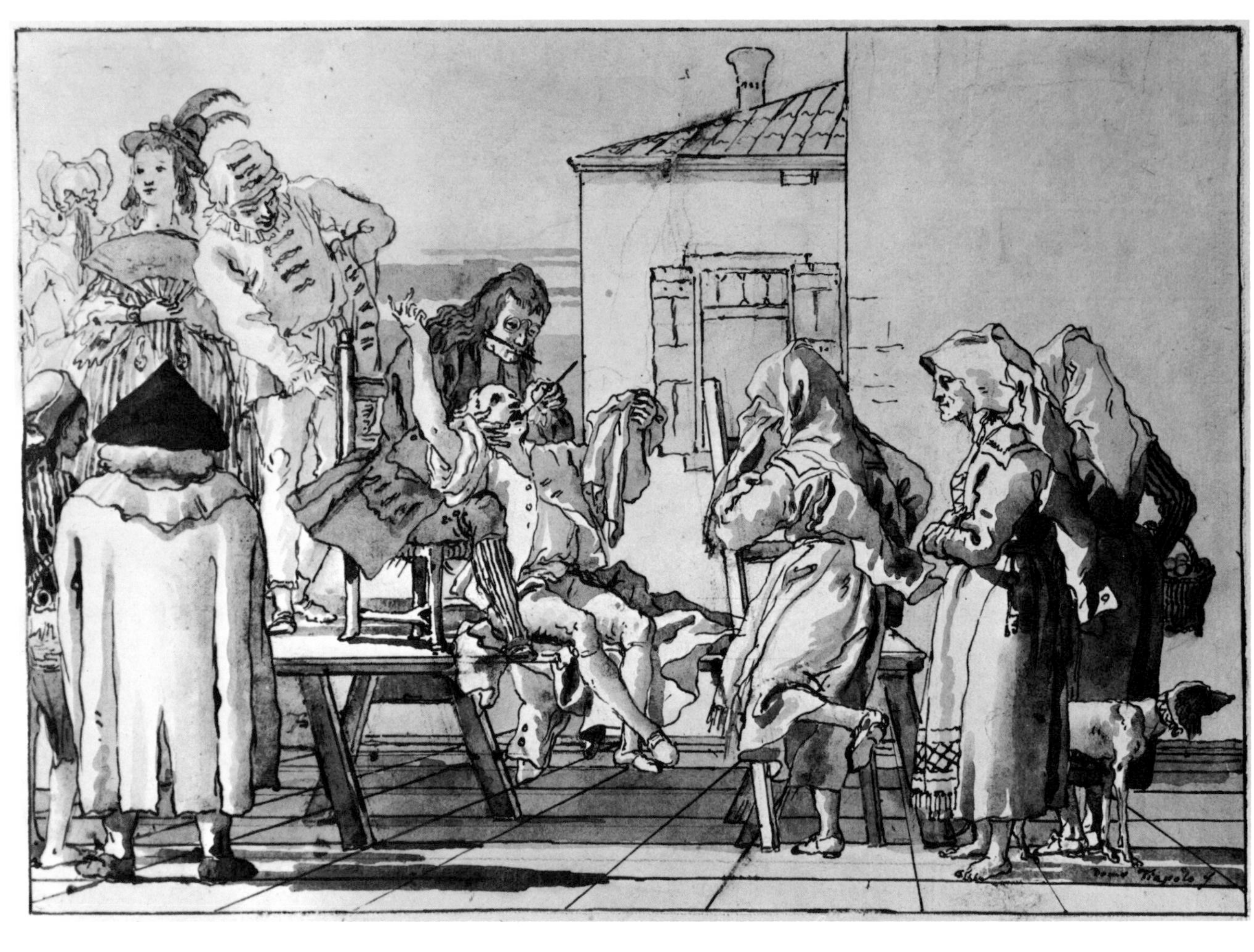

• 37 •

Giovanni Domenico Tiepolo (Italian, 1727–1804)

ITINERANT DENTIST TREATING A PATIENT, WITH SEVERAL OBSERVERS, possibly c. 1790

Brown ink and gray and brown washes over traces of black chalk on off-white antique laid paper, 14$\frac{5}{8}$ x 19$\frac{13}{16}$" (37.2 x 50.3 cm)

Purchased: SmithKline Beckman Corporation Fund

1981-63-1

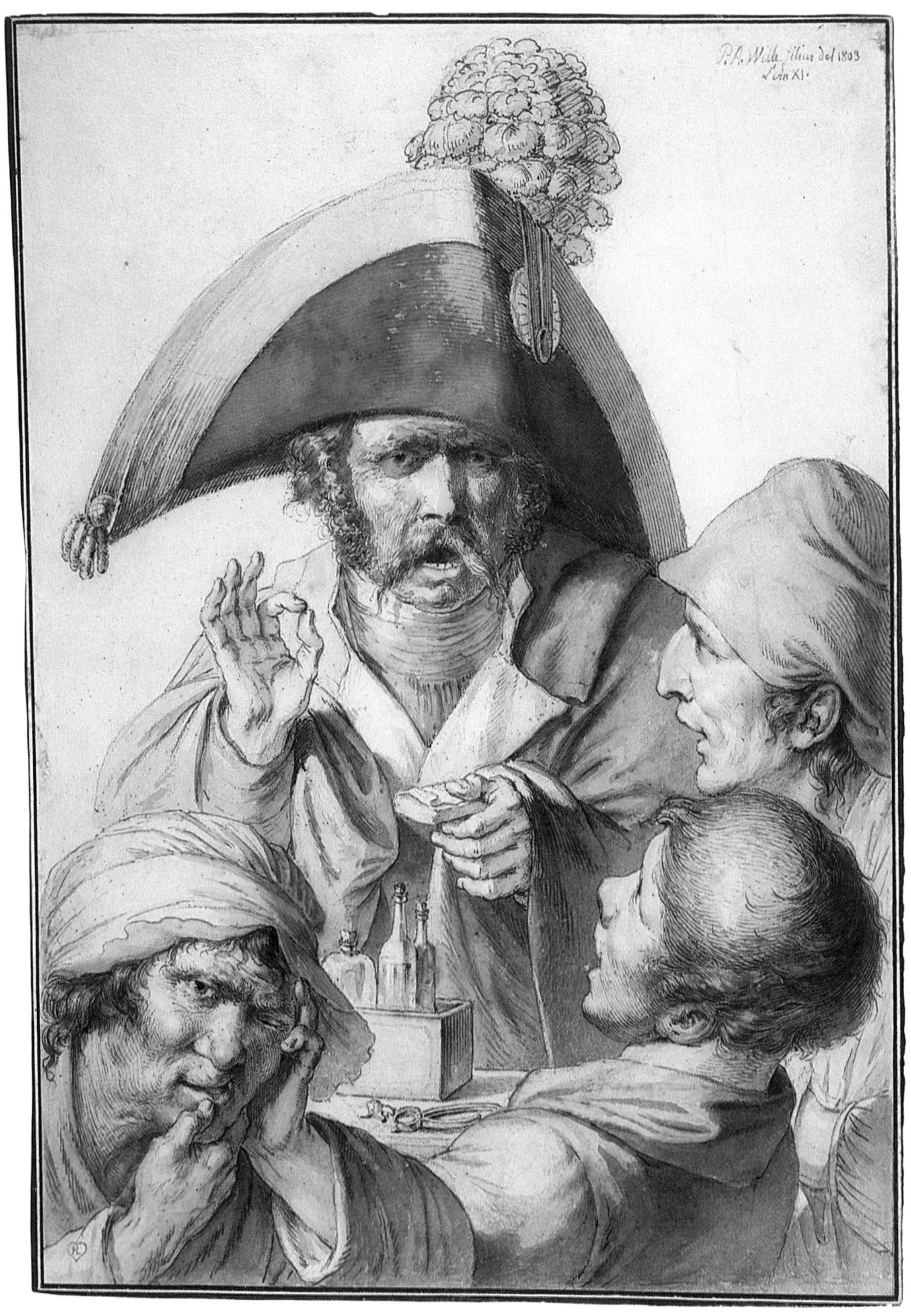

• 38 •

Pierre-Alexandre Wille (French, 1748–1837)

ITINERANT DENTIST WITH HIS PATIENT AND TWO OBSERVERS, 1803

Brown ink and colored washes over traces of black chalk on cream wove paper, 13 1/16 x 9 1/4" (33.2 x 23.5 cm)

Purchased: SmithKline Beckman Corporation Fund

1984-81-1

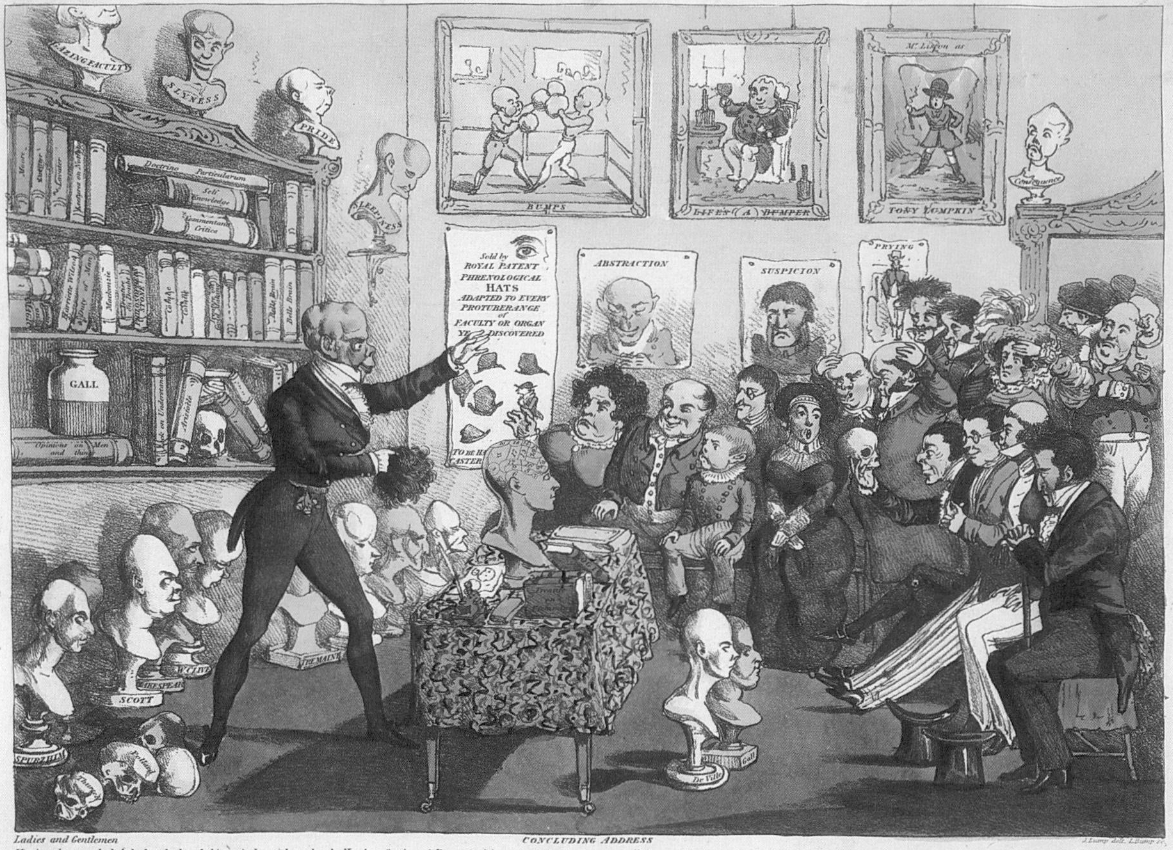

• 39 •

Henry Alken (English, 1785–1851)

CALVES' HEADS AND BRAINS, OR A PHRENOLOGICAL LECTURE, 1826

Hand-colored soft-ground etching, etching, and engraving, 9¾ x 12¾" (24.8 x 32.4 cm)
Purchased: SmithKline Beckman Corporation Fund
1984-12-1

L'imagination. N° 15.

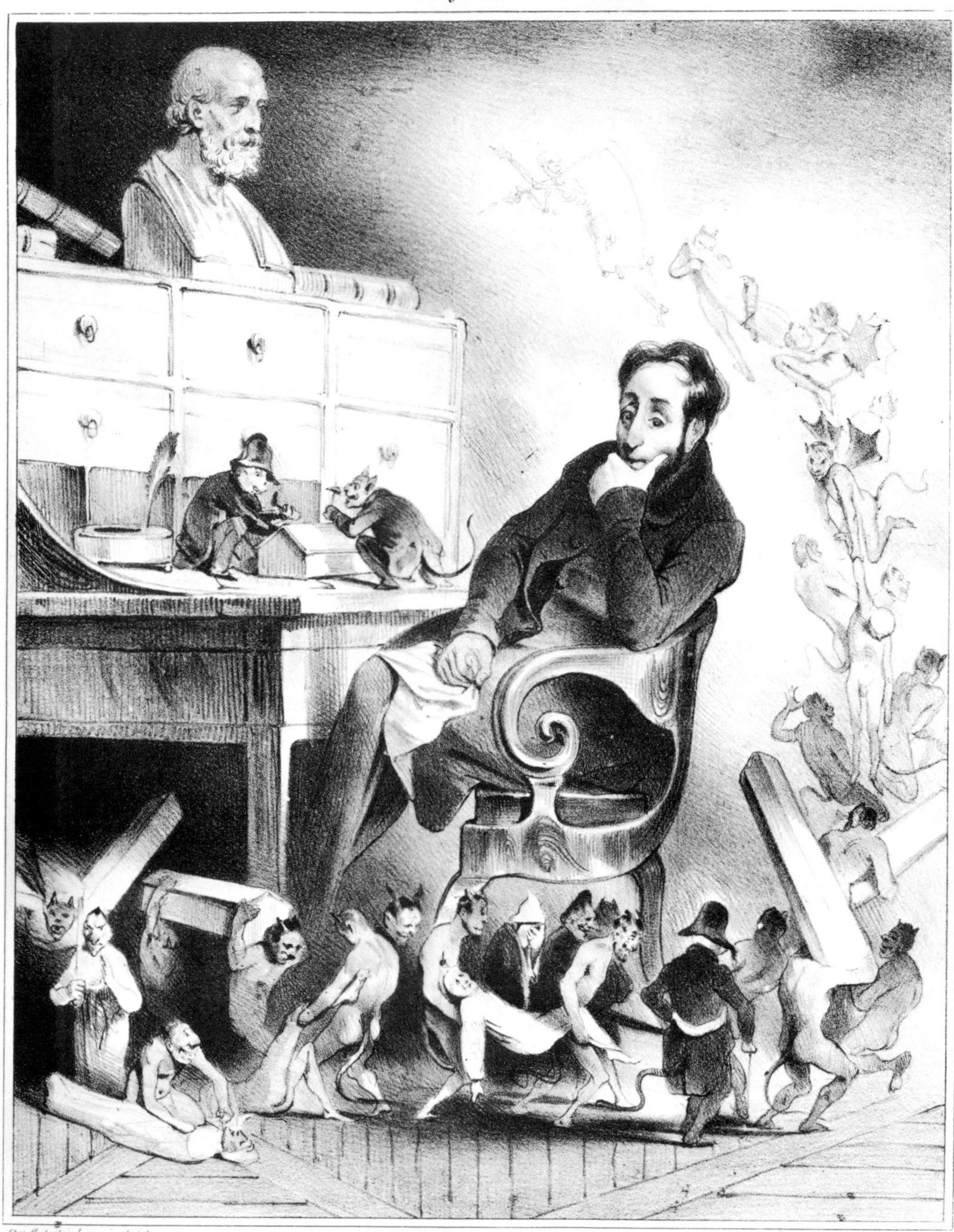

Chez Aubert galerie véro dodat. L. de Benard rue de l'Abbaye 4

Le médecin,

Pourquoi, diable! mes malades s'en vont ils donc tous?........ j'ai beau les saigner,
les purger, les droguer......... je n'y comprends rien!

• 40 •

Honoré Daumier (French, 1808–1879)

THE PHYSICIAN: WHY THE DEVIL!
ARE ALL MY PATIENTS DEPARTING THIS WAY? . . . , 1833

Published in *Le Charivari*, August 19, 1833
Lithograph, 11⁵⁄₁₆ x 8″ (28.7 x 20.3 cm)
Gift of Carl Zigrosser
68-162-20

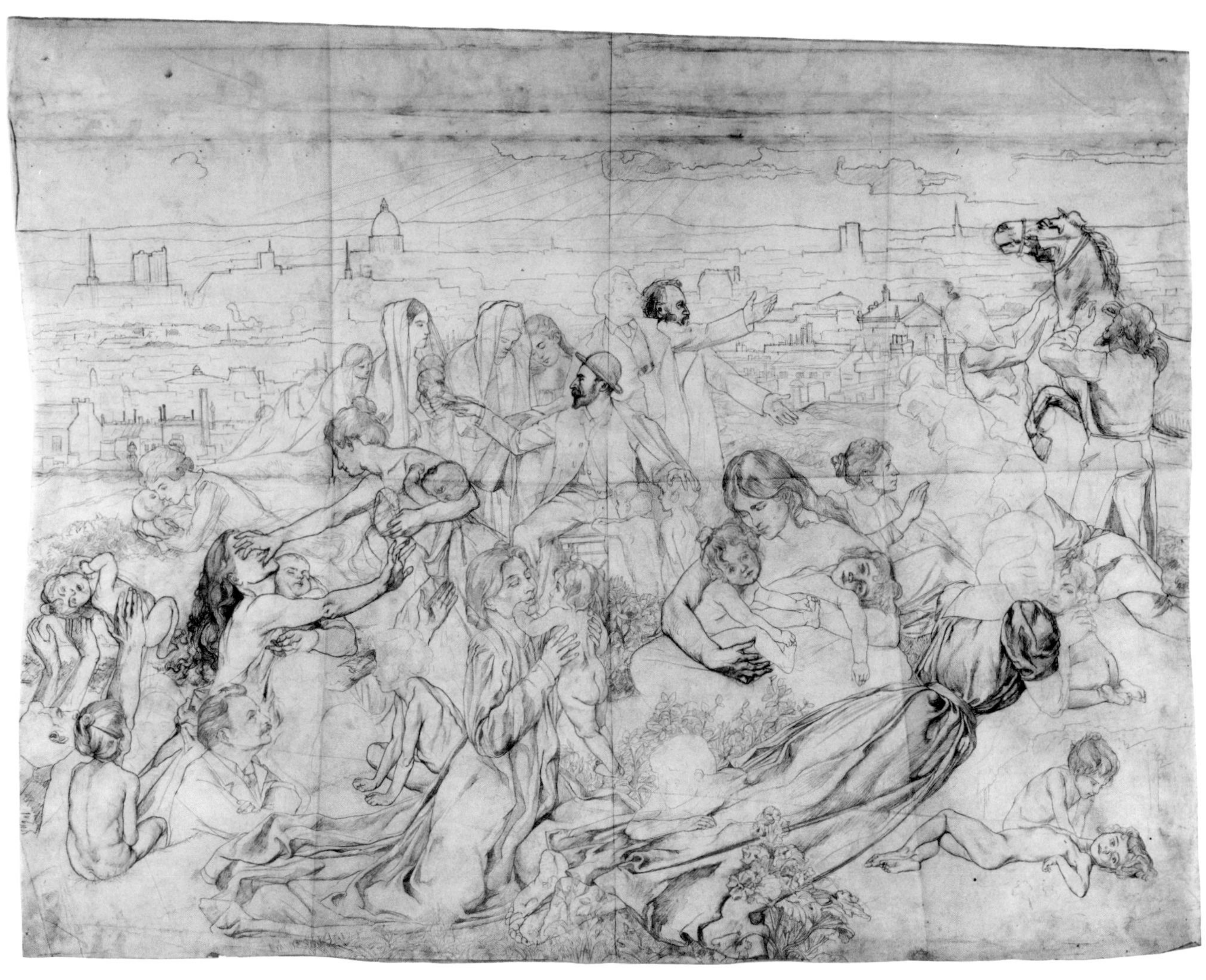

• 41a •

Charles Maurin (French, 1856–1914)

Study for SERUM THERAPY, 1895

Graphite on architects' linen, 31⁹⁄₁₆ x 40⅜" (80.2 x 102.6 cm) (irregular)

Purchased: SmithKline Beckman Corporation Fund

1984-19-2

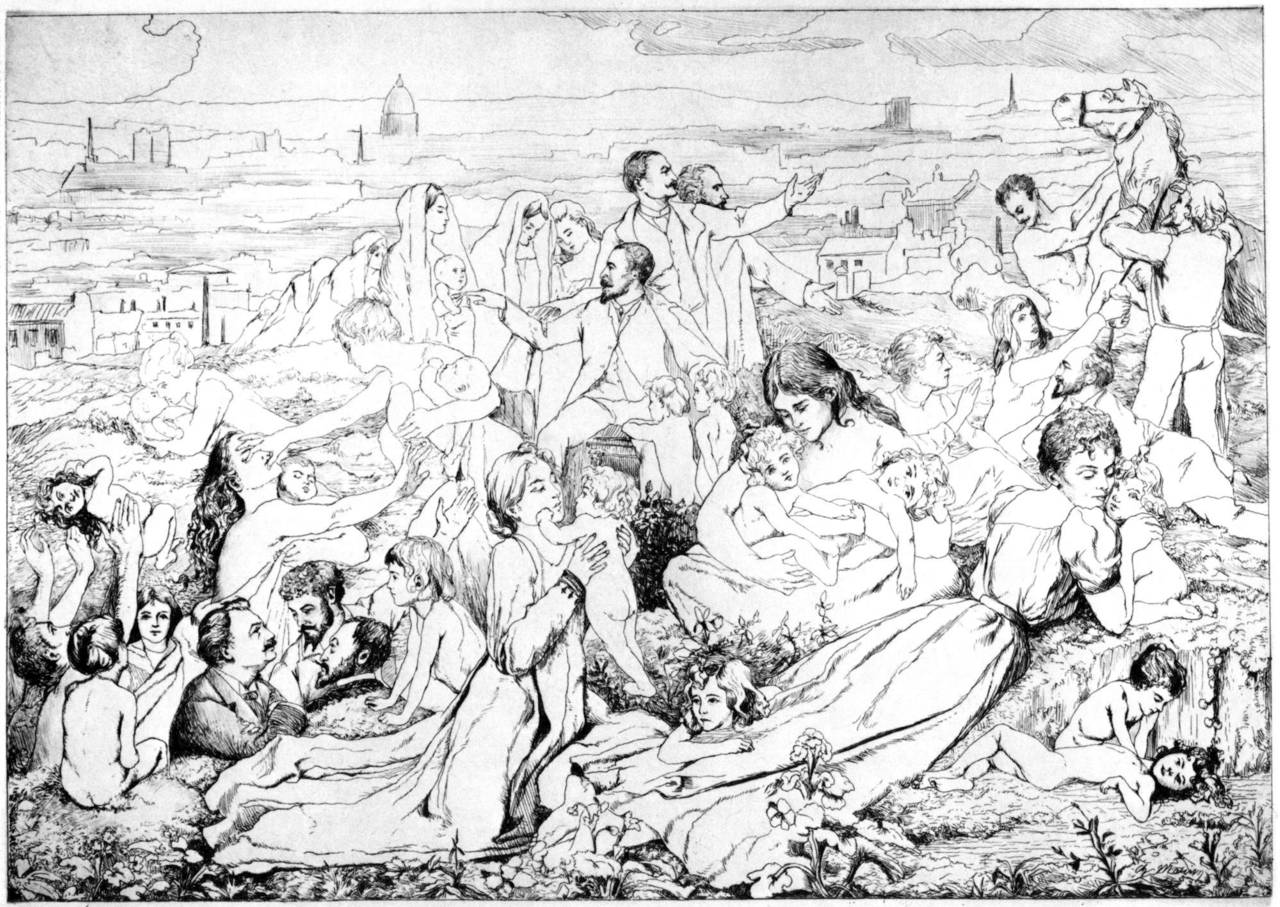

• 41b •

Charles Maurin (French, 1856–1914)

SERUM THERAPY, c. 1896

Etching and drypoint, 13⅝ x 15⁹⁄₁₆" (34.6 x 39.6 cm)

Purchased: SmithKline Beckman Corporation Fund

1984-19-1

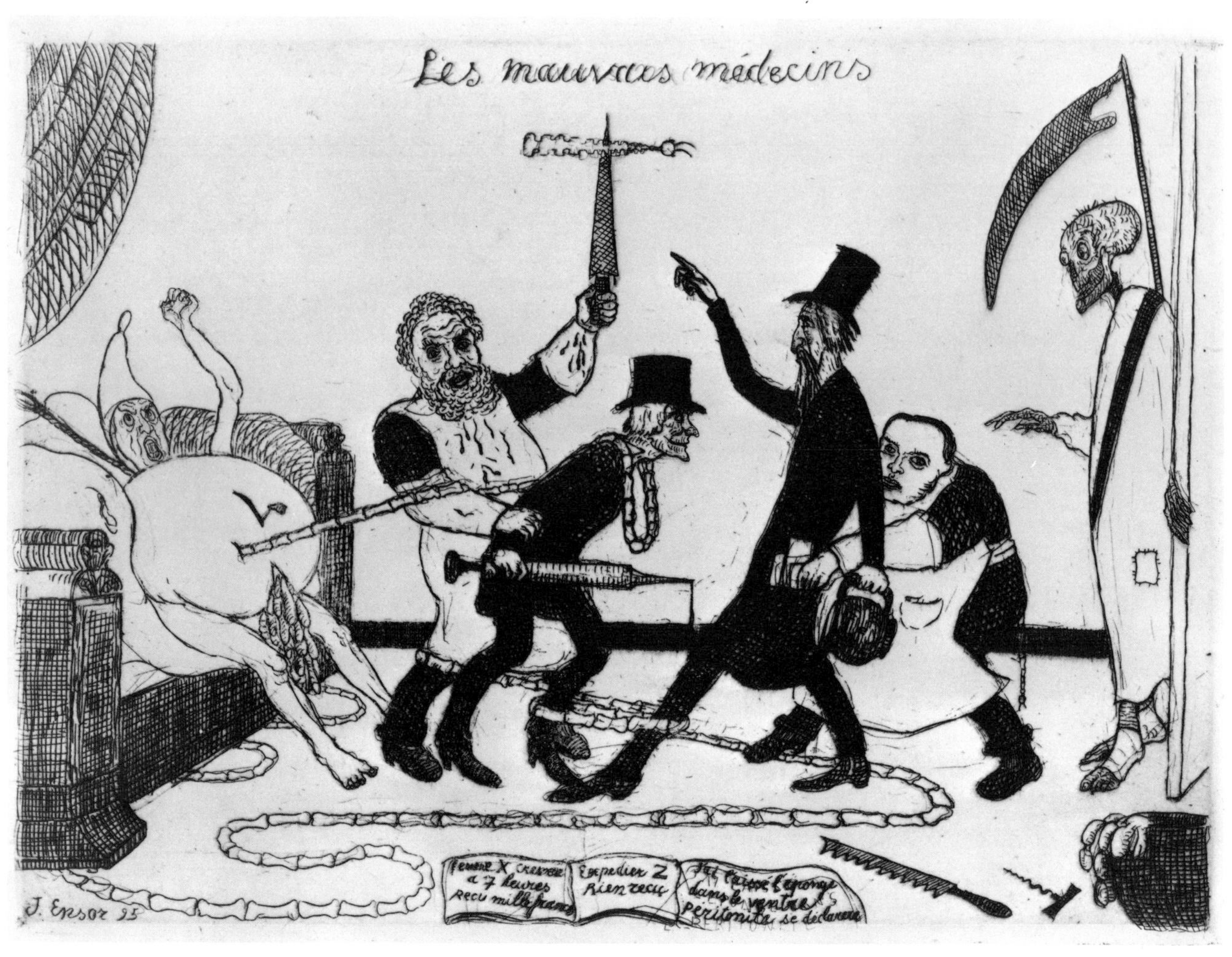

• 42 •

James Ensor (Belgian, 1860–1949)

THE BAD DOCTORS, 1895

Etching, 7 1/16 x 9 15/16" (17.9 x 25.2 cm)

Purchased: SmithKline Beckman Corporation Fund

68-166-1

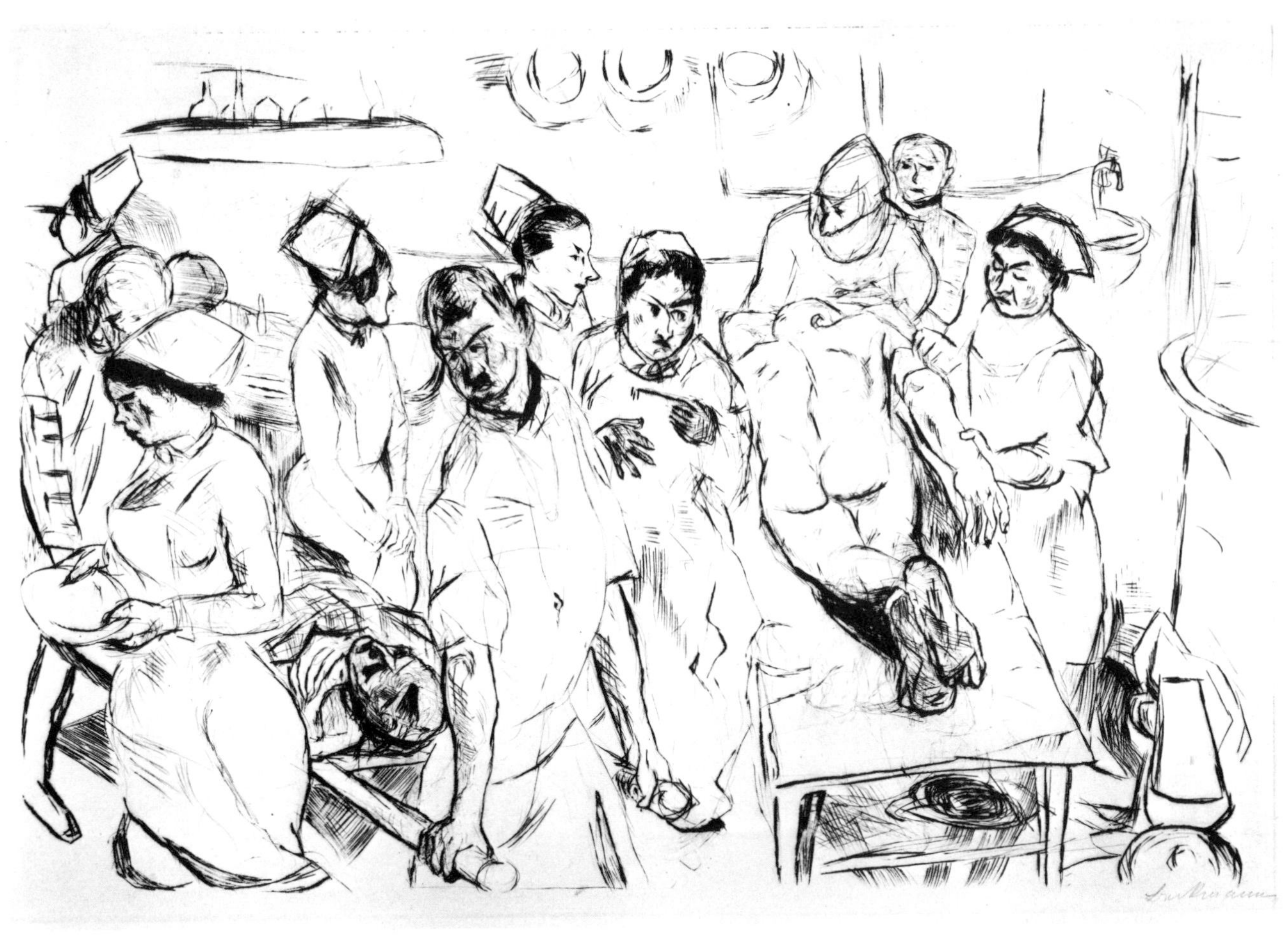

• 43 •

Max Beckmann (German, 1884–1950)

THE LARGE OPERATION, 1914

From *Gesichter* (Munich: R. Piper, 1919)

Drypoint, 11 11/16 x 17 11/16" (29.7 x 44.9 cm)

Purchased: SmithKline Beckman Corporation Fund

70-191-6

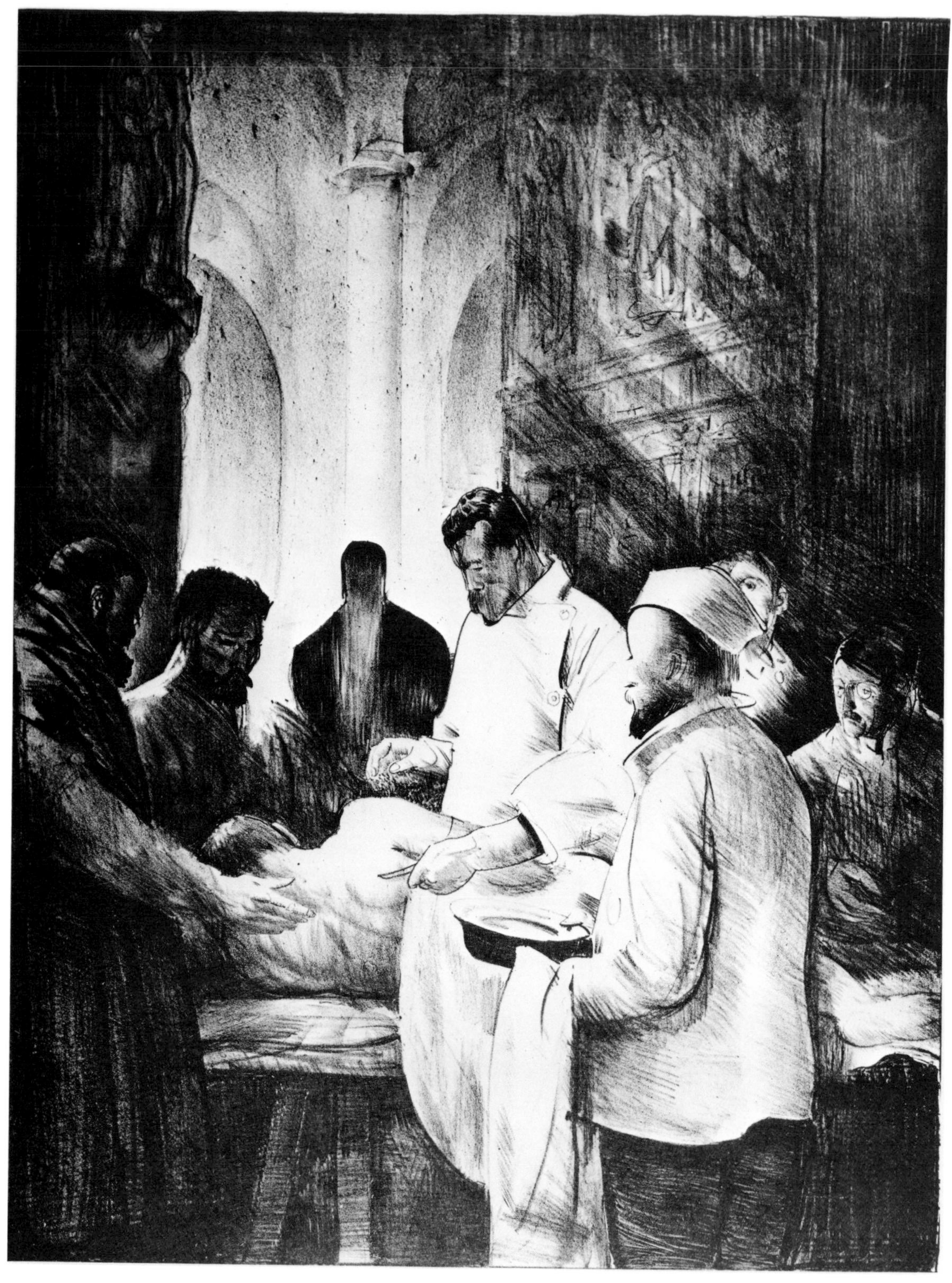

• 44 •

George Bellows (American, 1882–1925)

BASE HOSPITAL (second version), 1918

From "War Series," 1918

Lithograph, 17⅝ x 13⁹⁄₁₆" (44.7 x 34.4 cm)

Purchased: SmithKline Beckman Corporation Fund

1980-52-1

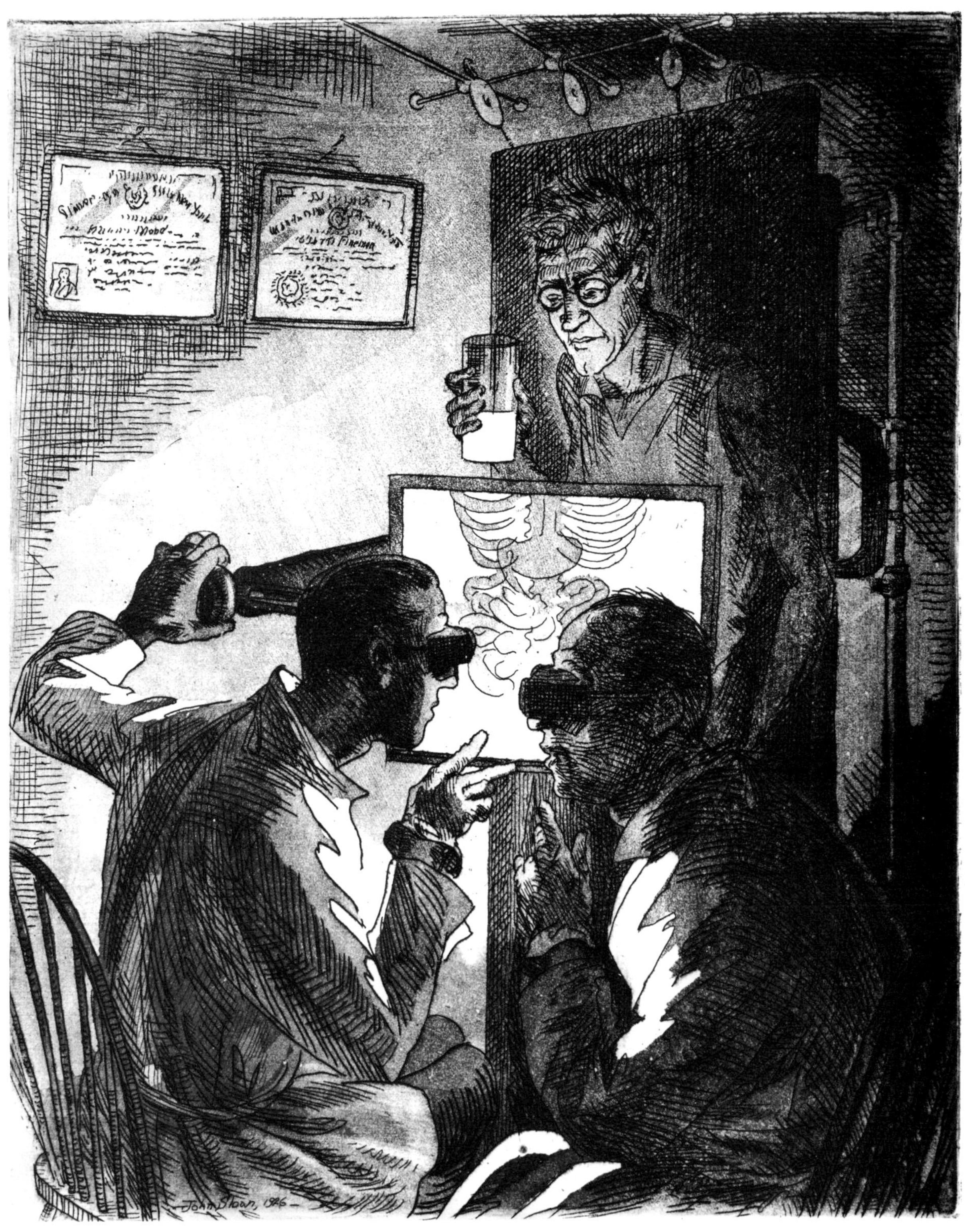

• 45 •

John Sloan (American, 1871–1951)

X-RAYS, 1926

Etching and aquatint (ii/ii), 9¾ x 7¹⁵⁄₁₆" (24.8 x 20.1 cm)

Purchased: Katharine Levin Farrell Fund and funds contributed by Lessing J. Rosenwald

56-35-137

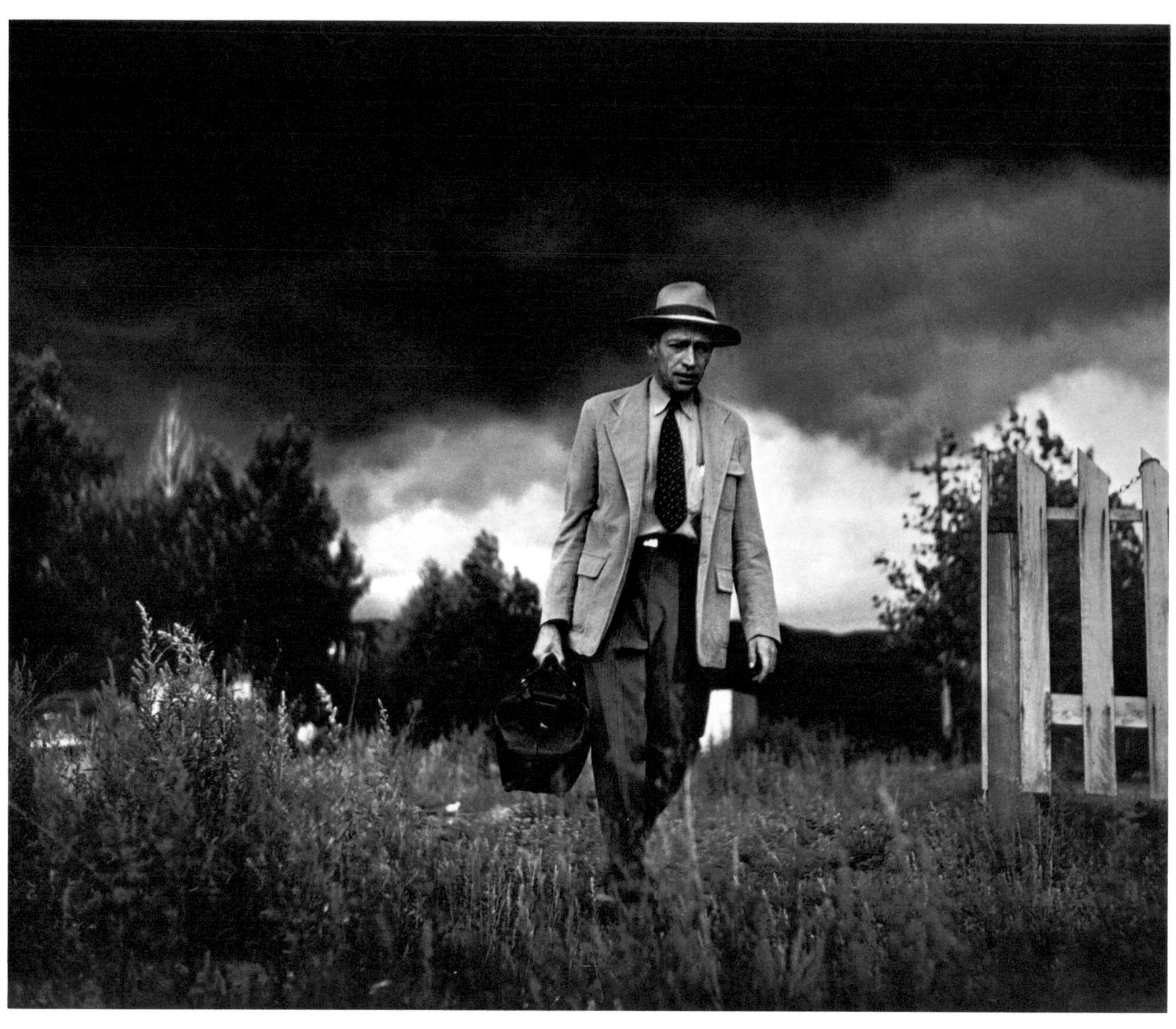

• 46a •

W. Eugene Smith (American, 1918–1978)

DR. CERIANI MAKING A HOUSE CALL, 1948

From "Country Doctor," 1948

Gelatin silver print, 19⅜ x 23⁷⁄₁₆" (49.2 x 59.5 cm)

Purchased: SmithKline Beckman Corporation Fund

1981-13-1

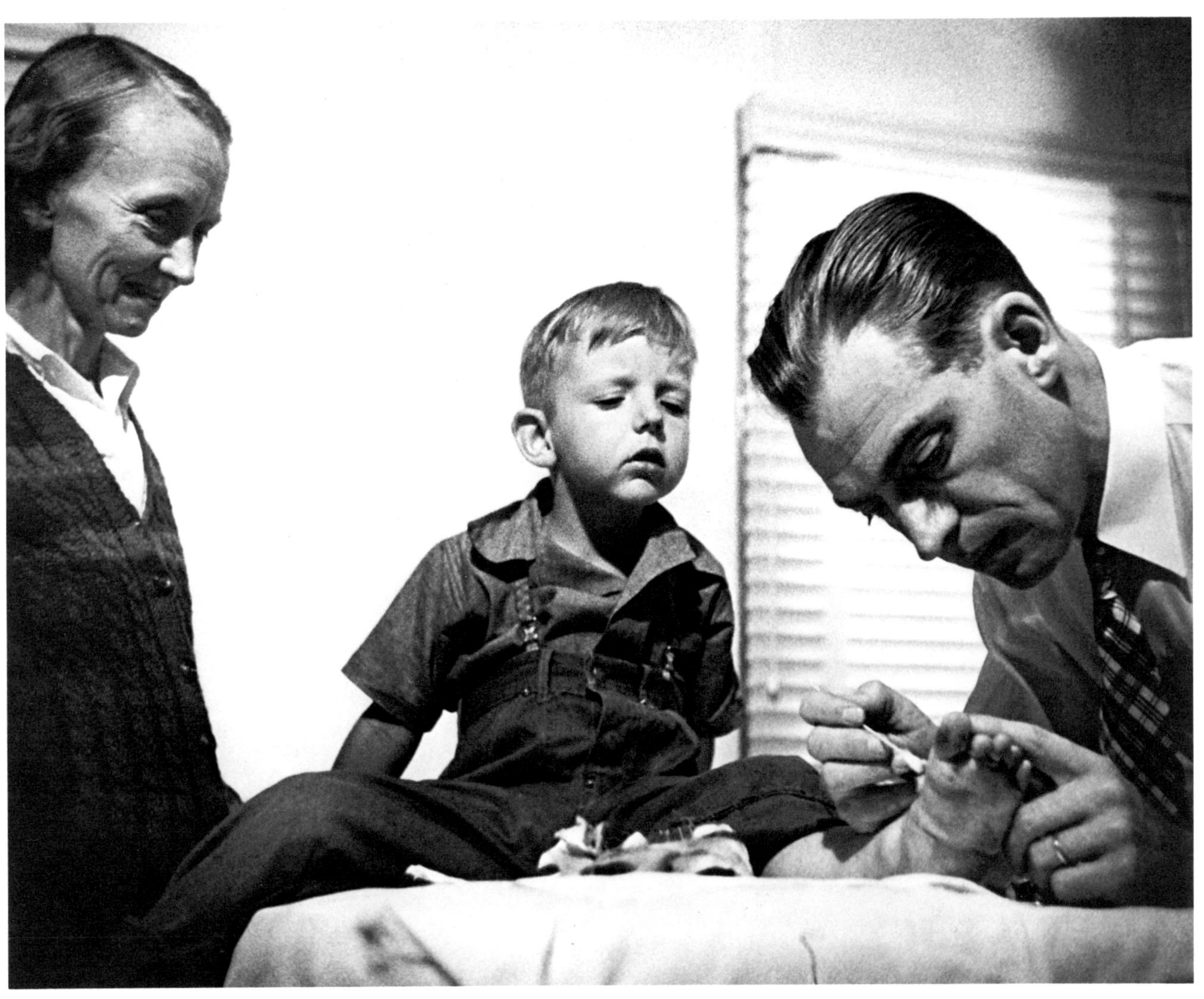

• 46b •

W. Eugene Smith (American, 1918–1978)

DR. CERIANI AND PATIENT, 1948

From "Country Doctor," 1948

Gelatin silver print, 10%16 x 13½" (26.8 x 34.3 cm)

Purchased: SmithKline Beckman Corporation Fund

1984-55-1

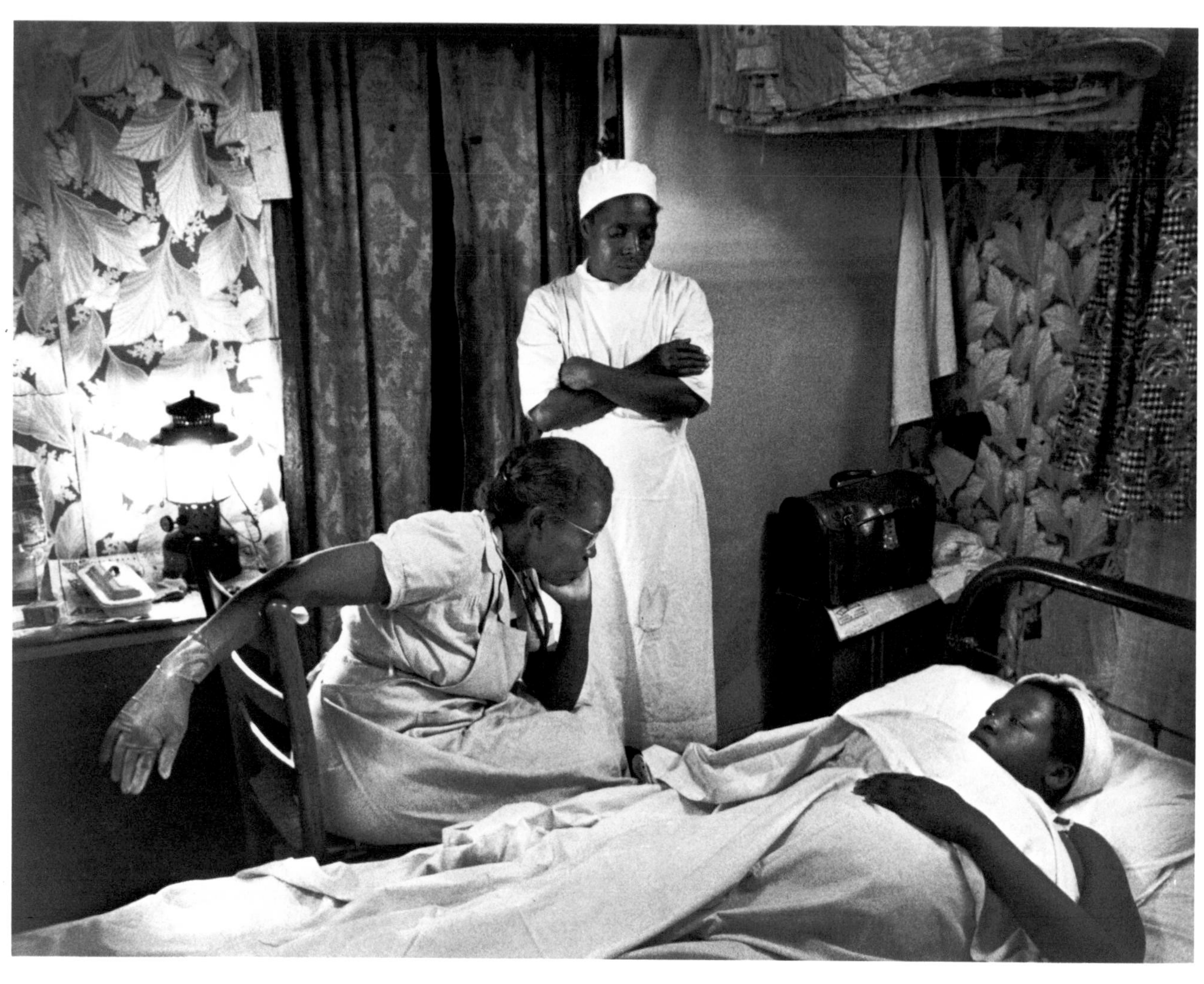

• 47 •

W. Eugene Smith (American, 1918–1978)

MAUDE CALLEN, 1951

From "Nurse Midwife," 1951

Gelatin silver print, 10⅜ x 13⁷⁄₁₆" (26.3 x 34.1 cm)

Purchased: SmithKline Beckman Corporation Fund

1982-35-7

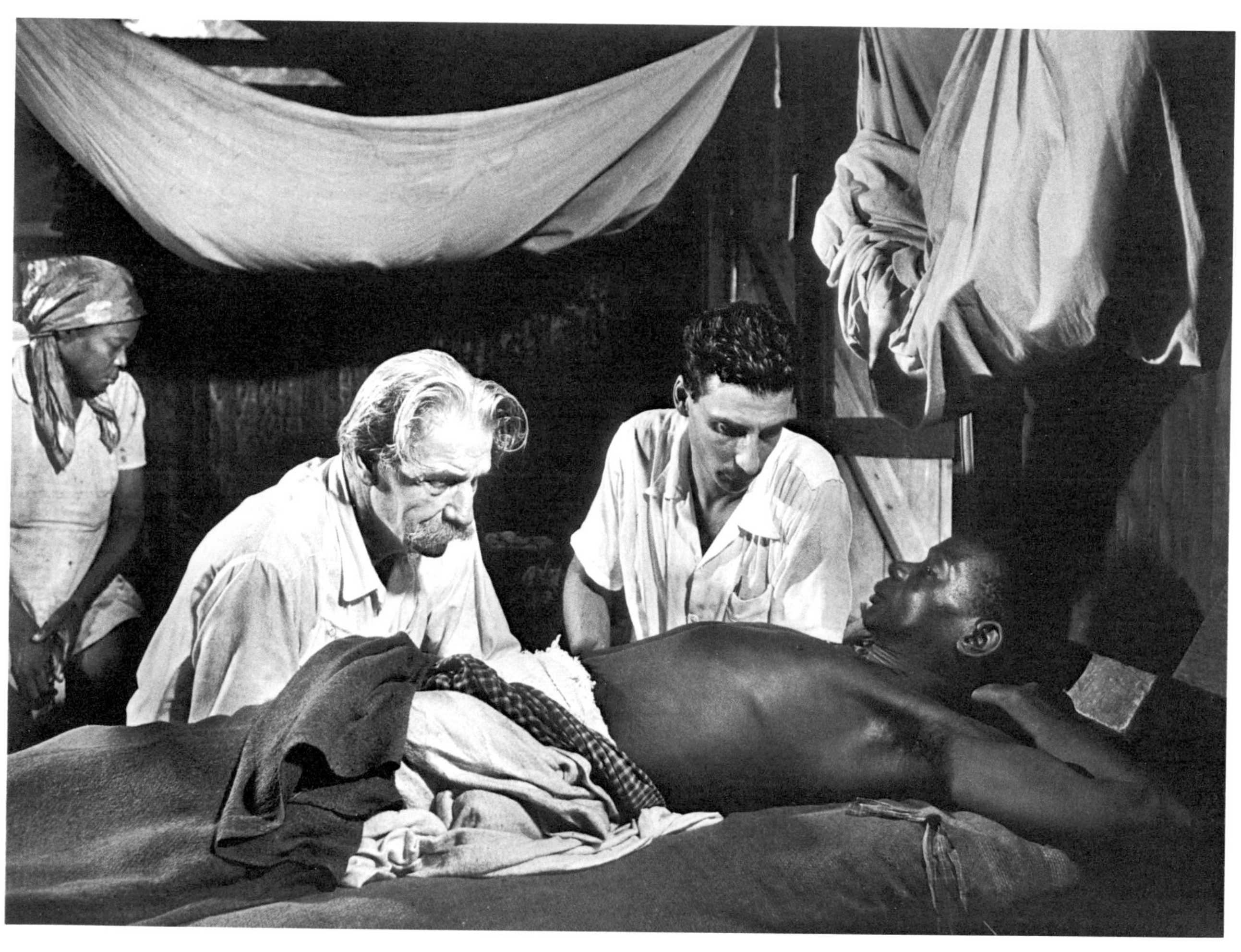

• 48 •

W. Eugene Smith (American, 1918–1978)

ALBERT SCHWEITZER, 1954

From "A Man of Mercy," 1954

Gelatin silver print, 9⁹⁄₁₆ x 13⁷⁄₁₆" (24.3 x 34.1 cm)

Purchased: SmithKline Beckman Corporation Fund

1978-146-1

DISEASE, DISABILITY, AND MADNESS

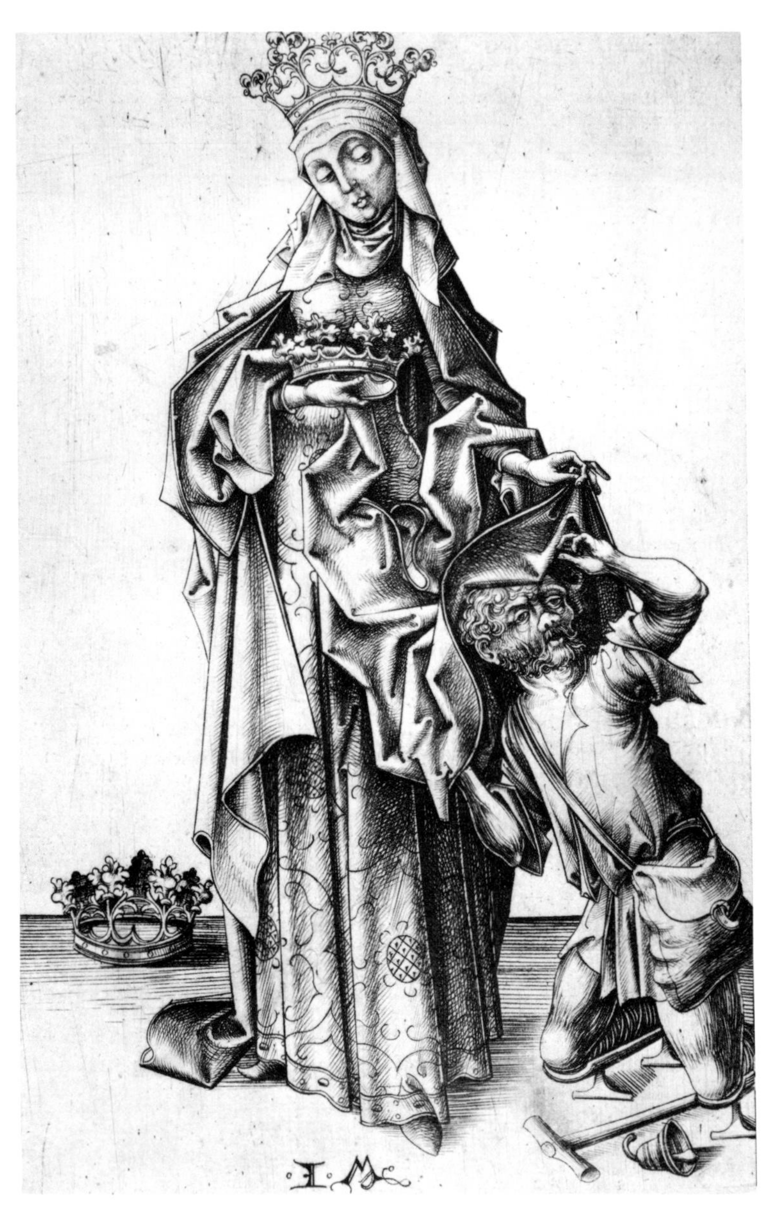

• 49 •

Israhel van Meckenem (German, c. 1445–1503)

SAINT ELIZABETH OF THURINGIA, c. 1475–80

Engraving (i/ii), 6⅛ x 4⅟₁₆" (15.5 x 10.3 cm) (trimmed)
Purchased: SmithKline Beckman Corporation Fund
1984-53-1

Diß künd iſt geboren worden zu Tettnang

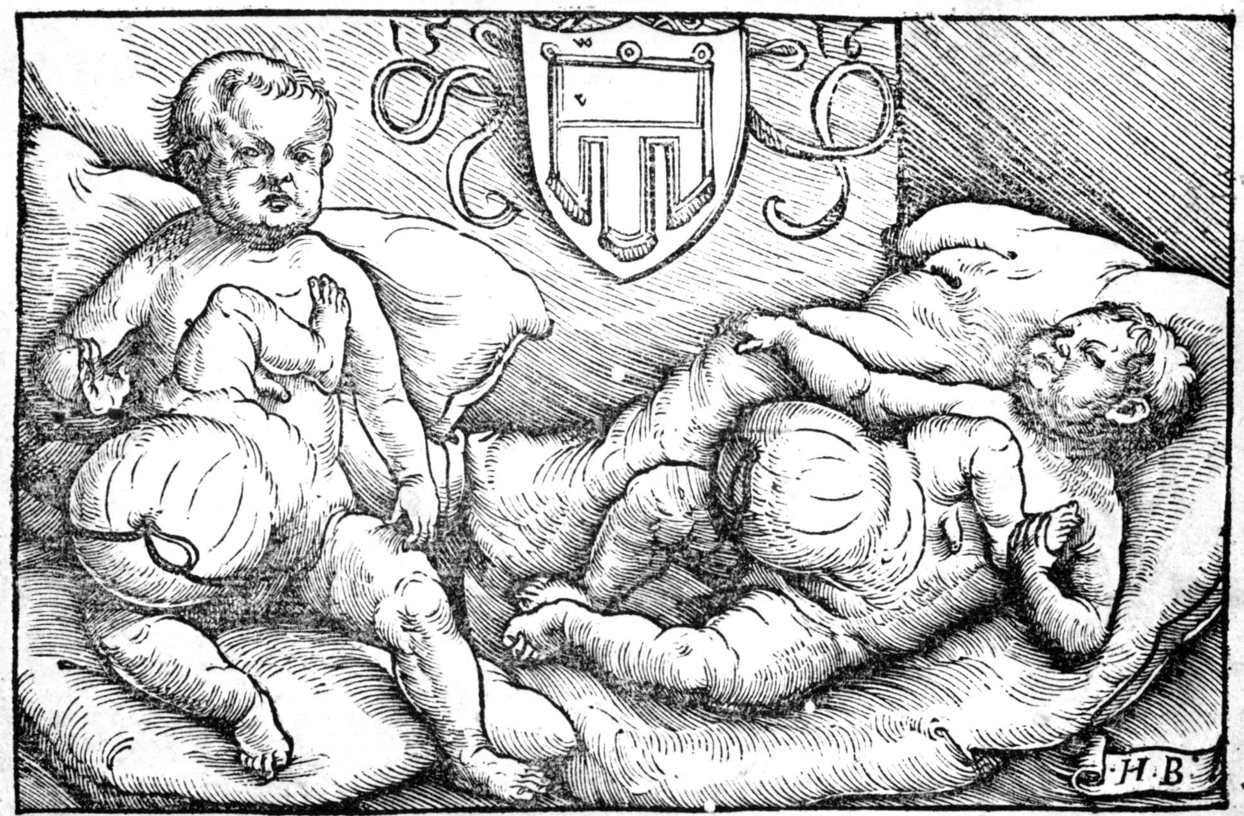

Vff den Achten tag des monats Apprillen von der geburt Jheſu Chriſti/ als man zalt/fünffzehenhundert vnd Sechtzehen Jare/jnn der halben ſtunnd als nach mit nacht die glock ains geſchlagenn hat iſt in des wolgebornenn Herren herrn Vlrich Graue zů Muntfort vnnd ſtat Tettnang vonn ainer frawen mit namen Anna Bingerin / Conradenn Millers da ſelbs Eewirtin ain ſolch künd wie ob ſtet/mit dem fießlin vnnd ſchwentzel an ſeiner prüſt auch groſſem plafarben gewechs an ſeinem bauch auſſen her vm̃ Ain Retin vñ Rotfarbe ſtraumen darüber wie ain geſchwer geborn worden/So des/ſelbig künd wachend/ſeine Bain von ain ander/vnnd ſo es ſchlaffend auch der maſſen gelegen/aber alwegen das fießlin in der hand haltend vnd iſt ain döchterlin vnnd biß an/den Neünden tag lebendig geweſen/ſolich künd hat der ob beſtimbt Herr vnnd Grauff ſeinen maller Mayſter Matheyſen miller Maler burger zů Lindaw mit fleyß hayſen verzaychnen oder konterfenn vnd zů trucken ver ortnen wie oben geſehen wirt.

• 50 •

Hans Burgkmair (German, 1473–1531)

After Mathis Miller (German, active early sixteenth century)

CHILD WITH THREE LEGS, 1516

Woodcut, 7¹¹⁄₁₆ x 6¹³⁄₁₆″ (19.5 x 17.3 cm) (trimmed)

Purchased: SmithKline Beckman Corporation Fund

1982-42-1

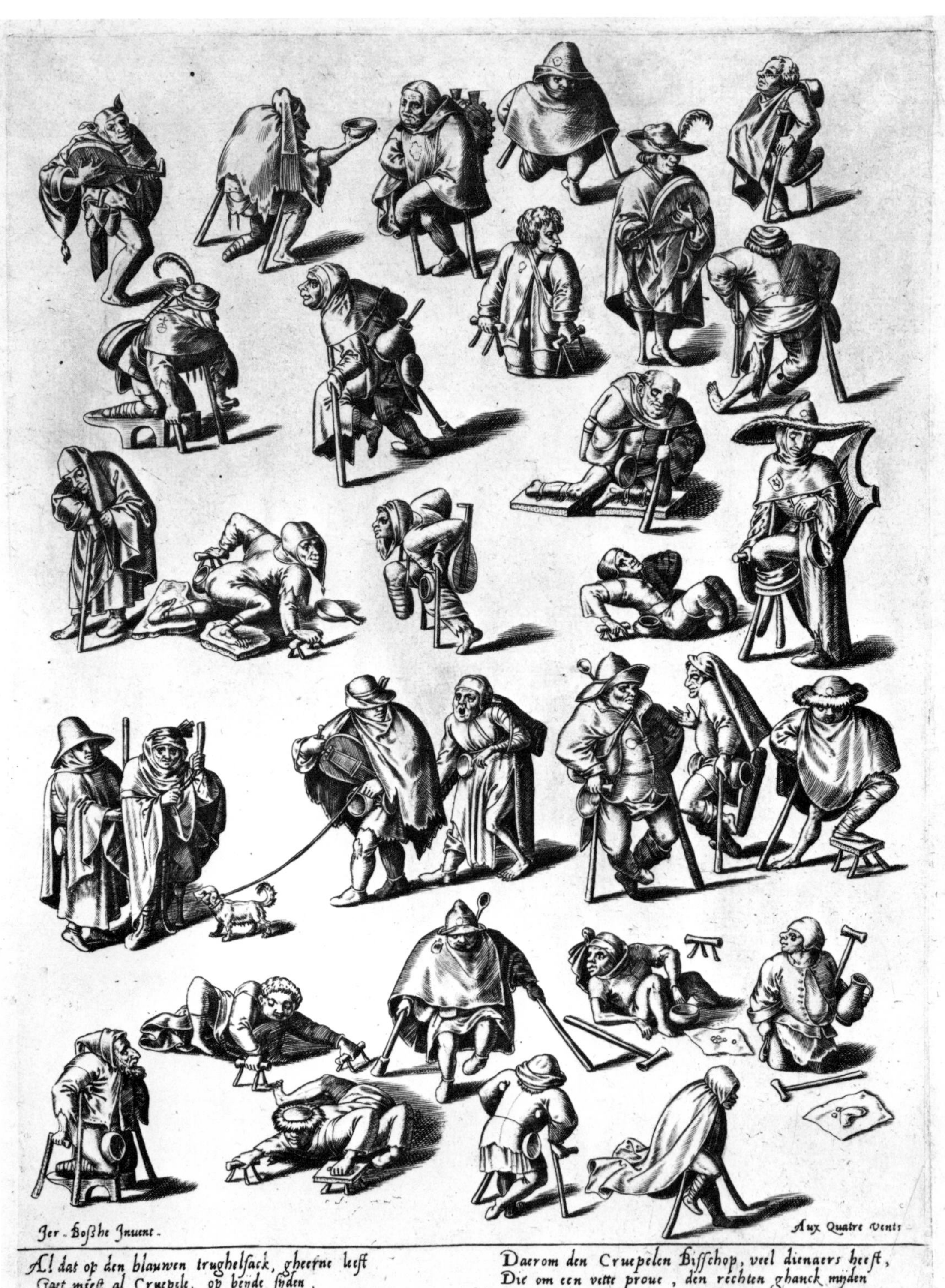

• 51 •

Hieronymus Cock (Flemish, c. 1520–1570)
After Hieronymus Bosch (Dutch, c. 1450–1516)
BEGGARS, mid-sixteenth century

Engraving (i/ii), 11¾ x 8¹¹⁄₁₆" (29.8 x 22.1 cm)
Purchased: SmithKline Beckman Corporation Fund
1983-32-1

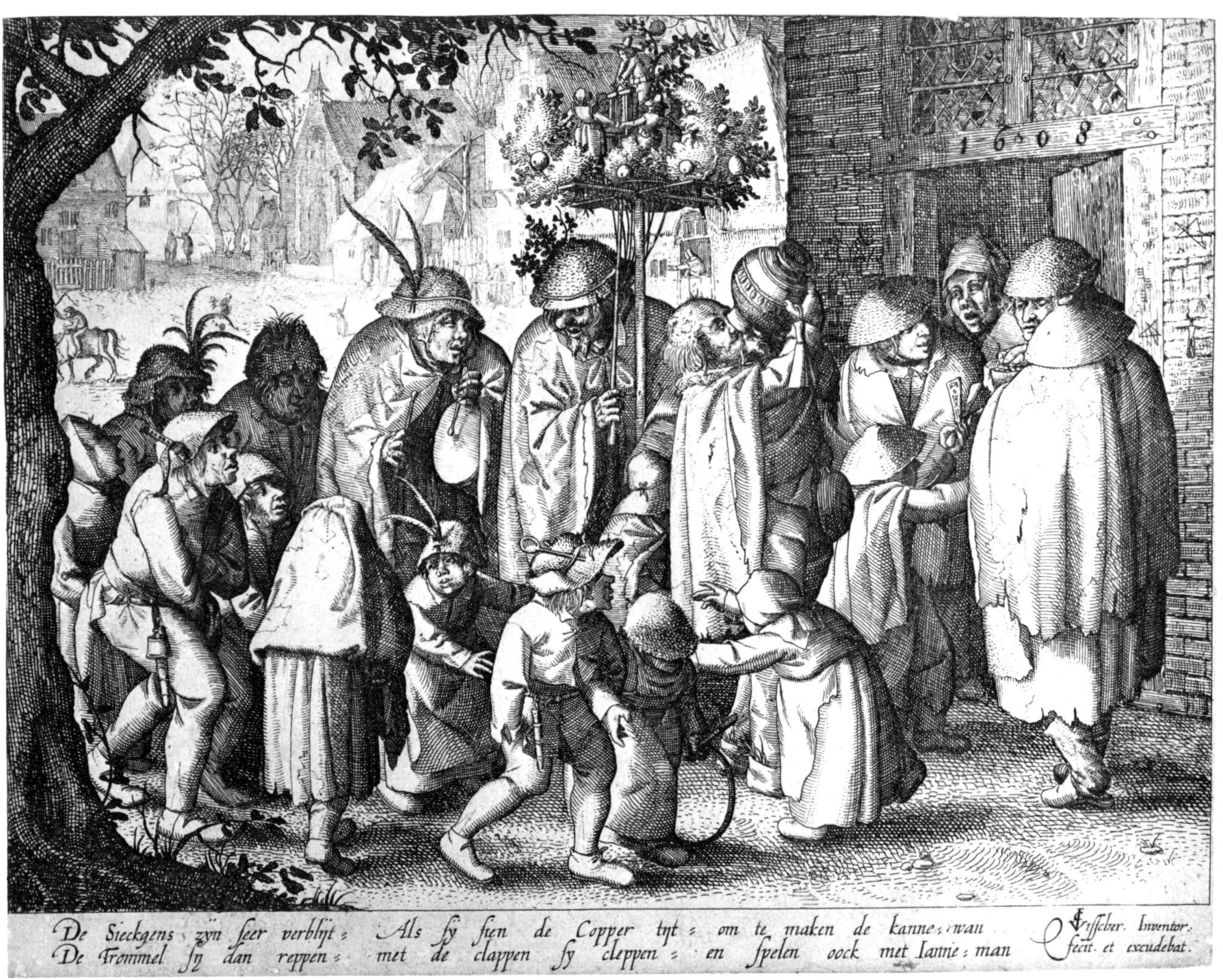

• 52 •

Claes Jansz. Visscher the Younger (Dutch, 1586–1652)

PROCESSION OF LEPERS ON COPPER MONDAY, 1608

Etching, 6¾ x 8⅞" (17.1 x 22.5 cm) (trimmed)

Purchased: SmithKline Beckman Corporation Fund

1983-73-1

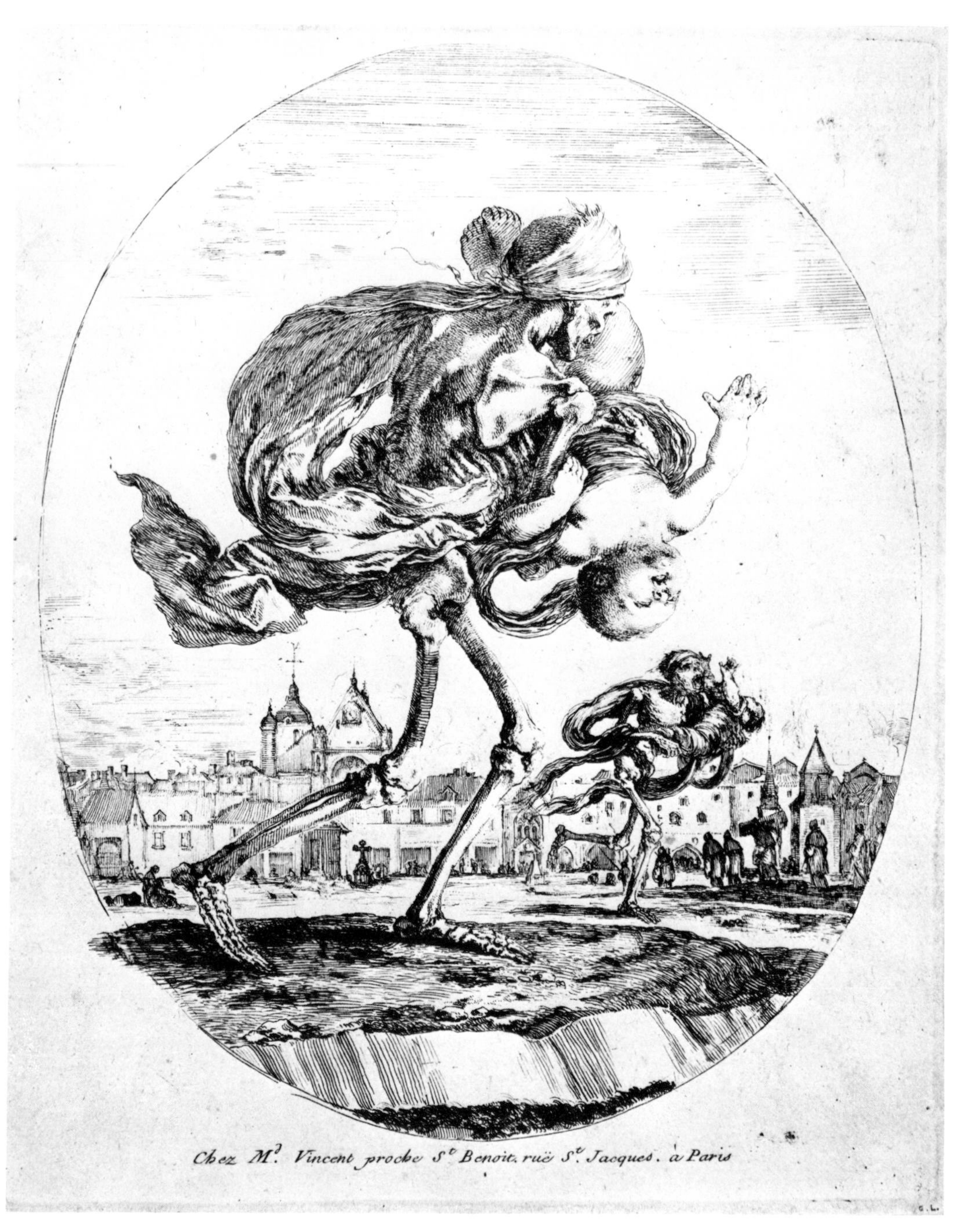

• 53 •

Stefano della Bella (Italian, 1610–1664)

PLAGUE, c. 1648

From "The Five Deaths," c. 1648
Etching (iii/iii), 7$\frac{3}{16}$ x 5$\frac{7}{8}$" (18.3 x 14.9 cm)
Purchased: SmithKline Beckman Corporation Fund
68-215-24

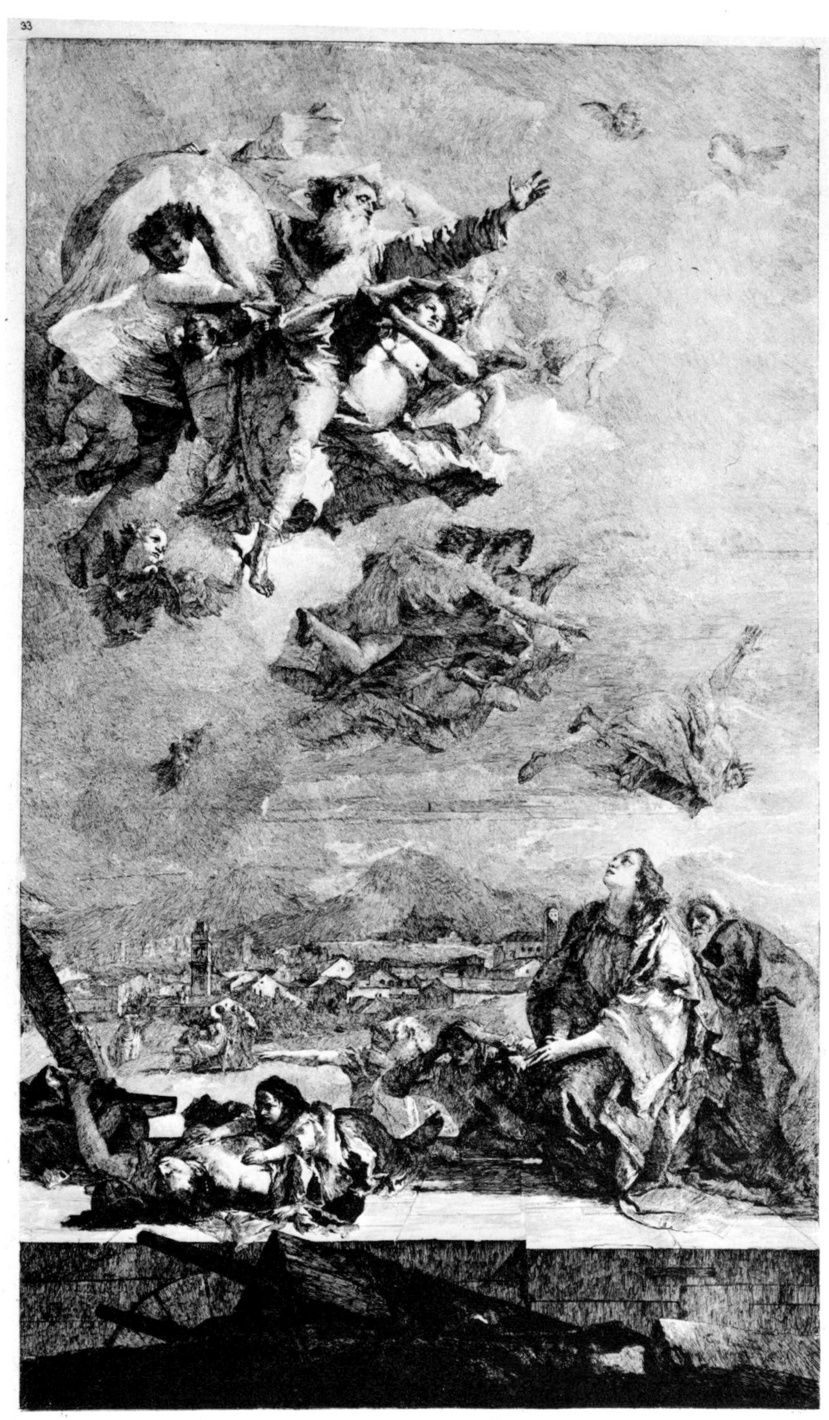

Joannes Batta Tiepolo inv. et pin.
Laurentius Tiepolo filius del. et inc.

• 54 •

Lorenzo Baldissera Tiepolo (Italian, 1736–before 1776)
After Giovanni Battista Tiepolo (Italian, 1696–1770)
SAINT THECLA PRAYING FOR THE END OF THE PLAGUE IN THE CITY OF ESTE, c. 1759

Etching (ii/ii), $27\frac{13}{16}$ x $15\frac{7}{8}$" (70.6 x 40.3 cm)
Purchased: SmithKline Beckman Corporation Fund
1982-83-1

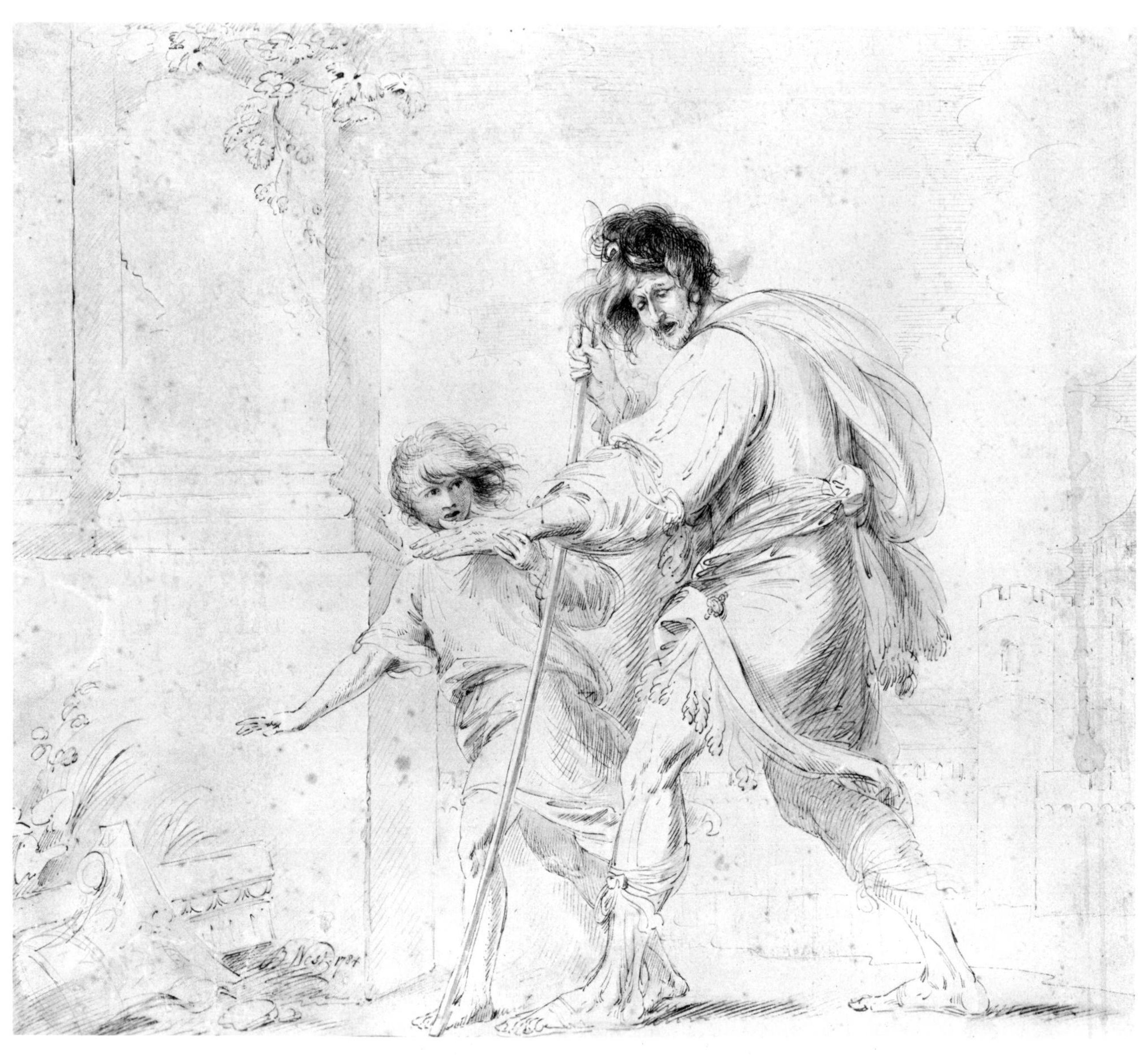

• 55 •

Benjamin West (American, active England, 1738–1820)

THE BLIND BELISARIUS LED BY A BOY, 1784

Brown ink and brown and pale blue washes with stylus lines on buff laid paper, 17³⁄₁₆ x 19½" (43.6 x 49.5 cm)

Purchased: SmithKline Beckman Corporation Fund

66-9-1

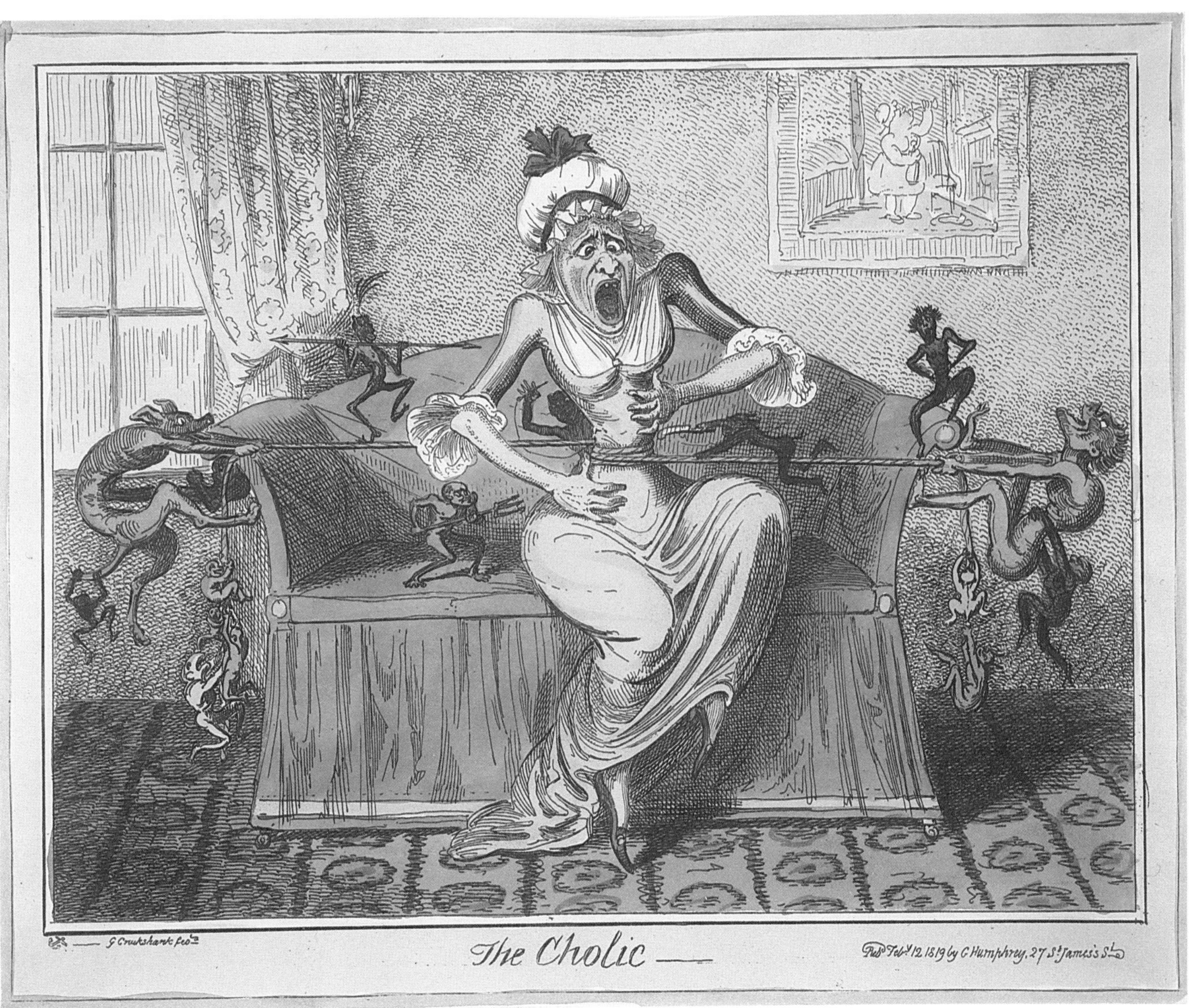

• 56 •

George Cruikshank (English, 1792–1878)

THE CHOLIC, 1819

Hand-colored etching (i/ii), 8⅛ x 10⅛" (20.7 x 25.7 cm) (trimmed)

Purchased: SmithKline Beckman Corporation Fund

1983-96-1

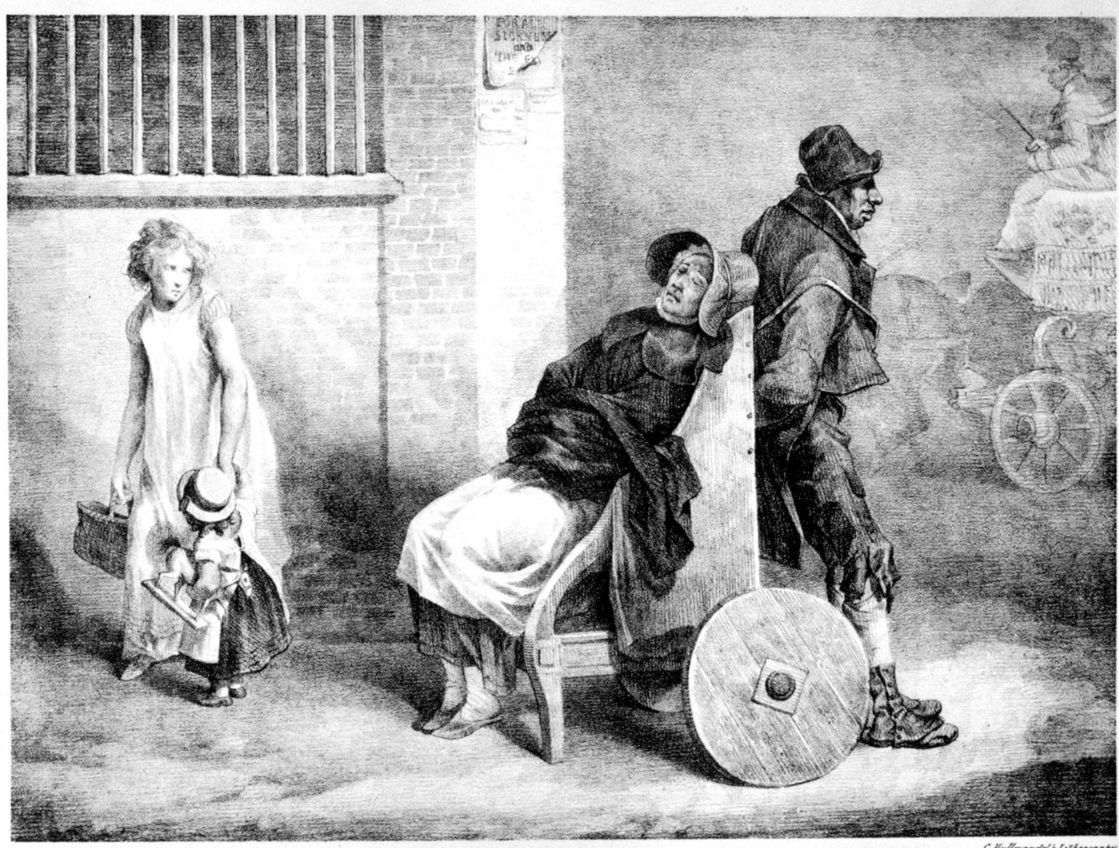

• 57 •

Jean-Louis-André-Théodore Géricault (French, 1791–1824)

A PARALEYTIC WOMAN, 1821

From *Various Subjects Drawn from Life and on Stone* (London: Rodwell & Martin, 1821)

Lithograph, 9⁹⁄₁₆ x 12⁷⁄₁₆" (24.3 x 31.6 cm)

Purchased: SmithKline Beckman Corporation Fund

1982-117-1

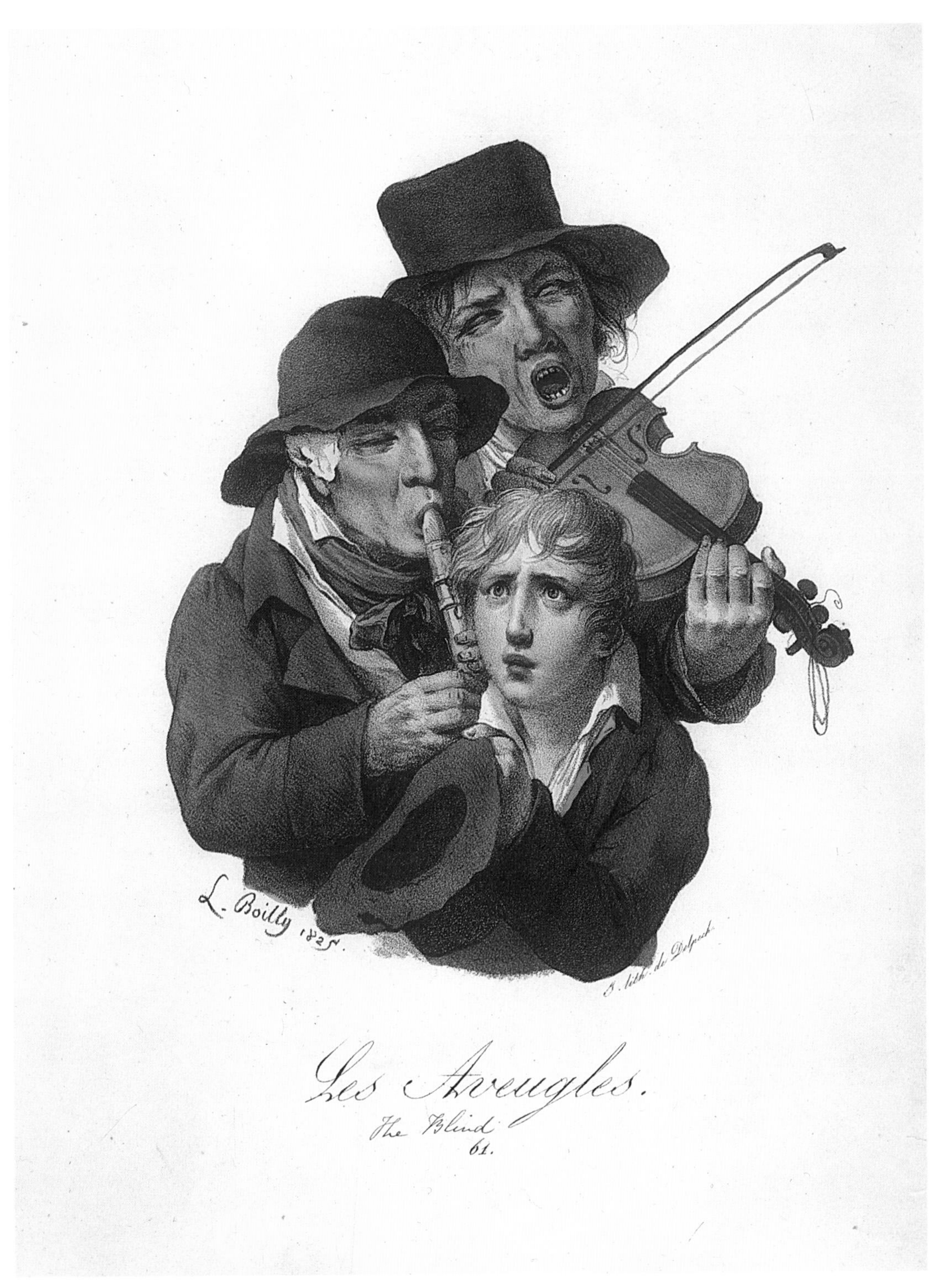

• 58 •

Louis-Léopold Boilly (French, 1761–1845)

THE BLIND, 1825

From "The Collection of Grimaces," 1823–28

Hand-colored lithograph, $10\frac{7}{16}$ x $7\frac{5}{16}$" (26.5 x 18.6 cm)

Purchased: SmithKline Beckman Corporation Fund

1978-25-2

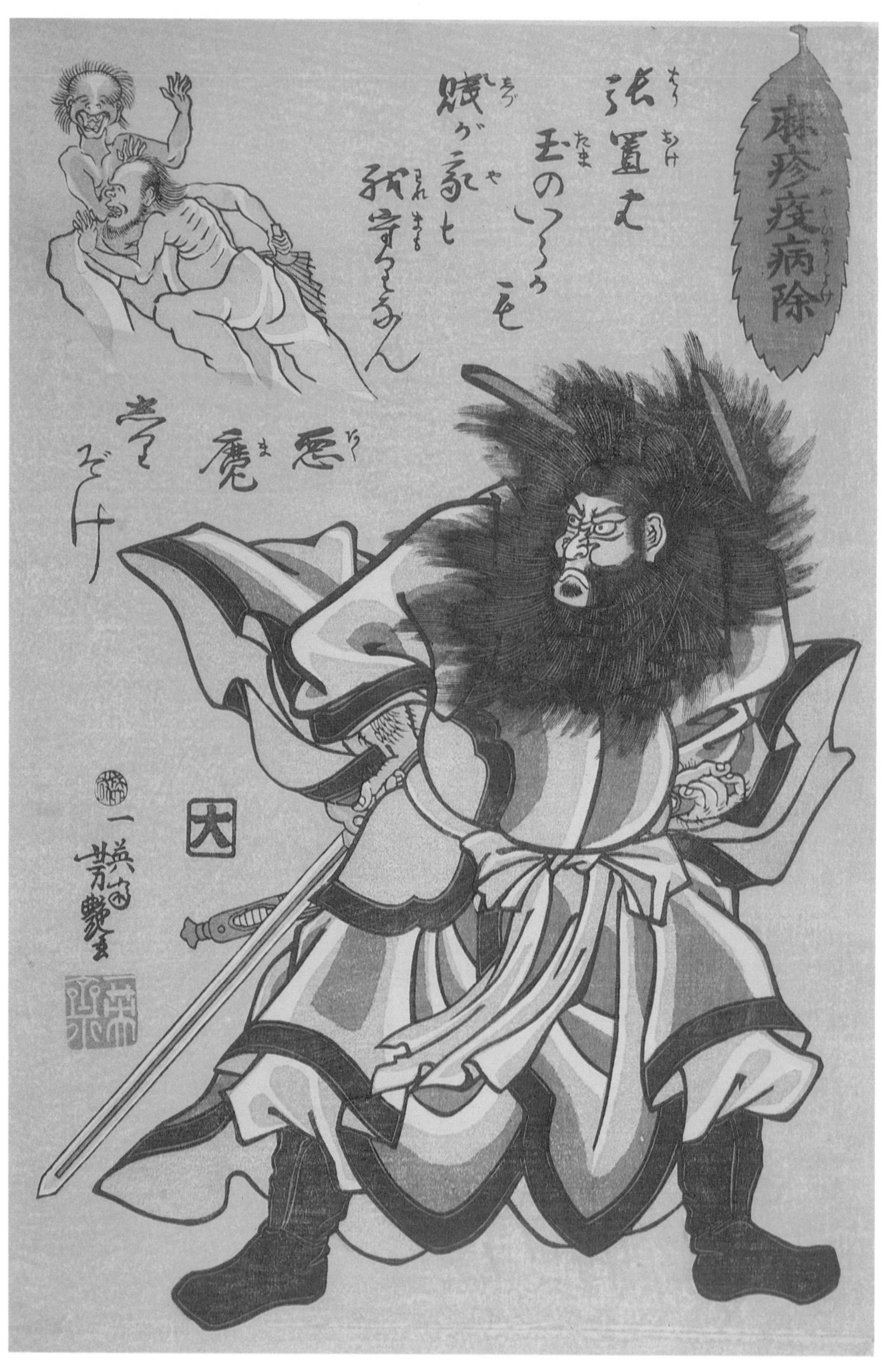

• 59 •

Utagawa Yoshitsuya, known as Ichieisai (Japanese, 1822–1866)

PROTECTION FROM THE MEASLES EPIDEMIC, 1862

Color woodcut, 14 7/16 x 9 3/4" (36.7 x 24.8 cm)
Purchased: SmithKline Beckman Corporation Fund
1978-87-1

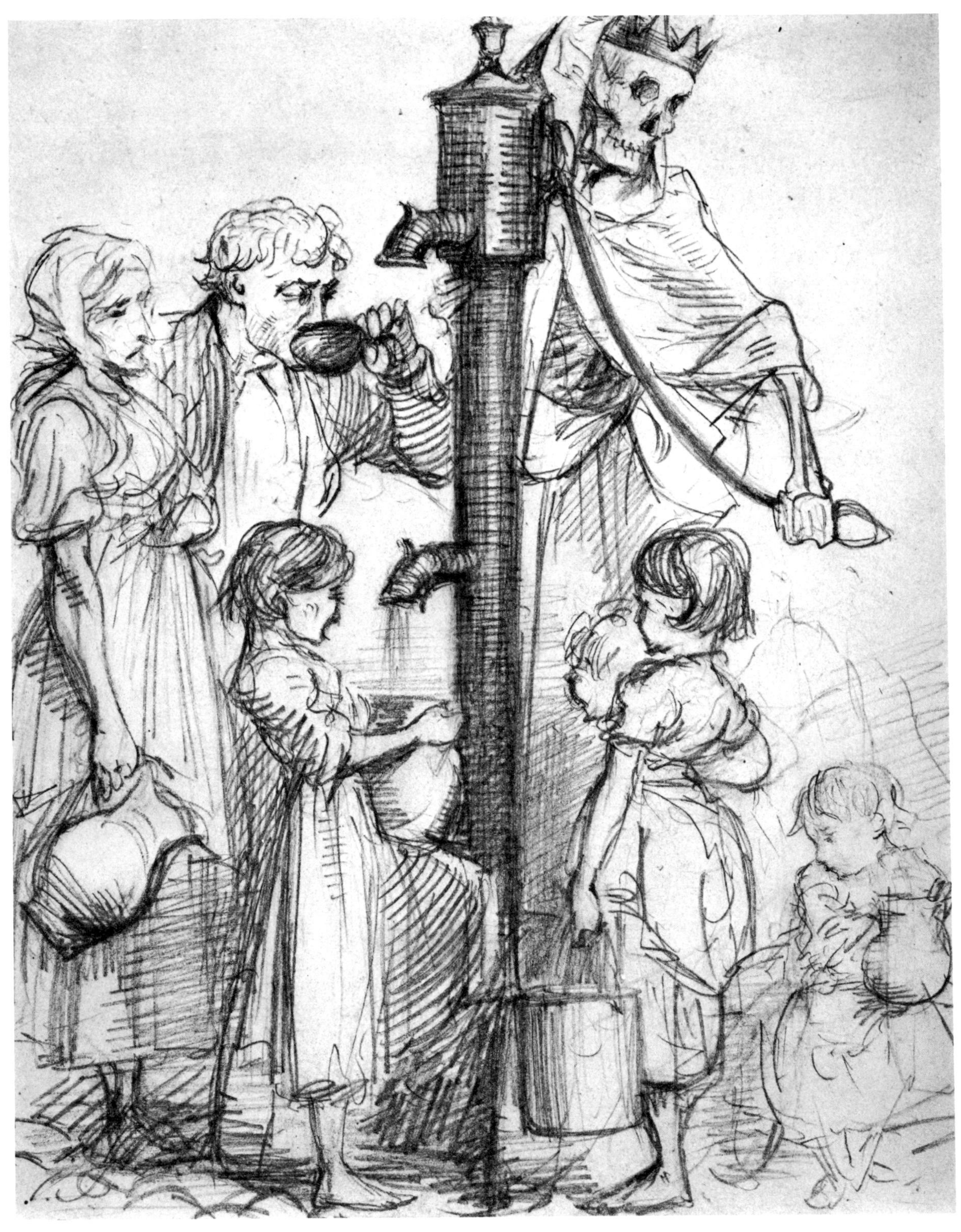

• 60 •

George John Pinwell (English, 1842–1875)

DEATH'S DISPENSARY, c. 1866

Graphite on light buff wove paper, 7 15/16 x 6 5/16" (20.2 x 16.1 cm)

Purchased: SmithKline Beckman Corporation Fund

1984-17-1

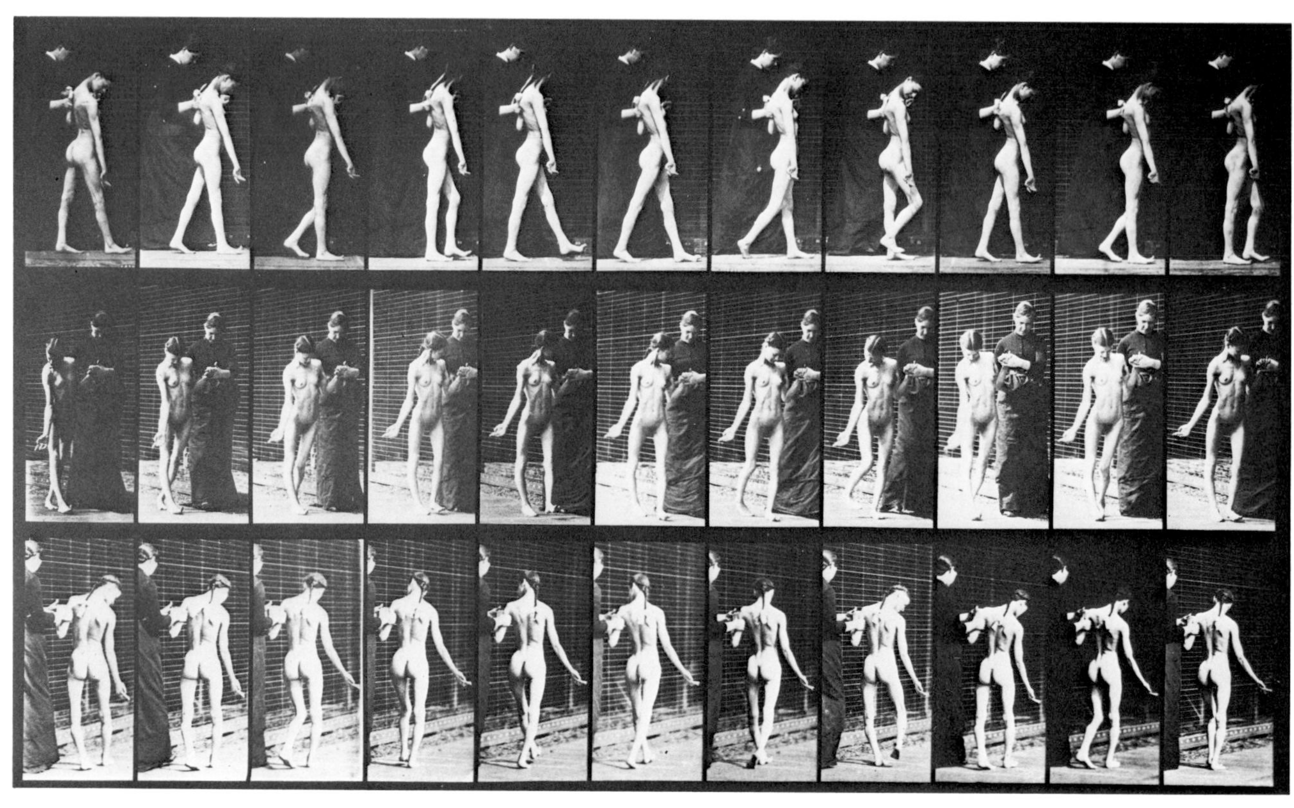

• 61 •

Eadweard Muybridge (American, born England, 1830–1904)

SPASTIC WALKING, 1885

From Eadweard Muybridge, *Animal Locomotion: An Electro-Photographic Investigation of Consecutive Phases of Animal Movements* (Philadelphia: University of Pennsylvania, 1887)

Collotype, 8¼ x 14⅛" (20.9 x 36 cm)

Gift of the City of Philadelphia Trade & Convention Center, Department of Commerce

62-135-242

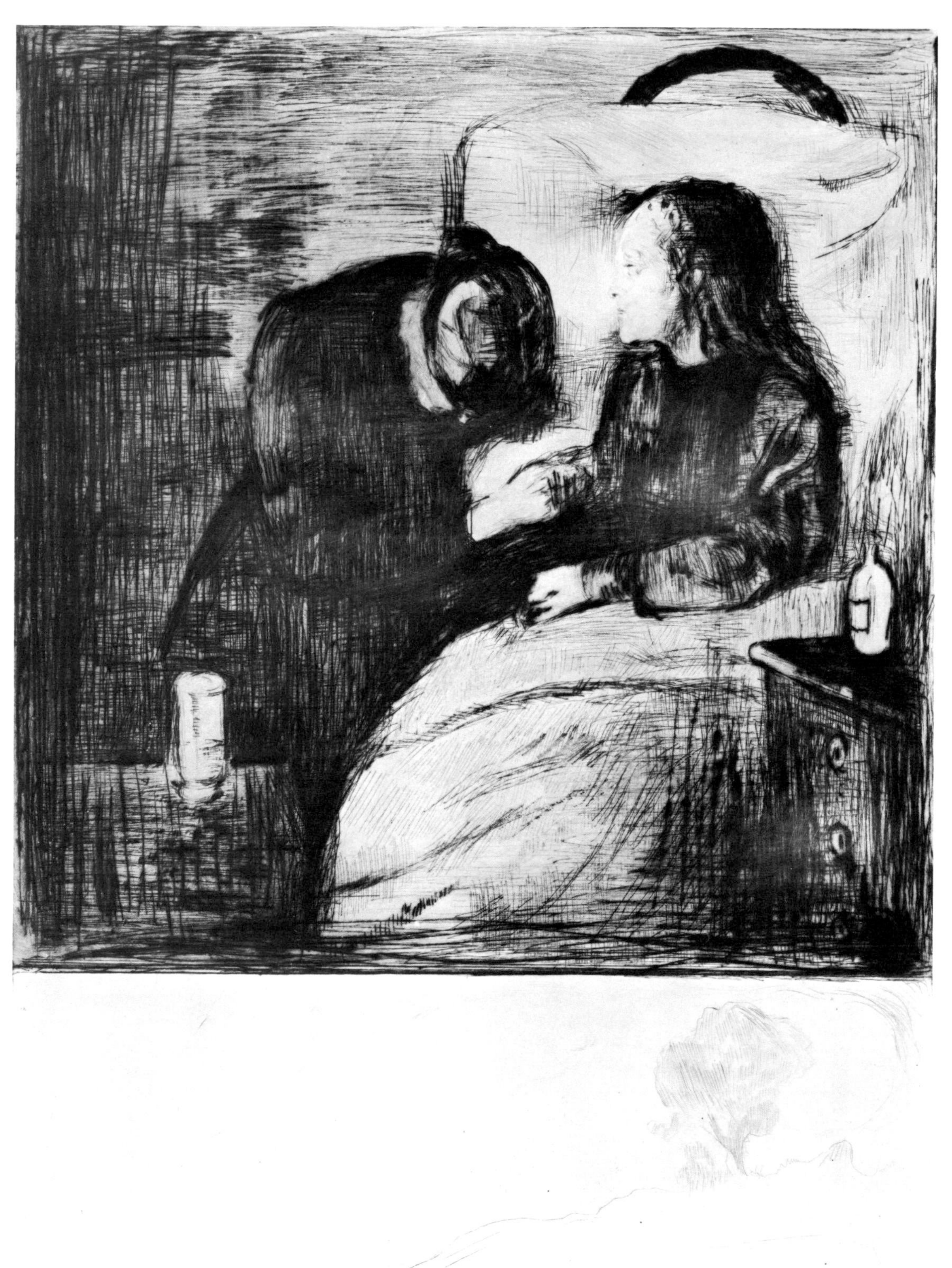

• 62 •

Edvard Munch (Norwegian, 1863–1944)

THE SICK CHILD, 1894

Drypoint (v/v/c), 15³⁄₁₆ x 11⁷⁄₁₆" (38.6 x 29 cm)
Purchased: SmithKline Beckman Corporation Fund
49-97-38

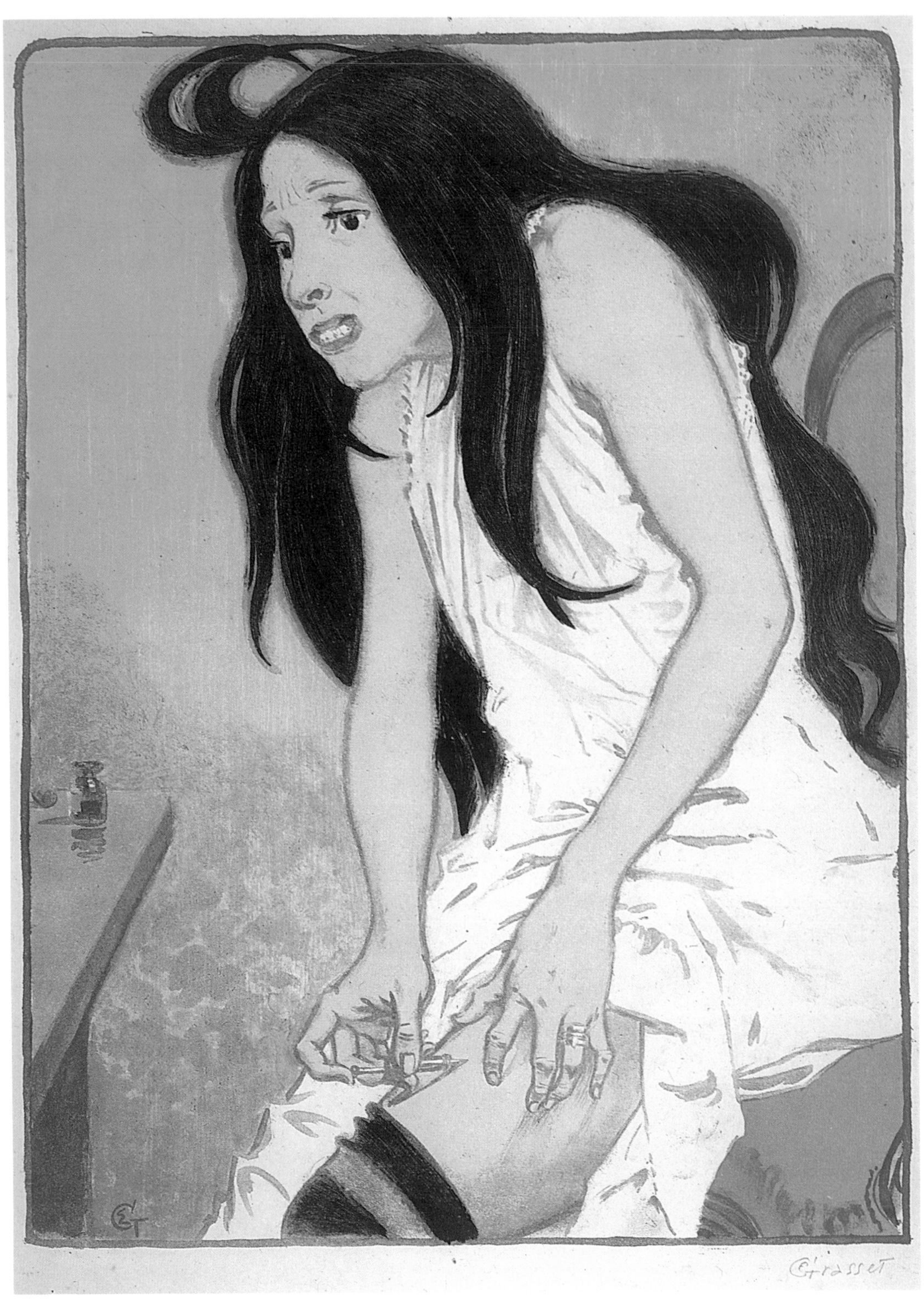

• 63 •

Eugène-Samuel Grasset (French, born Switzerland, 1841–1917)

MORPHINOMANIAC, 1897

From *L'Album des peintres-graveurs* (Paris: Ambroise Vollard, 1897)

Color lithograph, 16 5/16 x 12 3/8" (41.4 x 31.4 cm)

Purchased: SmithKline Beckman Corporation Fund

1983-99-1

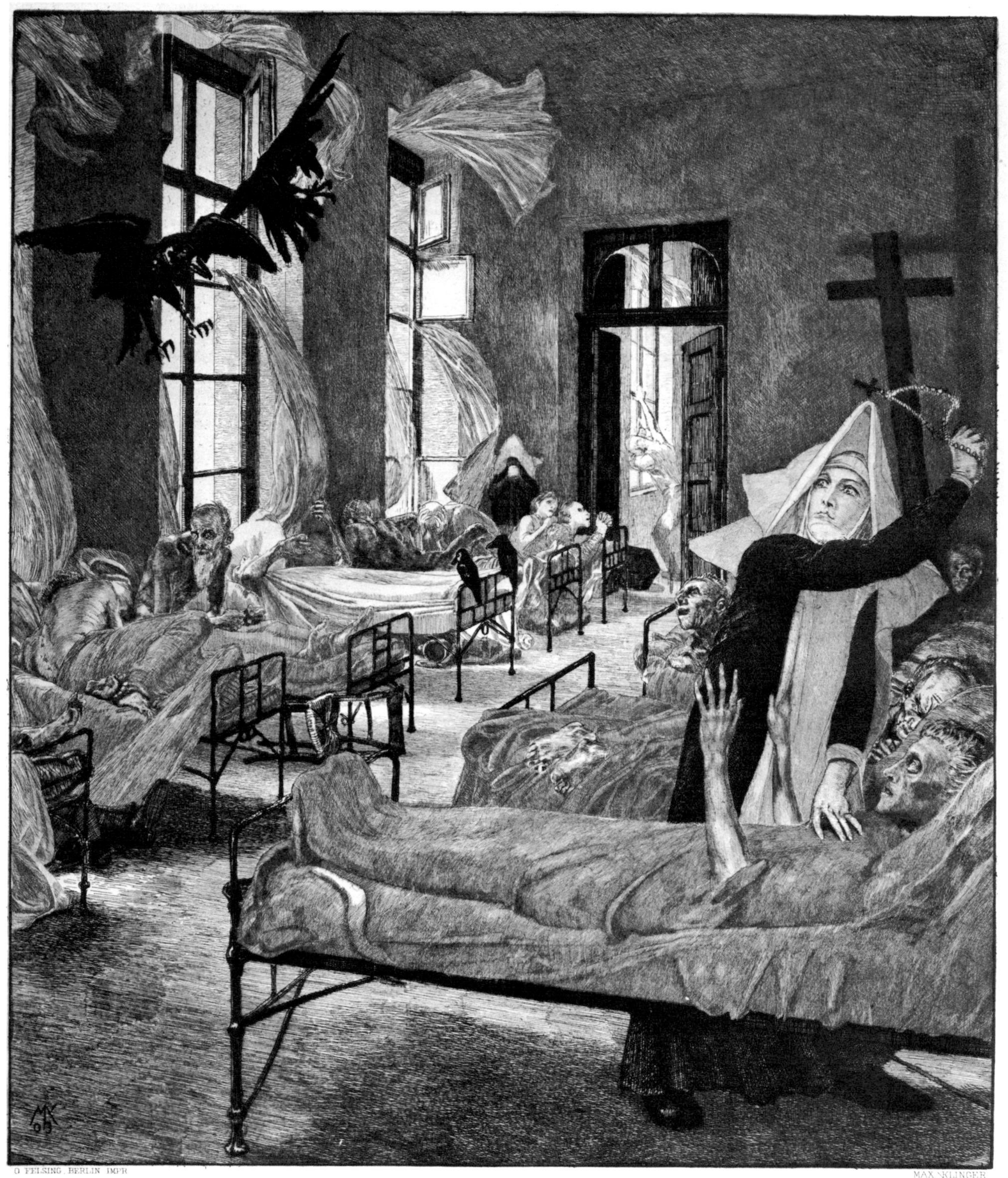

• 64 •

Max Klinger (German, 1857–1920)

THE PLAGUE, 1903

From "On Death, Part II," 1898–1909

Etching and drypoint, 16$\frac{13}{16}$ x 13$\frac{1}{4}$" (42.7 x 33.6 cm)

Purchased: SmithKline Beckman Corporation Fund

1980-51-1

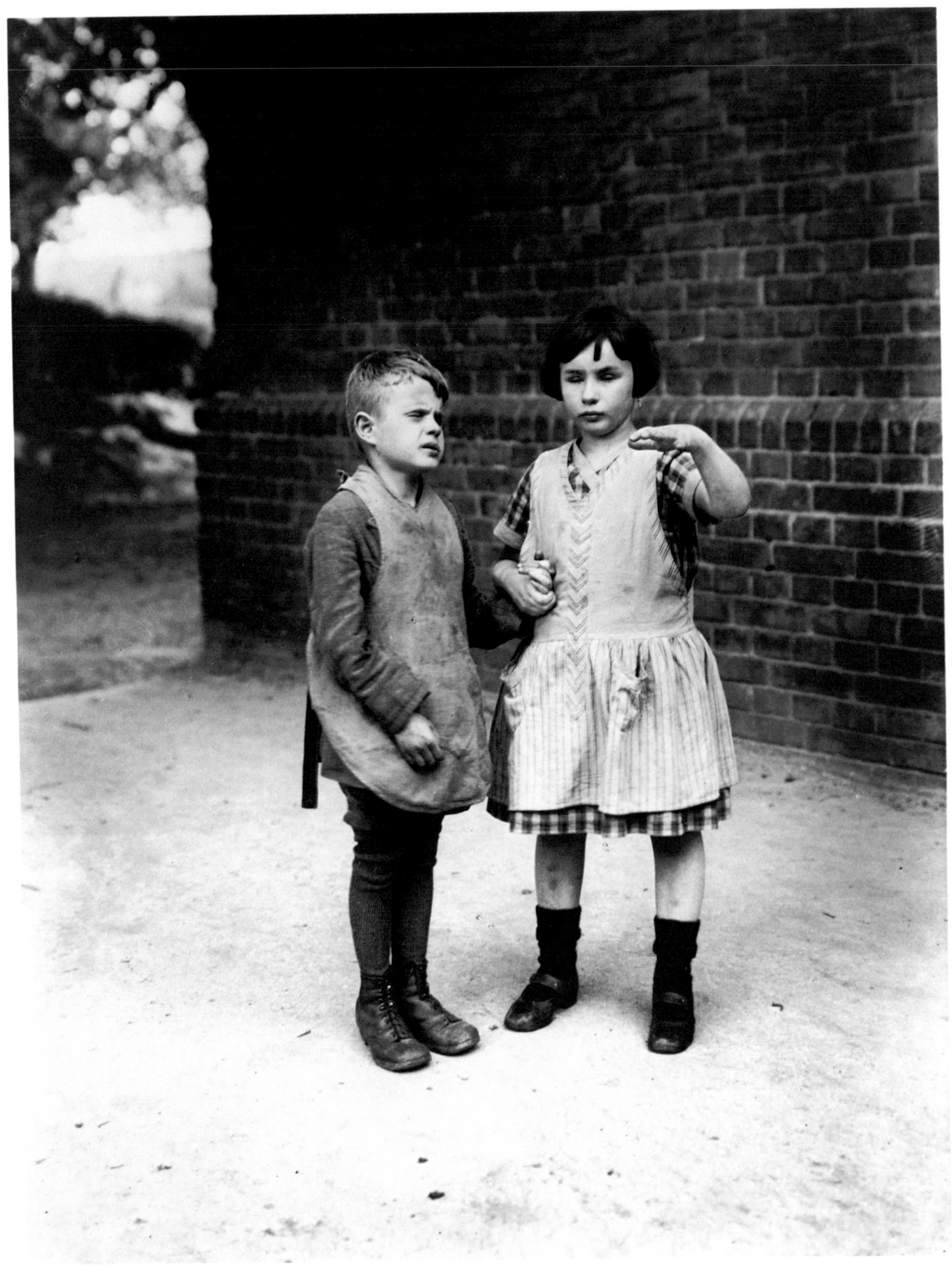

• 65 •

August Sander (German, 1876–1964)

CHILDREN IN A HOME FOR THE BLIND, DUREN, 1930

From "Man of the Twentieth Century"

Gelatin silver print, 11⅞ x 9" (30.2 x 22.9 cm)

Purchased: SmithKline Beckman Corporation Fund

1980-97-1

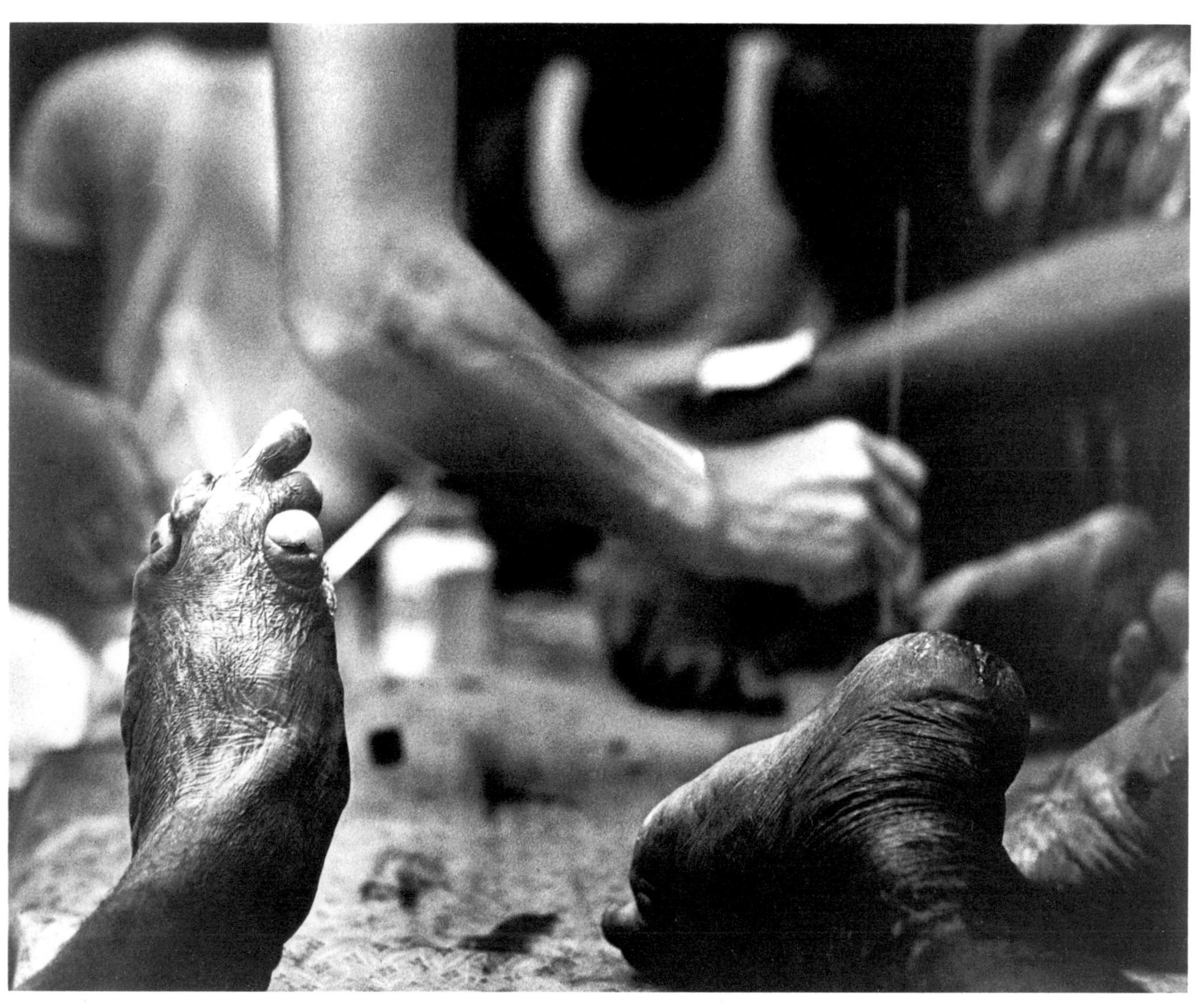

• 66 •

W. Eugene Smith (American, 1918–1978)

LEPROSY, 1954

From "A Man of Mercy," 1954

Gelatin silver print, 10 7/16 x 13 7/16" (26.5 x 34.1 cm)

Purchased: SmithKline Beckman Corporation Fund

1978-95-4

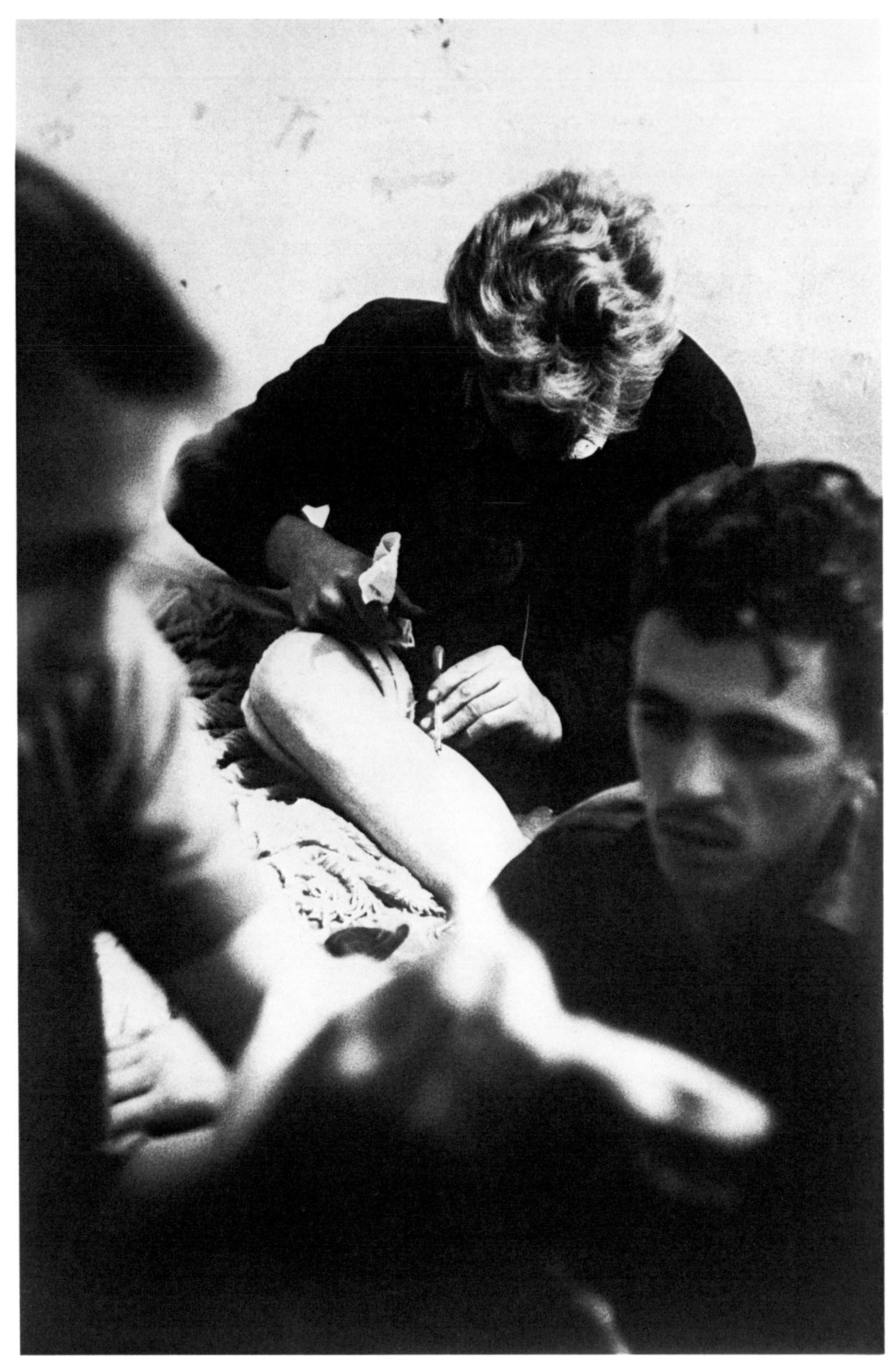

• 67a •

Larry Clark (American, born 1943)

UNTITLED, 1963–70

From "Tulsa," 1963–70

Gelatin silver print, 11 15/16 x 8" (30.3 x 20.3 cm)

On extended loan from Milton J. Green

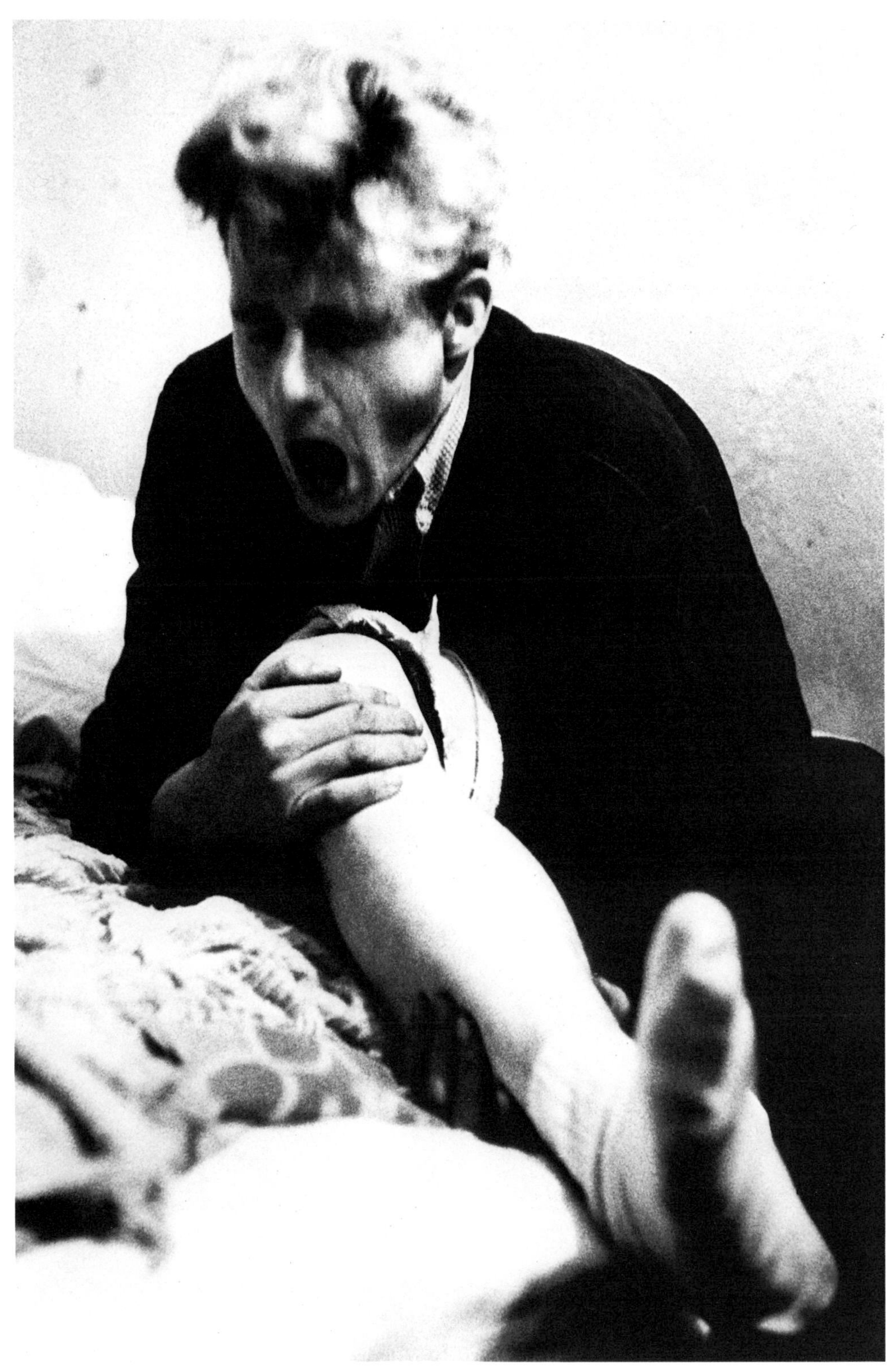

• 67b •

Larry Clark (American, born 1943)

UNTITLED, 1963–70

From "Tulsa," 1963–70

Gelatin silver print, 12¼ x 8⅟16" (31.1 x 20.5 cm)

On extended loan from Milton J. Green

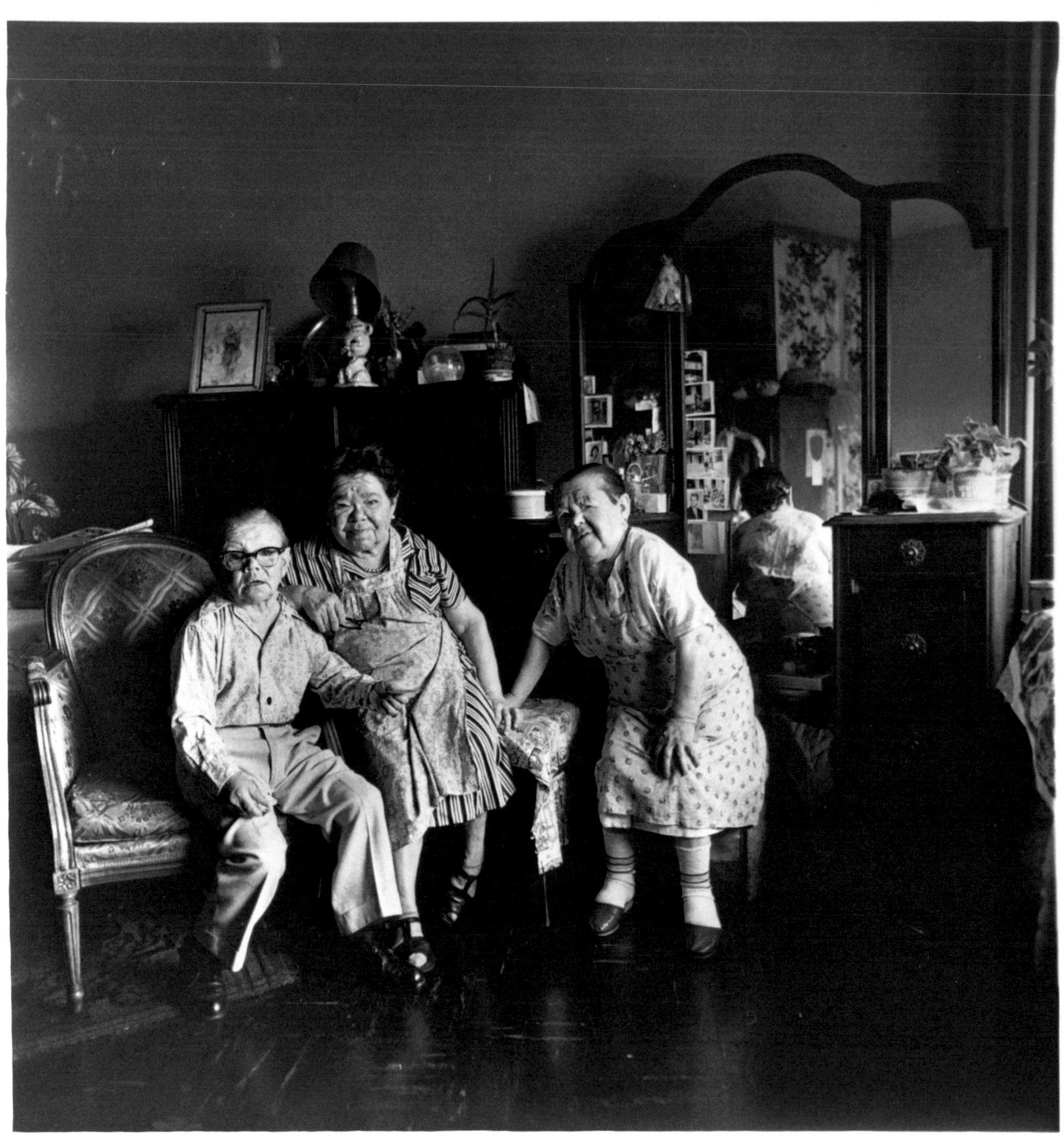

• 68 •

Diane Arbus (American, 1923–1971)

RUSSIAN MIDGET FRIENDS IN A LIVING ROOM ON 100TH STREET, NEW YORK CITY, 1963

Gelatin silver print, 8⁹⁄₁₆ x 8⅜" (21.7 x 21.2 cm)
Purchased: SmithKline Beckman Corporation Fund
1984-49-2

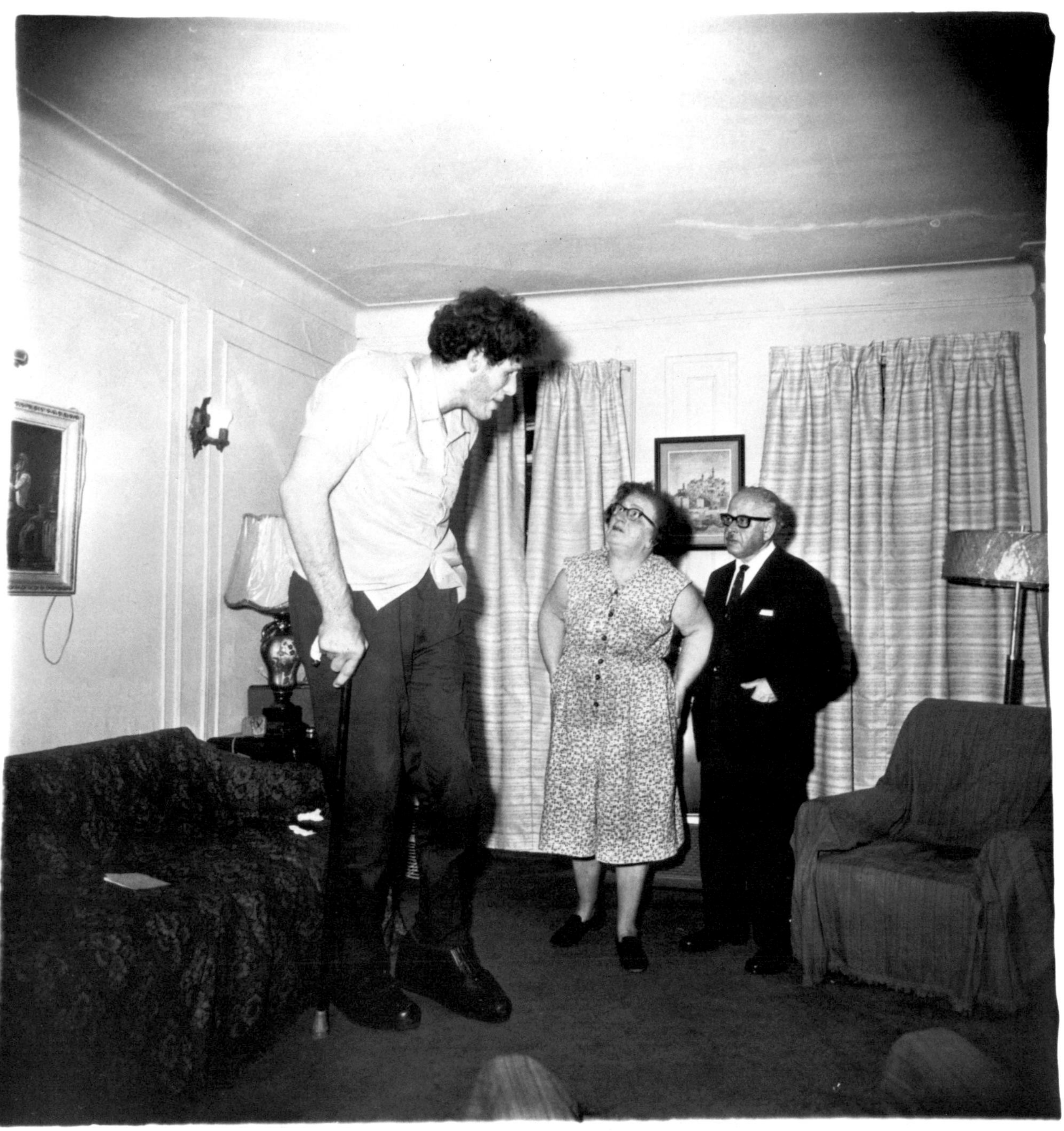

Diane Arbus (American, 1923–1971)

JEWISH GIANT AT HOME WITH HIS PARENTS IN THE BRONX, 1970

Gelatin silver print, 14⅞ x 14¾" (37.8 x 37.5 cm)
Purchased: SmithKline Beckman Corporation Fund
1984-49-3

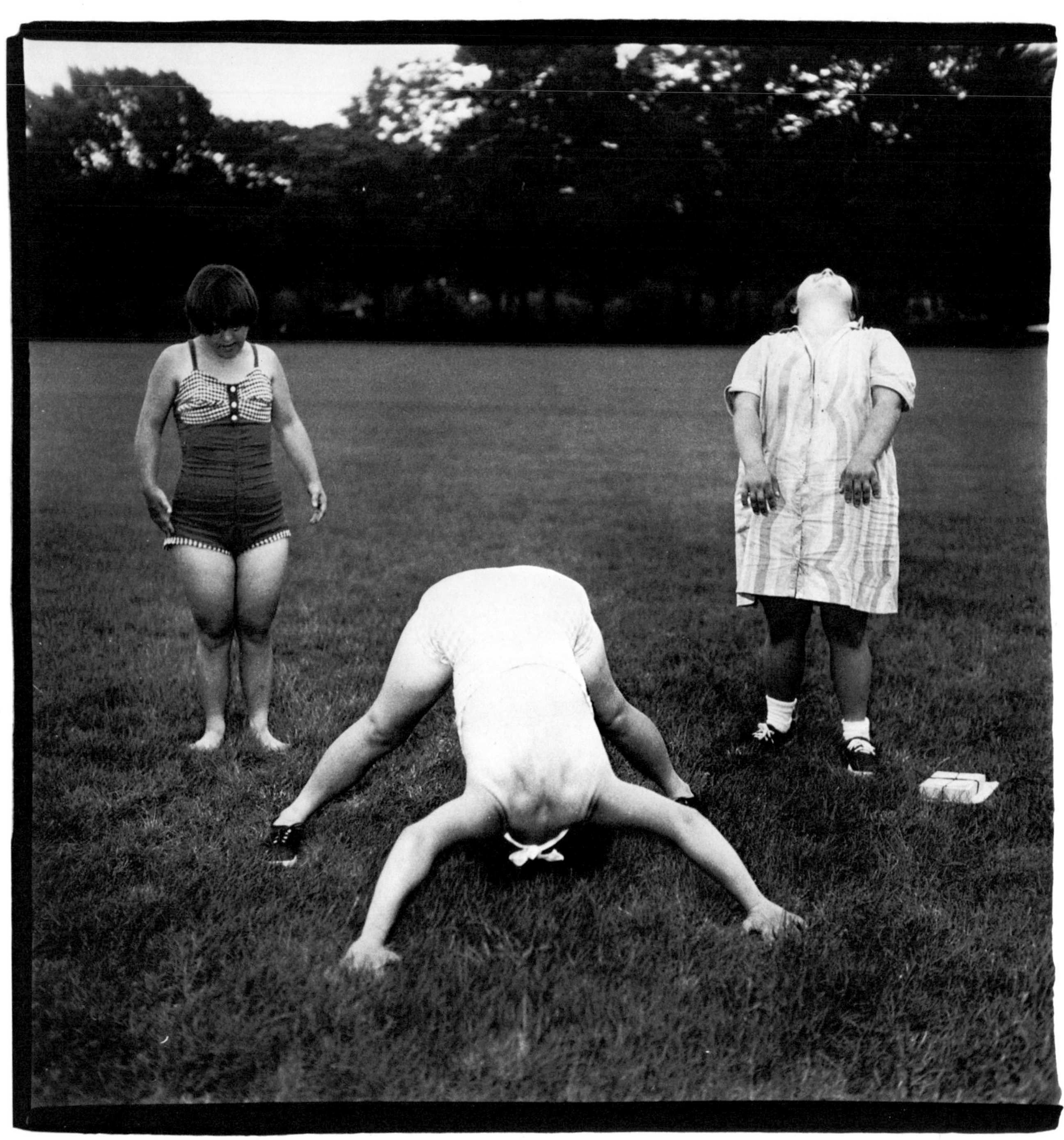

• 70 •

Diane Arbus (American, 1923–1971)

UNTITLED (6), 1970–71

Gelatin silver print, 15⅞ x 15⅜" (40.3 x 39 cm)

Purchased: SmithKline Beckman Corporation Fund

1984-49-1

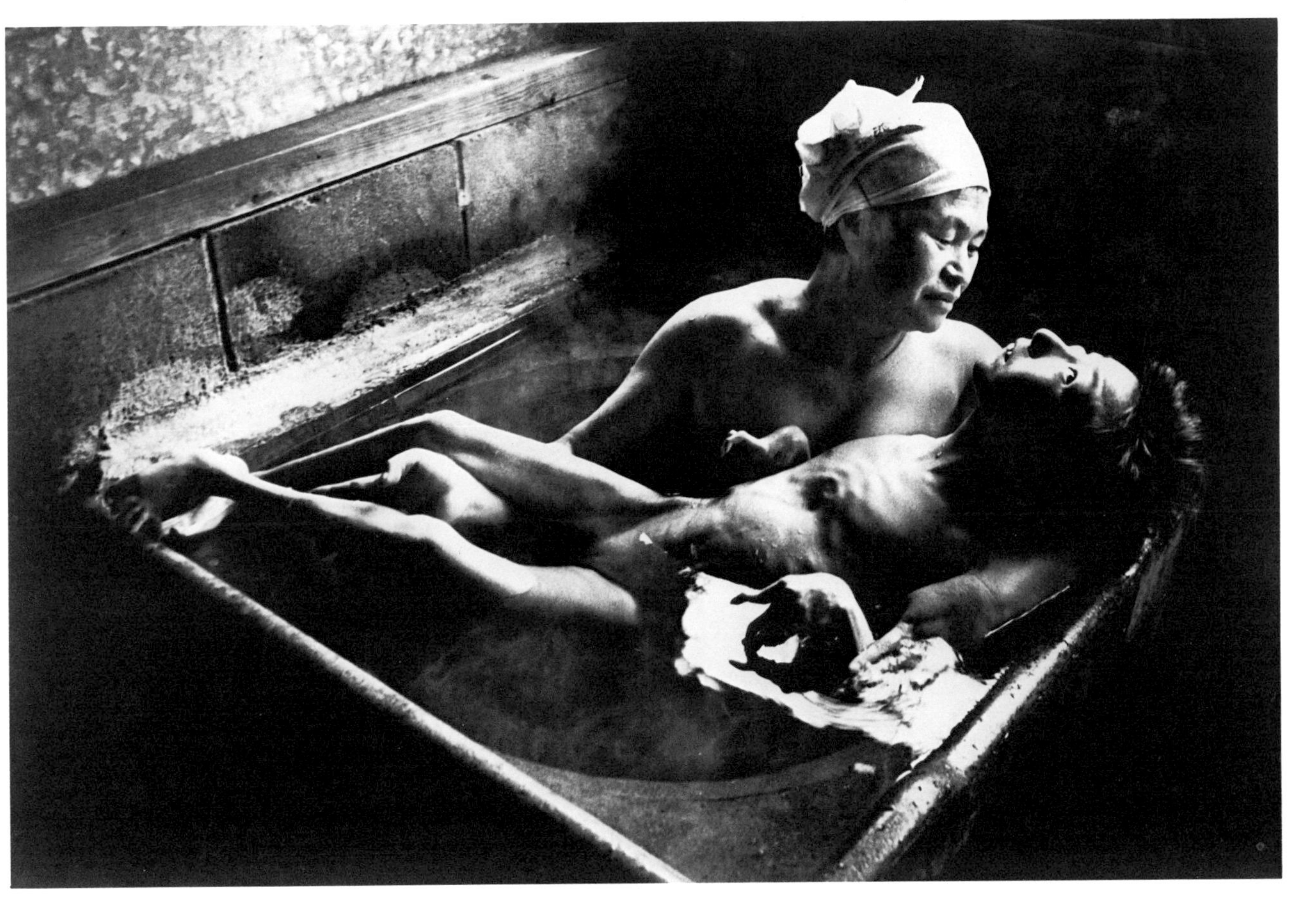

• 71 •

W. Eugene Smith (American, 1918–1978)

TOMOKO IN BATH, 1972–75

From "Minamata," 1972–75

Gelatin silver print, 8 7/16 x 13 1/4" (21.4 x 33.6 cm)

Purchased: SmithKline Beckman Corporation Fund

1979-144-5

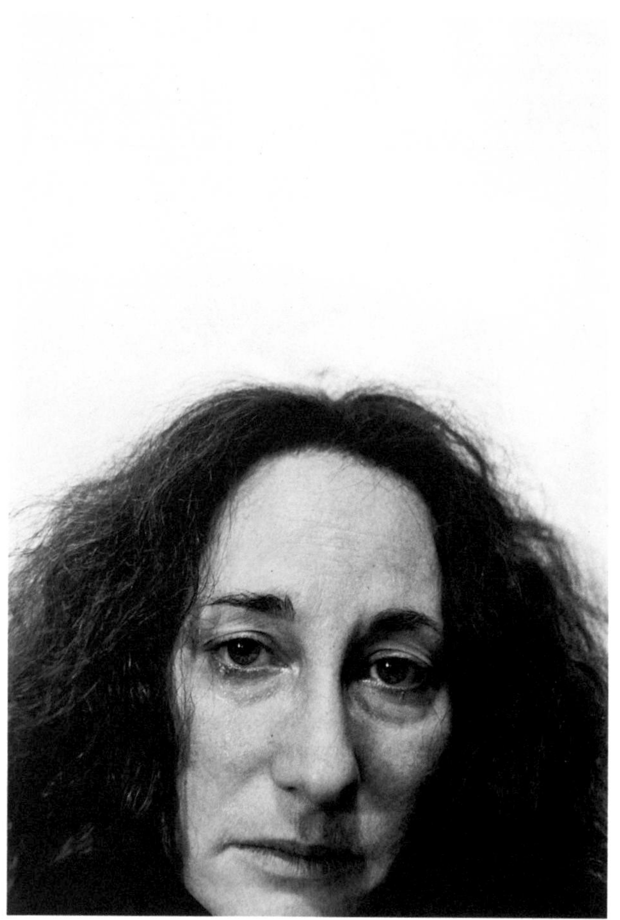

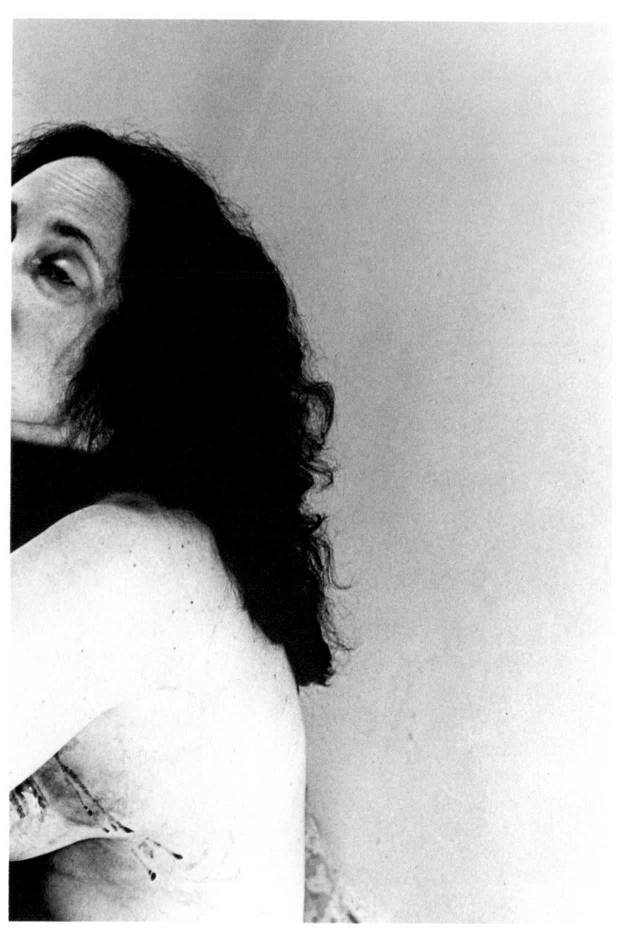

• 72a–b •

Eugene Richards (American, born 1944)

a: DOROTHEA, AFTER THE DISCOVERY OF A LUMP, 1978;

b: DOROTHEA'S BIOPSY, 1978

From "Exploding into Life," 1978–79

Gelatin silver prints, a and b: 17 13/16 x 11 15/16" (45.3 x 30.4 cm)

Purchased: SmithKline Beckman Corporation Fund

1984-161-3,2

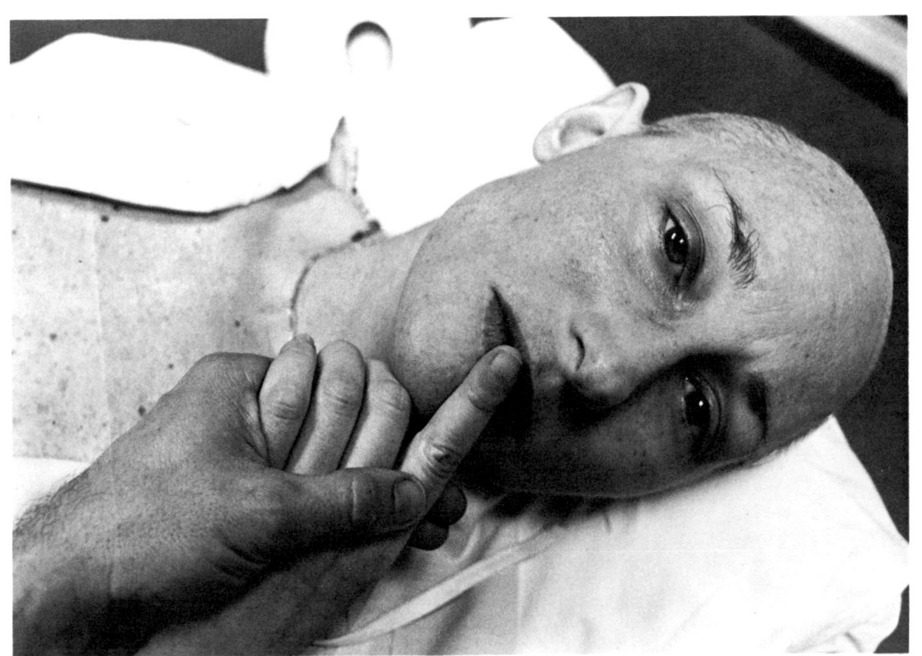

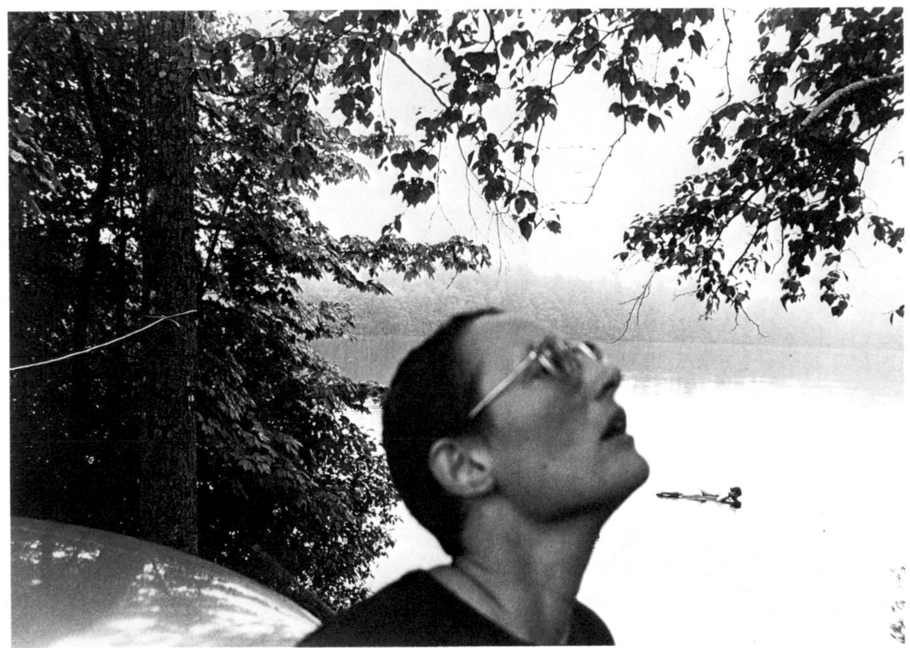

• 72c–d •

Eugene Richards (American, born 1944)

c: DOROTHEA AND I, 1978;

d: DOROTHEA'S FIRST MILE RUN, MAINE, 1979

From "Exploding into Life," 1978–79

Gelatin silver prints; c: 12⁵⁄₁₆ x 18⅛" (31.2 x 46 cm), d: 12 x 17¹⁵⁄₁₆" (30.5 x 45.5 cm)

Purchased: SmithKline Beckman Corporation Fund

1984-161-1,4

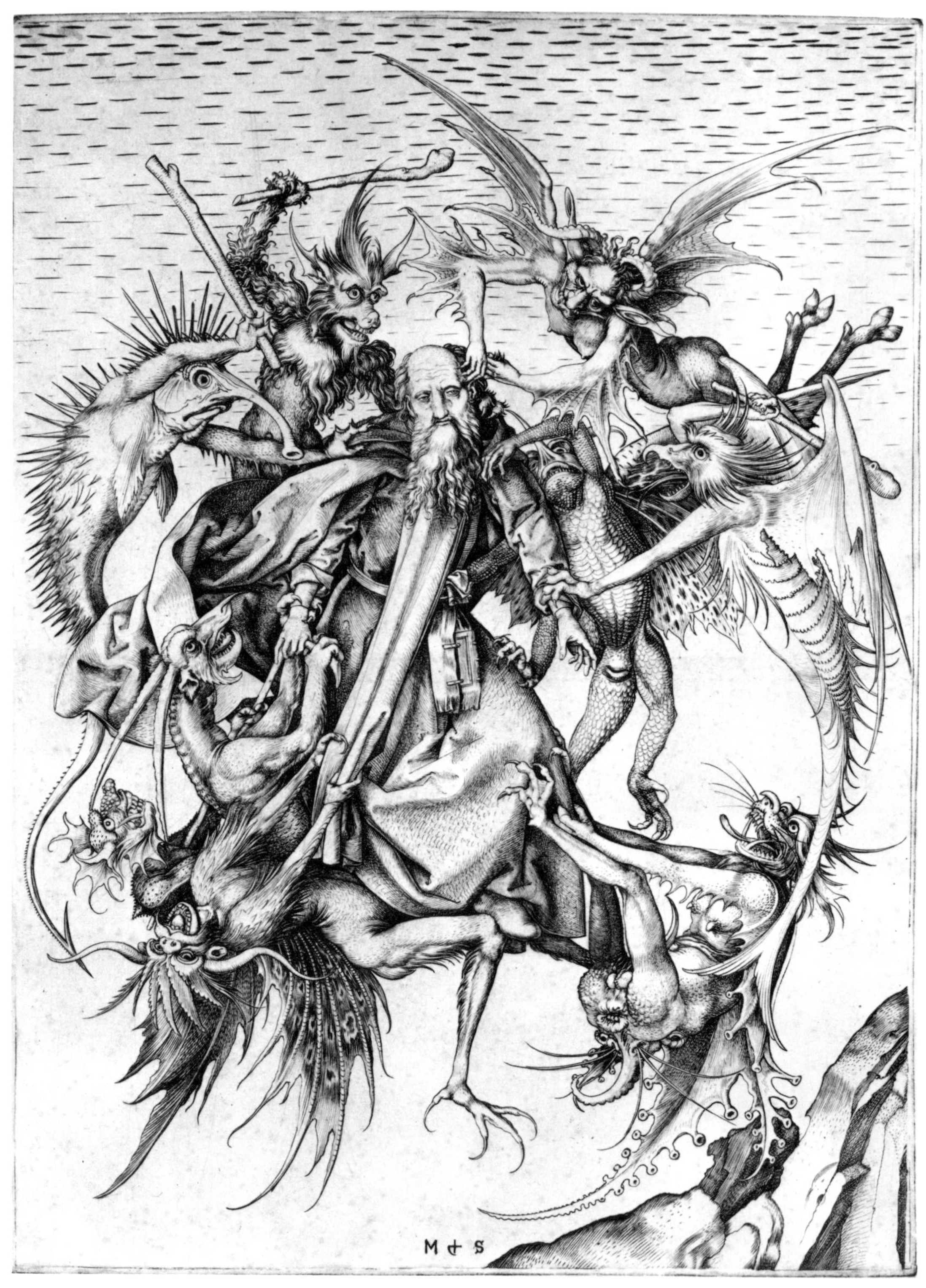

• 73 •

Martin Schongauer (German, c. 1450–1491)

THE TRIBULATIONS OF SAINT ANTHONY, c. 1470–75

Engraving (ii/ii), 12¼ x 9 1/16″ (31.1 x 23 cm) (trimmed)

The W. P. Wilstach Collection

W'50-4-9

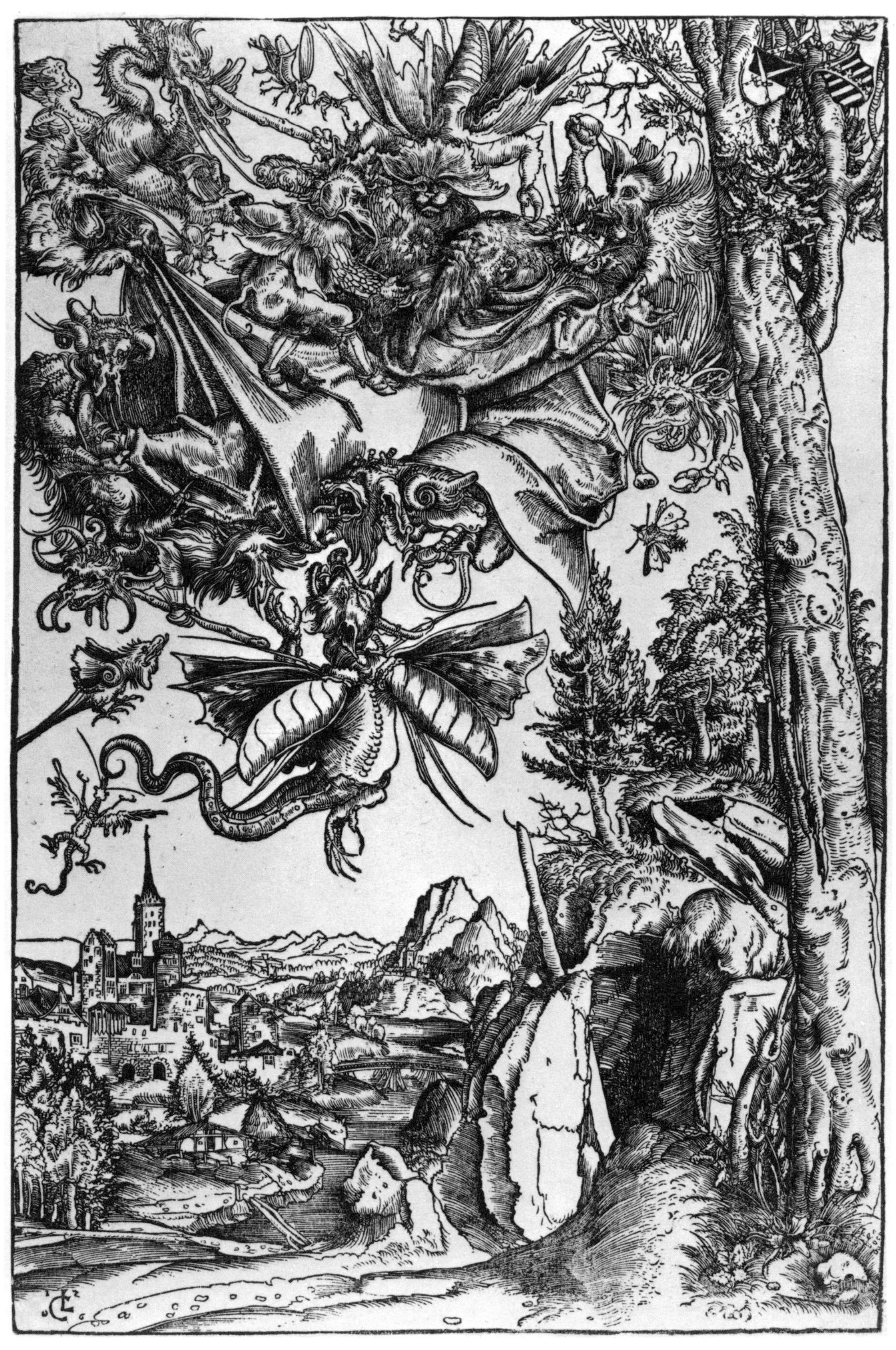

• 74 •

Lucas Cranach the Elder (German, 1472–1553)

THE TRIBULATIONS OF SAINT ANTHONY, 1506

Woodcut (ii/ii), 16 x 11″ (40.7 x 28 cm)
Purchased: Thomas Skelton Harrison Fund
71-238-1

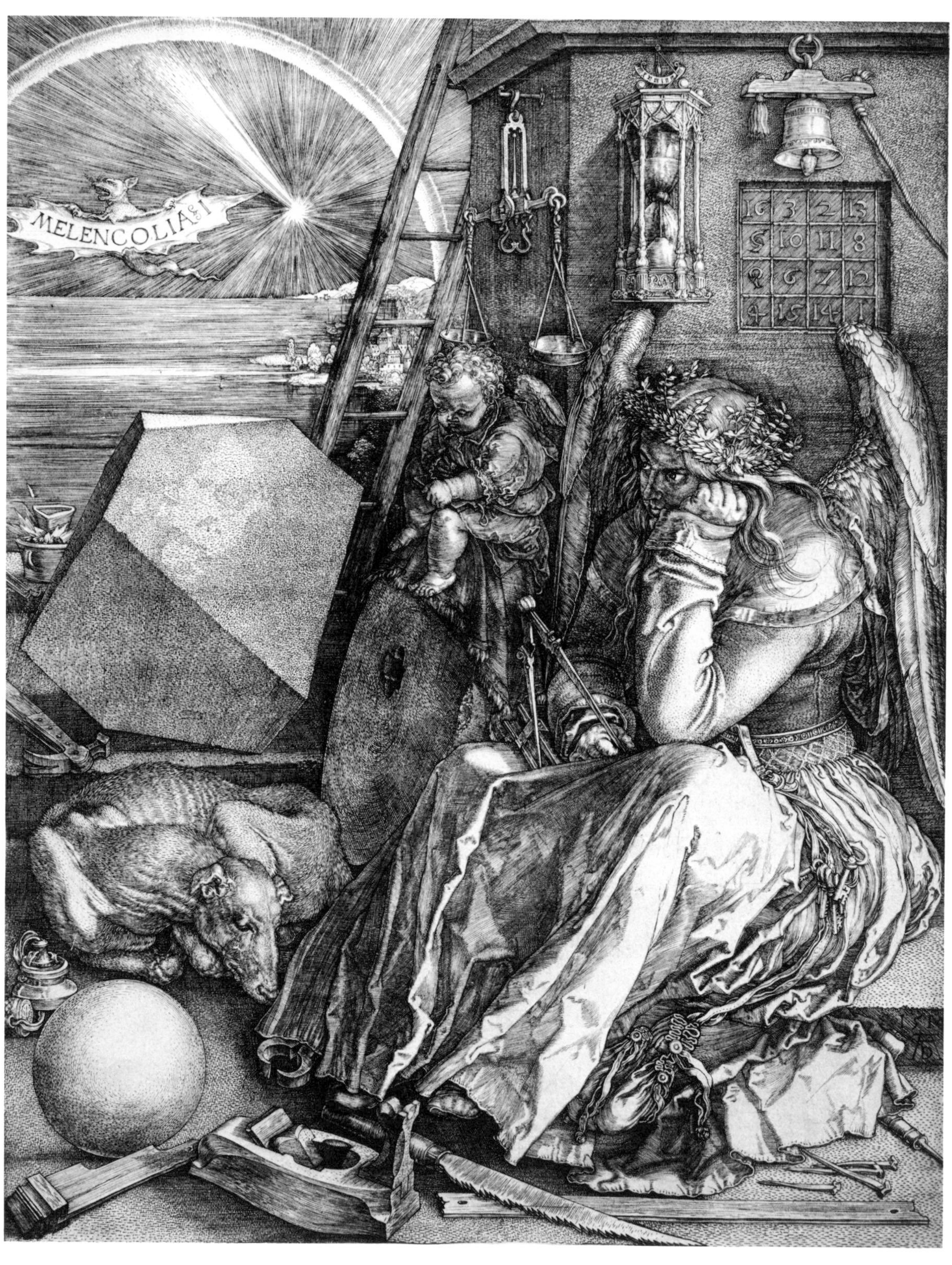

• 75 •

Albrecht Dürer (German, 1471–1528)

MELENCOLIA I, 1514

Engraving (ii/ii, e), 9½ x 7 5/16" (24.1 x 18.5 cm) (trimmed)

Purchased: Lisa Norris Elkins Fund

51-96-5

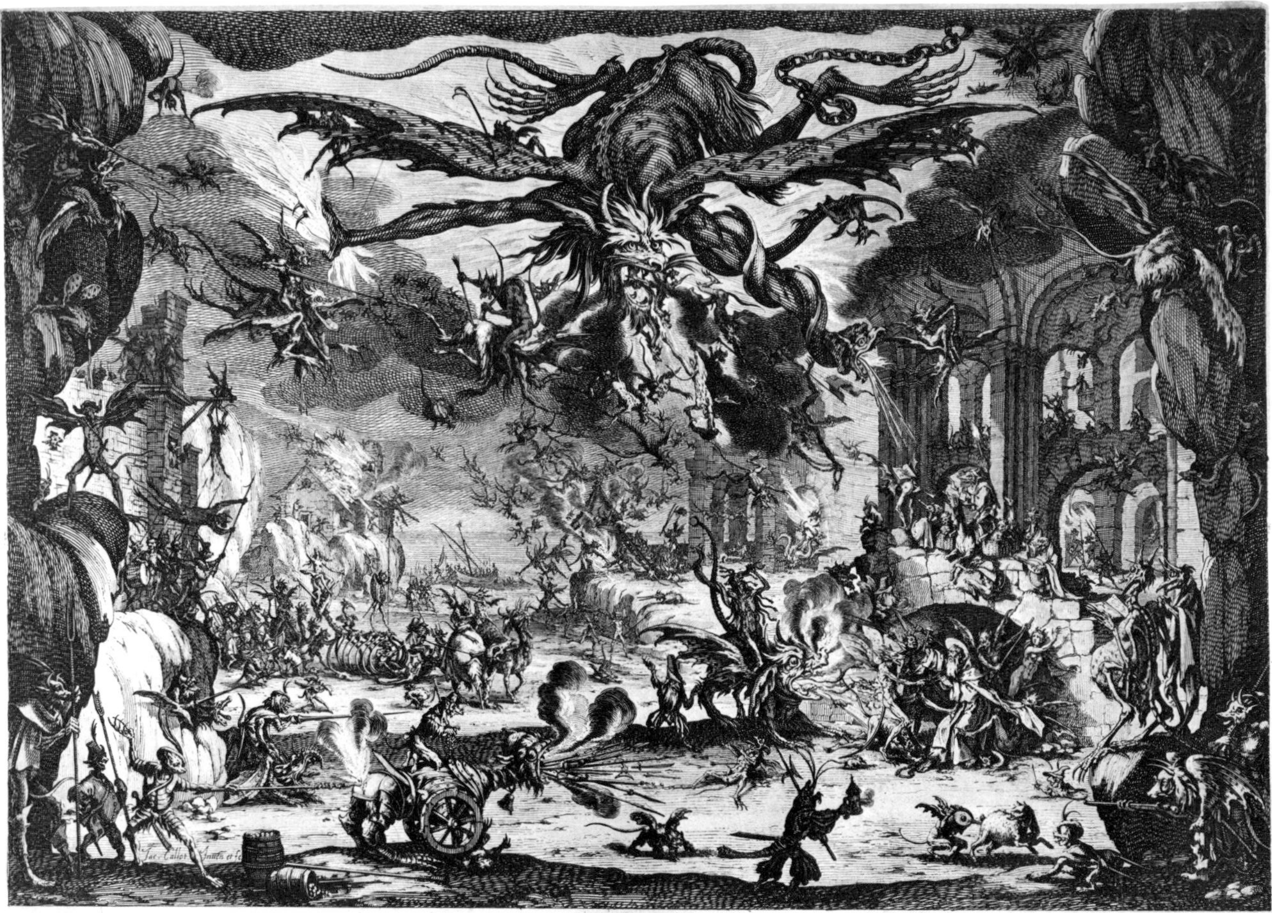

• 76 •

Jacques Callot (French, 1592–1635)

THE TRIBULATIONS OF SAINT ANTHONY (second version), 1635

Etching (iv/v), 14 x 18⅛" (35.6 x 46 cm) (trimmed)
Charles M. Lea Collection
28-42-791

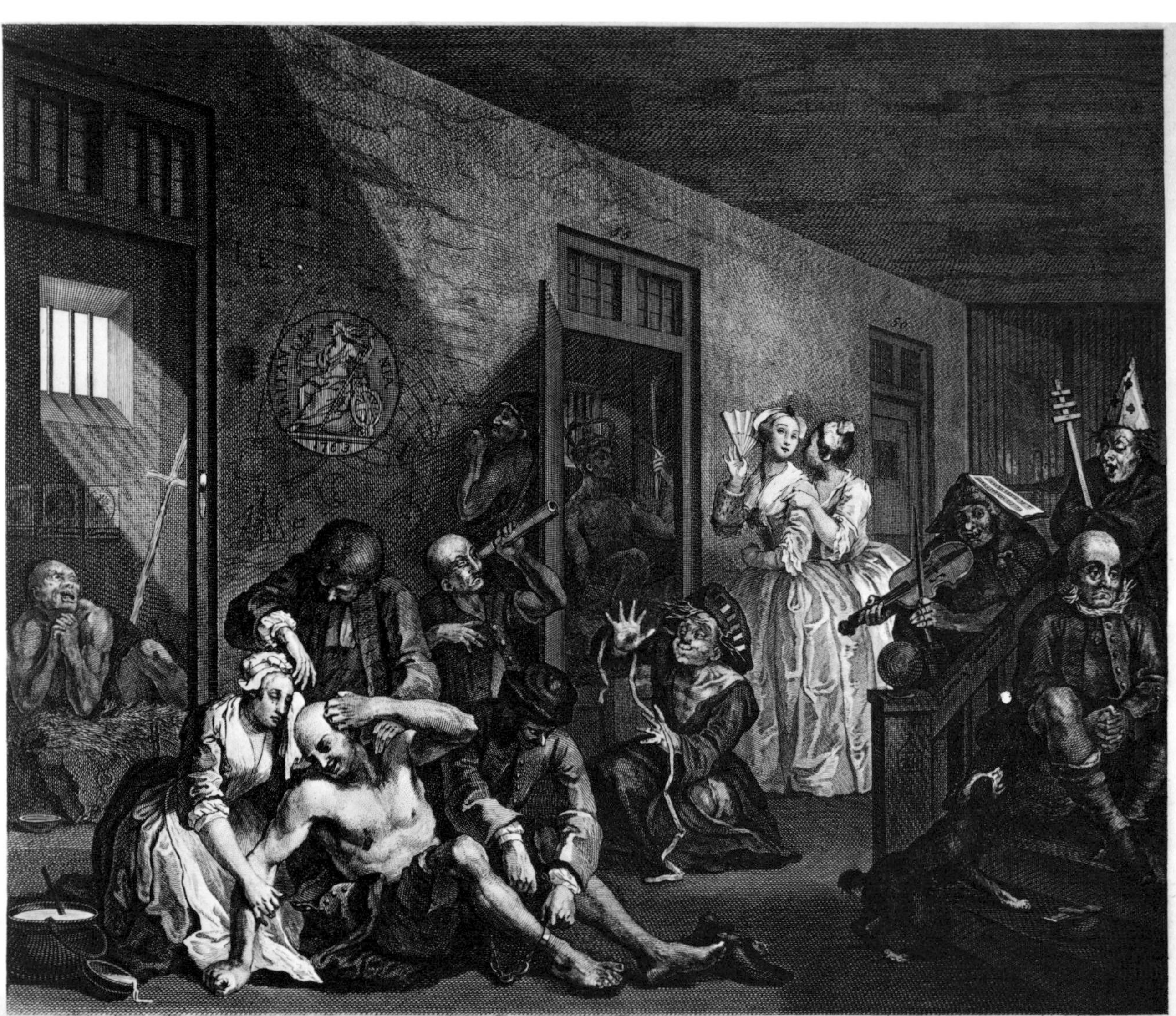

• 77 •

William Hogarth (English, 1697–1764)

IN BETHLEHEM HOSPITAL (BEDLAM), 1735, reworked 1763

From "A Rake's Progress," 1735

Engraving and etching (iii/iii), 14 1/16 x 16 1/4" (35.7 x 41.3 cm)

Gift of Boies Penrose

40-11-20

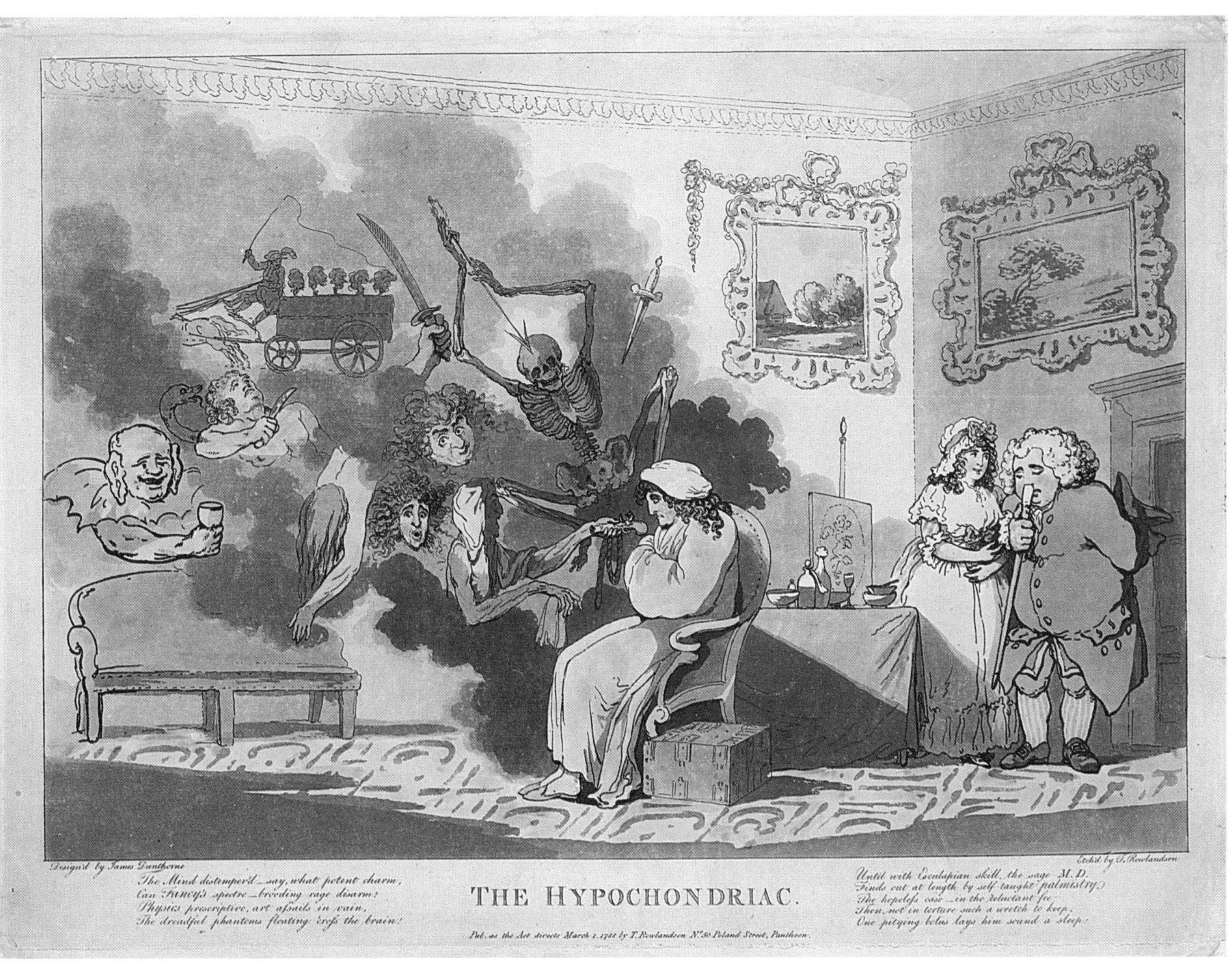

• 78 •

Thomas Rowlandson (English, 1756–1827)
After James Dunthorne (English, 1730–1815)
THE HYPOCHONDRIAC, 1788

Hand-colored etching, 16⁷⁄₁₆ x 22¾" (41.7 x 57.8 cm)
Purchased: SmithKline Beckman Corporation Fund
69-190-54

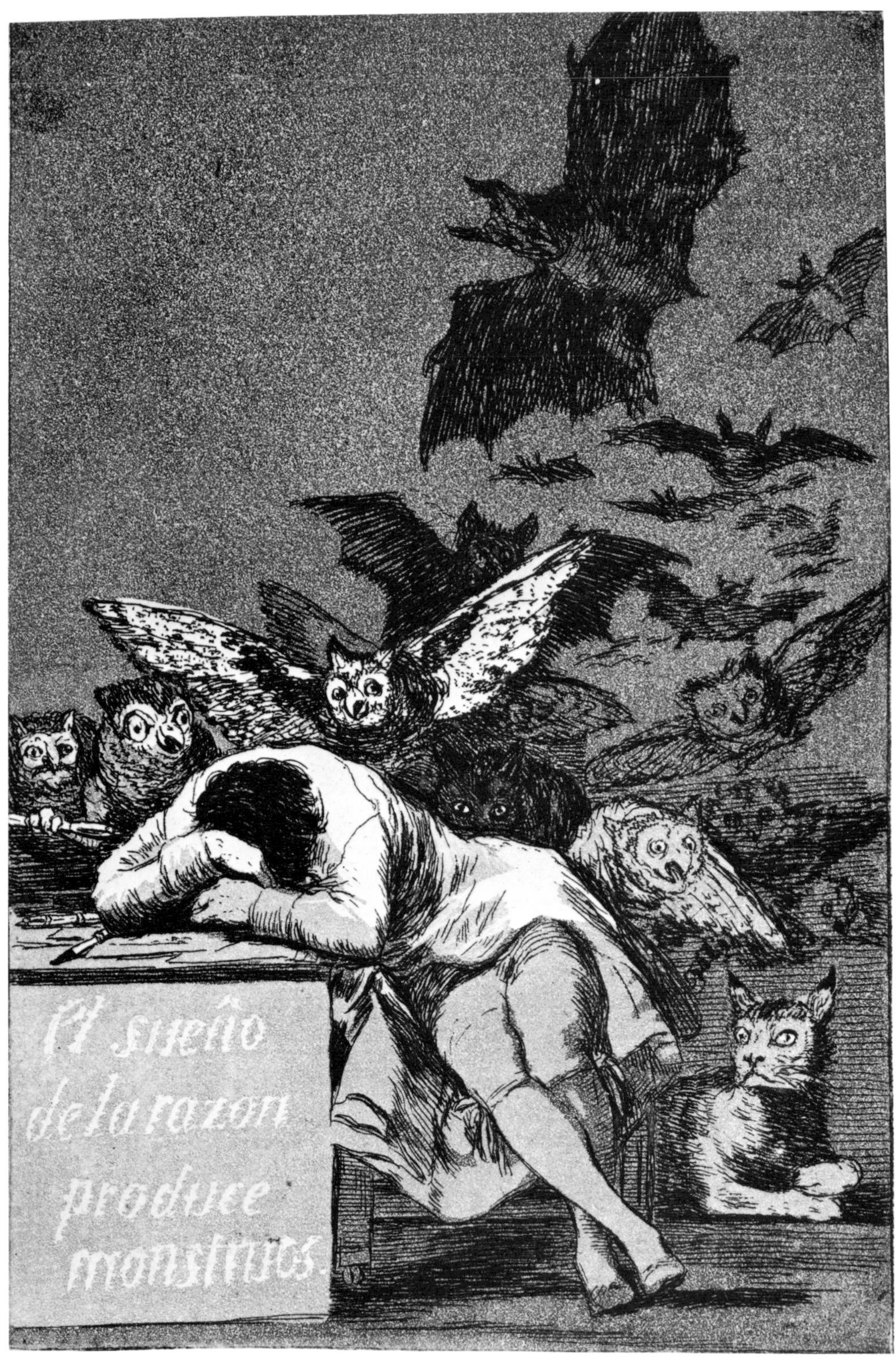

• 79 •

Francisco José de Goya y Lucientes (Spanish, 1746–1828)

THE SLEEP OF REASON PRODUCES MONSTERS, 1797–98

From *Los Caprichos* (Madrid, 1799)

Etching and aquatint, $8\frac{7}{16}$ x $5\frac{15}{16}$" (21.4 x 15 cm)

Purchased: SmithKline Beckman Corporation Fund

49-97-9

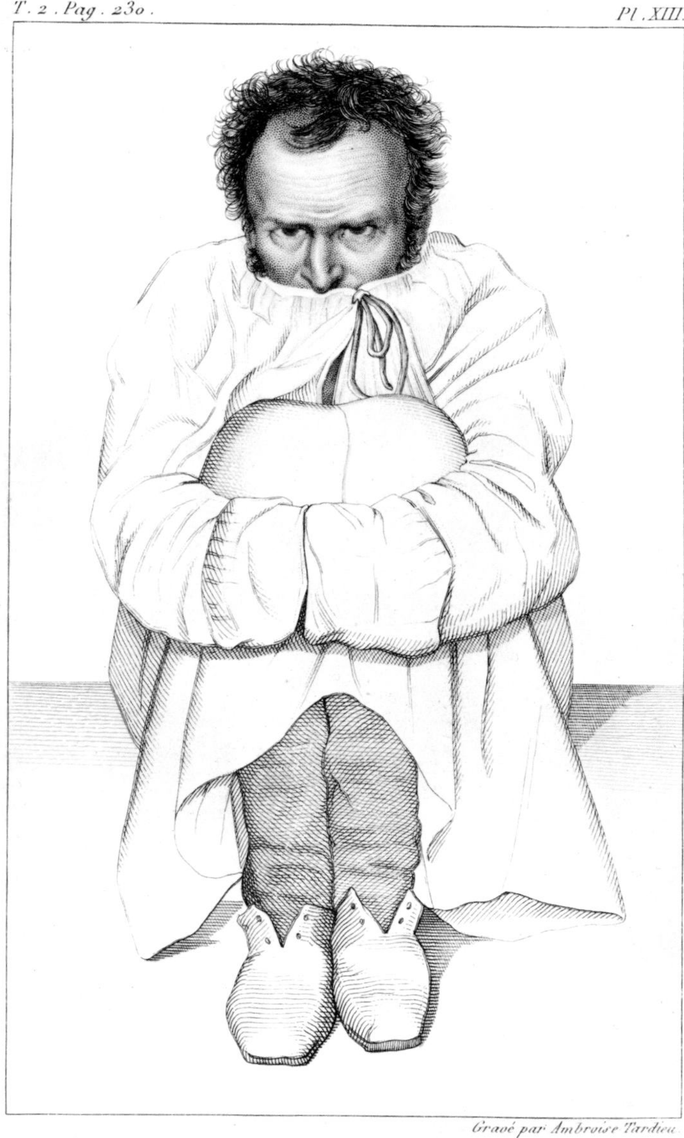

• 80 •

Ambroise Tardieu (French, 1788–1841)

MANIA SUCCEEDED BY DEMENTIA, 1838

From Jean-Etienne-Dominique Esquirol, *Des Maladies mentales considérées sous les rapports médical, hygiénique et médico-légal,* vol. 2 (Paris: J.-B. Baillière, 1838)

Etching, stipple etching, and engraving, 6 x 3¹¹⁄₁₆" (15.2 x 9.4 cm)

Purchased: SmithKline Beckman Corporation Fund

68-109-4b

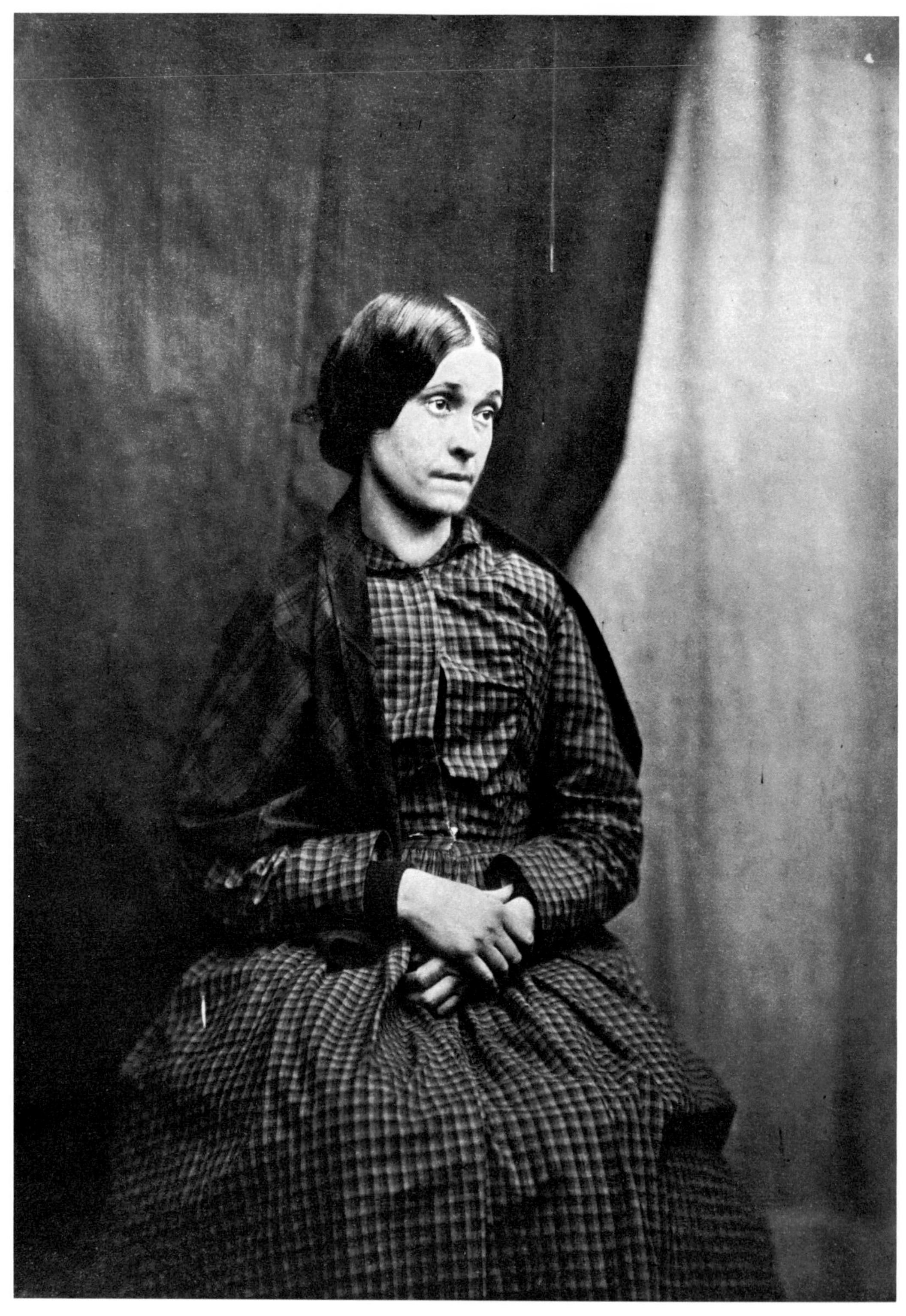

• 81 •

Hugh Welch Diamond (English, 1809–1886)

FEMALE PATIENT, SURREY COUNTY LUNATIC ASYLUM, c. 1850

Albumen print, 7 x 5³⁄₁₆″ (17.6 x 13.1 cm)

Purchased: SmithKline Beckman Corporation Fund

1984-93-1

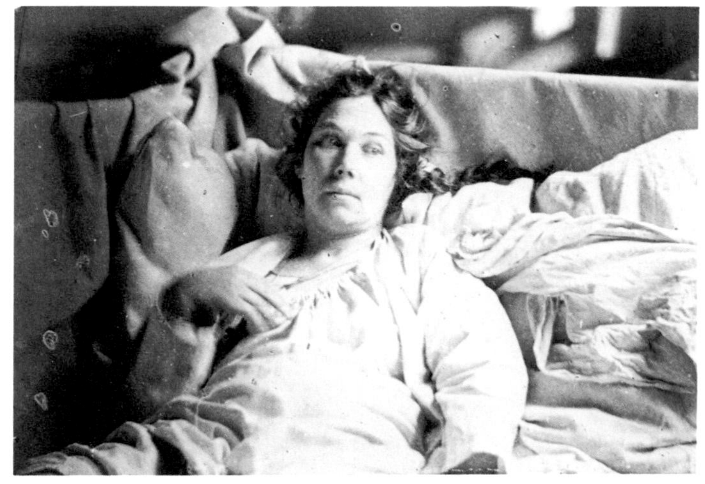

• 82 •

Désiré Magloire Bourneville (French, active late nineteenth century) and
Paul Regnard (French, active late nineteenth century)
TERMINAL STAGE: MELANCHOLIA, 1877

From Désiré Magloire Bourneville and Paul Regnard, *Iconographie photographique de La Salpétrière*, vol. 1 (Paris: Bureaux du Progrès Médical & V. Adrien Delahay & Cie, 1877)
Albumen print, 2⅜ x 3¹¹⁄₁₆" (6 x 9.3 cm)
Purchased: SmithKline Beckman Corporation Fund
71-116-2a

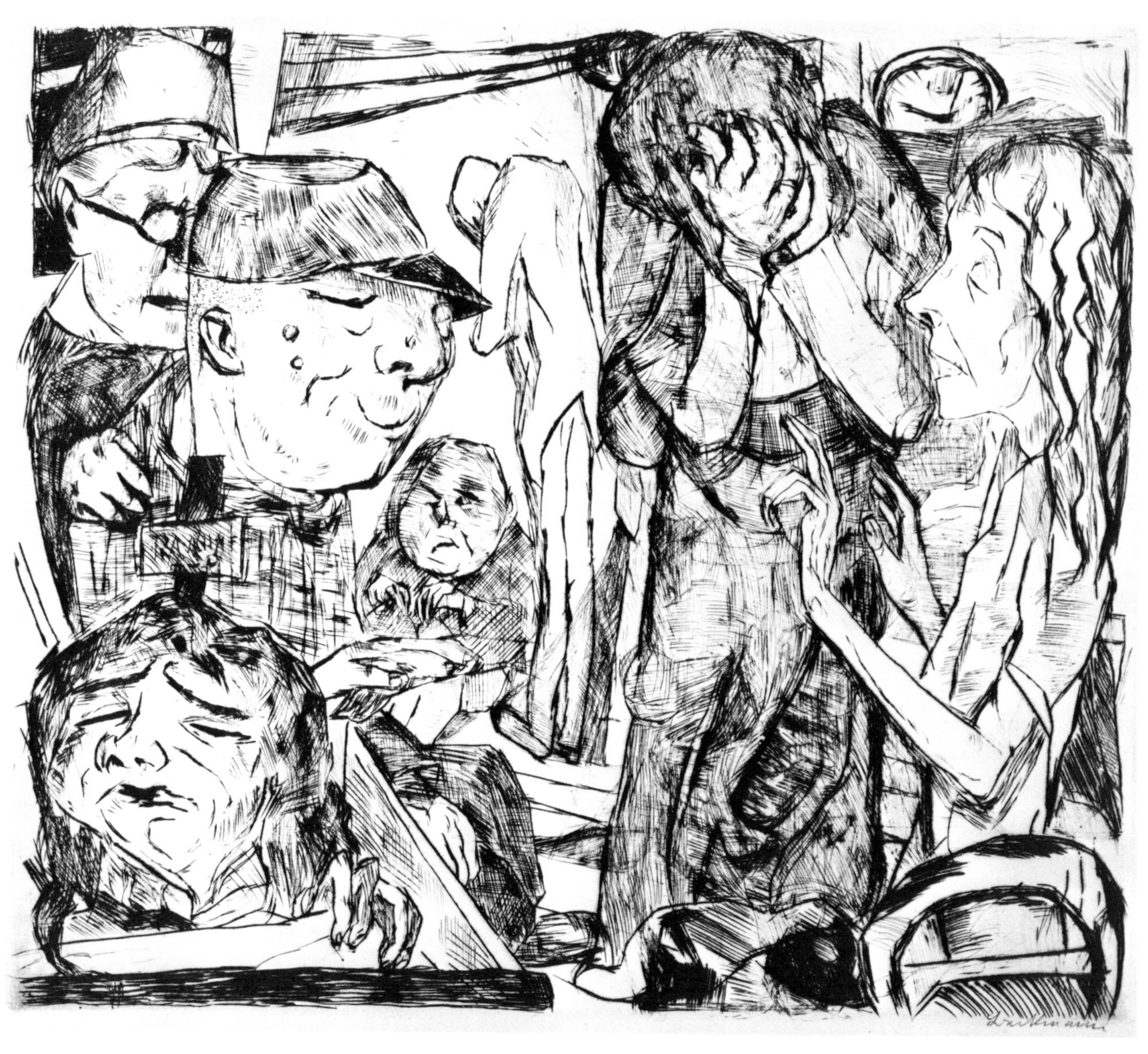

• 83 •

Max Beckmann (German, 1884–1950)

THE MADHOUSE, 1918

From *Gesichter* (Munich: R. Piper, 1919)

Drypoint, 10¼ x 12⅛" (26 x 30.8 cm)

Purchased: SmithKline Beckman Corporation Fund

1983-93-1

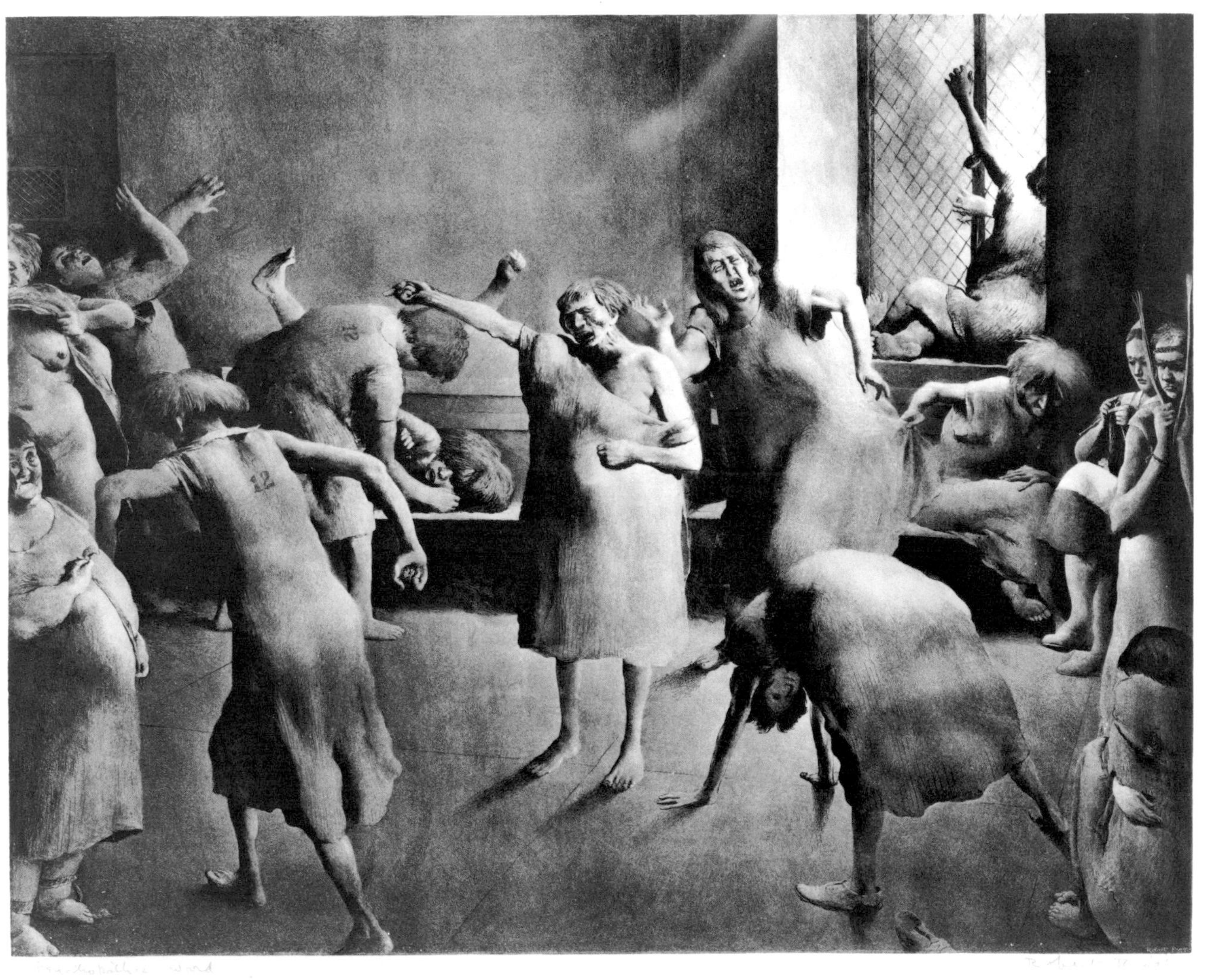

• 84 •

Robert Riggs (American, 1896–1970)

PSYCHOPATHIC WARD, 1940

Lithograph, 14⁵⁄₁₆ x 18⁷⁄₈" (36.3 x 47.9 cm)

Gift of R. Sturgis Ingersoll

46-80-8

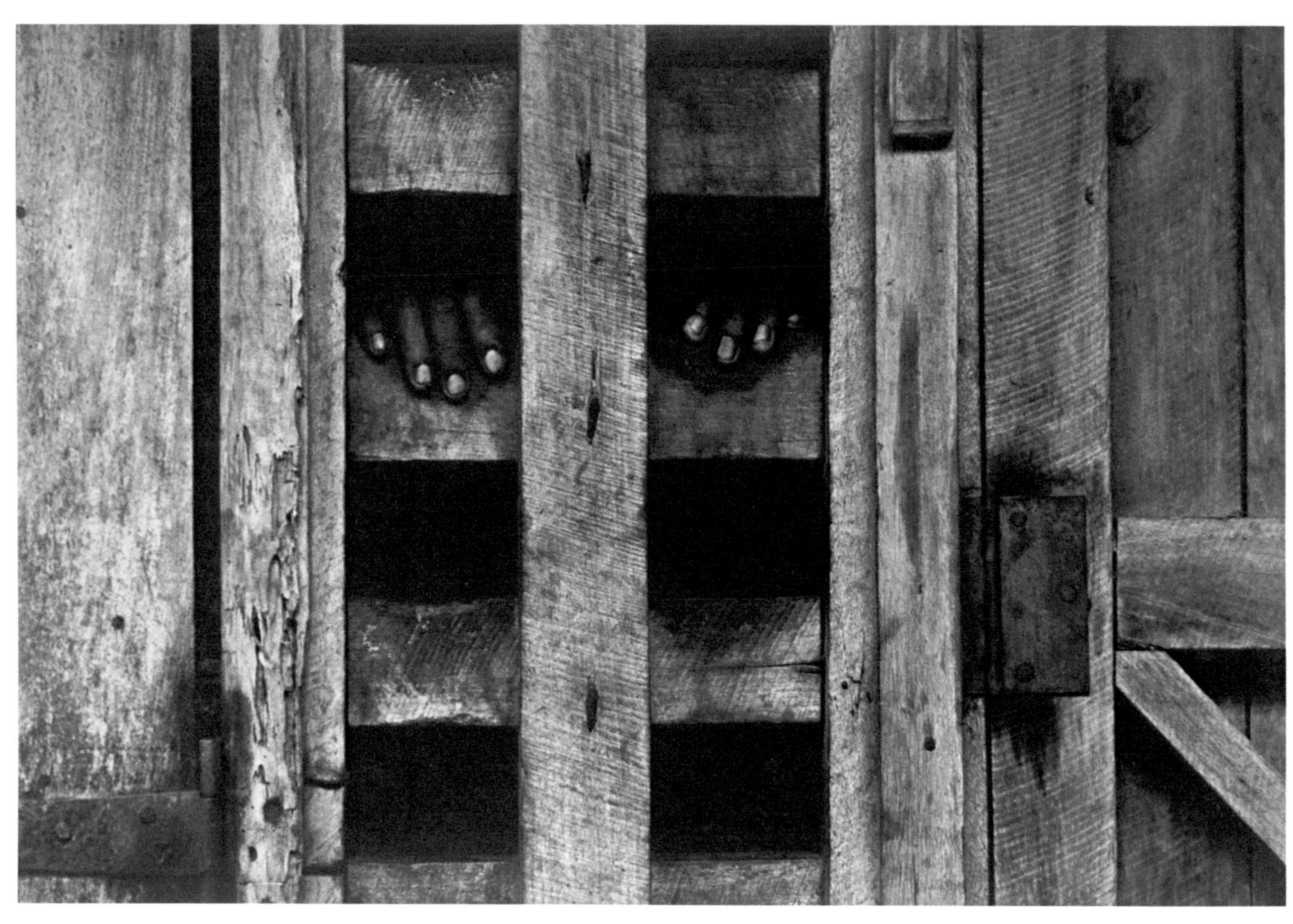

• 85 •

W. Eugene Smith (American, 1918–1978)

INSANE COMPOUND, LAMBARENE, 1954

From "A Man of Mercy," 1954
Gelatin silver print, 9 x 13½" (22.9 x 34.3 cm)
Purchased: SmithKline Beckman Corporation Fund
70-33-2

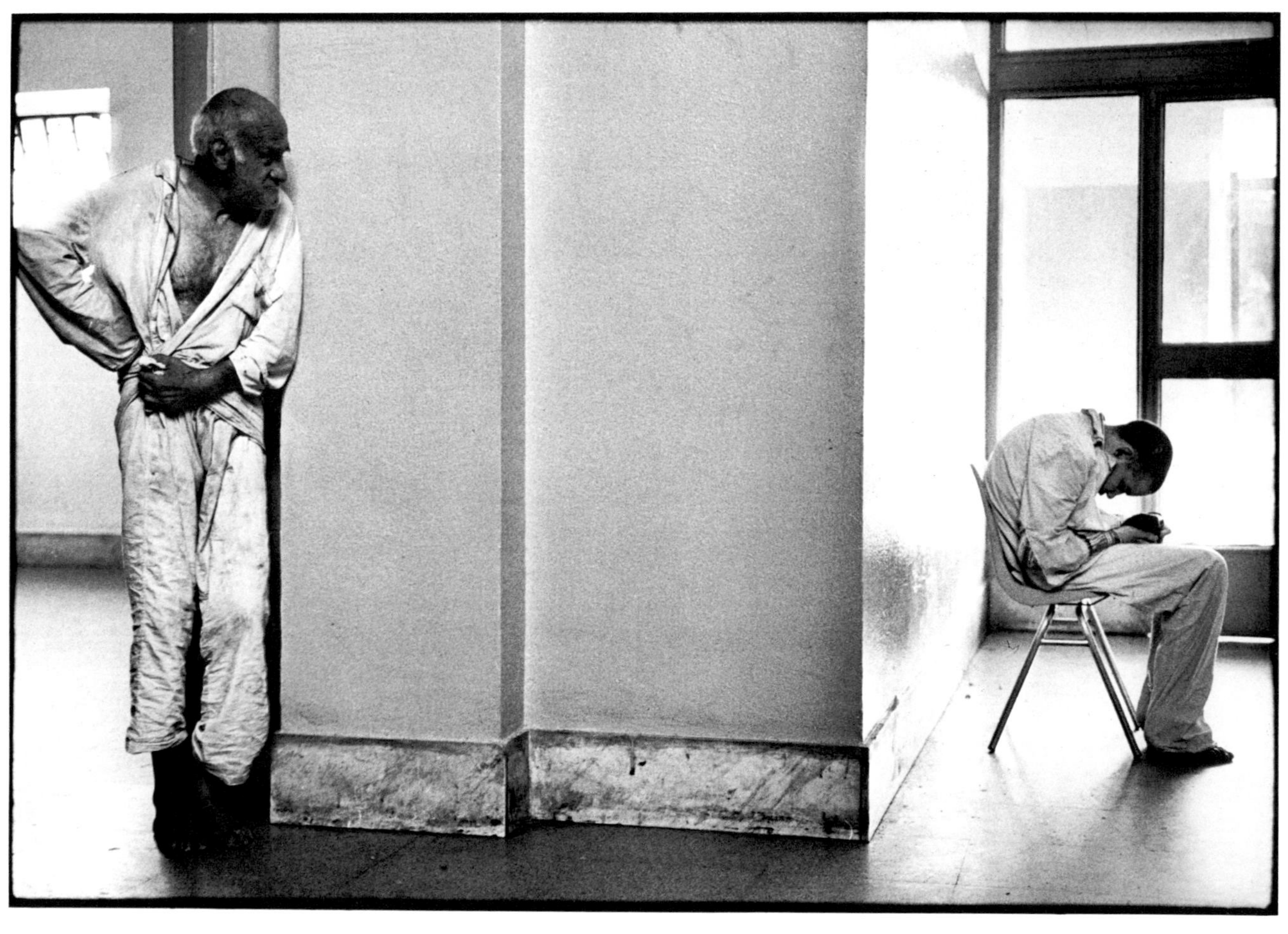

• 86a •

Raymond Depardon (French, born 1942)

UNTITLED, 1977–79

From "Insane Asylums in Italy," 1977–79

Gelatin silver print, 9 7/16 x 14 1/4" (24 x 36.2 cm)

Purchased: SmithKline Beckman Corporation Fund

1983-30-10

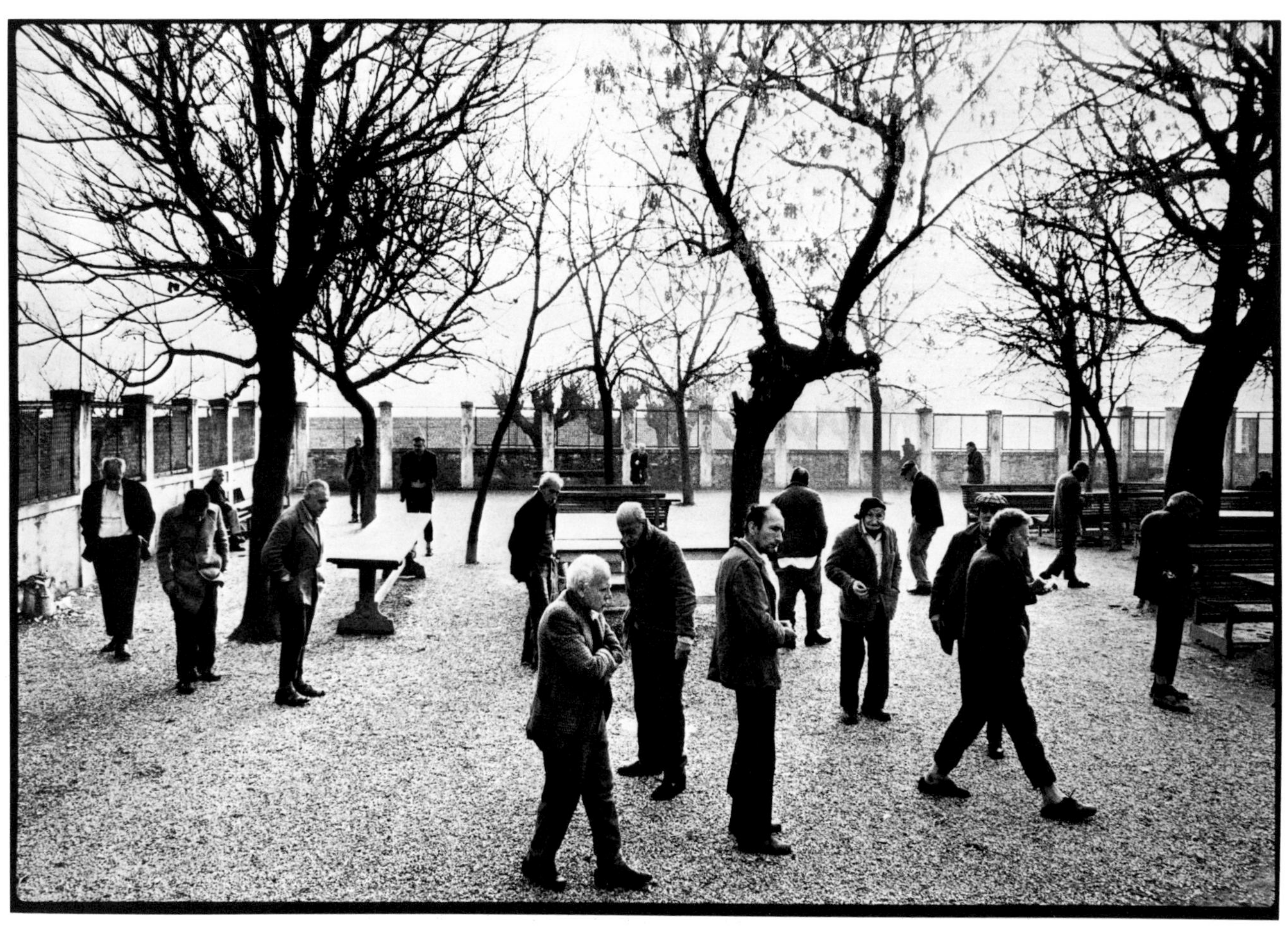

• 86b •

Raymond Depardon (French, born 1942)

UNTITLED, 1977–79

From "Insane Asylums in Italy," 1977–79

Gelatin silver print, 9⁹⁄₁₆ x 14³⁄₁₆" (24.4 x 36 cm)

Purchased: SmithKline Beckman Corporation Fund

1983-30-11

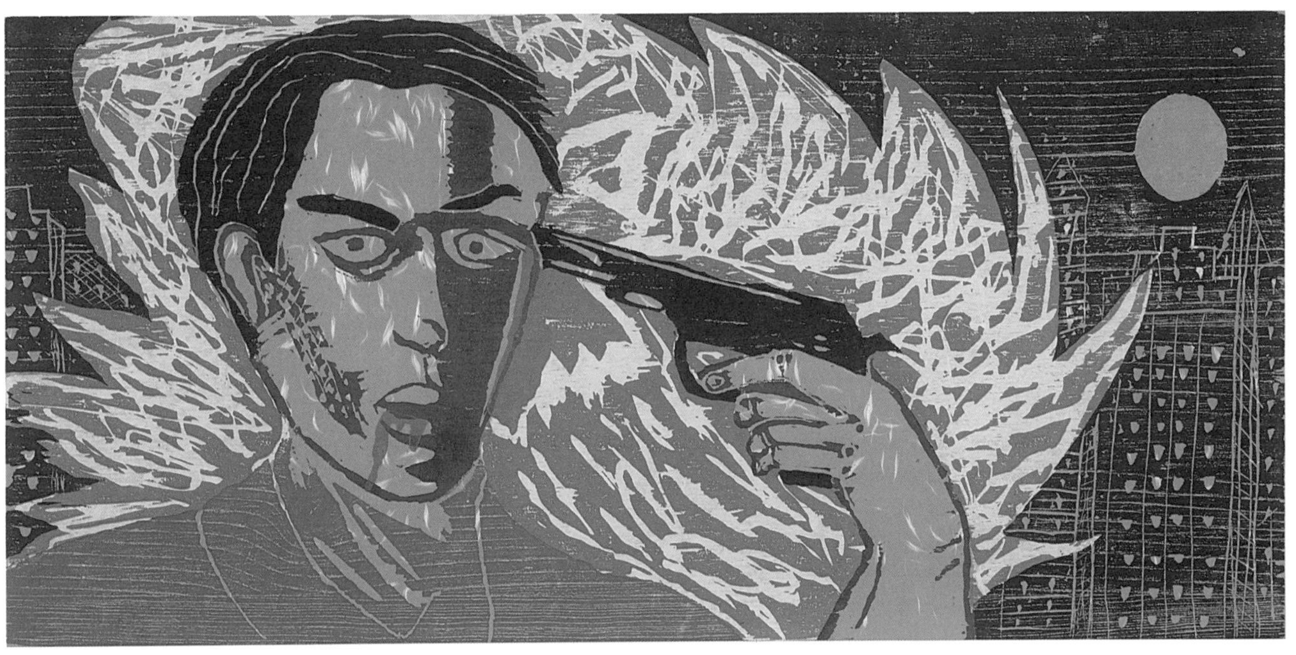

• 87 •

Richard Bosman (American, born 1944)

SUICIDE, 1980–81

Color woodcut, 13³⁄₁₆ x 27⁹⁄₁₆" (33.5 x 70 cm)

Purchased: SmithKline Beckman Corporation Fund

1982-115-1

THE CYCLE OF LIFE

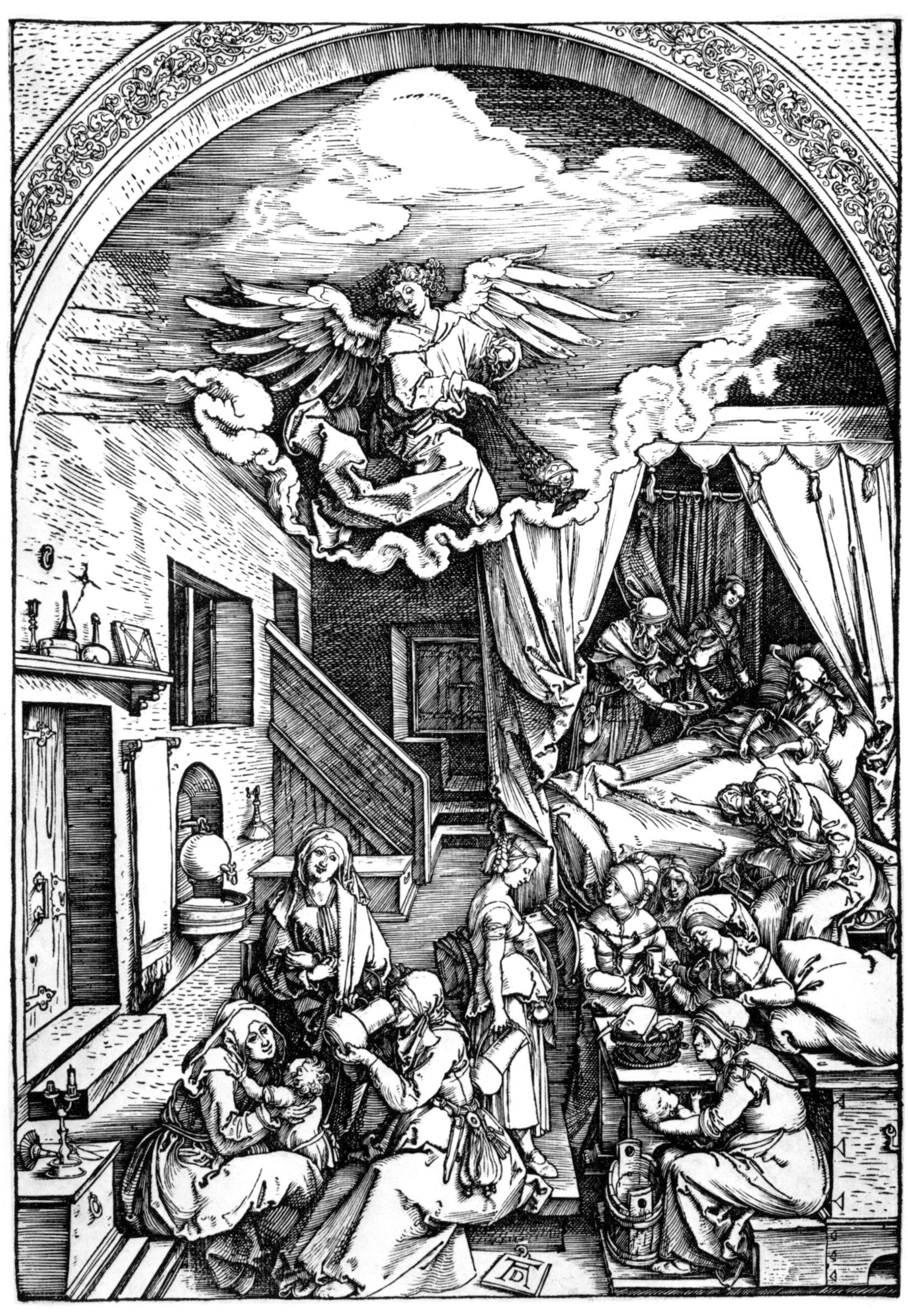

• 88 •

Albrecht Dürer (German, 1471–1528)

BIRTH OF THE VIRGIN, c. 1503–4

From "The Life of the Virgin," 1502–10

Woodcut (b/b), 11¹¹⁄₁₆ x 8³⁄₁₆" (29.7 x 20.8 cm)

Gift of Lessing J. Rosenwald

50-8-5

De natiuitate Antechristi.

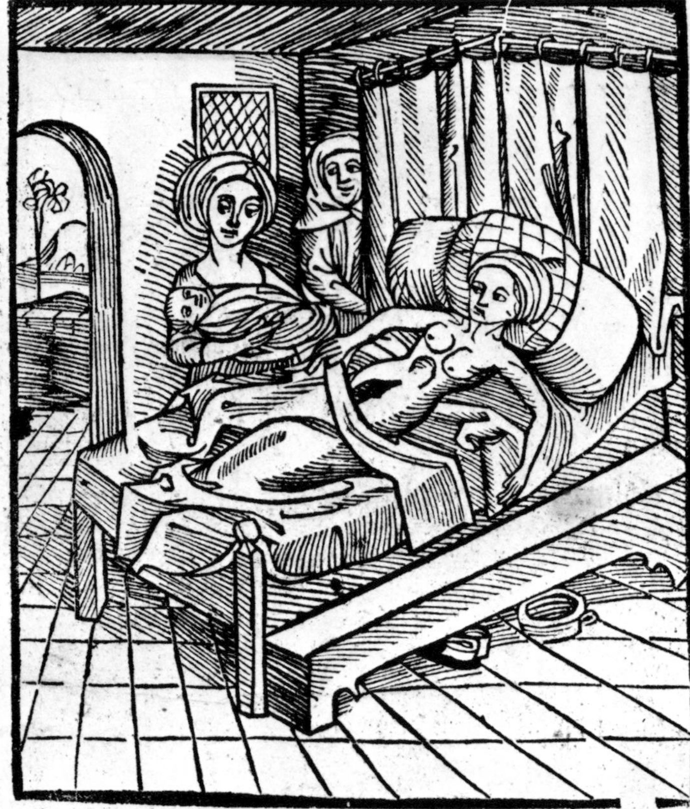

Post ebdomodã vo tpis cũ cõphenderint ciuitatẽ Jopen. mittet dñs de⁹ vnũ ex pncipib⁹ militie sue ꝛ pcutiet eos i vno momẽto tẽpis. Et post hec descẽdet rex Romanoꝝ ꝛ demorabit i hierlm septiana tẽpoꝝ ꝛ dimidia. qđ ẽ. x. anni ꝛ dimidiũ. Et cũ cõplebũt. x. anni ꝛ dimidi⁹. ꝛ apparebit fili⁹ pditionis. Hic nascet i Chorosai ꝛ nutriet i Bethsaida. ꝛ regñbit Capharnaũ. Et letabit Chorosai eo ꝙ in ea ẽ. Et Betsaida ppter qđ nutrit⁹ est in ea. Et Capharnaũ eo ꝙ regnauerit in ea. Propter hãc causaꝫ in euangelio dñs tertio sententiã dedit dicens. Ve tibi Chorosaim: ve tibi Betsaida: ꝛ tibi Capharnaum: si vsqꝫ in celum exaltaberis vsqꝫ ad infernũ descendes.

De Jopen ciuitate habet Actuũ. x. caplo et Ezech. 39. ca. Jopen est ciuitas ꝛ porta maris illis transfretantib⁹ de nr̃is terris pro mare ad irlm et terrã pmissionis quã ciuitataꝫ Japhet ꝛ tertius fili⁹ ipius Noe primo fundauit. Natiuitas antechristi.

d ij

• 89 •

Anonymous (Swiss, early sixteenth century)

CAESAREAN BIRTH, c. 1506

Woodcut, 7 13/16 x 5 15/16" (19.9 x 15.1 cm)

Purchased: SmithKline Beckman Corporation Fund

71-54-2

LIBER QVARTVS.

DE VARIETATIBVS NON NA-turalis partus, & earundem curis.

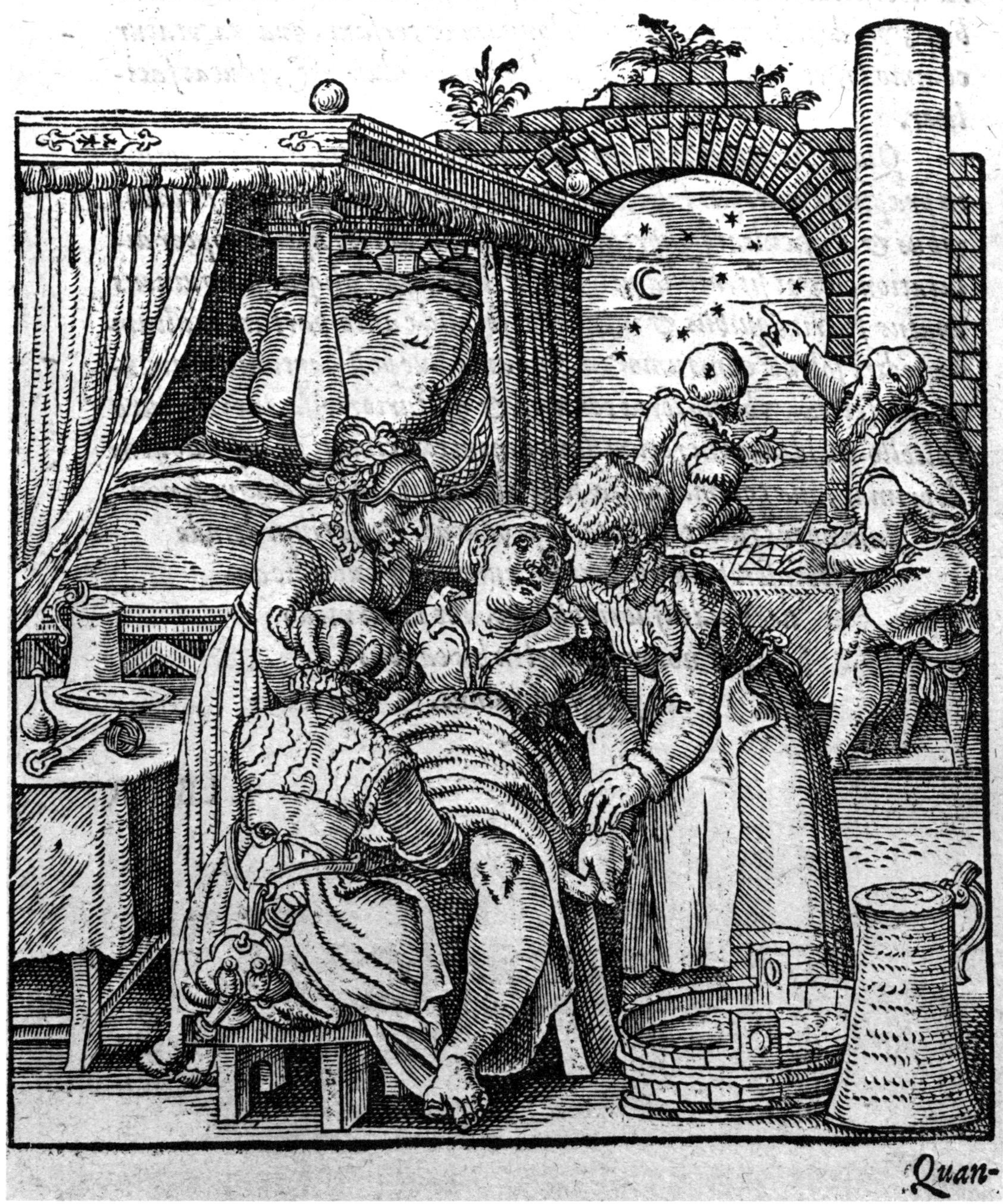

• 90 •

Jost Amman (Swiss, active Germany, 1539–1591)

CHILDBIRTH, 1580

From Jacob Rueff, *De Conceptu et Generatione Hominis* . . . (Frankfort on the Main: Sigismundi Feyerabendius, 1580)

Woodcut, 7 11/16 x 5 7/8" (19.5 x 14.9 cm)

Purchased: SmithKline Beckman Corporation Fund

49-97-12a

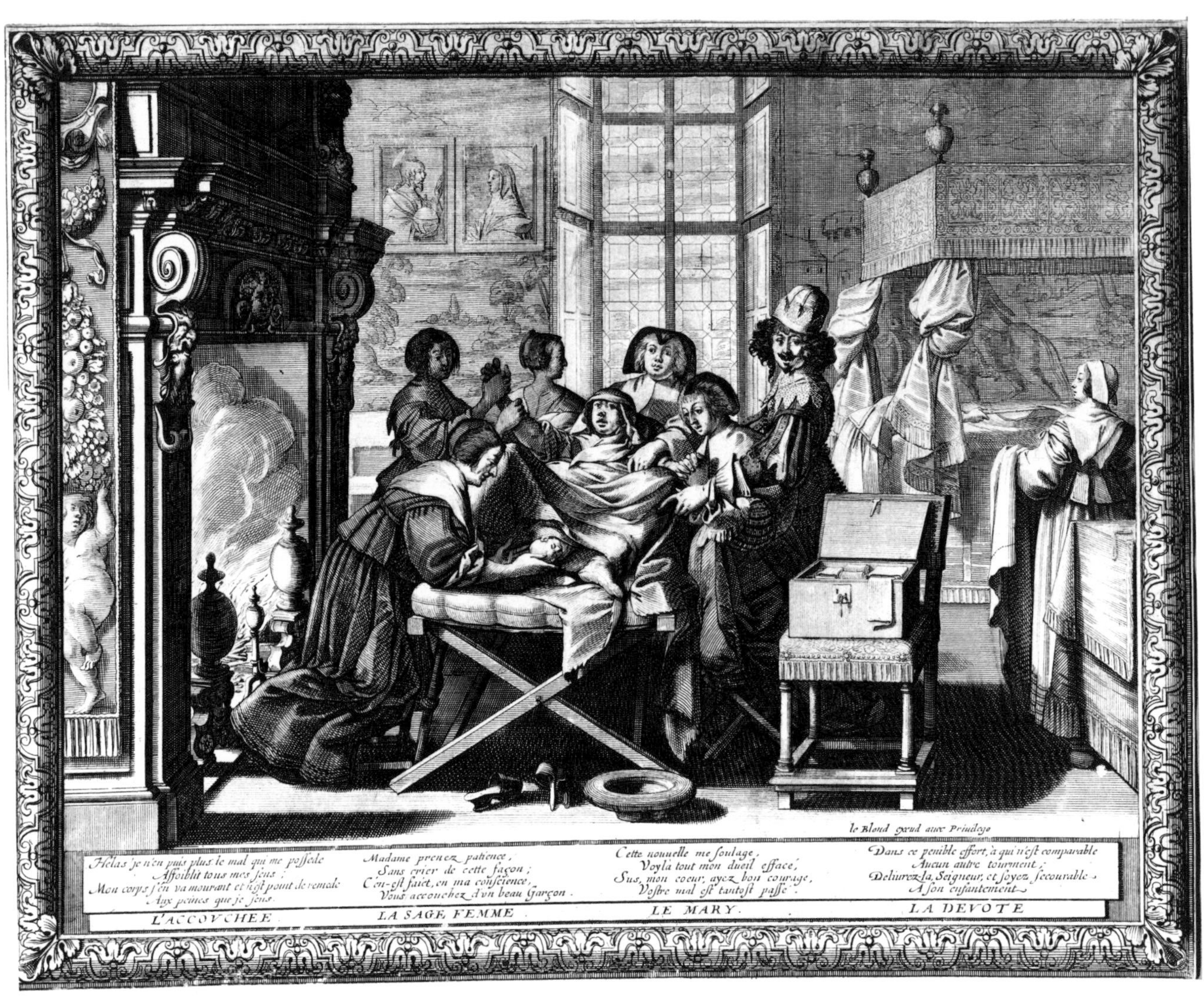

• 91 •

Abraham Bosse (French, 1602–1676)

CHILDBIRTH, 1633

From "The City Marriage," 1633

Etching, 10¼ x 13¼" (26 x 33.5 cm) (trimmed)

Purchased: SmithKline Beckman Corporation Fund

49-97-13

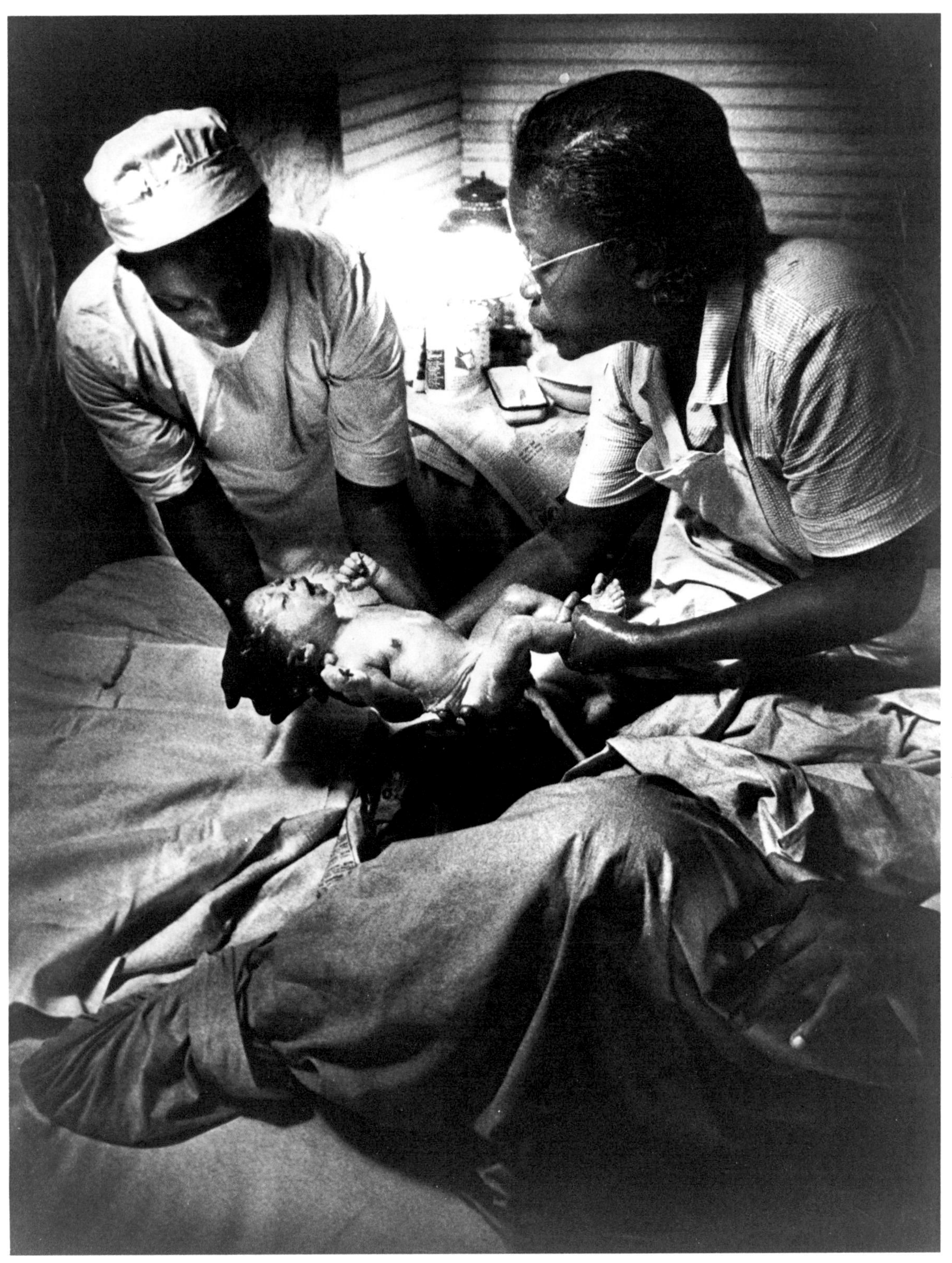

• 92 •

W. Eugene Smith (American, 1918–1978)

MAUDE CALLEN, 1951

From "Nurse Midwife," 1951

Gelatin silver print, 12 13/16 x 9 7/8" (32.7 x 25 cm)

Purchased: SmithKline Beckman Corporation Fund

1978-95-15

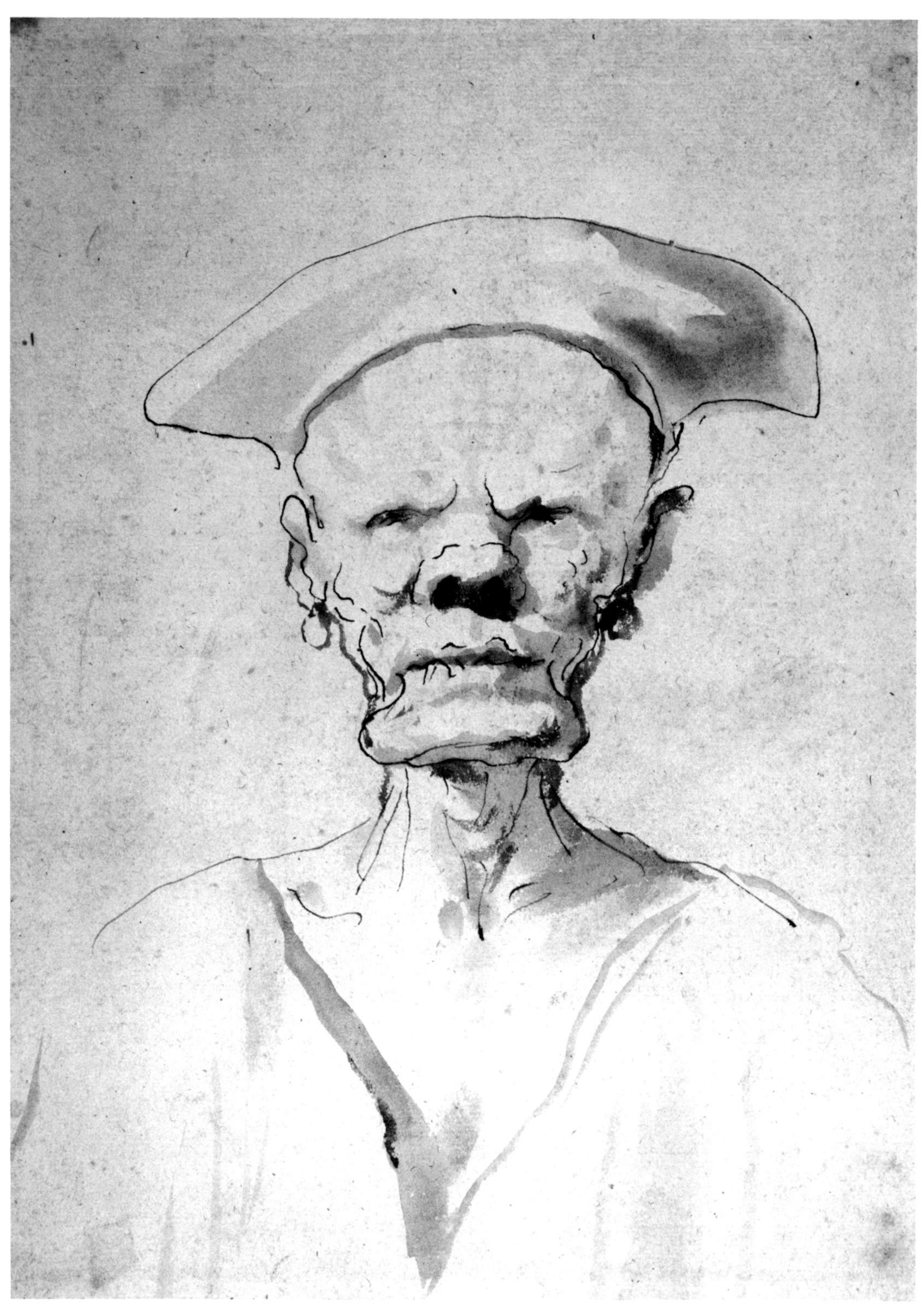

• 93 •

Giovanni Francesco Barbieri, known as Il Guercino (Italian, 1591–1666)

CARICATURE OF AN EMACIATED OLD MAN

Brown ink and brown washes on light buff antique laid paper, 11⅜ x 8¼" (29 x 21 cm)

Purchased: SmithKline Beckman Corporation Fund

1984-77-1

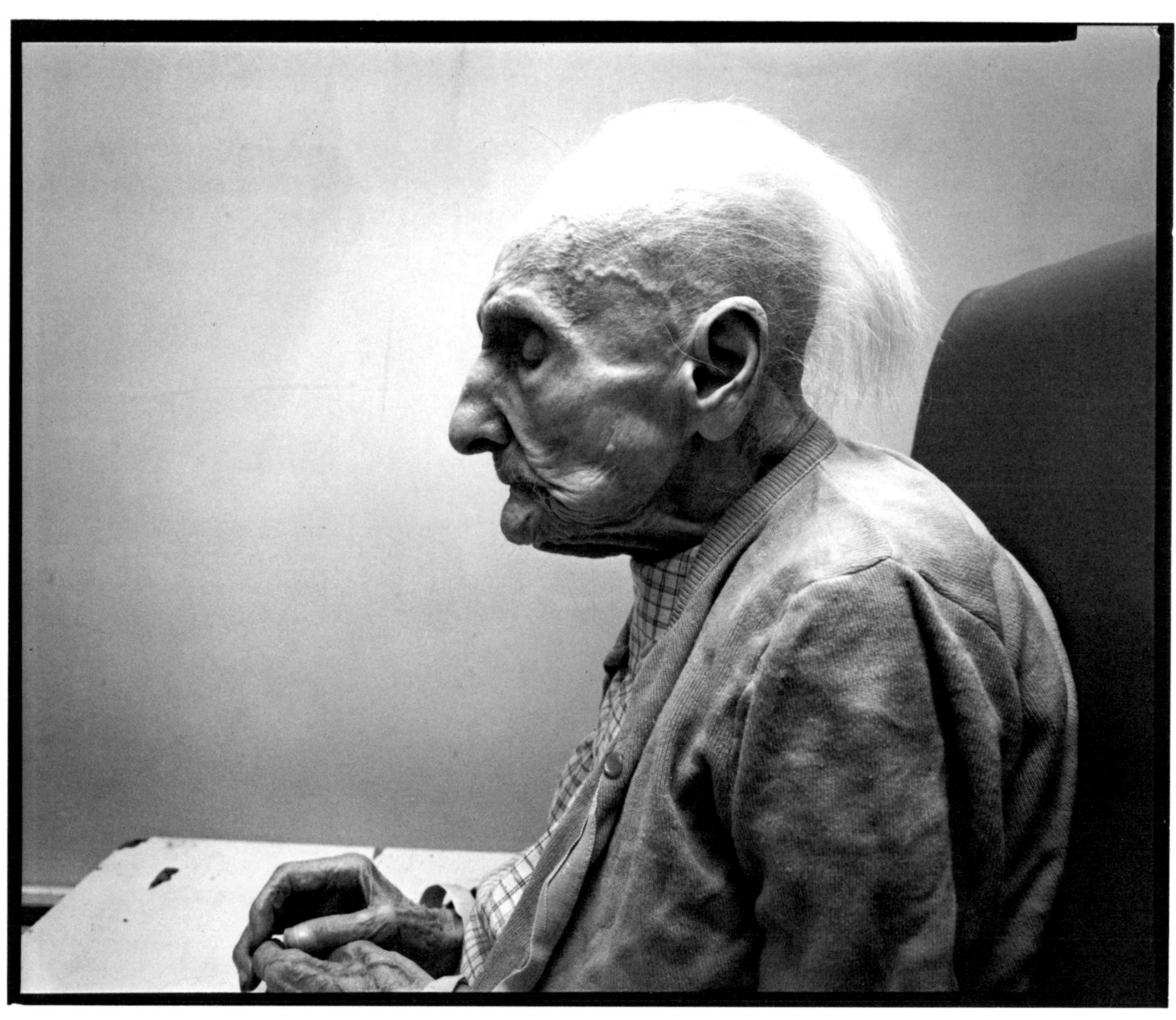

• 94 •

Nicholas Nixon (American, born 1947)

C. C., BOSTON, 1983

Gelatin silver print, 8 x 9 15/16" (20.3 x 25.2 cm)

Purchased: SmithKline Beckman Corporation Fund

1985-17-1

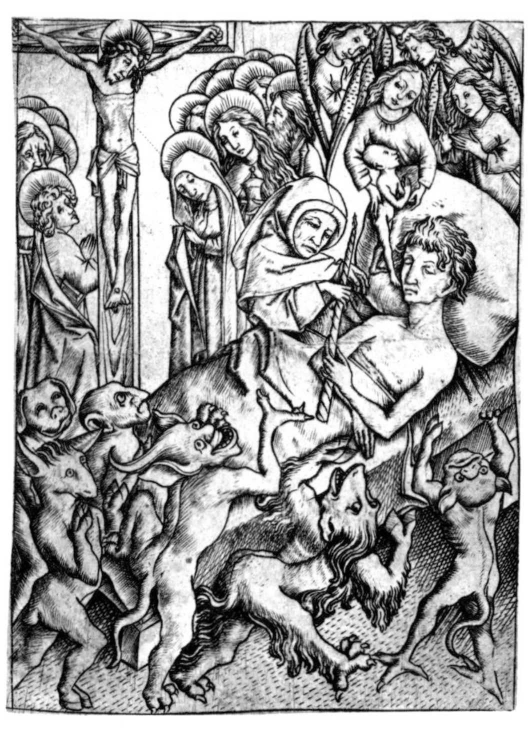

· 95 ·

Master E. S. (German, active c. 1450–67)

TRIUMPH OVER TEMPTATION, c. 1450

From the *Ars Moriendi,* c. 1450

Engraving, 3 7/16 x 2 9/16" (8.7 x 6.5 cm) (trimmed)

Purchased: SmithKline Beckman Corporation Fund

1983-72-1

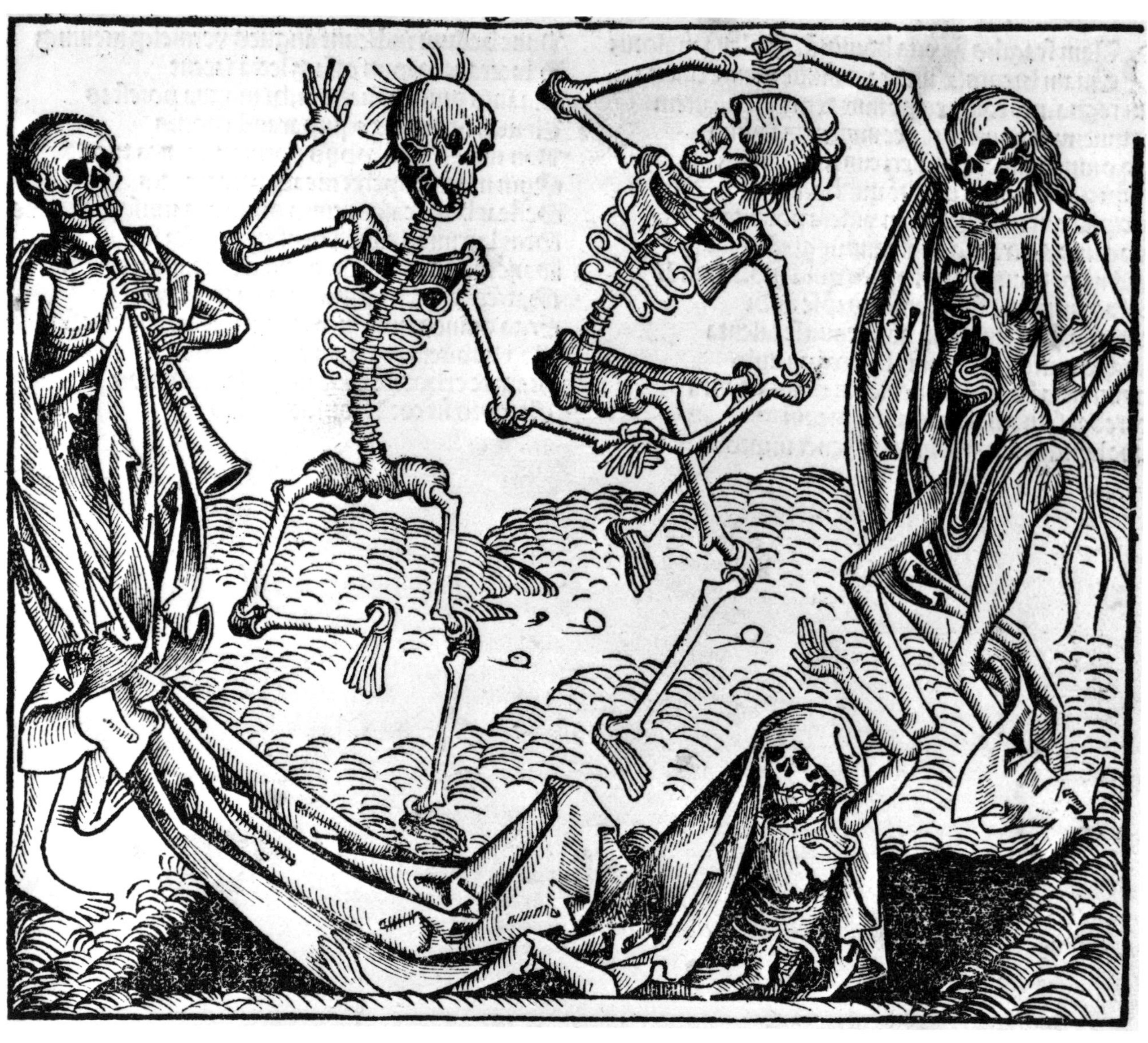

• 96 •

Wilhelm Pleydenwurff (German, active 1482/83–died 1494)

After Michel Wolgemut (German, 1434–1519)

IMAGO MORTIS: DANCE OF THE DEAD, 1493

From Hartmann Schedel, *Liber Chronicarum . . . ab Inicio Mundi . . .* (Nuremberg: Anthonius Koberger, 1493)

Woodcut, $7\frac{15}{16} \times 9\frac{3}{16}$" (20.1 x 23.3 cm)

Gift of Carl Zigrosser

74-179-511

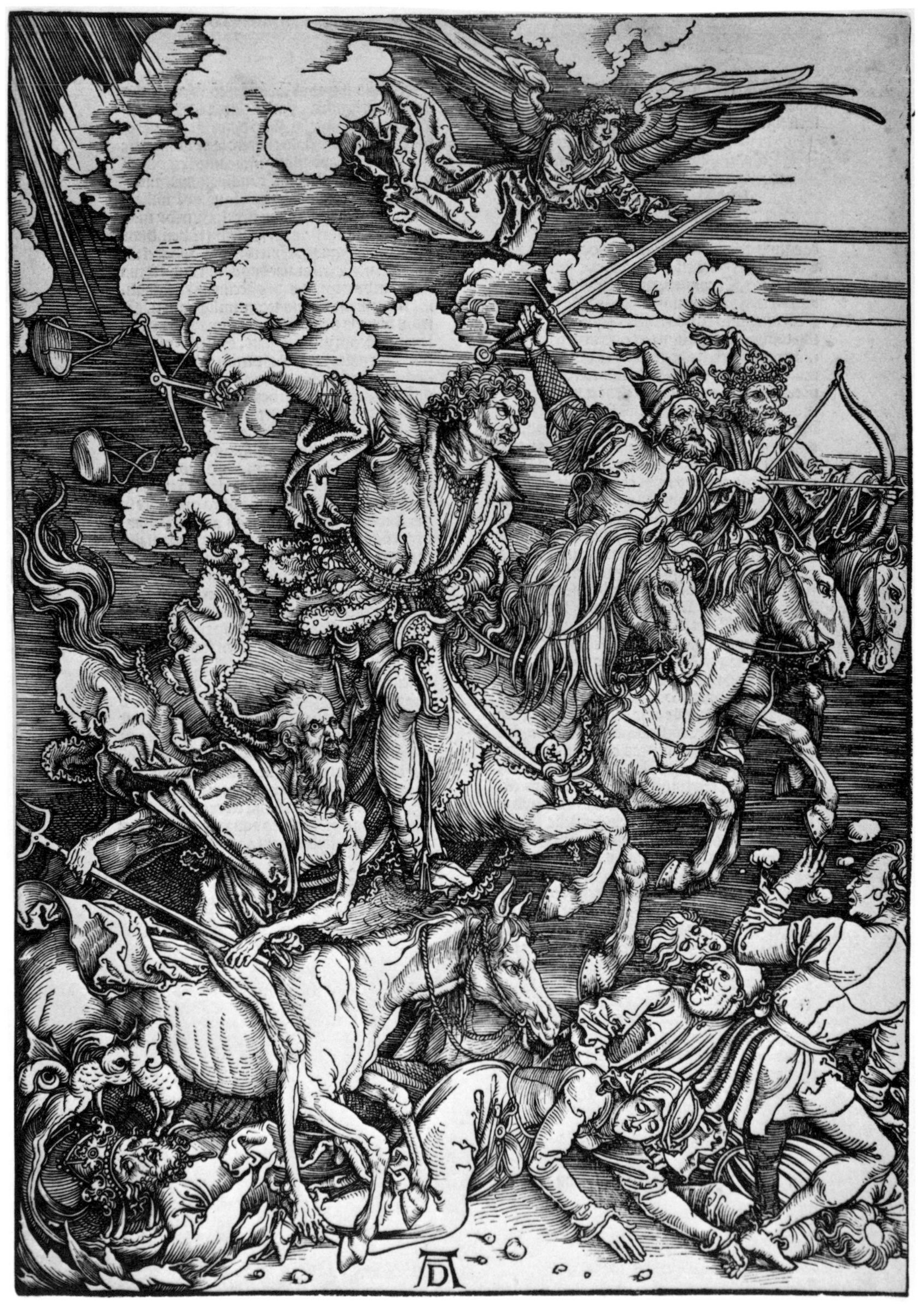

• 97 •

Albrecht Dürer (German, 1471–1528)

THE FOUR HORSEMEN OF THE APOCALYPSE, 1498

From *Apocalipsis* (Nuremberg: Albrecht Dürer, 1498)
Woodcut, 15⁹⁄₁₆ x 11¹⁄₁₆" (39.5 x 28.1 cm)
Purchased: SmithKline Beckman Corporation Fund
1984-51-1

Medice, cura te-ipſum.

LVCAE IIII.

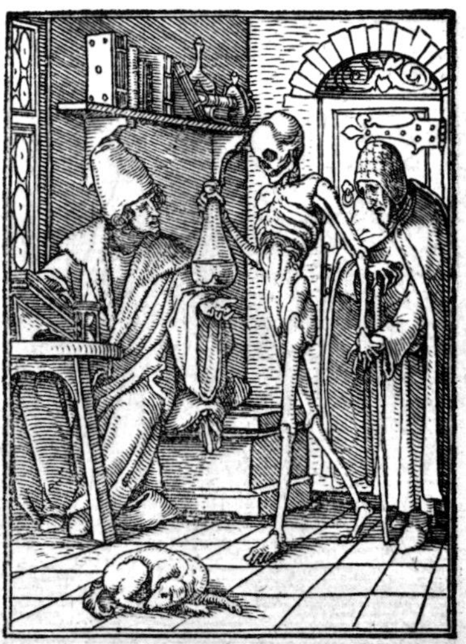

Tu bene cognoſcis morbos, artemq́; medendi
Qua ſimul ægrotis ſubueniatur, habes.
Sed caput ô ſtupidum, cùm fata aliena retardes
Ignoras morbi quo moriere genus.

• 98 •

Hans Lützelburger (Swiss, died 1526)
After Hans Holbein the Younger (German, 1497/98–1543)
DEATH AND THE PHYSICIAN, c. 1524–26

From Hans Holbein the Younger, *Imagines Mortis* . . . (Lyons: Ioannes & Franciscus Frellonii, 1545)
Woodcut, 5⅝ x 3¹³⁄₁₆" (14.3 x 9.7 cm)
Purchased: SmithKline Beckman Corporation Fund
49-97-16b

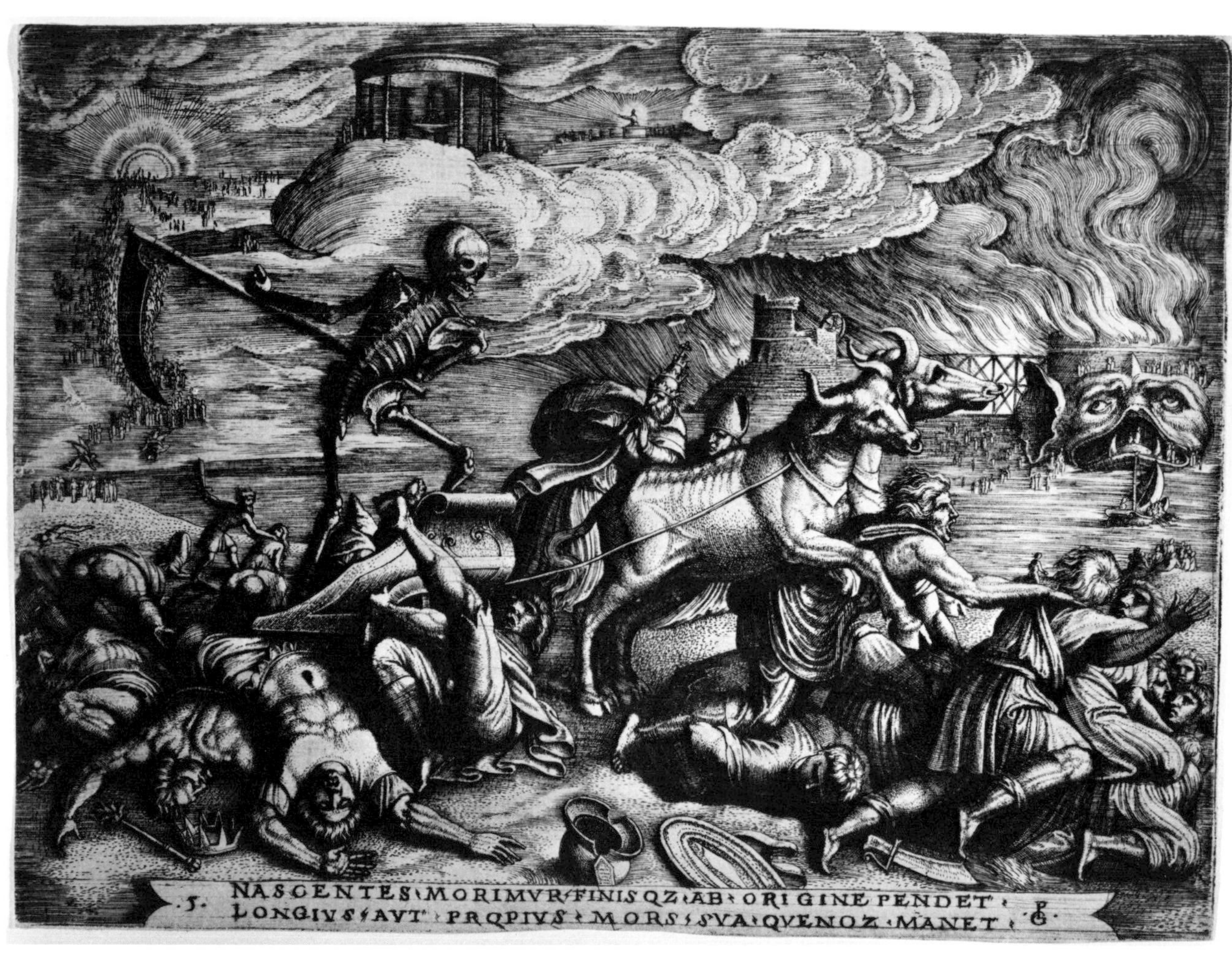

• 99a •

Georg Pencz (German, 1500–1550)

THE TRIUMPH OF DEATH, c. 1540

From "The Six Triumphs of Petrarch," c. 1540
Engraving, 5 15/16 x 8 1/4″ (15.1 x 21 cm) (trimmed)
William S. Pilling Collection
33-72-1744

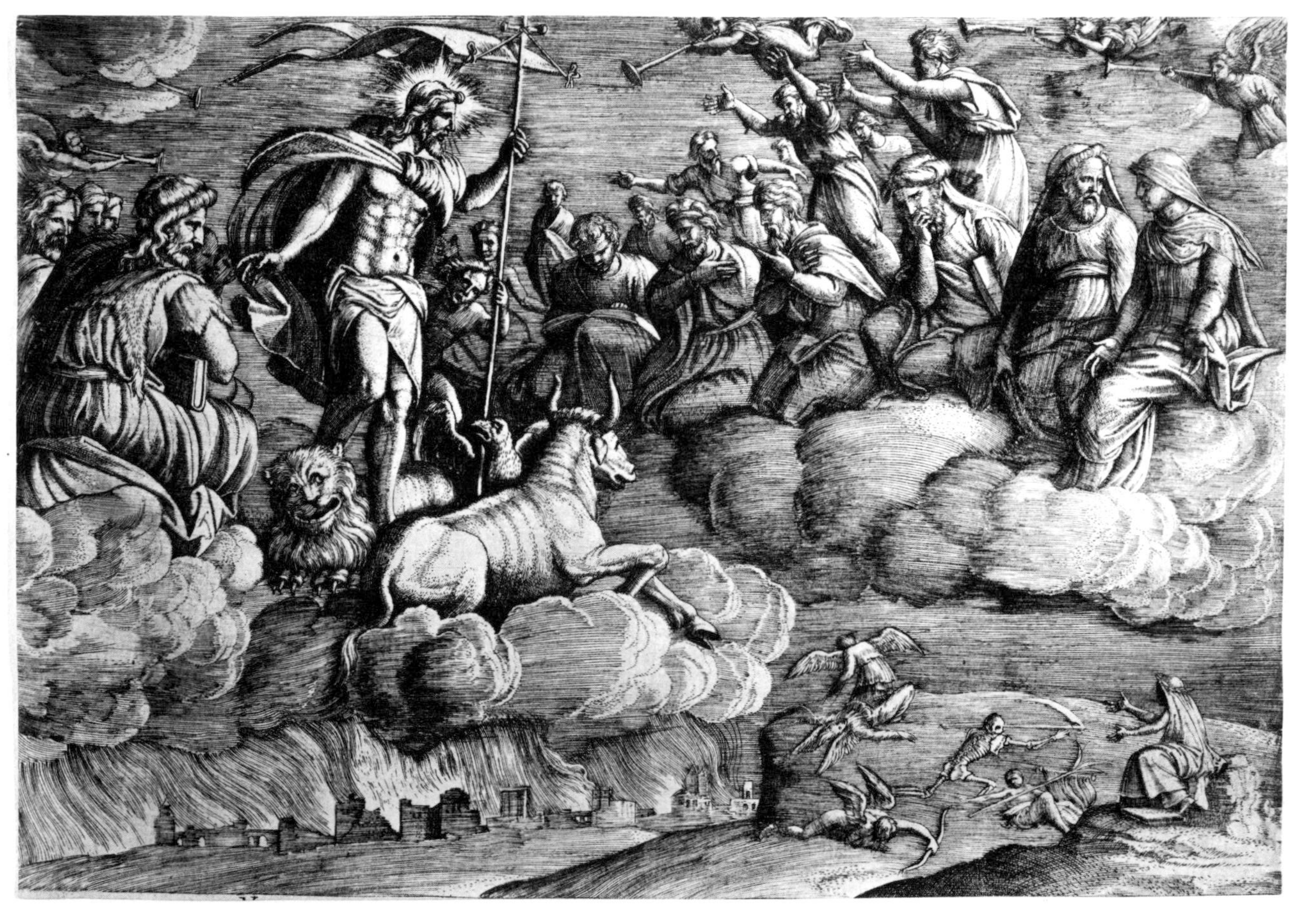

• 99b •

Georg Pencz (German, 1500–1550)

THE TRIUMPH OF ETERNITY, c. 1540

From "The Six Triumphs of Petrarch," c. 1540

Engraving, 5 15/16 x 8 1/4" (15.1 x 21 cm) (trimmed)

William S. Pilling Collection

33-72-1746

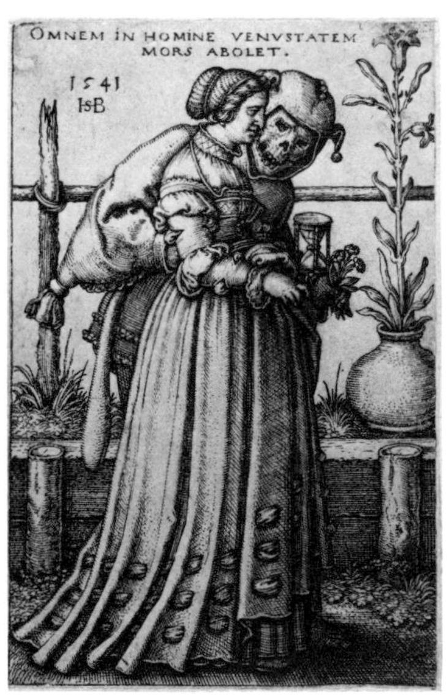

• 100 •

Hans Sebald Beham (German, 1500–1550)

YOUNG WOMAN ACCOMPANIED BY DEATH AS A JESTER, 1541

Engraving (ii/iii), 3 1/16 x 2" (7.8 x 5.1 cm) (trimmed)
Purchased: SmithKline Beckman Corporation Fund
1983-94-1

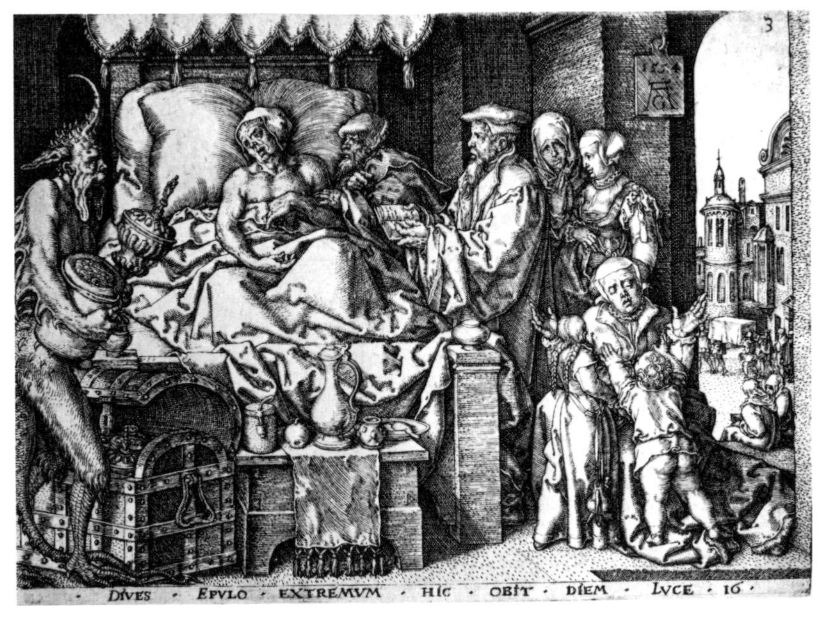

• 101 •

Heinrich Aldegrever (Trippenmeker) (German, 1502–c. 1560)

THE RICH MAN AND THE DEVIL, 1554

From "The Parable of the Rich Man and Lazarus," 1554

Engraving, $3\frac{1}{16}$ x $4\frac{3}{16}$" (7.8 x 10.6 cm) (trimmed)

Purchased: SmithKline Beckman Corporation Fund

1983-31-1

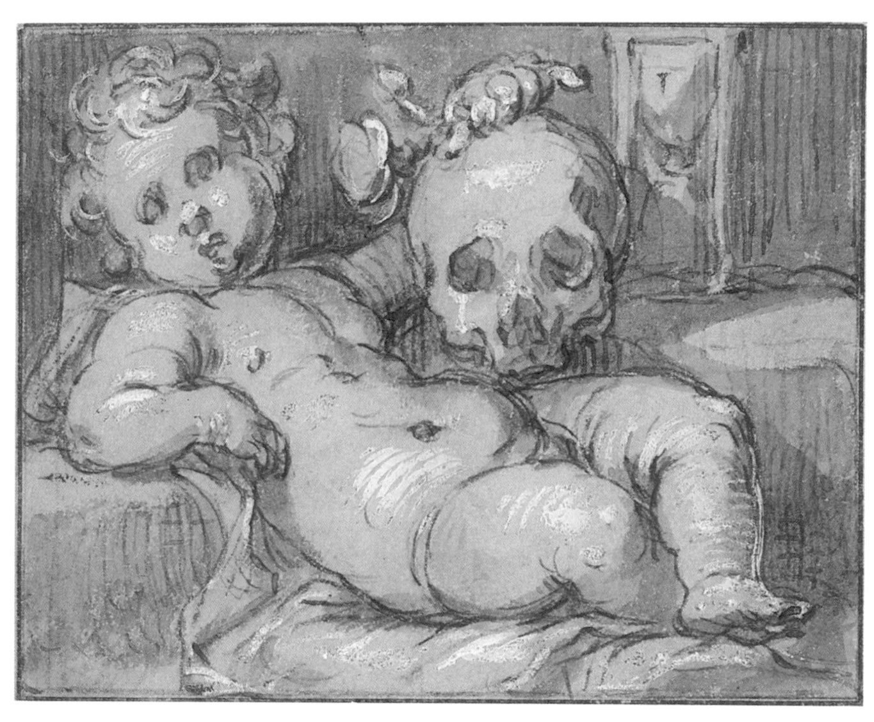

• 102 •

Abraham Bloemaert (Dutch, 1564–1651)

PUTTO WITH SKULL, ROSE, AND HOURGLASS, c. 1610

Black ink and blue and gray washes over traces of black chalk, heightened with opaque white watercolor, on light buff laid paper, 3⁹⁄₁₆ x 4⁹⁄₁₆" (9.1 x 11.5 cm)

Purchased: SmithKline Beckman Corporation Fund

1984-15-1

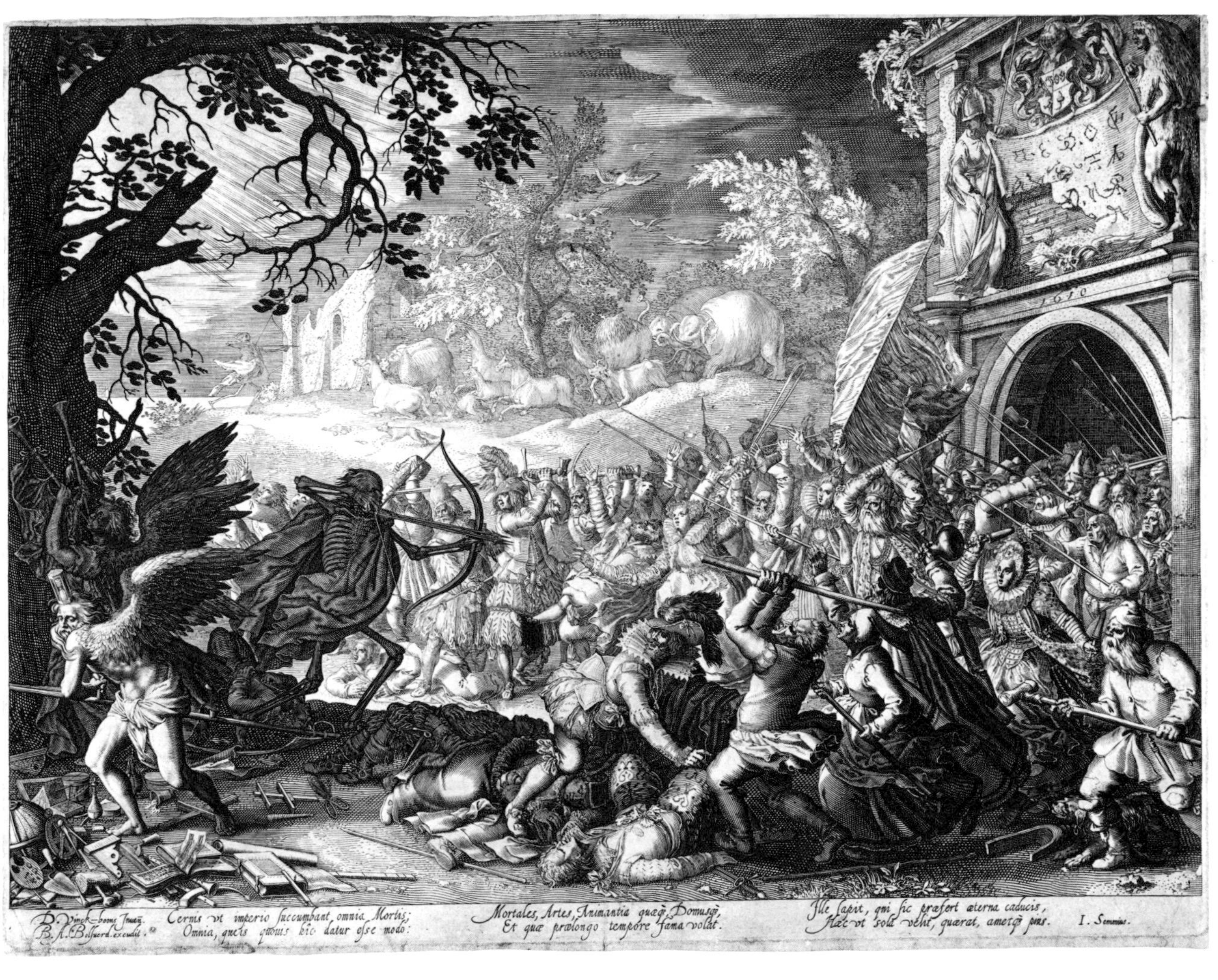

• 103 •

Boetius Adam van Bolswert (Dutch, 1580–1633)
After David Vinckboons (Flemish, 1576–1629)

ALL-CONQUERING DEATH, 1610

Engraving, 10 15/16 x 14 7/8" (27.8 x 37.8 cm) (trimmed)
Purchased: SmithKline Beckman Corporation Fund
1983-95-1

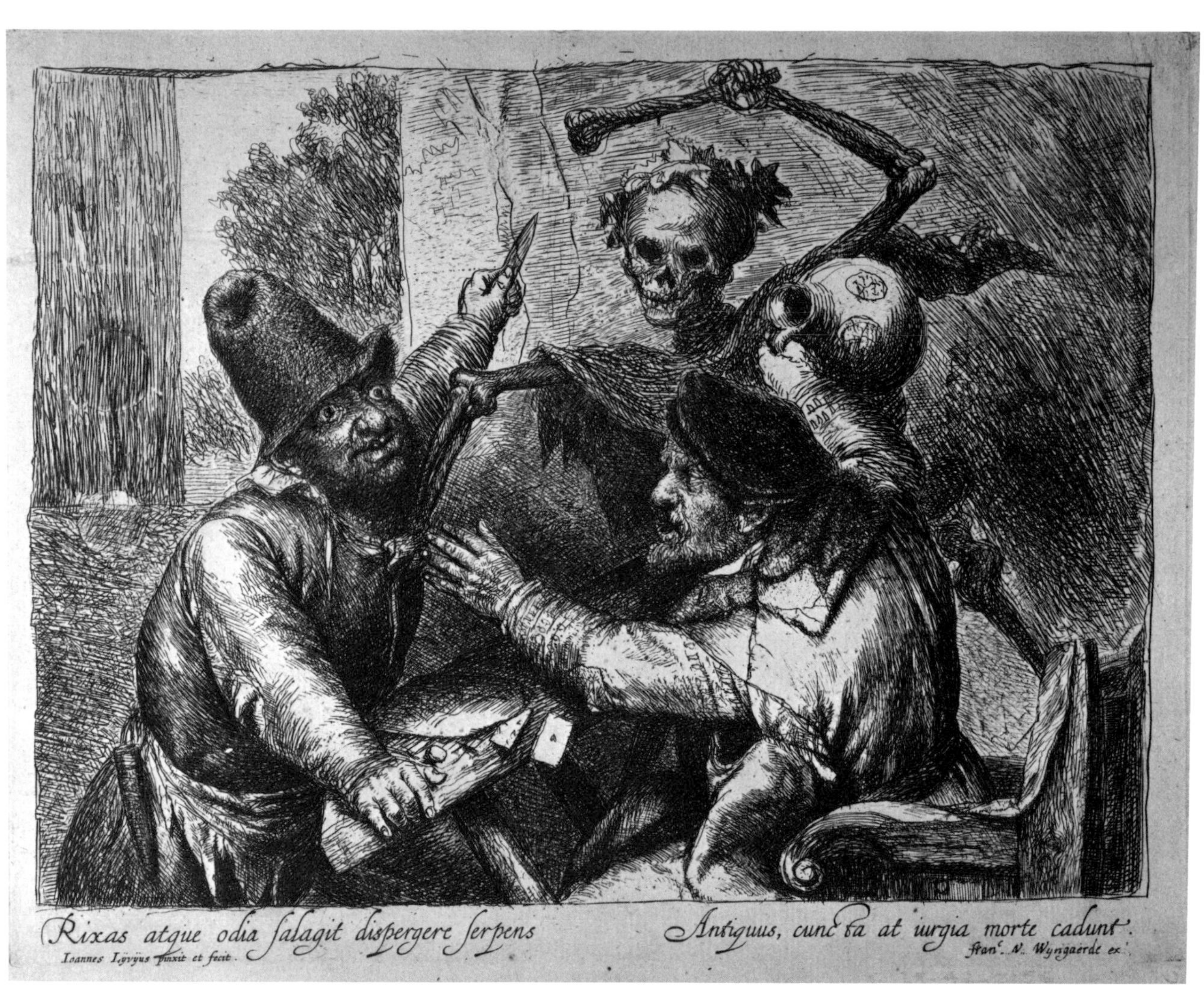

• 104 •

Jan Lievens (Dutch, 1607–1674)

QUARRELING CARD PLAYERS AND DEATH, c. 1635

Etching (iii/iii), 7$\frac{15}{16}$ x 10$\frac{9}{16}$" (20.2 x 26.8 cm)

Charles M. Lea Collection

28-42-2156

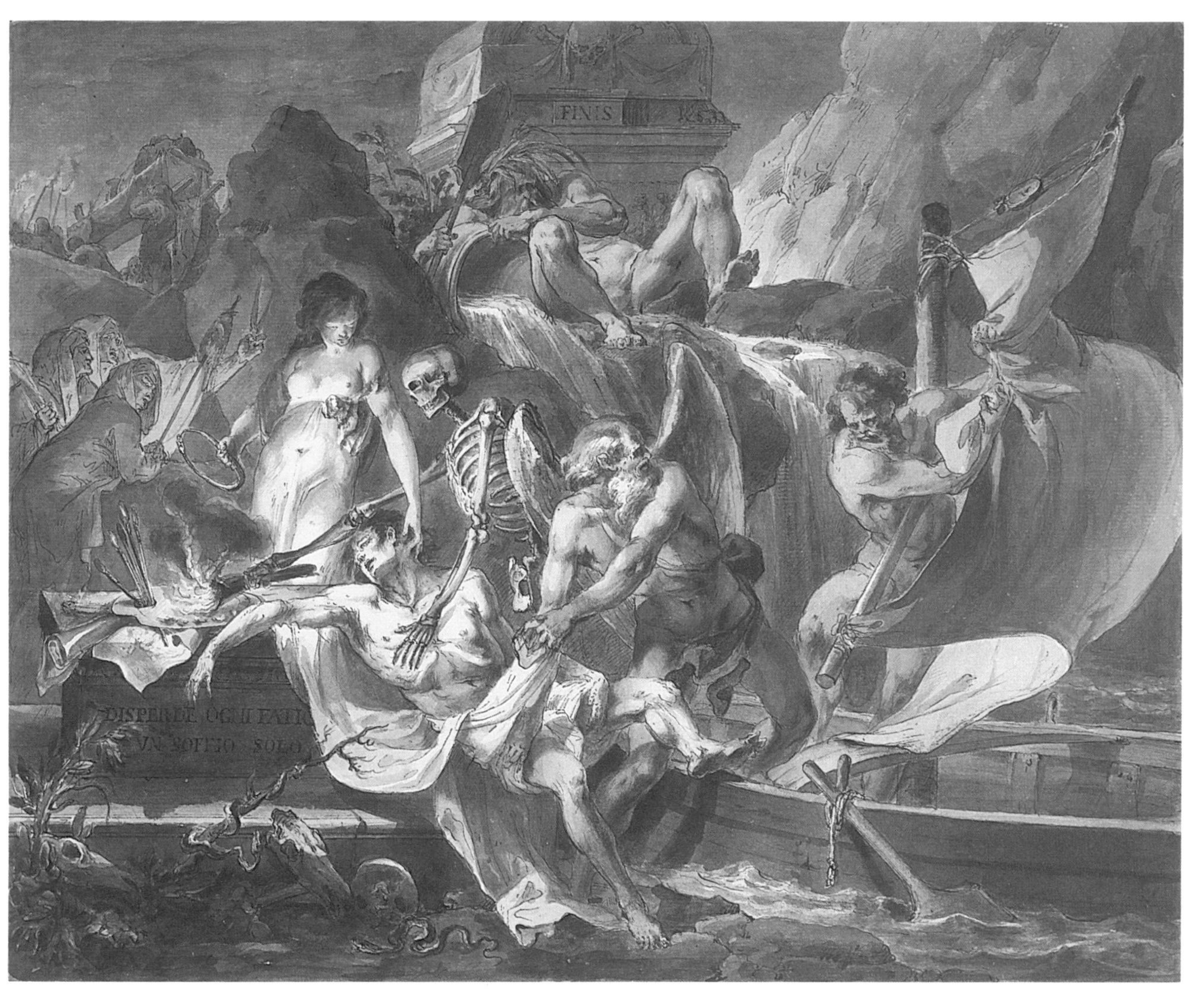

• 105 •

Attributed to Giovanni David (Italian, 1743–1790)

ALLEGORY OF THE DEATH OF AN ARTIST, 1780–90

Ink with colored washes over traces of black chalk on off-white antique laid paper, 13 5/16 x 16½" (33.8 x 41.9 cm)

Purchased: SmithKline Beckman Corporation Fund

1978-62-2

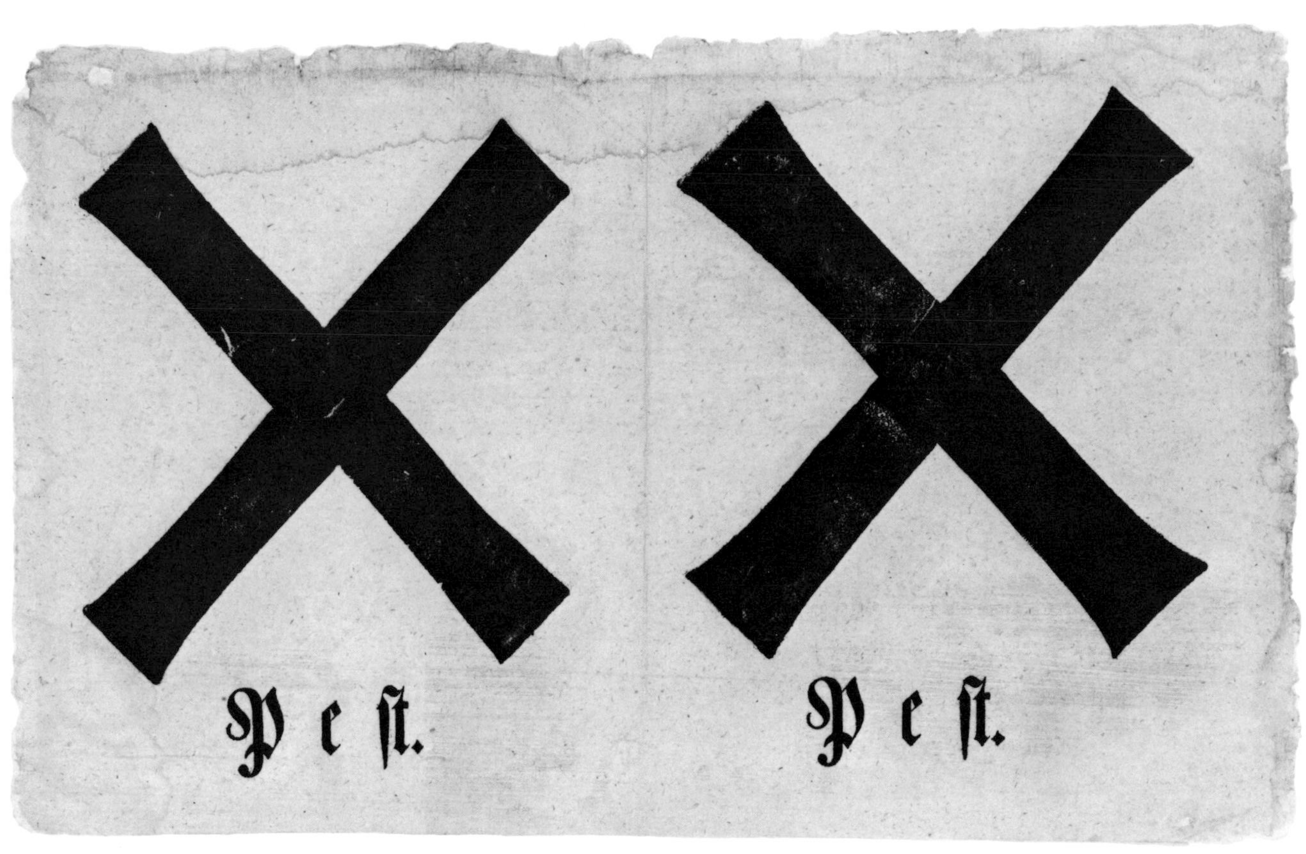

• 106 •

Anonymous (German, seventeenth century)

QUARANTINE SIGN, c. 1683

Woodcut, $6\frac{1}{16} \times 12\frac{11}{16}$" (15.4 x 32.2 cm)
Purchased: SmithKline Beckman Corporation Fund
71-116-1

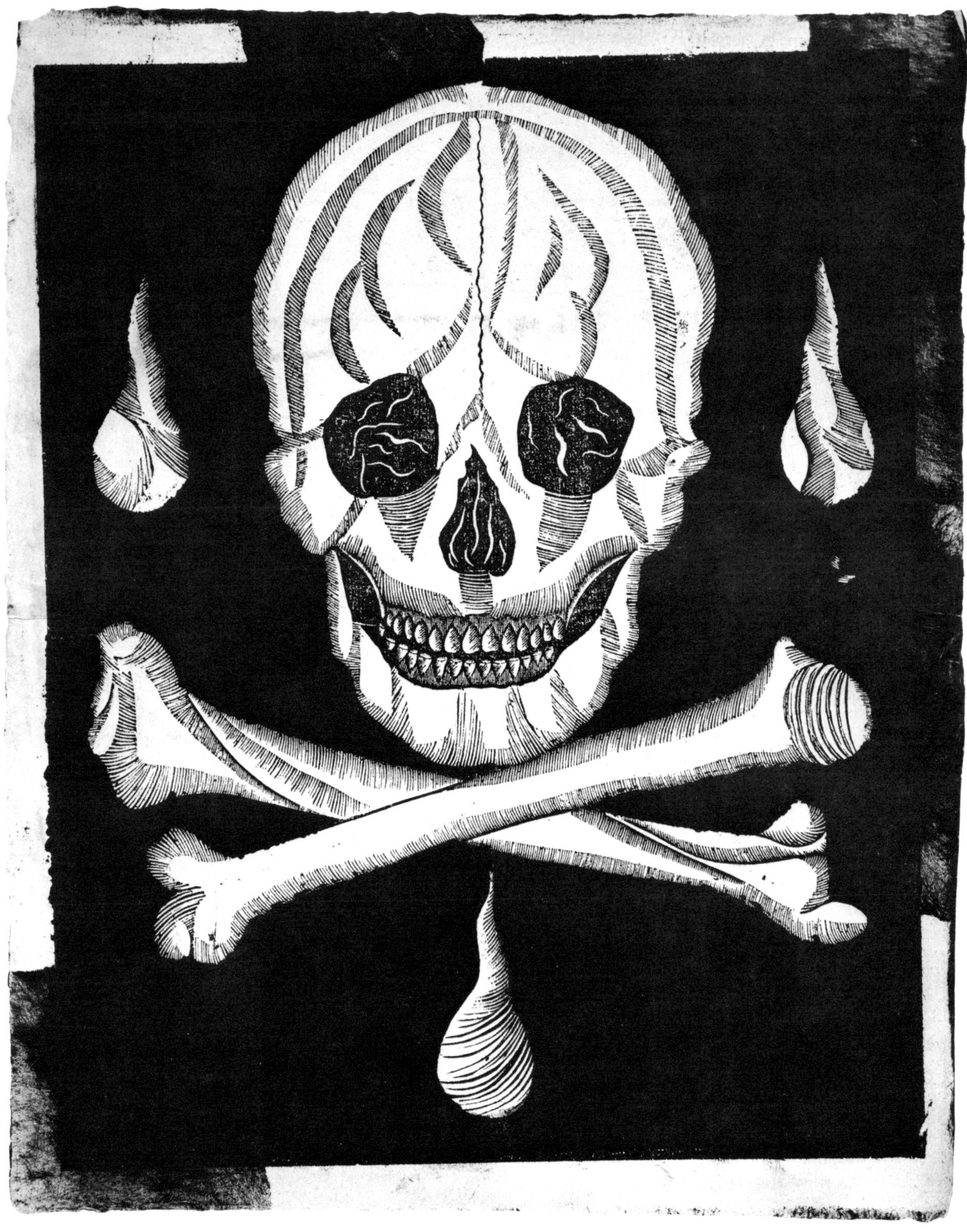

• 107 •

Anonymous (French, seventeenth century)

SKULL AND CROSSBONES, seventeenth century

Woodcut, 15¼ x 12$^{13}/_{16}$" (38.8 x 32.5 cm)

Purchased: SmithKline Beckman Corporation Fund

1982-118-1

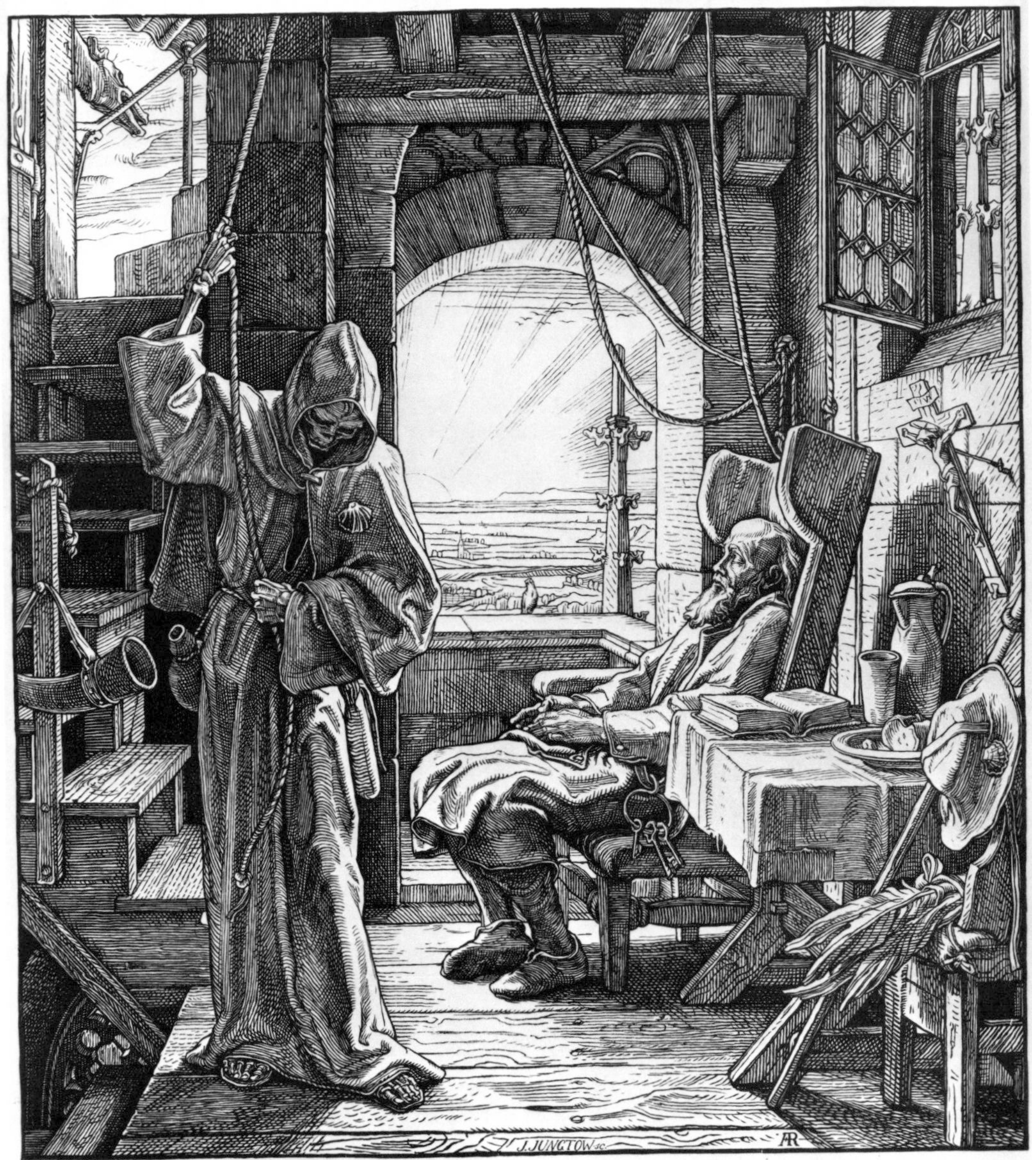

Der Tod als Freund.

Herausgegeben aus der Akademie der Holzschneidekunst von H. Bürkner in Dresden.

Erschienen bei Ed. Schulte (J. Buddeus'sche Buch- und Kunsthandl.) in Düsseldorf.

• 108a •

Richard Julius Jungtow (German, 1828–after 1851)

After Alfred Rethel (German, 1816–1859)

DEATH AS A FRIEND, c. 1851

Wood engraving, 12 x 10¾″ (30.5 x 27.3 cm)

Purchased: SmithKline Beckman Corporation Fund

58-150-20

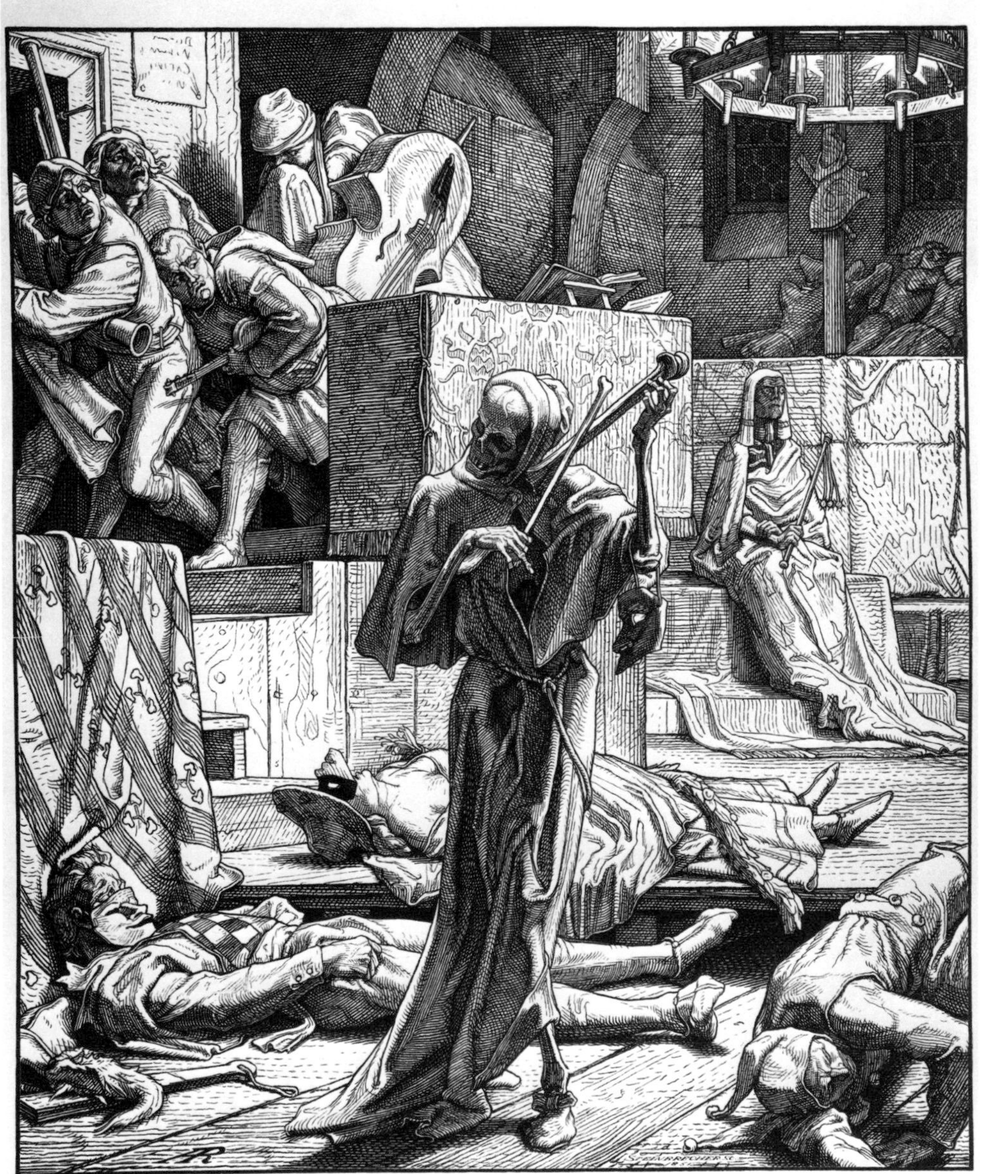

Der Tod als Erwürger.

Erster Auftritt der Cholera auf einem Maskenball in Paris 1831.

Herausgegeben aus der Akademie der Holzschneidekunst von H. Bürkner in Dresden.

Erschienen bei Ed. Schulte (J. Buddeus'sche Buch- und Kunsthandl.) in Düsseldorf.

• 108b •

Gustav Richard Steinbrecher (German, 1828–1887)
After Alfred Rethel (German, 1816–1859)
DEATH AS AN ENEMY
(THE FIRST OUTBREAK OF CHOLERA AT A MASKED BALL IN PARIS, 1831),
1851

Wood engraving, 12¼ x 10⅞" (31.1 x 27.6 cm)
Purchased: SmithKline Beckman Corporation Fund
58-150-19

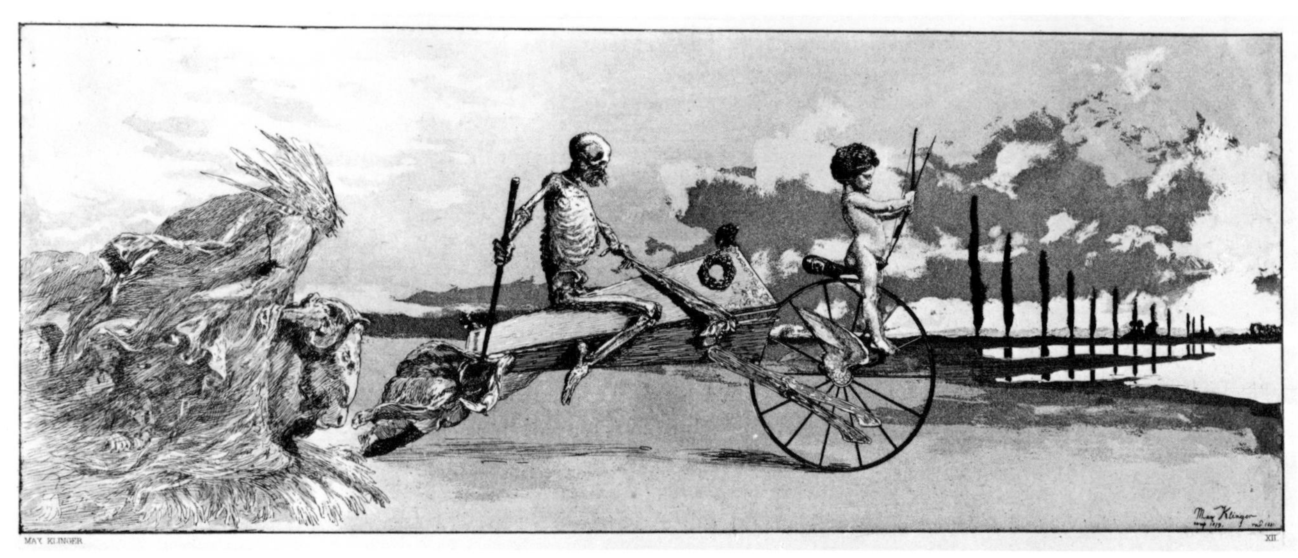

• 109 •

Max Klinger (German, 1857–1920)

CUPID, DEATH, AND THE BEYOND, 1881

From *Intermezzi* (Munich: Theo. Stroefer, 1881)
Etching and aquatint (iii/iii), 7¾ x 16⅝" (19.7 x 42.2 cm)
Purchased: SmithKline Beckman Corporation Fund
1984-18-1

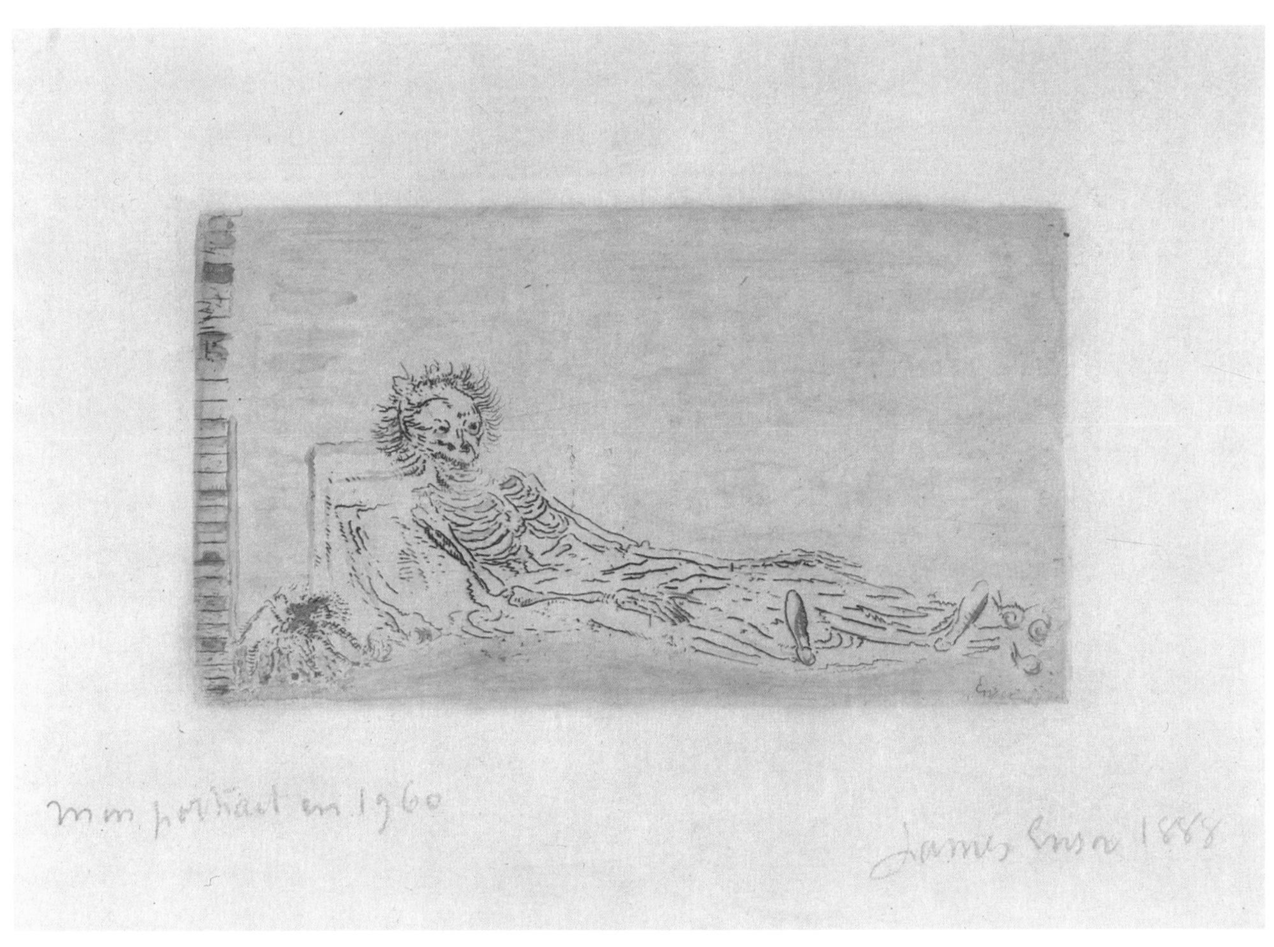

• 110 •

James Ensor (Belgian, 1860–1949)

MY PORTRAIT IN THE YEAR 1960, 1888

Hand-colored etching, 2¾ x 4¾" (7 x 12.1 cm)

Purchased with funds given by Derald H. Ruttenberg and Robert A. Hauslohner

72-216-1

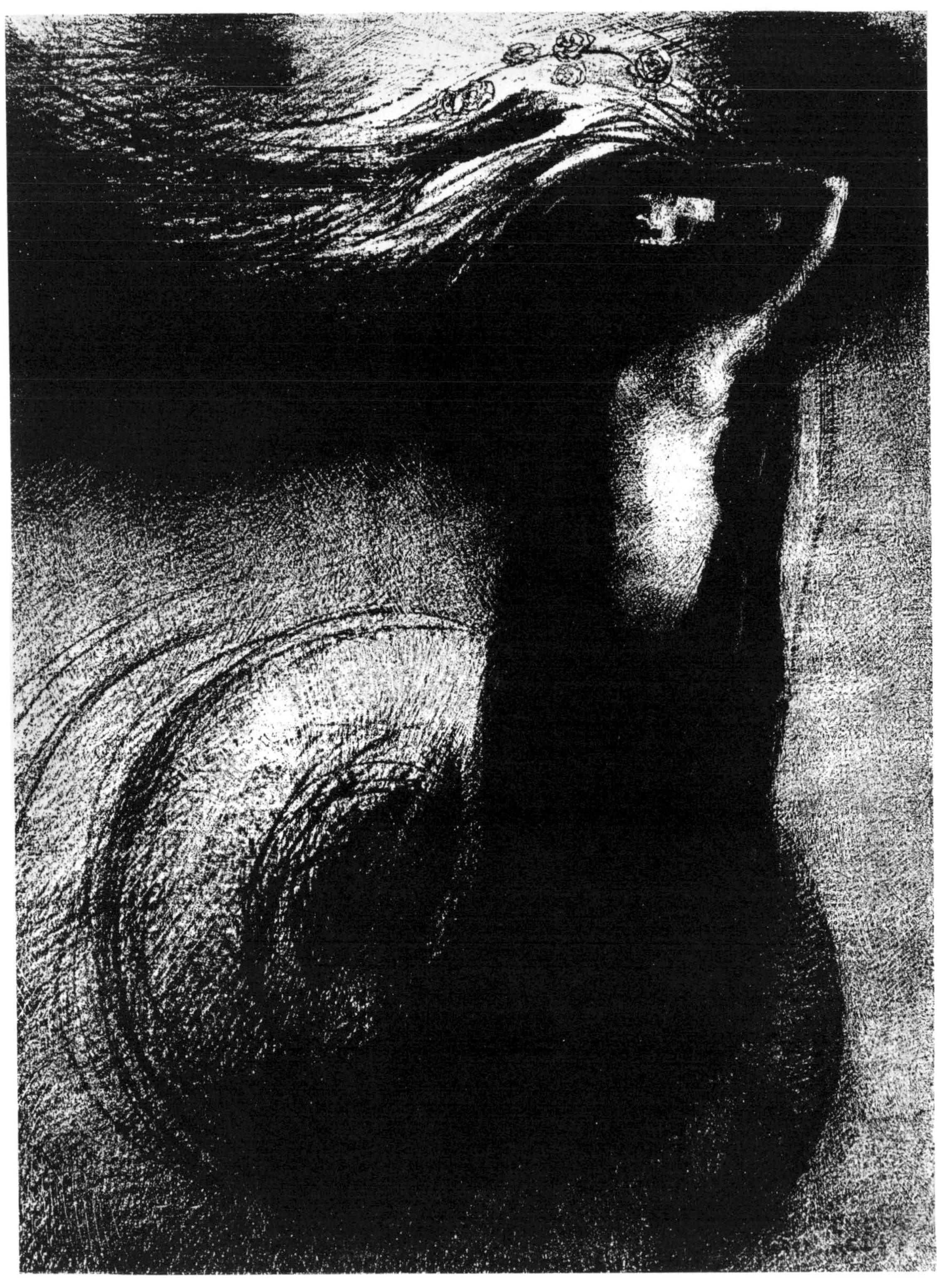

• 111 •

Odilon Redon (French, 1840–1916)

DEATH: MY IRONY SURPASSES ALL OTHERS, 1889

From *A Gustave Flaubert: Six Dessins pour la "Tentation de St.-Antoine"* (Paris, 1889)
Lithograph (proof before letters), 10$\frac{5}{16}$ x 7$\frac{5}{8}$" (26.2 x 19.3 cm)
Purchased: SmithKline Beckman Corporation Fund
1984-20-1

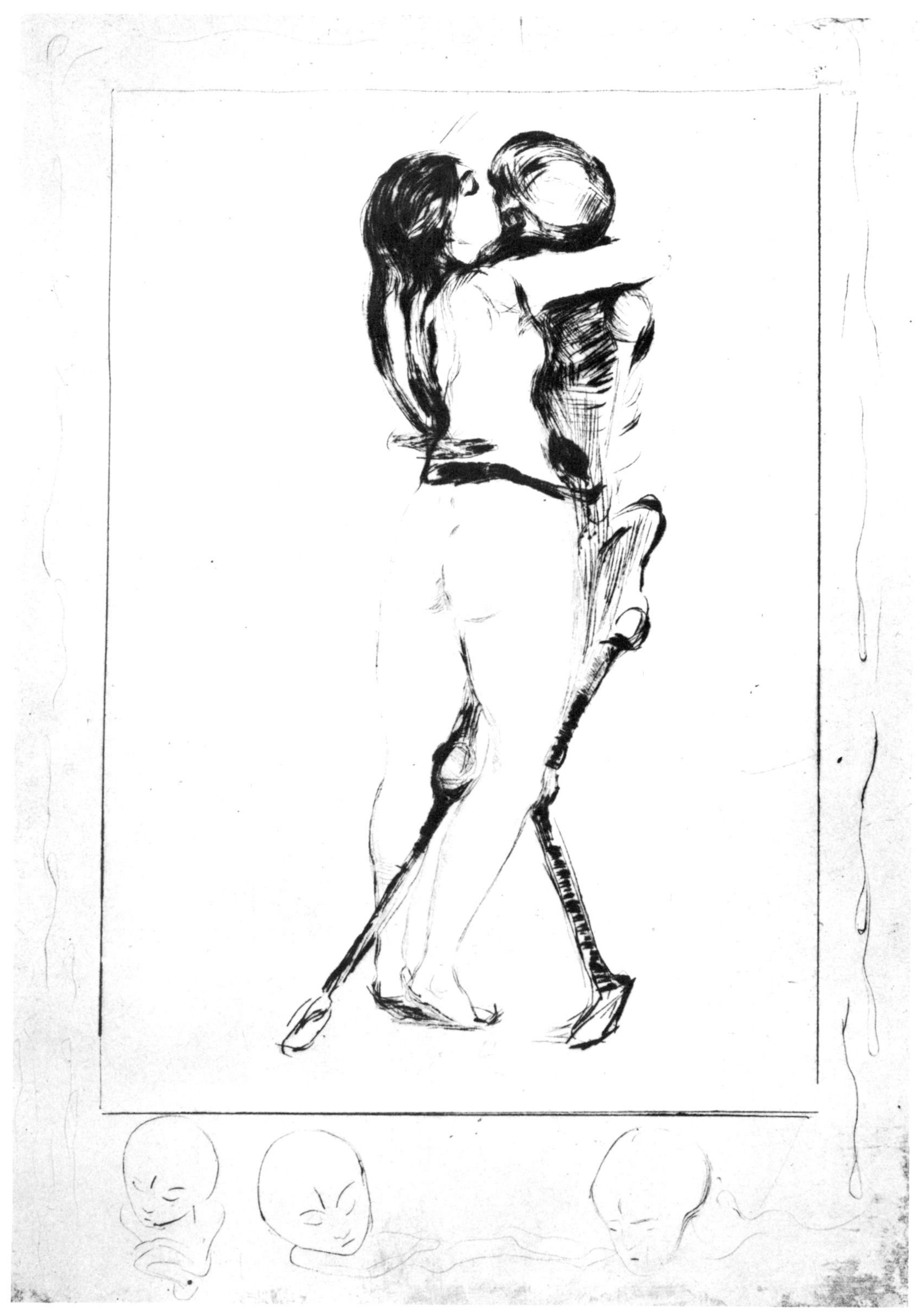

• 112 •

Edvard Munch (Norwegian, 1863–1944)

DEATH AND THE MAIDEN, 1894

Drypoint (ii/ii/b), 12 x 8¾" (30.5 x 22.2 cm)

Purchased: SmithKline Beckman Corporation Fund

1983-36-1

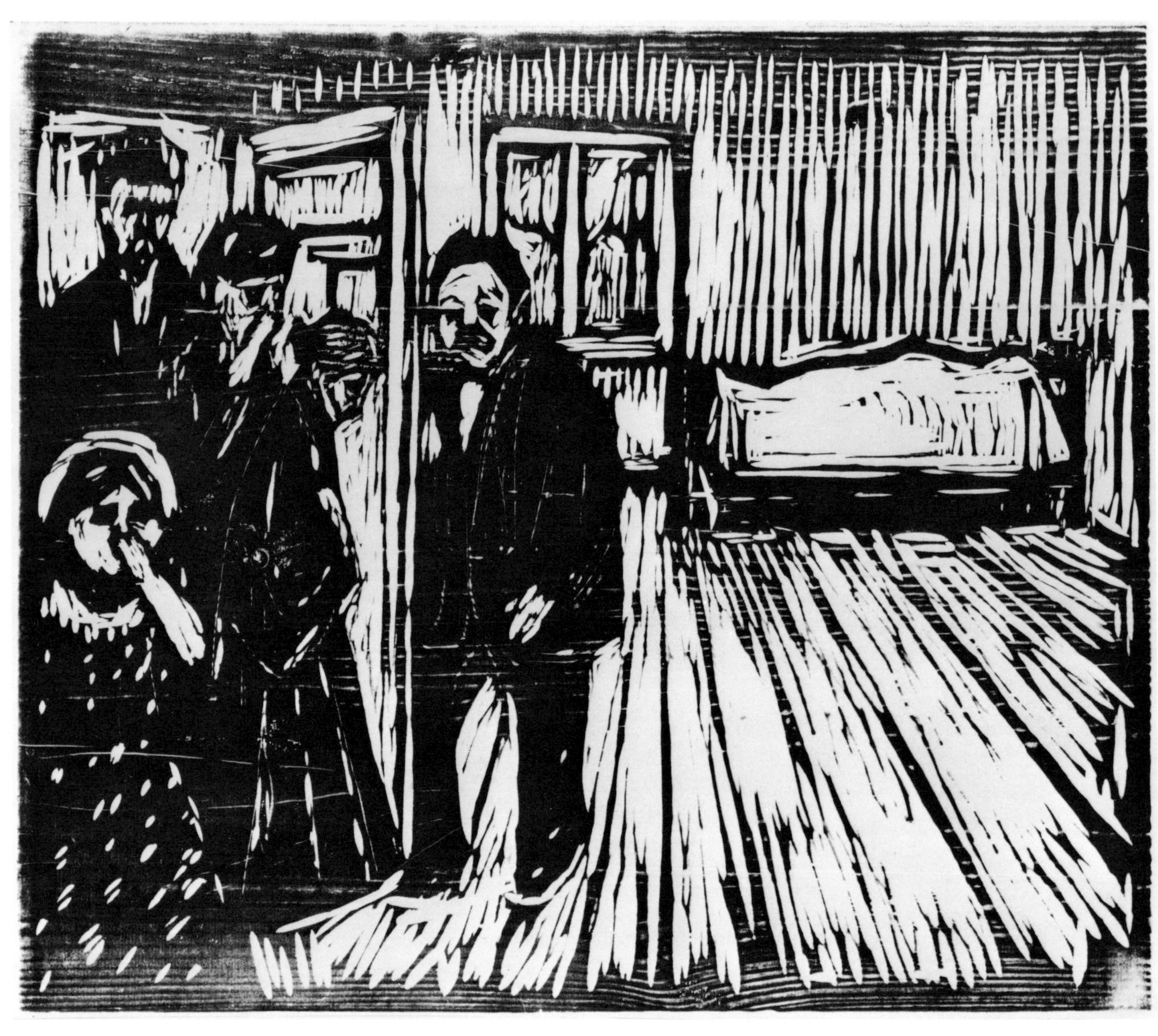

• 113 •

Edvard Munch (Norwegian, 1863–1944)

VISIT OF CONDOLENCE, 1904 (inscribed 1912)

Woodcut, 19½ x 23½″ (49.5 x 59.7 cm)

Purchased: SmithKline Beckman Corporation Fund

1980-18-3

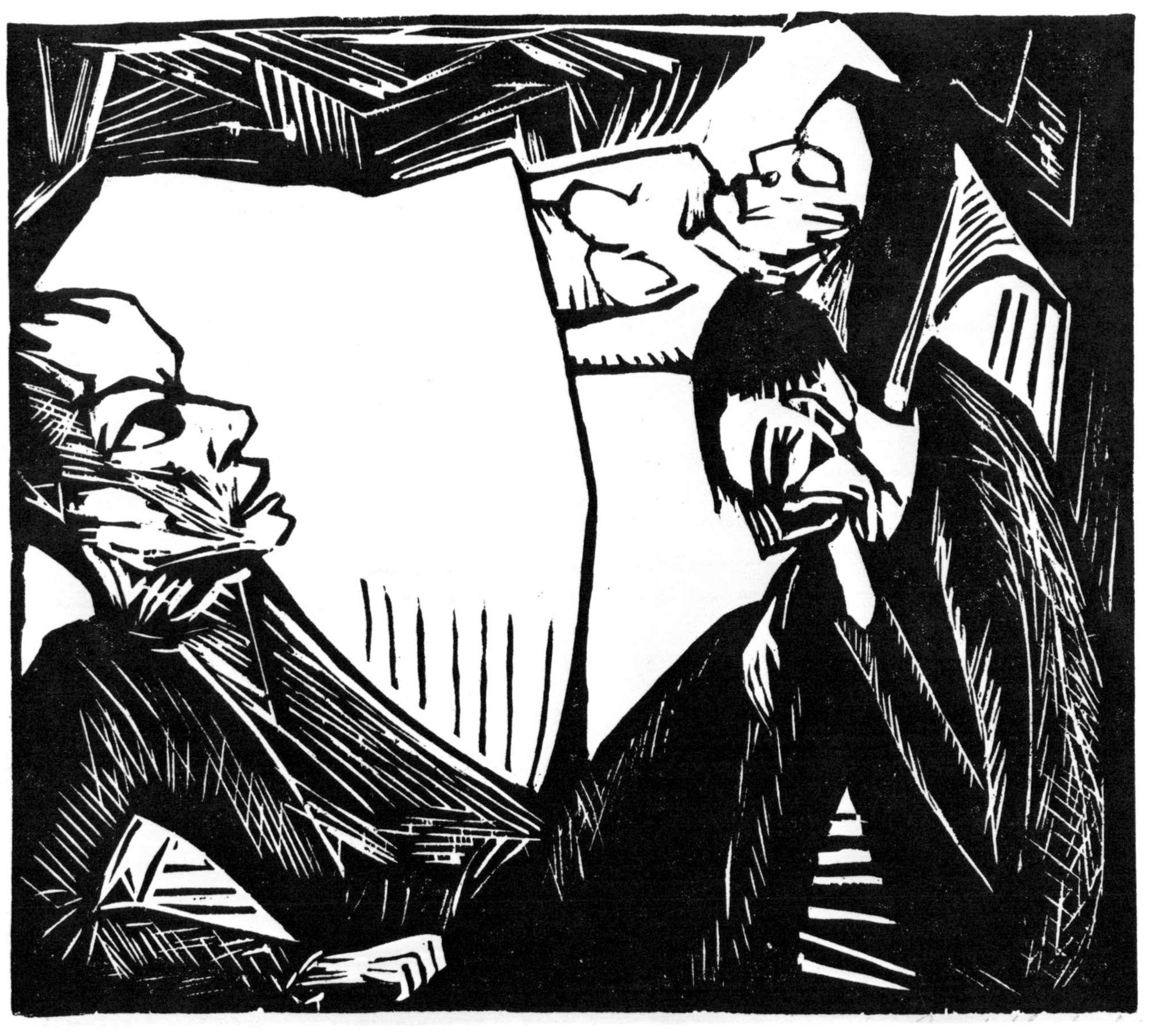

• 114 •

Erich Heckel (German, 1883–1970)

THE DEAD WOMAN, 1912 (inscribed 1919)

Woodcut (ii/ii), 9 13/16 x 11 11/16" (24.9 x 29.7 cm)

Purchased: SmithKline Beckman Corporation Fund

1983-35-1

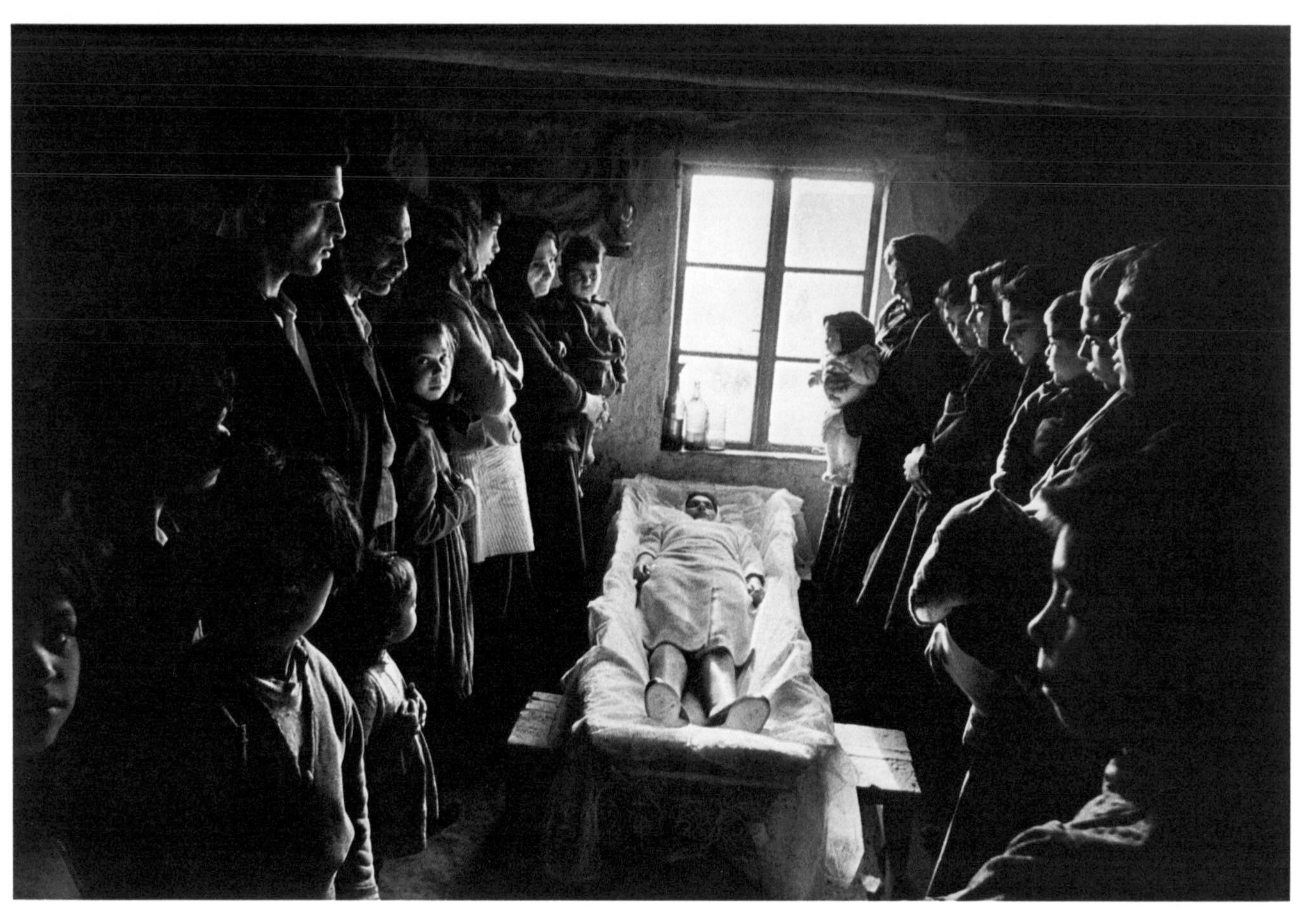

• 115 •

Josef Koudelka (Czechoslovakian, born 1938)

JARABINA, 1963

Gelatin silver print, 9³⁄₁₆ x 14¹⁄₁₆" (23.4 x 35.8 cm)

Purchased: The Contemporary Photographers Exhibition Fund

1977-231-1

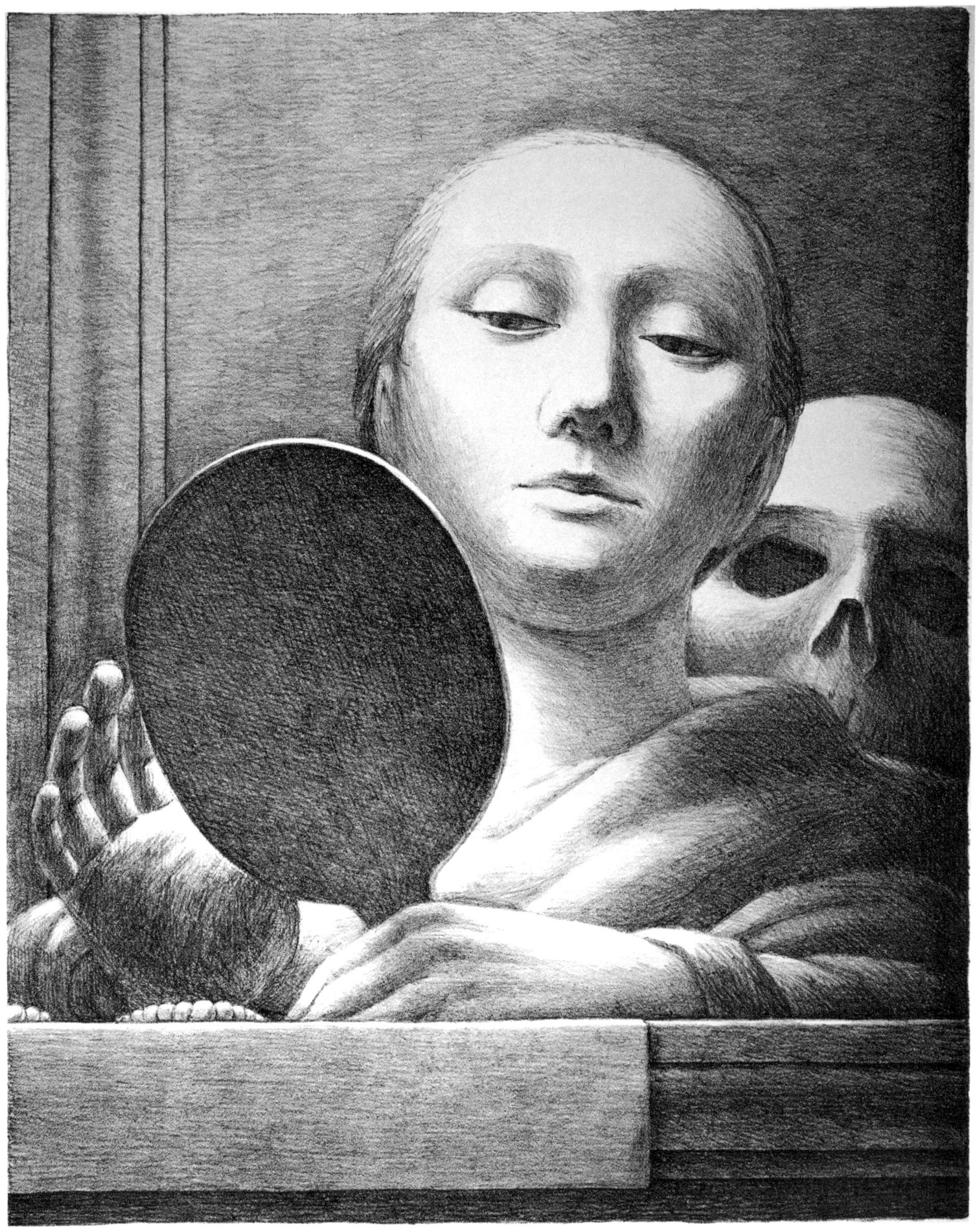

• 116 •

George Tooker (American, born 1920)

THE MIRROR, 1975

Color lithograph, 19 15/16 x 16 1/8" (50.6 x 41 cm)

Purchased: SmithKline Beckman Corporation Fund

1982-116-1

ANATOMY

1

Anonymous (Italian, late fifteenth century)
ZODIAC MAN, 1493

From Johannes de Ketham, *Fasciculus Medicinae* (Venice: Cesarem Arrivabenum, 1522)
Woodcut, 11 7/16 x 8 5/16" (29.1 x 21.1 cm)
Purchased: SmithKline Beckman Corporation Fund
49-97-3e

This elegant and ingenious image, which synthesizes ancient astrological elements with modern Renaissance realism, is from the 1522 edition of an illustrated medical treatise, the *Fasciculus Medicinae*, first published in Latin in Venice in 1491. The edition history of the work between 1491 and 1523 attests to its enormous if transitory popularity: During those years no less than fourteen editions appeared, in both Latin and Italian. The work was a landmark in anatomical literature because, for the first time, the illustrations were accorded a place of honor on a par with the text.

The 1491 Latin text consisted of a compilation of earlier writings on anatomy and dissection. The first Italian edition of 1493 was considerably expanded with the addition of the *Anothomia* by the noted fourteenth-century Bolognese physician Mondino de' Luzzi (Mundinus). That edition also boasted several lively and realistic narrative scenes (see nos. 2 and 24) as well as newly designed and cut blocks for some of the more traditional subjects, such as this *Zodiac Man.*

In overall format this figure is modeled on the Zodiac Man in the 1491 edition, but here the man and the zodiacal representations are less schematic and the entire composition is better integrated. The charmingly relaxed figure of Aquarius the Water-Bearer casually pours water into the hole in the ground (grave?), Gemini the Twins are balanced on the man's arms, and Leo the Lion and Taurus the Bull are drawn realistically. All this is in contrast with the earlier version, in which the drawing and cutting were cruder and the zodiacal details were incongruously applied to the main figure.

This and other standard figures in the anatomical and medical literature of the time such as the Wound and Bloodletting Manikins (see nos. 4a,b), which served as treatment charts for the physician, are diagrams that describe locations and functions (or malfunctions) of the organs and body parts. Zodiac Man also incorporated notions of the localized power of astrological signs over anatomy and disease. He is closely linked to the Bloodletting Manikin in that both provided directions for bloodletting sites, with diagnosis based on examination of the blood. Zodiac Man was also consulted as a guide for other purgation treatments, as an aid to dietary recommendations and proscriptions, and as a tool for predicting the patient's future, sometimes even the probable mode of death.

Although the history of bloodletting as an all-purpose remedy can be traced back to classical antiquity, the incorporation of astrological wisdom in medical treatises apparently was of oriental origin and arrived on the scene of late medieval Western medicine by way of Greek manuscripts. Manuscript illustrations that served as bloodletting charts appeared in the thirteenth century and continued with increasing frequency until, by the mid-fifteenth century, they had become an essential part of the practitioner's equipment. They were so common that in Germany, from the mid-fifteenth century on, annual printed almanacs of bloodletting and purging were illustrated with diagrams such as Zodiac Man.

M.C.

2

Anonymous (Italian, late fifteenth century)
Possibly after designs by Gentile Bellini (Italian, c. 1429–1507)
ANATOMY LESSON, 1495

From Johannes de Ketham, *Fasciculus Medicinae* (Venice: Cesarem Arrivabenum, 1522)
Woodcut, 11 7/16 x 8 1/4" (29.1 x 20.9 cm)
Purchased: SmithKline Beckman Corporation Fund
49-97-3d

The addition of Mondino de' Luzzi's *Anothomia* to the 1493 edition of the *Fasciculus Medicinae* (see no. 1) enabled the publishers to include this remarkable woodcut of a dissection scene. Because the illustration immediately precedes the Mondino text, it is thought to be an imaginary depiction of the Bolognese physician himself conducting an anatomy lesson—an anachronism since the figures are in contemporary dress and Mondino had died in 1326. The dynamic realism of this and the other illustrations newly designed for the edition parallels the editor's introduction to Mondino's text: "Here begins the most worthy Fasciculus of Medicine in the vulgar tongue. It treats of all the infirmities of man, the body of man, and the anatomy thereof." This was a proud and ambitious claim in the full Renaissance sense, made regardless of the fact that the text was traditional.

In this illustration the physician sits in the cathedra of the university, lecturing while the dissection proceeds on the lower plane. The chief protagonists are the demonstrator on the right, pointing to the cadaver and giving directions, and the dissector who, with sleeves rolled up, actually does the work. The dissection scene that had appeared in the 1493 edition in color, which had been added by stencil, was recut for the third edition of 1495, perhaps because the block had broken. This recut print, somewhat cruder than the original of 1493, does not have color additions. The distinctive portraits are altered, perhaps to show a new dramatis personae, and the original *risus sardonicus* (sardonic smile) on the corpse's face, a pathetic clinical manifestation of rigor mortis, is lost. The positions of the participating physicians are changed, and one who had been youthful and bearded is somewhat older.

Much has been written about this illustration as graphic evidence of the medieval distinction between the anatomist-physician reading from classical texts and the menials to whom the actual process of dissection was relegated. In fact, this traditional view is being modified: Mondino, by his own account, dissected, as did other major predecessors of Vesalius, such as his teacher Sylvius. The strength of this image lies in the unity, not the separation, of the physician and dissectors. Stylistically, all the actors in the drama are rendered with equal attention to almost portraitlike verisimilitude, and they exist in a rational space, which is given a sense of locale with its view out the window.

M.C.

3

Anonymous (German, early sixteenth century)
EXACT ANATOMY OF THE BONE STRUCTURE OF MAN, 1517

Inserted in Hans von Gersdorff, *Feldtbuch der Wundartzney* . . . (Strasbourg: Hans Schotten, 1540)
Hand-colored woodcut, 11 5/16 x 9 1/4" (28.7 x 23.5 cm)
Purchased: SmithKline Beckman Corporation Fund
49-97-11a

The Alsatian surgeon Hans von Gersdorff's *Feldtbuch der Wundartzney*, first published in 1517, offered the physician and surgeon a well-organized handbook for the care of those wounded in combat. The beautiful, hand-colored woodcuts in this volume illustrated surgical scenes, medical instruments, and methods of treatment (see nos. 25a, b). By the early sixteenth century certain traditional figures (see no. 1), which were used as guides for treatment, had become standard in medical and anatomical texts;[1] among those that appeared in von Gersdorff's handbook are this diagrammatic skeleton structure and Wound and Bloodletting Manikins (see nos. 4a, b).

Although its conception may be of an earlier date,[2] this skeleton was first issued in 1517 by the Strasbourg printer Hans Schotten as a loose anatomic sheet, perhaps as a broadside to be used by barbers and surgeons. This and a separate bloodletting figure (no. 4b) were folded and inserted into the first edition of von Gersdorff's handbook.[3] In its original format, a lengthy title was printed above the skeleton and verses of poetry reflecting on death were included below. Such a reference, a memento mori, or reminder of death, relating the skeleton and death, often appears in anatomic illustrations as well as in numerous artists' prints.

Entitled *Exact Anatomy of the Bone Structure of Man,* the skeleton demonstrates the early sixteenth-century concept of human skeletal structure. The most noticeable inaccuracies are the pinched-bowl effect of the pelvis, with its unsocketed hips, and the free-floating lower ribs. While some effort was made to model the skeleton, it appears to lie flat on the page, no more a demonstration of three-dimensional structure than the randomly aligned legend notations that surround it.

1. See Charles Singer, "Description of the *Fasciculo di Medicina,* Venice," in Johannes de Ketham, *The Fasciculo di Medicina* (1493; facsimile reprint, Florence, 1925), vol. 1, p. 18.
2. The format for this skeleton may have been drawn from the sepulcher created in the 1490s for Duke Albrecht, Bishop of Strasbourg, in the Marienkapelle at Zabern, as is indicated by the original title printed above the skeleton.
3. It was also used in Laurentio Phryesen von Colmar's *Spiegel der Artzny* . . . , published by Johannes Grieninger in Strasbourg in 1518; see Josef Benzing, "Bibliographie der Schriften des Colmarer Arztes Lorenz Fries," *Philobiblon*, vol. 6, no. 2 (June 1962), pp. 129–32.

D.K.

4a

Anonymous (German, early sixteenth century)
WOUND MANIKIN, 1517

From Hans von Gersdorff, *Feldtbuch der Wundartzney* . . . (Strasbourg: Hans Schotten, 1540)
Hand-colored woodcut, 10⁵⁄₁₆ x 7³⁄₁₆" (26.2 x 18.3 cm)
Purchased: SmithKline Beckman Corporation Fund
49-97-11m

4b

Anonymous (German, early sixteenth century)
BLOODLETTING MANIKIN, 1517

From Hans von Gersdorff, *Feldtbuch der Wundartzney* . . . (Strasbourg: Hans Schotten, 1540)
Hand-colored woodcut, 9¹³⁄₁₆ x 6¹⁵⁄₁₆" (24.9 x 17.7 cm)
Purchased: SmithKline Beckman Corporation Fund
49-97-11b

Hans von Gersdorff's handbook for the treatment of those wounded in battle—the *Feldtbuch der Wundartzney* (see no. 3), first published in 1517 and reprinted in several later editions—included among its illustrated guides for medical care Wound and Bloodletting Manikins.

Man's earliest notions about human anatomy were based in part on experience with wounds, most often inflicted in combat. During the Middle Ages the Wound Manikin had become a popular graphic treatment used to aid in such observation, serving as both a catalogue of frequent injuries and a chart indicating locations for the ligation of arteries. The inscription above this illustration from von Gersdorff's field manual (no. 4a) describes the manikin as a model for the medical treatment of the foot soldier, who is said to suffer the price of his profession. The wounded man's body is pierced by arrows, swords, spears, and clubs[1]—weapons the soldier typically encountered in battle. The diagram's simplicity expanded the possibilities for its use, and the manikin was intended to serve as a guide for the barber-surgeon performing bloodlettings in the bathhouse as well as the surgeon on the battlefield.

The *Bloodletting Manikin* (no. 4b) was perhaps redesigned and recut to replace a chart that, along with the skeleton figure (no. 3), was originally published in 1517 as a single sheet that was then folded and inserted in the first edition of the *Feldtbuch*. Although the image may have been reworked on a smaller block to correspond to the size of the book, both the larger, folded sheet and the smaller version can be found in 1517 editions of the handbook. This figure illustrated Guy de Chauliac's fourteenth-century surgical treatise that was published in von Gersdorff's book.

In this woodcut, as in many early bloodletting figures, the sites for bloodletting are marked with letters that correspond to sections of the text, and the abdominal and thoracic cavities are opened to render more strikingly the relationships of the internal organs. The hand coloring of the print beautifies the cut as it clarifies and reinforces these relationships.

Moving away from the mere repetition of earlier anatomical images, the artist has joined traditional stylized formats with new data obtained from actual observation to provide the most accurate rendering of the viscera *in situ* available in printed form at the time. The significance of this approach toward the representation of the human body is underlined by the fact that verses beneath the original version of the figure explained that the image was drawn from observations of a dissection performed in 1517 on the body of a hanged criminal. The manikin's abdomen contains a spherical stomach, slipper-shaped spleen, and simplified gall bladder, kidney, and vessels, all made visible by the movement of the intestines to one side. The trilobed liver, although still not completely accurate, is a marked improvement over the traditional five-lobed organ derived from the descriptions written by Galen in the second century A.D. The treatment of the thoracic area also shows that the artist had seen an actual dissection, for the lungs are prominent and fill the cavity surrounding the heart.

1. Karl Sudhoff ("Der 'Wundenmann' in Frühdruck und Handschrift und sein erklärender Text: Ein Beitrag zur Quellengeschichte des 'Ketham,'" *Archiv für Geschichte der Medizin*, vol. 1 [1908], pp. 351–61) has compared the Wound Manikin to images of Saint Sebastian, whose form of martyrdom may have been a model for these multipunctured figures.

D.K.

5a

Anonymous, possibly by François (Jean) Jollat (French, active 1502–50)
After Perino del Vaga (Italian, 1501–1547) and possibly Etienne de la Rivière (French, died 1569)
FEMALE FIGURE, 1530–39

From Charles Estienne, *La Dissection des parties du corps humain* . . . (Paris: Simon de Colines, 1546)
Woodcut, 14⅞ x 9⁵⁄₁₆" (37.8 x 23.7 cm)
Purchased: SmithKline Beckman Corporation Fund
1980-93-2

5b

Anonymous, possibly by François (Jean) Jollat (French, active 1502–50)
Possibly after Etienne de la Rivière (French, died 1569)
MUSCLES OF THE BACK, 1530–39

From Charles Estienne, *La Dissection des parties du corps humain* . . . (Paris: Simon de Colines, 1546)
Woodcut, 14¹⁵⁄₁₆ x 9½" (38 x 24.1 cm)
Purchased: SmithKline Beckman Corporation Fund
1980-93-5

5c

Anonymous, possibly by François (Jean) Jollat (French, active 1502–50)
Possibly after Etienne de la Rivière (French, died 1569)
PERIPHERAL NERVOUS SYSTEM, 1530–39

From Charles Estienne, *La Dissection des parties du corps humain . . .* (Paris: Simon de Colines, 1546)
Woodcut, 14 15/16 x 9 3/8" (38 x 23.8 cm)
Purchased: SmithKline Beckman Corporation Fund
1980-93-3

De Dissectione Partium Corporis Humani, a collaborative effort between Charles Estienne, Humanist author, poet, publisher, and physician, and Etienne de la Rivière, surgeon and anatomist, has angered, delighted, and bemused historians of anatomical illustration for some years. The illustrations have been called hideous, distorted, and ugly, with bodies "placed in queer and repulsive positions."[1] At the same time the elegance of certain figures has rightly been identified as the product of a sophisticated artist, a master in the French Renaissance tradition.

The earliest of the woodcut illustrations is dated 1530; the plates were complete and the text was printed up to midway in Book Three (the final book) by 1539. The fact that *De Dissectione* did not actually appear until 1545—the French edition shown here was published the next year—was due to a lawsuit brought by Rivière against Estienne over the credit to be given to each in the final publication. As the title page shows, the courts decided that the credit was to be shared equally. In the process, however, six years were lost, which affected later critical assessment of the book because it was published after Vesalius's *Fabrica* (see nos. 8a–g). Vesalius, who studied in Paris from 1533 to 1536, would have been aware of Estienne's work and would probably have seen some of the illustrations, issued first as single-sheet woodcuts.

A number of innovative features that were to influence later illustrated anatomical works through Vesalius's widely acclaimed and distributed book did in fact make their first appearance in this work. Among them were the illustration of dissection in serial progression; the discussion and illustration of the total human organism (muscles, bones, internal organs, venous and arterial systems, cranium, nerves, glands, and joints); the mode of illustrating the visceral organs as cutout sections within a "living" torso; directions for mounting a skeleton; setting the figures in a fully developed panoramic landscape (a concept that had been seen in rudimentary form in the anatomical works of Jacopo Berengario da Carpi twenty years earlier); and a comprehensive index.

One factor that has surely contributed to the wildly diverging critical opinion on *De Dissectione* is that the book lacks the imagistic coherence of the *Fabrica*. However, despite the variation in quality—from crude to exquisite—from image to image, the best illustrations are superb examples of the French Mannerist drawing and woodcut tradition, and the quality of the typography, the paper, and the general presentation equals the highest standard of French book production of the period.

The remarkable images from the gynecological series in Book Three show women in exaggerated poses of physical abandon on ornate chairs or beds, most set in rich if perspectively incorrect domestic interiors. An odd feature of the prints is that the parts of the blocks showing the dissected uterus, as well as the plaques containing the anatomical texts, were cut separately and set into the main block for printing. It has been suggested that the blocks were originally intended for another anatomical publication, possibly one that Vasari says was begun by the Italian Mannerist artist Rosso Fiorentino before his arrival in France in 1530.[2] The argument is based on hypothesis, however, and final proof is lacking.

A direct correlation does exist, however, between the female figures in Book Three and the amorous goddesses in the illustrations for a slightly earlier series of prints, "The Loves of the Gods," engraved by Gian Giacomo Caraglio after drawings by Rosso Fiorentino and Perino del Vaga.[3] The male partners have been eliminated and most of the action has been moved indoors, but the frankly erotic poses were retained and from this the resulting images gain their strange power. The synthesis of sexual activity and anatomical dissection, the implicit statement that both represent incursions into personal space on an intimate level, was brilliant. *Female Figure* (no. 5a), from a design by Perino for Doris and Neptune embracing, is particularly poignant in this respect, as a comparison with the figure of Doris shows. In the anatomical print the position of the right arm has been altered as if to ward off either the onlooker or the dissector; her features, hidden in the Caraglio print by the face of Neptune who kisses her, gain an expression of pain and lassitude here, exacerbated by the deep shadows around her eye. Faint and highly sophisticated echoes of sadism have crept in. This element recurs over the centuries, particularly in female dissection, but it is seldom stated as frankly as in Estienne's work.

The identity of the artists who did the Estienne illustrations remains obscure. Three monograms that occur throughout the book indicate that an artist by the name of Jollat—or perhaps two artists with that name—was responsible for them, but Jollat's particular involvement as designer or engraver remains enigmatic.[4] The consistently high level of woodcut technique (with the possible exception of some of the insets mentioned above) is so at odds with the great variation in the quality of the drawings from which the cutter worked that one is tempted to posit the existence of a number of designers-draftsmen and one skilled studio of cutters-craftsmen.

The illustration of the muscles of the back (no. 5b) from Book One, which depicts standing male figures in varying degrees of dissection and shows, image by image, the muscle layers, nerves, and skeletons, points up the difficulty in assigning artistic responsibility for the images. In contrast to the enigmatic and tormented figures of men and women undergoing dissection in Books Two and Three, and even compared with other figures in Book One, it is stiff and unconvincing. Although the portrayal and identification of the muscles indicate that it was done from actual dissection, it is nonetheless artistically inept—the arms and hands, for example, are disproportionately large in comparison with the feet—yet the engraving technique is of high quality. It is part of a group that includes some plates with the monogram of Jollat, who may have been responsible for cutting the block, possibly working from an anatomist's diagram rather than from an artist's drawing.

The two nerve men, the anterior and this posterior view (no. 5c), follow the skeleton in the dissection sequence of Book One. The idea of combining the representation of the nervous system with the skeleton was novel; the resulting images are some of the most engaging, although this undoubtedly was not Estienne's intention. The frivolity of the nerve men stems partly from their jaunty stance in the landscape and partly from the drawing of the nerves, depicted almost as decorative bits of knotted ribbon appropriate to a sixteenth-century costume.

The problem that faced the artist commissioned with such a subject is almost impossible to comprehend. There was no artistic precedent to aid him in the task of rendering in clear linear form some image that would be intelligible to the block cutter. Aside from dissection, the method then used to reduce the human body to bones and nerves, which was suggested by Mondino and apparently practiced by Rivière, was to place a cadaver in a cask drilled with holes and submerge it in a river for a period of time.[5] The resulting chaotic mass would have reduced any artist to the decorative solution that Estienne's artist did, in fact, choose.

1. Ludwig Choulant, *History and Bibliography of Anatomic Illustration*, ed. and trans. Mortimer Frank, rev. ed. (1945; reprint, New York, 1962), p. 153.
2. C. E. Kellett, "A Note on Rosso and the Illustrations to Charles Estienne's *De dissectione,*" *Journal of the History of Medicine*, vol. 12 (July 1957), pp. 325–36.
3. C. E. Kellett, "Perino del Vaga et les illustrations pour l'anatomie d'Estienne," *Aesculape*, vol. 37, no. 4 (April 1955), pp. 74–89.
4. See Robert Herrlinger, *History of Medical Illustration from Antiquity to A.D. 1600* (Nijkerk, The Netherlands, 1970), pp. 88–101.
5. C. E. Kellett, "Two Anatomies," *Medical History*, vol. 8 (1964), pp. 344–46.

M.C.

6
Monogrammist M. F. Possibly after Melchior Meier (German/Swiss, active 1580s) APOLLO AND MARSYAS, sixteenth century

Engraving, 9 x 12¼" (22.8 x 31.1 cm) (trimmed)
Purchased: SmithKline Beckman Corporation Fund
1982-36-1

This rare and striking print, which bears a cartouche with the date of 1536 and the initials *MF*, is one of the most fascinating in the history of early anatomical illustration. The identity of Monogrammist M. F. is still a mystery. The composition of the print is identical (in reverse) to that of an engraving bearing the date 1581 and the initials *MM*, attributed to a sixteenth-century German-born artist, Melchior Meier.[1] The almost fifty-year discrepancy in dates between the two prints would seem to suggest that the Meier print is a copy of the M. F., but the matter is not so simple. A stylistic comparison between certain details seen in both prints—such as the origins and insertions of Marsyas's muscles, the handling of the cloud formations and the landscape background, the delineation of facial features in the crowd of onlookers, and the foreground rock and tree-stump shapes—suggests that the artist responsible for the 1581 print had a better comprehension both of human anatomy and of the engraver's technique than did his ostensible predecessor, Monogrammist M. F. Also, the Meier engraving shows Apollo holding his flaying knife quite realistically in his right hand, whereas in the M. F. print he holds it, oddly, in his left.[2] Was the print that bears the earlier date in fact copied from the one that is dated later? This would imply a falsified date, which is difficult to explain. A more interesting hypothesis is that both prints could have been done independently on the basis of an original drawing, perhaps itself bearing a 1536 date, which can no longer be traced. These questions have important implications for the history of anatomical illustration, as the anatomical accuracy of the flayed Marsyas would be extraordinarily advanced for a date of 1536, seven years before the appearance of Vesalius's *Fabrica* (see nos. 8a–g). Several scholars, in fact, have attempted to prove that the famous standing *écorché* holding his own skin in Juan de Valverde's *Anatomia* of 1556 (one of his few images not copied from Vesalius) was drawn from the Apollo in the M. F. print, a most convincing proposal had it been borne out by the dates.[3]

The composition of the M. F. engraving demonstrates an important feature more characteristic of the High Renaissance than late-sixteenth-century art in its front-plane, friezelike composition.[4] Moreover, it seems improbable that a mere craftsman would have been capable of either the marvelously inventive composition or the high quality of draftsmanship seen here.

Equally remarkable is the selection and treatment of

the subject itself. The story, from the sixth book of Ovid's *Metamorphoses,* tells how the satyr Marsyas had the bad judgment to challenge the god of music, Apollo, to a contest pitting his flute against Apollo's lyre. The outcome was predictable, and Apollo claimed his right to punish the satyr by flaying him alive, to the distress of his satyric comrades. The subject (along with its religious counterpart, the Flaying of Saint Bartholomew) was often used by artists as a vehicle for demonstrating their skills at portraying the superficial muscle layers. This particular presentation, largely because of the detailed depiction of the cadaver (for that is what it is), can also be read as a subtle reference to the two major sources of inspiration and erudition for Renaissance man: classical antiquity (the figure of Apollo certainly has the proportions and, to some extent, the pose of the Apollo Belvedere) and empirical observation, signified by the act of dissection.

1. Adam Bartsch, *Le Peintre graveur,* vol. 16 (Vienna, 1818), pp. 246–47. This print is dedicated to Francesco de' Medici, which suggests that Meier also worked in Italy.
2. I am indebted to Janet Byrne, Curator, Department of Prints, The Metropolitan Museum of Art, New York, for these observations, as well as for having kindly informed me that A. Hyatt Mayor, former Curator of Prints at the Metropolitan, had written on the mat of the M. F. print: "Date 1536 probably wrong, as this seems to be copied from Melchior Meier's engraving, 1581. The dissection looks post-Vesalian" (Byrne to Cazort, December 19, 1983). Apparently the first scholar to cast doubt upon the date was Eugen Holländer in *Die Medizin in der klassischen Malerei* (Stuttgart, 1913), vol. 2, p. 11.
3. L. H. Wells discusses the matter thoroughly in two articles: "A Note on the Valverde Muscle-Man," *Medical History*, vol. 3 (1959), pp. 212–14, figs. 1–5; and "The 'M. F.' Engraving and the Valverde Muscle-Man: A Correction," *Medical History*, vol. 5 (1961), p. 197.
4. This has been suggested by Diane Karp.

M.C.

7a

Hans Baldung Grien (German, 1484/85–1545)
DISSECTION OF THE SCALP AND EXPOSURE OF THE HEMISPHERES OF THE BRAIN, 1541

From Walter Hermann Ryff, *Des aller fürtrefflichsten . . . gschöpffs aller Creaturen . . . beschreibung oder Anatomi* (Strasbourg: Balthasar Beck, 1541)
Hand-colored woodcut, 12 x 15⅛" (30.5 x 38.4 cm)
Purchased: SmithKline Beckman Corporation Fund
1982-40-1h,i

7b

Hans Baldung Grien (German, 1484/85–1545)
REMOVAL OF THE PIA MATER AND A CROSS-SECTION OF THE BRAIN, 1541

From Walter Hermann Ryff, *Des aller fürtrefflichsten . . . gschöpffs aller Creaturen . . . beschreibung oder Anatomi* (Strasbourg: Balthasar Beck, 1541)
Hand-colored woodcut, 12 x 15⅛" (30.5 x 38.4 cm)
Purchased: SmithKline Beckman Corporation Fund
1982-40-1j,k

This series of woodcuts came from an illustrated volume on anatomy compiled by Walter Ryff and published in 1541. The illustrations are by the Strasbourg artist Hans Baldung Grien, who may have worked in the shop of Albrecht Dürer in his youth. For the format of these woodcuts depicting the anatomy and dissection of the head and brain, the artist depended on Johann Dryander's *Anatomiae*, published in 1537, but greatly improved and enlarged the quality of the images.

The series demonstrates the successive stages of dissection of the cranium: In the first two illustrations shown here (no. 7a), the scalp is peeled back to reveal the cranium; then, with the tools drawn below, the upper part of the cranium is removed to uncover the hemispheres of the brain. The next two (no. 7b) demonstrate the removal of the pia mater to reveal a schematized cross-section of the left and right hemispheres. Each layer—dermis, epidermis, duramater (the fibrous membrane enveloping the brain), and so forth—is clearly distinguished and marked, and again the tools for the procedure are pictured underneath. The head is masterfully rendered in convincing three-dimensional volume with only an outline and short, parallel lines for modeling. The hand coloring, contemporary to the woodcuts, adds a marked dimensionality to each plate. It has been suggested that these prints are so heavily soiled because they were frequently used by surgeons during actual operations.

D.K.

8a

Anonymous, possibly by Jan Stevensz. van Calcar (Flemish, c. 1499–c. 1550)
VESALIUS CONDUCTING AN ANATOMICAL DISSECTION, 1543

From Andreas Vesalius, *De Humani Corporis Fabrica* (Basel: Johannes Oporinus, 1543)
Woodcut, 15¹⁵⁄₁₆ x 10⅝" (40.5 x 27 cm)
Purchased: SmithKline Beckman Corporation Fund
49-97-41a

8b

Anonymous, possibly by Jan Stevensz. van Calcar (Flemish, c. 1499–c. 1550)
THE FIRST PLATE OF MUSCLES, 1543

From Andreas Vesalius, *De Humani Corporis Fabrica* (Basel: Johannes Oporinus, 1543)
Woodcut, 15¹⁵⁄₁₆ x 10⅝" (40.5 x 27 cm)
Purchased: SmithKline Beckman Corporation Fund
49-97-41f

8c

Anonymous, possibly by Jan Stevensz. van Calcar (Flemish, c. 1499–c. 1550)
THE NINTH PLATE OF MUSCLES, 1543

From Andreas Vesalius, *De Humani Corporis Fabrica* (Basel: Johannes Oporinus, 1543)
Woodcut, 15 15/16 x 10 5/8" (40.5 x 27 cm)
Purchased: SmithKline Beckman Corporation Fund
49-97-41d

8d

Anonymous, possibly by Jan Stevensz. van Calcar (Flemish, c. 1499–c. 1550)
THE SEVENTH PLATE OF MUSCLES, 1543

From Andreas Vesalius, *De Humani Corporis Fabrica* (Basel: Johannes Oporinus, 1543)
Woodcut, 15 15/16 x 10 5/8" (40.5 x 27 cm)
Purchased: SmithKline Beckman Corporation Fund
49-97-41h

8e

Anonymous, possibly by Jan Stevensz. van Calcar (Flemish, c. 1499–c. 1550)
THE THIRTEENTH PLATE OF MUSCLES, 1543

From Andreas Vesalius, *De Humani Corporis Fabrica* (Basel: Johannes Oporinus, 1543)
Woodcut, 15 15/16 x 10 5/8" (40.5 x 27 cm)
Purchased: SmithKline Beckman Corporation Fund
49-97-41i

8f

Anonymous, possibly by Jan Stevensz. van Calcar (Flemish, c. 1499–c. 1550)
ANTERIOR VIEW OF THE SKELETON, 1543

From Andreas Vesalius, *De Humani Corporis Fabrica* (Basel: Johannes Oporinus, 1543)
Woodcut, 15 15/16 x 10 1/2" (40.5 x 26.7 cm)
Purchased: SmithKline Beckman Corporation Fund
49-97-41c

8g

Anonymous, possibly by Jan Stevensz. van Calcar (Flemish, c. 1499–c. 1550)
DELINEATION OF THE VENA CAVA, 1543

From Andreas Vesalius, *De Humani Corporis Fabrica* (Basel: Johannes Oporinus, 1543)
Woodcut, 15 15/16 x 10 5/8" (40.5 x 27 cm)
Purchased: SmithKline Beckman Corporation Fund
49-97-41e

Two books, published in Basel in 1543, have come to signify the seamless collaboration of scientist, artist, craftsman, and publisher that has been repeatedly cited as typical of peak Renaissance achievement. *De Humani Corporis Fabrica* and *Epitome* have been known collectively ever since as "Vesalius," after the anatomist and entrepreneur Andreas Vesalius of Brussels (1514–1564). *Fabrica*, the more elaborate of the two, consists of seven *libri* (chapters) that present the structure of the human body through woodcut illustrations accompanied by a Latin text and keyed to indices that label various body parts. *Epitome*, a slender volume of the same-size format that has a number of the same woodcuts used in *Fabrica*, is more general and was aimed at students and a less specialized market. *Epitome* also contains plates showing internal organs and arterial and venous structures, with instructions on how to cut out the printed pieces and partially glue them onto the full-figure male and female images so that, by raising the small flaps, the reader could obtain an idea of the relationship of all the parts.

The books rapidly achieved international fame, as indicated by the fact that they were instantly plagiarized. For several centuries they continued to exercise enormous influence on the mode of presenting and illustrating anatomical material for the use of both anatomists and artists. With the development of medical history as a serious discipline in the late nineteenth century, the status of Vesalius was elevated to a position just short of celestial by scholars, who isolated his achievement and claimed that his work "established with startling suddenness the beginning of modern observational science and research."[1]

Until fairly recently the general tendency was to give full credit to Vesalius himself for the conception, and sometimes even the illustrations, of the work. Recent research by scholars trained in the disciplines of both medical and art history has begun to shift the emphasis from Vesalius back to his unknown artists, as it is increasingly acknowledged that the power of the book resides more in the woodcuts than in the text, which remains obscure and has yet to be translated out of the late Humanistic Latin in which it was written. Further recent research has revealed the existence of an underlying plan in the ordering of the illustrations, which suggests that Vesalius had access to a comprehensive design by some as yet unidentified artist, which he then failed to incorporate in the final publications while still using the original images.

The elaborate title page for the first edition of *De Humani Corporis Fabrica* (no. 8a) shows Vesalius performing a dissection before a crowd of students, fellow doctors, the general public, animals, and assorted imaginary classical figures in a fanciful architectural setting. Vesalius's identity can be established by the fact that his portrait was included as the frontispiece of the first and second editions of *Fabrica*, of 1543 and 1555, as well as in the Latin and German editions of *Epitome*, both of 1543. The portrait was copied many times, both as prints and in paintings, and is the chief source of information as to Vesalius's actual appearance.

The title page is a stunning monument to Venetian sixteenth-century book illustration, both in the complexity of its design and iconography and in the skill with which it was executed. Aside from the skeleton usually associated with anatomical illustration, which signifies the result of a successful dissection and a memento mori (reminder of death), there are dogs and apes, symbols of the old, rejected anatomy of the second-century A.D. Greek physician Galen, whose descriptions of human anatomy were usually based on animal dissection in contrast to the new Renaissance anatomy, the result of human dissection. The subject of the dissection is, interestingly, a woman, derived from Vesalius's anatomy of a woman in Book Five of *Fabrica*. Although all the anatomies of internal organs in Book Five are drawn in the framework of classical torsos (a brilliant visual pun synthesizing the two major sources of anatomical knowledge for Renaissance artists—dissection and antiquity), this image is one of only two in all of "Vesalius" in which the body is recumbent and thus probably drawn directly from the cadaver. Female cadavers were hard to come by, and according to Vesalius's own account, this particular dissection necessitated a rather lurid adventure in grave robbing.

By far the best known of the illustrations to Vesalius's *Fabrica* are the full-figure dissection images, which consist of the three prints of mourning skeletons that complete Book One and the set of fourteen muscle men that initiates Book Two. It has recently been suggested that the intention of the unknown designer of the series was to arrange the muscle figures in such a way as to reflect the actual sequence of a dissection from the superficial muscle layer inward (an order reversed in the Vesalian publication).[2] If this convincing hypothesis is correct, *The First Plate of Muscles* (no. 8b) would actually have been the second in the progression of anterior views of the muscle men. It shows a frontal view of a male *écorché* at the initial stage of dissection. It has also been suggested that the woodcuts, as printed, did not take into account the right-left direction of the figures as envisaged by the original designer. Ascertaining the original context of the individual figures is important in order to understand not only the progressive anatomical revelations but also the stately and melancholy drama of the underlying concept, a drama unaccountably ignored by Vesalius in his final ordering of the images and his preparation of the text.

These figures demonstrate a basic characteristic of the Vesalian illustrations, namely the illusion of life in a body that is otherwise clearly dead, a paradox that must surely account for the hypnotic appeal of the works. Close examination of the muscle series, along with careful reading of the text available to those who do not read late Humanistic Latin, leads one to marvel at the ingenuity of the unknown artist who could fabricate the illusion of a living body in a dramatic pose out of bits of slack muscle tissue (when the messy fragments could even be seen in a crowded and hasty dissection), splicing in pieces of anatomy that in some instances only occur in animals, yet producing a convincing image.

The landscape background in the muscle series has been discussed extensively. There is general consensus that the landscapes and figures were drawn as separate entities and then joined according to a preconceived plan. It seems likely that they were the work of two separate artists. The figures are possibly by Jan Stevensz. van Calcar, a Fleming who had been a student of Titian in Venice, while the name of Domenico Campagnola (c. 1484–c. 1563), another artist from the workshop of Titian, has been suggested for the landscapes. The treatment of topography and foliage is in accord with the mid-century Venetian landscape tradition, but the inclusion of monumental Roman ruins, rotundas, pyramids, and obelisks suggests that the artist responsible was familiar with Rome, or at least with contemporary prints or drawings made in Rome. Attempts have also been made to identify the site of the Vesalian landscapes as a specific locale near Padua, but the argument is not entirely convincing.

The Ninth Plate of Muscles (no. 8c) is the corollary in terms of degree of dissection of the previous *écorché* figure. Vesalius himself designated these particular plates as being of use to artists as well as to anatomists.

In the reconstruction of the order of the series, *The Seventh Plate of Muscles* (no. 8d) would have been penultimate in the progressive dissection of the male body as seen anteriorly. It is also the first in which the figure is deprived of life despite the pathetic, artificial semblance of vitality conferred by the drooping contrapposto that the rope suspension provides: It is quite dead, propped against the wall. The dissection has probed to the interior of the chest area, although the organs are not shown. Vesalius provided an odd explanation for this image: He claimed that the figure's lax position is due to the slack position of the rope (as if he had had no control over the positioning of the figure). He also offered a quaint explanation for the peculiar detail of organic form shown flat against the wall on the right: It is the diaphragm, excised from the body, which is "owing to its flexibility, adhering to the wall,"[3] as if the ruined wall, the landscape, and other fictive elements were actually there.

The Thirteenth Plate of Muscles (no. 8e), depicting the deeper spinal muscles, would be, according to the reconstruction, the penultimate of the posterior views in the muscle series. In contrast to the anterior views, the posterior figures remain self-supporting to the bitter end.

The skeletal figures were among the most frequently copied of all the Vesalian illustrations. Although the standing, gesturing skeleton as the end product of dissection and a grim reminder of mortality (no. 8f) did not make its initial appearance in "Vesalius," the

Fabrica images are among the most poignant in all the history of anatomical illustration. If the reconstruction of the order of the plates is accepted, which would conclude the series with the three skeletons, then the drama as originally conceived is even more moving as, by this reading, the skeletons as culmination to the muscle series continue to walk and weep even after death has claimed them.

The third book of *Fabrica* is devoted to an exposition of the veins and arteries. The plate depicting the venous system (no. 8g) and its companion plate on the arterial system are the only ones in Book Three to show the full human figure, the contours of which repeat those of the graceful figure of Adam that appears in *Epitome*. The Vesalian illustrations seem to be the earliest indications in anatomical illustration that the artist, in making his drawings, used tracings to provide him with standard and repeatable full figures within which various aspects of the dissection could be shown. The procedure may have been suggested by the earlier "flap anatomies," crude figures with a series of partially glued-on overlays, and tracings were later utilized with great precision by Jan Wandelaer (see no. 13) in eighteenth-century Leiden. A simple exercise with the use of tracing paper shows that, for instance, the legs bearing the body's weight in both figures (that is, Vein Man's right and Adam's left) are precise mirror images of each other, and other sections of contour are likewise identical. It is known that sixteenth-century artists used oiled paper for tracings and image reversal. The trick was employed repeatedly throughout the Vesalian editions with considerable virtuosity in rotating the tracing, reversing some parts, and so forth.

The iconography of Vein Man, like that of the Wound Manikin (see no. 4a) and Zodiac Man (see no. 1), has its roots in medieval treatment literature. Although it is included in *Fabrica* in the context of dissection, it was of special significance to Vesalius, who had earlier been involved in a controversy, the passion of which is incomprehensible to us now: preferred bloodletting sites in relation to the afflicted body part. Since antiquity phlebotomy had been, and was to remain for several centuries, a highly regarded therapeutic practice.

1. J. B. deC. M. Saunders and Charles D. O'Malley, *The Illustrations from the Works of Andreas Vesalius of Brussels* (1950; reprint, New York, 1973), p. 9.
2. See G.S.T. Cavanagh, "A New View of the Vesalian Landscape," *Medical History*, vol. 27 (1983), pp. 77–79; and Marielena Putscher, "Ein Totentanz von Tizian: Die 17 grossen Holzschnitte zur Fabrica Vesals (1538–1542)," in *Festschrift für Professor Hans Schadewaldt zur Vollendung des 60. Lebensjahres* (Dusseldorf, 1983), pp. 30–31, pl. 15.
3. Vesalius, as translated and quoted in Saunders and O'Malley, *Illustrations from the Works of Andreas Vesalius*, p. 104.

M.C.

9
Anonymous, possibly by Juste de Juste (French, 1505–1559)
PYRAMID OF SIX MEN, 1542–48

Etching, 10⁹⁄₁₆ x 8⅛" (27 x 20.6 cm)
Purchased: SmithKline Beckman Corporation Fund
1984-52-1

The circulation of engravings of Michelangelo's *Last Judgment* in the Sistine Chapel almost immediately after it was unveiled in 1541 made its twisted, strained, and plunging nude figures accessible to artists throughout Europe. With this inspiration and the visual documentation of the human body that became available with the publication of Vesalius's *Fabrica* in 1543 (see nos. 8a–g), artists were free to portray the figure in virtually any position with an anatomical authority that lent credibility to even seemingly impossible compositions.

The fantastic grouping and exaggerated positions described in this etching, which explores the human body as an expressive medium, would have appeared foolish had the artist not understood the anatomic mechanisms that affect such actions. The six attenuated male nudes balance precariously in a "pyramid" of interlocked limbs; each figure is built up of simple etched lines and modeled with crosshatching to display the flexion and extension of the muscles. For all the implausibility of this composition its reality is convincing because of the muscular interaction of the figures that fill the entire space of the plate. The artist allowed the hand and heels to overhang just a bit at the bottom edge of the print, giving additional tension to the already dynamic composition set against a space that is remarkably undefined.

This is one of five etchings of human pyramids that may possibly be connected with Juste de Juste, a sculptor active at the château of Fontainebleau during the period of its enlargement and lavish embellishment under Francis I, king of France from 1515 to 1547. Its attenuated, elegant forms are associated with the school of Fontainebleau, where an etching workshop is assumed to have been active between 1542 and 1547 or 1548.[1] Very few impressions from this series exist and even fewer have the brilliance and freshness of this print. It is a tour de force of wit, balance, and etching technique and reveals how vital the knowledge of human anatomy had become to the artist by the mid-sixteenth century.

1. See Henri Zerner, *The School of Fontainebleau: Etchings and Engravings* (London, 1969), p. 16.

D.K.

10

Hendrik Goltzius (Dutch, 1558–1617)
THE LARGE HERCULES, 1589

Engraving (i/ii), 22⅜ x 16″ (56.8 x 40.7 cm)
Charles M. Lea Collection
28-42-1596

Hendrik Goltzius has been regarded by his own and later generations as one of the outstanding artists of his time, noted especially for his brilliant and innovative handling of the engraver's burin and for the individuality of his Mannerist style. Goltzius's large engraving of *The Large Hercules* was probably done as a bravura demonstration of the artist's skill. He created this extraordinary work, which is a masterpiece among his more than four hundred prints, at a time when he was experiencing ill health and depression, conditions that waxed and waned for most of his life. This powerful, massive image, rendered in great detail, seems to be a statement of the artist's will to dominate the physical and emotional problems that tormented him.

Goltzius, like most Dutch artists of the sixteenth and seventeenth centuries, studied anatomy in life-drawing groups such as those established at the Academy in Haarlem and by observing dissection at the University of Leiden,[1] so that the external musculature of this figure, while exaggerated and stylized with bulges, is still anatomically correct. So clearly defined is the external anatomy that this engraving was utilized as demonstration material in anatomical lectures at the university, whose chair of anatomy was established by Pieter Paaw (see no. 12) in 1589, the same year that Goltzius engraved this dramatic print.

The subject of the print is explained in the caption:

> *Who is unaware of the valor of Amphitryon's son on land and sea?*
> *Or of the cruel stepmother, source of such great wrong?*
> *He was exposed to so many monsters, to the Hydra, to triple-bodied*
> *Geryon, and to you, flame-breathing Cacus.*
> *Here he overcomes Antaeus, and you, two-horned Achelous;*
> *But the Naiads bless its stem with fertile fruit.*[2]

Hercules stands between exploits, two of which are seen in the distance. At right, he wrestles Antaeus, poised at the moment he lifts Antaeus free from the earth and brings about his demise; at left, Hercules fights with the bull Achelous, his ultimate victory attested to by the horn he holds in his hand. Hercules stares intently to the left with a serious, dramatically shadowed face. Goltzius may have intended to suggest this as the moment between labors when, according to Euripedes' fifth-century B.C. play *Alcestis*, Apollo chose to send Hercules to rescue Alcestis from death. Wrestling Alcestis free at the gates of Hades, Hercules thus began his role as the savior of those bound for the courts of the dead. The inclusion in the lower left of the plant foxglove, used for a variety of medicinal purposes, may serve to reinforce his ability to save man from death.

1. It is known that Pieter Paaw invited Goltzius to watch his second dissection in Leiden. See I. Q. van Regteren Altena, *Jacques de Gheyn: Three Generations* (The Hague, 1983), vol. 2, p. 43.
2. Translation by Frederick F. Kempner.

D.K.

11

Anonymous (Northern, active early seventeenth century)
MUSCLES OF THE BACK, c. 1600–1616

From Adriaan van den Spieghel, *Opera Quae Extant, Omnia*, ed. Johannes Antonides van der Linden (Amsterdam: Johannem Blaeu, 1645)
Engraving, 16¾ x 10¹⁵⁄₁₆″ (42.6 x 27.8 cm)
Purchased: SmithKline Beckman Corporation Fund
1982-41-1bb

The book from which this engraving is taken is usually referred to as "Spigelius," after the Latinized name of the author of the text, Adriaan van den Spieghel. Credit for the illustrations belongs rather to the Northern Italian anatomist Giulio Casserio, also known by his Latinized name, Casserius, as it was under his supervision that the copperplates from which the prints were taken had been prepared some years before the first edition of the book was printed in Venice in 1627.[1]

The publication has a complicated history. Van den Spieghel succeeded to the chair of anatomy at the University of Padua at Casserio's death in 1616, and when he himself died in 1625, he requested in his will that his manuscript, *De Humani Corporis Fabrica*, be published by a young associate in Padua, the physician Daniel Rindfleisch, known as Bucretius. Despite the fact that van den Spieghel had specified that the book contain no illustrations, Bucretius sought from Casserio's heirs the seventy-seven unpublished plates that he had had made, commissioned twenty more, and published them with van den Spieghel's text. The fascinating group of full figure studies, which includes this engraving of the muscles of the back, was part of the original Casserian lot, produced probably in the early years after 1600. It is not known why the anatomist did not issue the prints during his lifetime. Innovative both anatomically and artistically, the illustrations mark the first significant deviation from the Vesalian prototypes established over half a century earlier (see nos. 8a–g). Like Vesalius, Casserio wanted to illustrate total human anatomy through the use of successive images of dissection, and like Vesalius, he was astute in his choice of artists, but there the similarity ends. A major difference between the two anatomists is that Casserio chose to have his plates made by the technique of copper engraving, which allows for greater and more subtle detail than had been possible in the woodcut process used by Vesalius.

The unknown draftsman who produced the designs from which the engraver worked imprinted them with his distinctive artistic personality and, far from repeating the by then hackneyed images of the post-Vesalian illustrators, infused his figures with the new spirit of the Baroque. The title page, a rather tiresome recital of standard anatomical iconography, bears the names of the Bolognese-Venetian artists Odoardo Fialetti as its designer and Francesco Valesio as the engraver. This fact has led to the unjustified assumption in literature that these artists were responsible for all the illustrations, even though the title page would have been engraved specifically for the first Venetian edition of 1627 and it is known that the Casserian plates were produced some years earlier. The Casserian engraver was technically far advanced over most Italian engravers of the period around 1600 in his skillful manipulation of the burin and his virtuosity with the tapered line, techniques that had recently been introduced into Italy from the North. Several of the images in the figure series do, in fact, derive directly from specific engravings by Hendrik Goltzius: All stylistic evidence thus points to the designer and the engraver being Northern rather than Italian.[2]

This illustration of an early stage in the dissection of the back muscles is typical of the series as it shows the subject, comfortably seated in a landscape, participating in the dissection by agreeably holding up a portion of his own anatomy as if it were a bit of festive costume, a convention that goes back to the illustrations for Jacopo Berengario da Carpi's anatomical works published in the early 1520s. The Casserian plates may be unique in anatomical illustration in combining dissection with humor.

1. I am indebted to Kenneth B. Roberts, John Clinch Professor of the History of Medicine, Memorial University, St. John's, Newfoundland, for much of the information on the Casserian illustrations, as well as for kindly allowing me access to his personal copy of "Spigelius."
2. In the text for his *De Vocis* of 1601, Casserio stated that from 1593 he had had in his house and working for him a German artist named Joseph Maurer. Ludwig Choulant (*History and Bibliography of Anatomic Illustration*, ed. and trans. Mortimer Frank, rev. ed. [1945; reprint, New York, 1962], p. 223) considered this artist to be Josias Maurer, the brother of the better-known Christoph Maurer, a Swiss-German designer of stained glass and a draftsman of considerable merit, but this has yet to be proved.

M.C.

12

Andries Jacobsz. Stock (Dutch, c. 1580–after 1648)
After Jacques de Gheyn II (Flemish, 1565–1629)
THE ANATOMY LESSON OF DR. PIETER PAAW, 1615

First inserted in Pieter Paaw, *Primitiae Anatomicae. De Humani Corporis Ossibus* (Leiden: Justi à Colster, 1615)
Engraving, 11⅝ x 9" (29.5 x 22.9 cm) (trimmed)
Charles M. Lea Collection
28-42-4554

This engraving, inserted in Pieter Paaw's *Primitiae Anatomicae* of 1615,[1] shows the doctor presiding over a dissection for an audience of professors, students, and the curious general public, which includes children and dogs. Foreign doctors (note the costumed men at upper left, who might be identified as a Pole and a Hungarian, and those at lower right) also attended.[2] Historical personages are alluded to as well: The prelector (the man in glasses at the right, reading from an anatomy book) appears to be the second-century Greek physician Galen, whose work dominated anatomy before and even after Vesalius; Scaliger, Dousa, and Lipsius, professors and librarians at Leiden, all of whom were dead by 1615, are shown seated in the front row.[3] This practice of including figures from the history of medicine was not uncommon and may be a reference to the title page of Vesalius's famous text of 1543 (see no. 8a). Like Vesalius, Paaw is presented at the center of a busy dissection scene demonstrating firsthand.

Anatomy lessons, part of the medical school curriculum (which otherwise dealt with disease only theoretically), were great events, often advertised in newspapers and held with much fanfare. The anatomists themselves were quite famous among intellectuals and scientists for their knowledge, and Paaw (1564–1617) in particular was highly esteemed. Not only did he edit a new edition of Vesalius's *Epitome* in 1616 but he also made a number of important contributions to craniology and osteology. The volume in which this engraving appeared was perhaps the first osteological work published in the Netherlands. Paaw was the founder of the anatomical theater established in 1597 at the University of Leiden and a professor of anatomy and botany at the university, but he is perhaps best known as the teacher of Dr. Tulp, the physician made famous by Rembrandt in his painting of 1632 (Mauritshuis, The Hague).

Most of the figures gesture toward the cadaver, which, as was the custom at public anatomies until 1684, was that of a criminal.[4] Underlying this theme is an emblem to which no one looks—the animated, articulated skeleton holding a banner with an inscription from the Roman poet Horace: "Death is the line that marks the end of all."[5] This phrase, along with the skeleton, the skulls beneath the dissecting table, and the cadaver, serves as a memento mori, or reminder of death. The anatomy lesson thus was more than an intellectual, didactic, or social event: It was part of a moral decree.

Seventeenth-century prints, drawings, and written descriptions of the amphitheater of Leiden, which had six galleries and seating for several hundred observers, and of Paaw performing anatomy lessons indicate that several animated skeletons with messages of moralizing intent were actually displayed there. The theater also housed a collection of natural history: skeletons of animals, birds, and reptiles; stuffed heads of animals; and flayed human skins.[6] That these are not illustrated here is explained in the text accompanying some versions of the print that states that the amphitheater was largely dismantled before a dissection to allow for a larger audience.[7]

The designer of the print, Jacques de Gheyn II, lived in Leiden for a short time after his marriage in 1595 (until 1596 or possibly 1598), and would have known the city's famed anatomical theater and Paaw.[8] De Gheyn, who was a student of Hendrik Goltzius (see no. 10), also worked in Haarlem and the Hague as a painter, draftsman, and engraver, but is best known for his lyrical ink drawings. Andries Jacobsz. Stock, a student of de Gheyn, executed the print after the latter's design. The print is the only one of its subject executed by either artist.

1. A full sheet of the print contains a poem written by P. Scriverius and dated 1615; see I. Q. van Regteren Altena, *Jacques de Gheyn: Three Generations* (The Hague, 1983), vol. 2, p. 43.
2. William S. Heckscher, *Rembrandt's "Anatomy of Dr. Nicolaas Tulp"* (New York, 1958), p. 26.
3. According to the text of the print, not illustrated here (Altena, *De Gheyn*, vol. 2, p. 44).
4. Heckscher, *Rembrandt's "Anatomy,"* p. 135 n. 58. The first public dissection of a body of a noncriminal was performed in Amsterdam on February 19, 1684.
5. Horace, *Satires, Epistles and Ars Poetica*, trans. H. Rushton Fairclough (Cambridge, Mass., 1929), Epistles 1.16.79.
6. The amphitheater (1597–1820) was described by J. J. Orlers in 1641; see Heckscher, *Rembrandt's "Anatomy,"* p. 184. It is reproduced in Rijksmuseum, Amsterdam, *Leidse Universiteit 400* (March 27–June 8, 1975), nos. B4–6.
7. Altena, *De Gheyn*, vol. 2, p. 43.
8. Ibid.

F.F.H./D.K.

13
Jan Wandelaer (Dutch, 1690–1759)
MUSCLE MAN, 1739

From Bernhard Siegfried Albinus, *Tabulae Sceleti et Musculorum Corporis Humani* (Leiden: J. & H. Verbeek, 1747)
Etching and engraving, 22¾ x 16⁵⁄₁₆" (57.8 x 41.4 cm)
Gift of Dr. Richard H. Chamberlain
73-83-1

The German-born anatomist Bernhard Siegfried Albinus was educated in Leiden and Paris and in 1721 returned to Leiden to serve the city's illustrious university as professor of surgery and anatomy until his death in 1770. The appearance in 1747 of the *Tabulae Sceleti et Musculorum Corporis Humani,* with text by Albinus and forty prints of skeletons and muscle men by Jan Wandelaer, established new standards for the illustrated anatomical atlas, as had Vesalius's *Fabrica* (see nos. 8a–g) two hundred years earlier. The author's attitudes toward the understanding and depiction of human anatomy can be seen in the cultural context of the Netherlands by the end of the seventeenth century: the intense pragmatism of the philosophers-scientists and an artistic climate in which the painters had brought to perfection their techniques of translating into two dimensions the structures, details, and sleek surfaces of visible reality.

Within this setting Albinus was precise in describing his intentions and methods. He wished to illustrate the anatomy of the *homo perfectus,* a single idealized human body based on the dissection of many examples so as to be truly typical and not idiosyncratic. Being aware of both the distortions inherent in the traditional conventions of perspective and foreshortening and the artist's tendency to interpret subjectively, he devised an ingenious double-grid system through which the anatomical subject could be viewed and measured as it was drawn. In Albinus's own words, his goal was

> *to reproduce, not free hand . . . as is customary, but from actual measure: to reproduce, not as the demonstrators of anatomy generally do, by merely placing before the eyes of the artist what they have uncovered, but by collecting (data) from one body after another, and making a composite according to rule so that the actual truth will be displayed.*[1]

The preparatory drawings for the *Tabulae,* conserved in the library of the University of Leiden, provide further insights into the production and resulting appearance of the prints.[2] The studies are primarily of two kinds. There are the life-size studies in black ink and gray wash that Wandelaer executed to establish the compositions of the major skeleton and muscle plates in their environmental settings. These very large drawings are dated 1728, after the artist had been working for Albinus for five years; the fact that it took another nineteen years to ready the material for publication indicates the meticulous and time-consuming work involved. The other studies in ink or fine red chalk, some bearing Albinus's own corrections, further document the repeated and painstaking measuring procedures used. For every pose a primary figure study was drawn and then etched in outline to serve as an endlessly repeatable template that the artist could use to develop his progressive and detailed studies.[3]

The crystalline detail in the *Tabulae* illustrations such as the *Muscle Man* only partially accounts for their appeal. The *écorchés* and skeletons stand about in lush gardens, as seen in this print, and glimpses of classical architecture are offered. Although such carefully arranged settings may be interpreted as an eighteenth-century comment on the harmony of man and nature or as the familiar palliative device used by anatomical illustrators to gloss over the repulsiveness of their subject matter, Albinus gives his own explanation for this feature:

> *He (Wandelaar* [sic]*) maintained that he required a certain color around the pictures [the anatomical images themselves]. . . . It was for this reason particularly that he added the ornaments, which, far from harming the pictures, are actually a help. He maintained that, in this way, he would preserve the proper light of the pictures, for if the space around the picture and between the parts should be white, the light of the pictures would suffer. . . . The ornaments in the pictures of the skeleton are lighter than in the pictures of the muscles,*

corresponding to the lightness of the skeleton, the solidity of the muscles . . . .[4]

1. Translated and quoted by Ludwig Choulant in *History and Bibliography of Anatomic Illustration*, ed. and trans. Mortimer Frank, rev. ed. (1945; reprint, New York, 1962), p. 277.
2. I am indebted to Dr. P.F.J. Obbema, Keeper of Western Manuscripts at the university, for having kindly shown me the drawings.
3. For a thorough discussion of the methods employed by Albinus and Wandelaer, see Hendrik Punt, *Bernard Siegfried Albinus (1697–1770), on "Human Nature": Anatomical and Physiological Ideas in Eighteenth Century Leiden* (Amsterdam, 1983).
4. Translated and quoted in Choulant, *History and Bibliography of Anatomic Illustration*, pp. 277–78.

M.C.

14
Jacques-Fabien Gautier-Dagoty (French, 1716–1785)
MUSCLES OF THE BACK, 1746

From Joseph Guichard Duverney, *Essai d'anatomie, en tableaux imprimés* . . . (Paris: Chez Le Sieur Gautier, 1745–48)
Color mezzotint, 23 15/16 x 18 1/8" (60.8 x 46 cm)
Purchased: SmithKline Beckman Corporation Fund
68-25-79m

In the early eighteenth century, the color theories advanced by Sir Isaac Newton inspired the German artist Jakob Christof Le Blon to produce color prints using three mezzotint plates inked in yellow, red, and blue—the primary colors identified by Newton—that were printed one over another. When he found that he needed a fourth, black-inked plate to blend the three colors, Le Blon had stumbled onto the four-color printing process still used today. After twenty-five years of peddling his invention for "printed paintings" in Holland and England with varying degrees of failure, the elderly Le Blon finally succeeded in winning the backing of the academic community in Paris. By 1737 he had obtained a royal privilege granting him the exclusive rights for making three-color prints. It was specifically recommended by the king that he use his novel method to print anatomical illustrations, and he was encouraged to train students in the mezzotint technique, which had yet to find favor in France.[1]

One of the assistants Le Blon hired was the young Jacques-Fabien Gautier-Dagoty,[2] who worked with Le Blon for only a few weeks in 1737 before leaving to set up a rival workshop. Because Le Blon was eager to have his method conform to Newton's theory of three primary colors, he was reluctant to admit to using the black plate, and thus the path was left open for Gautier-Dagoty to ignore Le Blon's special privilege and claim the invention of the four-color method for himself.

A few years after Le Blon's death in 1741, Gautier-Dagoty stopped making color reproductions of paintings and during the following four decades concentrated on publishing scientific works illustrated with his color mezzotints, including at least ten anatomy books. First printed in 1745, the eight mezzotints for Gautier-Dagoty's *Essai d'anatomie* were the first anatomical illustrations in color published in France. Gautier-Dagoty, who was a printmaker and not an anatomist, had chosen the surgeon Joseph Guichard Duverney to prepare the dissections and write the accompanying legends. Their pioneering work was supplemented by twelve additional color prints and new text published in 1746 as *Suite de l'essai d'anatomie,* and in 1746 the two parts were issued together in a comprehensive study of the muscles entitled *Myologie complètte.*[3] The images were remarkable both for the size of the plates and the novelty of the color printing, which greatly enhanced their didactic purpose. Particularly striking is the plate *Muscles of the Back,* which has been called the "anatomical angel" because of the combination of a demure feminine profile with the winglike appearance of the dissected torso.

1. Hans W. Singer, "Jakob Christoffel Le Blon," *Mittheilungen der Gesellschaft für Vervielfältigende Kunst*, supplement in *Die graphischen Künste,* vol. 24 (1901), p. 5.
2. See Hans Wolfgang Singer, "Der Vierfarbendruck in der Gefolgschaft Jacob Christoffel Le Blons mit Oeuvre-Verzeichnissen de Familie Gautier-Dagoty, J. Roberts, J. Ladmirals und C. Lasinios," *Monatshefte für Kunstwissenschaft*, vol. 10 (1917), pp. 177ff.
3. The Museum's copy of this work consists of both parts bound consecutively, but with only the title page for the first part, dated 1745. The last page of text following the twentieth plate carries a printer's address: *De l'Imprimerie de Quillau, rue Galande, à l'Annonciation, 1748.*

J.I.

15
John Bell (English, active mid-eighteenth century) After William Hogarth (English, 1697–1764)
THE REWARD OF CRUELTY, 1751

Woodcut, 18 1/8 x 15 1/4" (46.1 x 38.7 cm)
Purchased: SmithKline Beckman Corporation Fund
1980-18-2

Both painter and printmaker, William Hogarth is perhaps best known for his biting satires on life in early Georgian England. *The Reward of Cruelty* is the last scene in his series of engravings entitled "The Four Stages of Cruelty," which depicts the life of Tom Nero, a heartless young man who is eventually hanged for murder. The first and second plates show Nero cruelly torturing animals and the third shows him being arrested after violently murdering his lover. In the fourth engraving, after he has been hanged, Nero's body, with his initials on his arm clearly identifying him and with the hangman's noose still around his neck, is turned over to a company of surgeons for dissection.

Printed by John Bell under Hogarth's supervision, this woodcut reproduces the engraved version of *The Reward of Cruelty*, which Hogarth published early in 1751. He planned to issue all four of the images in woodcut in the belief that this traditionally popular medium would attract an even wider audience for his prints, but woodcutting turned out to be too expensive and only the third and fourth plates were reproduced in this way.[1]

The woodcut follows the engraving closely, yet the coarser lines add a more strident tone to the scene, and the following moralizing verses, which were inscribed below the engraved version, are omitted (as are various other inscriptions):

Behold the Villain's dire disgrace!
Not Death itself can end.
He finds no peaceful Burial-Place;
His breathless Corse, no friend.

Torn from the Root, that wicked Tongue,
Which daily swore and curst!
Those Eyeballs, from their Sockets wrung,
That glow'd with lawless Lust!

His Heart, expos'd to prying Eyes,
To Pity has no Claim:
But, dreadful! from his Bones shall rise,
His Monument of Shame.

These last lines indicate that Nero's bones will eventually join the two skeletons identified in the engraving with inscriptions above the niches as those of James Field (on the left) and Macleane (on the right), two infamous criminals of the day, who point menacingly at each other. As a deterrent to crime, bodies of executed criminals were routinely offered to the Barber-Surgeons' Company of London for dissection, and the dissections were open to the public.[2] However, the actual scene represented here is a composite: The Surgeons and Barbers had separated in 1745 and the Surgeons were no longer allowed to use the Barber-Surgeons' Hall. Their new dissecting theater did not open until August of 1751.[3] While the niches holding the skeletons are probably taken from either the theater in the Barber-Surgeons' Hall or that in the newly erected but unused Surgeons' Hall, Hogarth seems to have incorporated other features from the Cutlerian Theatre of the Royal College of Physicians.[4] The arms atop the presiding surgeon's chair, for example, are based on those of the Royal College and depict a doctor's hand taking a pulse, an act of concern that sharply contrasts with the dissection scene below.

The scene is enlivened by Hogarth's emphasis on gruesome detail. Wearing birettas and mortarboards, the surgeons observe the dissection nonchalantly. In contrast, a layman at left points with a horrified expression to the skeleton of another criminal whose body had been similarly defiled. Seated on his chair and gesturing with his pointer, the presiding surgeon looks as if he is sitting in judgment on the unfortunate corpse. As if to repay him for the pain and suffering he caused, the dissecting surgeons treat Nero with brutal callousness. One gouges out his eye in much the same way as the boy in the first plate of the series gouges out the eye of a bird. Below the dissecting table a dog (one of the animals tortured by Nero) has fallen on his heart, and in the left foreground a cauldron of human remains is being boiled down to bones to create another articulated skeleton for anatomical demonstration and moral remonstration.

1. Lawrence Gowing, *Hogarth* (London, 1971), p. 69, no. 185.
2. Ronald Paulson, *Hogarth's Graphic Works* (New Haven, 1965), vol. 1, p. 215, no. 190.
3. Ibid., pp. 214–15.
4. William Brockbank and Jessie Dobson, "Hogarth's Anatomical Theatre," *Journal of the History of Medicine and Allied Sciences*, vol. 14 (July 1959), pp. 351–53.

D.K./K.R.

16

Pompeo Batoni (Italian, 1708–1787)
MALE NUDE LEANING ON A PEDESTAL, 1765

Black and white chalk on blue prepared paper, 20¹¹⁄₁₆ x 15¼"
(52.5 x 38.7 cm)
Bequest of Anthony Morris Clark
1978-70-171

The study of anatomy by artists during past centuries was by no means limited to probing beneath the surface of the human body in order to master its complexities. The most essential part of all artistic training since the Renaissance has been life drawing, studying the nude (usually male) body from a studio model who assumed a variety of standing, sitting, or reclining positions. By the seventeenth century in Italy such exercises were usually held in individual artists' studios or in the palaces of patrons and were known as "academies" *(accademie del nudo);* eventually, the drawings themselves were also called academies.[1] The mastery of representing the human figure was considered a fundamental part of a painter's or sculptor's education at least by the sixteenth century; students learned by drawing after prints, drawings, casts, sculptures, and the nude, and mature artists as well continued to draw from life.

This large and highly finished male academy is an example of the latter function of life drawing. Although most such sheets are anonymous, this one was considered of sufficient importance by its author to be accorded a signature and a date. By 1765, the year of its execution, Pompeo Batoni was the most celebrated painter active in Rome. After the deaths of Giovanni Battista Tiepolo and Anton Raphael Mengs in 1770 and 1779, respectively, Batoni was probably the best known living painter in Europe as well as the last eighteenth-century painter in Italy of considerable fame.

During his long career, Batoni produced great quantities of drawings, most of which were highly refined studies of heads, hands, feet, limbs, whole figures, and drapery related to his many figural compositions. Typically, these were executed in red, black, or white chalk—or a combination thereof—on papers sometimes washed or prepared in blue, yellow, or pinkish tones. The artist is known to have drawn from the model throughout his career in the studios of his first masters and later in those of his contemporaries, as well as during private life-drawing classes held in his own studio. The technical virtuosity of the elaborate crosshatching in this sheet and the masterful observation of the heavily muscled figure have led to the suggestion that such late academy drawings by Batoni were not studio exercises but demonstration pieces showing the artist's skill as a draftsman, and perhaps also for use as guides for students.[2] In any case, Batoni's emphasis on figural drawing falls within a continuum of Italian tradition that reaches back through earlier Roman masters such as Carlo Maratta and Andrea Sacchi to the Bolognese academic tradition of the Carracci family and ultimately to Raphael and Michelangelo.

1. See Nikolaus Pevsner, *Academies of Art: Past and Present* (Cambridge, 1940).
2. For Batoni and the place of drawing in his oeuvre, see Edgar Peters Bowron in Ulrich W. Hiesinger and Ann Percy, eds., *A Scholar Collects: Selections from the Anthony Morris Clark Bequest* (Philadelphia, 1980), pp. 43–44, 53–54, nos. 30, 42.

A.P./D.K.

17

T. C. Wilson (English, nineteenth century) After Thomas Rowlandson (English, 1756–1827) THE DISSECTING ROOM, early nineteenth century

Hand-colored lithograph, 11⁵⁄₁₆ x 14¹³⁄₁₆" (28.8 x 37.6 cm) (image)
Purchased: SmithKline Beckman Corporation Fund
68-215-34

Compared to Hogarth's *Reward of Cruelty* (no. 15), Thomas Rowlandson's *Dissecting Room* is an almost lighthearted depiction of a grisly subject. Indeed, were it not for the inscription below the image, it would be difficult to believe that Rowlandson produced this composition, which is curiously lacking in satire and very different from his other medical caricatures (see nos. 36 and 78).

The dissecting chamber is a somewhat bare attic room lit by a skylight. The rules for dissecting are posted, as are the prices paid for the bodies of male, female, and infant subjects. The men, most of whom are young and earnest looking, work with concentration on the corpses they are dissecting. The spectators appear serious and eager to learn, and even the corpses and skeletons are smiling. The only ghoulish note in the entire composition is struck by the corpse on the right, whose face is haunted by a horrible, ghostly expression.

D.K./K.R.

18a–c

Thomas Eakins (American, 1844–1916) a: JESSE GODLEY, b: THOMAS EAKINS, c: JOHN LAURIE WALLACE; 1883–84

Albumen prints; a: 3⁵⁄₁₆ x 7¹¹⁄₁₆" (8.4 x 19.5 cm), b: 3¹⁄₁₆ x 8⅜" (7.8 x 21.3 cm), c: 3⅛ x 7⁷⁄₁₆" (7.9 x 18.9 cm)
Purchased: SmithKline Beckman Corporation Fund
1984-89-6,3,1

18d

Thomas Eakins (American, 1844–1916) FIRST POSITION: GODLEY, EAKINS, AND WALLACE, 1883–84

Black, red, and blue ink with traces of graphite on tracing paper; two irregular sheets: 3¼ x 8½" (8.3 x 21.6 cm), 3¹¹⁄₁₆ x 2⁵⁄₁₆" (9.4 x 5.8 cm)
Purchased: SmithKline Beckman Corporation Fund
1984-22-7,8

These three serial photographs (nos. 18a–c) showing Thomas Eakins and two of his students at the Pennsylvania Academy of the Fine Arts in Philadelphia are from a recently discovered group of forty-two studies of nude male and female models, each pictured in standardized poses arranged in identical sequence and glued onto cardboard strips. The large number of subjects and their systematic presentation suggest that they were made to serve as a repertory of anatomical types for use in the study of the human figure. The evidence of various documentary sources indicates a date of 1883–84 for the group, which has been generally titled "The Naked Series" because of an entry in Eakins's journal for May 31, 1883, noting the cost of buying glass "for mounting naked series."[1] It is likely that these photographs are the ones referred to in the Academy's *Circular of the Committee on Instruction, 1883–1884:*

> *A number of photographs of models used in the Life Classes were made in cases in which the model was unusually good, or had any peculiarity of form or action which would be instructive, and a collection of these photographs will thus be gradually made for the use of the students.*[2]

Eakins's two small drawings based on tracings from the photographs (no. 18d) illustrate how the photographs were to be analyzed and compared and to what purpose. The inscription on the larger drawing explains that these views allow an artist to discover the distinctive centerline through the axes of weight and action, which vary with each individual. As Eakins stated at the end of his inscription: "Such lines form the only simple basis for a systematic construction of the figure."

By the time these drawings were made, Eakins, who had begun teaching at the Academy in 1876 and had been named director of its schools in 1882, had reshaped the curriculum with a philosophy that was described as early as 1879 as "radical."[3] He advocated that students eschew the traditional program that began with drawing from antique casts and start instead with painting figure studies. The Academy's anatomy lectures and demonstrations were already among the most comprehensive in America or Europe, utilizing skeletons, dissected cadavers, and living models, but Eakins, who viewed the study of art as a search for knowledge as much as a way to develop technique, insisted that advanced students, both men and women, should actually perform dissections. "To draw the human figure," he said, "it is necessary to know as much as possible about it, about its structure and its movements, its bones and muscles, how they are made, and how they act."[4]

Eakins's analytical turn of mind led him to use the medium of photography to help achieve his artistic goals. When the development of the dry-plate process made photography relatively convenient for the amateur, Eakins purchased a camera and made photographic studies for many of his landscape paintings in the 1880s. Alert to developments in photographic technique, he saw Eadweard Muybridge's experiments with instantaneous photography of moving horses soon after they appeared in 1879, and used them to establish the correct positions of the legs of trotting horses in his painting *The Fairman Rogers Four-in-Hand* (Philadelphia Museum of Art). When Muybridge carried out his photographs of humans and animals at the University of Pennsylvania in 1884–85 (see no. 61), Eakins was appointed to the commission to oversee the project and made his own photographic experiments with motion at the same time.

Eakins's interests as an artist were closely linked to his teaching, and although photography was not taught at the Academy, he encouraged his students to make photographs as aids for their own work. "The Naked Series" may have been inspired by Muybridge's motion studies, but as has been pointed out,[5] the static views of each figure in this series differ fundamentally from Muybridge's presentation of aspects of continuous motion. However, the concept of sequence and the format's potential for comparative analysis are common to both.

These photographs are of great interest as evidence of Eakins's teaching method, for they show him applying to the posed models of the life class the same intensive study that led him to insist that his students learn muscular and skeletal structure by actually dissecting cadavers. "The Naked Series" records and clarifies the transient process by which students in a life class perfected their ability to analyze their observations through the repetitive drawing or painting of a great variety of models. From this repetition and a preliminary understanding of anatomy, students could build their knowledge of the principles that govern the appearance of the human figure, which for Eakins was the single most important subject for art.

1. "Journal of Thomas Eakins (Self), 1883–1888," Daniel W. Dietrich II Collection (typescript, Eakins Archive, Department of American Art, Philadelphia Museum of Art).
2. Quoted in Ellwood C. Parry III and Robert Stubbs, *Photographer Thomas Eakins* (Philadelphia, 1981), n.p.
3. William C. Brownell, "The Art Schools of Philadelphia," *Scribner's Monthly*, vol. 18, no. 5 (September 1879), pp. 737–50.
4. Quoted in ibid., p. 745.
5. William I. Homer and John Talbot, "Eakins, Muybridge and the Motion Picture Process," *The Art Quarterly*, vol. 26, no. 2 (Summer 1963), pp. 194–216.

D.S.

19

John Sloan (American, 1871–1951) ANSHUTZ ON ANATOMY, 1912

Etching (vii/viii), 7⁹⁄₁₆ x 8¹⁵⁄₁₆" (19.2 x 22.7 cm)
Gift of Mrs. John Sloan
75-155-206

Thomas Anshutz was a student of Thomas Eakins at the Pennsylvania Academy of the Fine Arts in Philadelphia and became chief demonstrator of anatomy under him in 1881. When Eakins resigned from his position as director of the Academy's schools in 1886, Anshutz succeeded him as head of the life class. Eakins's insistence on the intensive study of human anatomy as a basis for figural composition (see nos. 18a–d) continued under Anshutz.

This etching of 1912 is John Sloan's record of an anatomy lecture Anshutz had presented some years earlier not at the Academy but to a group of Robert Henri's students at the New York School of Art. The place and date of this event may be indicated by the letters and numbers in the upper left corner: "NYSA 1905." Among the attentive observers are Sloan's friends, the painters Robert Henri, Maurice Prendergast, and George Bellows, and Sloan himself appears with glasses in the upper right. Anshutz stands before a skeleton and live model apparently discussing those aspects of anatomy that would be of interest to an artist. In his hand he holds a large piece of clay with which to form muscles on the bare skeleton. The human model served to demonstrate the external musculature and its variation in motion.[1]

For Sloan, etching was as important a medium as drawing or painting, and he often labored over a plate for weeks or even months, etching, burnishing, and hammering out the published state. This print went through eight states over a five-month period from February through June 1912 before Sloan was satisfied with his result.[2] It is one of his most famous prints.

1. Helen Farr Sloan, ed., *John Sloan: New York Etchings (1905–1949)* (New York, 1978), no. 18.
2. John Sloan, *John Sloan's New York Scene: From the Diaries, Notes and Correspondence, 1906–1913*, ed. Bruce St. John (New York, 1965), pp. 604–7.

D.K.

20

Jess (American, born 1923)
THE SUN: TAROT XIX, 1960

Collage of various lithographic illustrations, primarily offset, mounted on heavy wove paper, with a window-shade pull, 75½ x 45¾" (191.8 x 116.3 cm) (sight)
Purchased: SmithKline Beckman Corporation Fund
1984-78-1

First trained in the sciences, the contemporary California artist Jess subsequently turned to art as an antidote to the objective methodology of science. He chose collage as one of his chief mediums of expression at an early point in his career, and the development of his highly individual approach to this technique was influenced by his purchase of Max Ernst's 1934 Surrealist collage-book *Une Semaine de bonté* in 1952. His association with San Francisco's "beat generation" of the 1950s, particularly with its literary focus, also had a formative impact on Jess, who has maintained frequent collaborations with writers.

Jess's collages, which he calls "paste-ups," are the products of a lengthy process he has referred to as "a magical happening."[1] Varying greatly in scale, with *The Sun: Tarot XIX* being one of the largest, his paste-ups may take years to complete and sometimes conjoin hundreds of fragments cut from magazines, newspapers, engravings, book illustrations, greeting cards, scientific texts, and the like. The pieces of his most intricate compositions are first pinned into place, thus allowing "them to move throughout the whole field until these interactions of images and spaces have made a weave, by shuffling back and forth, have woven a tapestry."[2] The numerous pinholes, which are quite visible in the finished works, are reminiscent of both Renaissance cartoons and the process of anatomical dissection whereby layers of the body are pinned back to reveal the next level.

Jess has termed his overall field of juxtaposition a "flux-image,"[3] for relationships within this field constantly shift to produce an endless sequence of new realities. Associations between the various elements in a paste-up ebb and flow so that the entire composition may appear a little different upon each encounter with the image as new details assert themselves and new relationships emerge. Jess ideally wants viewers to experience new perspectives on themselves—on who and what they are beneath the surface.

Frequent references to mythology, the occult, ancient Egypt, and tarot appear throughout Jess's paste-ups, perhaps as a result of the artist's reaction against his early schooling in the sciences. Yet, ironically, the "scientific" aspect is what makes *The Sun: Tarot XIX* relevant in an Ars Medica context. The two large anatomical figures—the one at left demonstrating the nervous system and the one at right, the circulatory system—seem to be holding hands. Perhaps to acknowledge their original environment—the standard anatomy shades used as teaching tools in medical schools—Jess has suspended a window-shade pull in the center. This element also makes an entertaining pun on the title of the image, for a shade may either be pulled down to block the sun or pulled up to bring *The Sun* into a room. In the upper part of the composition, the two main figures are surrounded by a crowded tapestry created primarily of interlocking illustrations of anatomical sections. This collaged juxtaposition of the body in whole and in part on varying scales is a metaphor for the process of anatomical study used by both the artist and the scientist.

The sun is located at top center of this paste-up, and like every detail of this fantastic terrain it has many layers of possible meaning. Its rays are radiating spearheads that bear an odd resemblance to the weapons piercing the Wound Manikin of early medical treatises (see no. 4a). In conjunction with the propellers at the sun's center these rays also bring to mind the image of Apollo, the ancient sun god whose chariot daily propelled him across the sky and whose arrows were believed to have brought disease to the earth.

Jess has long been fascinated with the Egyptian Book of the Dead, a mystical form of picture language, and it was perhaps in reference to this interest that he included Egyptian tomb motifs at the center of this work. Below the Egyptian architectural design that divides the collage horizontally, the background of anatomical elements is abandoned for a dreamlike world of disparate and bizarrely juxtaposed objects.

Tarot, to which the title refers, is one of the oldest card games known to man and contains aspects of theology, mythology, astrology, and history that reflect many of the artist's interests. Just as tarot cards can be shuffled and redealt to yield new arrangements and relationships, so have the pictorial parts of this paste-up been shuffled and reshuffled to create an arrangement from which the viewer can gain insights. In tarot the nineteenth card is the sun, a symbol of truth and insight that is often presented with the same compositional organization as this collage: the sun at top center, with two figures in the space below. In addition to *The Sun: Tarot XIX,* Jess's other paste-ups of tarot are *The Wheel of Fortune: Tarot X* and *The Hanged Man: Tarot XIII.*

1. Quoted in Michael Auping, *Jess: Paste-Ups (and Assemblies) 1951–1983* (Sarasota, Fla., 1983), p. 16.
2. Jess, quoted in ibid.
3. Quoted in ibid., p. 12.

D.K.

21

Robert Rauschenberg (American, born 1925)
BOOSTER, 1967

From "Booster and Seven Studies," 1967
Color lithograph and silkscreen, 72 x 35⁹⁄₁₆" (182.9 x 90.3 cm)
Purchased with funds contributed by the International Graphic Arts Society in honor of Carl Zigrosser
67-183-1

Robert Rauschenberg has sought to explore the "gap" between art and life by incorporating into his work fragments, objects, and common images from the day-to-day world. In 1949 or 1950 he used the female body and other objects to create powerful images on huge sheets of blueprint paper, exploring in the life-size *Female Figure (Blueprint)* the shapes and relationships of the external anatomy of a model. Some eighteen years later, in this lithograph and silkscreen print, *Booster*, he delved into the internal anatomy of his own body.

Booster's central skeletal image is composed of x-rays of the artist's body, taken when he was wearing little more than a pair of hobnailed boots. The x-ray segments are assembled in order to reinforce, not mask, their source, and stand, somewhat precariously, as the structural support system for the print. The skeletal structure has been reassembled without attention to the actual scale of part to part, and as a result a rather small pelvis sits somewhat foolishly above a pair of large legs. Laid over the photolithographed x-ray figure is a bright red silkscreen printing of the time, or sky, chart for 1967, the year of the print's publication, bringing the relationship of man, time, and the universe into a single visual format. This element is likewise a reference to the ancient concept of the power of astrological signs over man, represented as well in the Renaissance image of the Zodiac Man (see no. 1).

Combined with the x-rays and the time chart are elements drawn from magazines and newspapers, transmuted by the artist into a strong comment on the society that supplied them. The solitary chair in blueprint tonality at top left and its ghostlike fragment at lower left appear as alternative supports for the precariously piled human bones in the x-rays and the ghostlike tracing of the up-ended skull at lower left. On the right, two spark plugs, whose shapes are reminiscent of the spaceships that by 1967 had become a part of everyday life, appear to hover in opposing rotational notation above the time chart. At lower right is an image of a pole vaulter caught in midjump, suggesting yet another symbol of man's desire to soar through the air.

In *Booster* Rauschenberg created an image of modern man that embraces art, science, and technology. The title conjoins these aspects in a clear way: In medicine a booster is an injection that helps reinforce the body's ability to fight disease, while the spark plugs, which boost an engine by providing the spark for combustion, as spaceship look-alikes refer to the imagination and technology that allow man to enter celestial orbit.

D.K.

22
Francesco Clemente (Italian, born 1952)
TELAMON #1, 1981

Etching, drypoint, soft-ground etching, and aquatint, 61¹⁄₁₆ x 19⅛"
(155.1 x 48.6 cm)
Purchased: SmithKline Beckman Corporation Fund
1982-80-2

The return of the figure and narrative content as focal points of contemporary art may sometimes accompany, as here, a renewed interest in the mechanisms of the human body. This etching is one of a pair of prints executed in 1981 by Francesco Clemente, a young Italian working in New York, Rome, and southern India, who has developed a highly personal mythology and imagery in his work of the past decade and a half. In *Telamon #1* the artist, whose images are often self-portraits, uses anatomical elements as vehicles for self-exploration.

In architectural terms, a telamon is an Atlas-like male figure used as a supporting column; in Greek mythology the Titan Atlas held up the pillars of heaven, his presence and strength acting to keep the sky from tumbling down. Clemente's telamones derive both from his individual, personal memory and a collective, historical memory of all antiquity and the classical past. The bottom section of *Telamon #1* is a back view (*Telamon #2* is seen from the front) that combines a self-portrait with a generalized or stylized depiction of parts of the upper body. All self-portraits are by nature introspective, but usually the face of the artist reveals the landscape of the mind. Here, by presenting his back, Clemente shows another side of introspection—the literal peering beneath the surface of one's own body. Clemente has included a stylized demonstration of the musculature of the arms and a strangely beautiful, abstracted dissection of the spinal column—the major element in man's structural and internal communication system. In this exploration of the realm of organic structure beneath the skin, rendered in etched lines, the very process of acid biting into the plate to produce the tense linear organization of the composition is a mirror of the act of cutting into the skin to reveal the structure of the body. Seen from behind and partially flayed to expose an abstracted and stylized view of his inner workings, man is presented not as a pillar of strength and support but as a figure whose many component parts conjoin in a vulnerable, human form.

The configuration above the telamon's head is that of a snake. Perhaps Clemente had in mind the role of the snake as the central figure in the Fall of Man and the Expulsion from the Garden of Eden—and thus as the one culpable for man's suffering, disease, and death—or perhaps the serpent's beneficial role as intercessor between Aesculapius, god of medicine, and his diseased supplicants in the healing centers of antiquity.

In the upper area of the print long, winding threads link fish, man's evolutionary ancestors, with fetal forms, perhaps referring to the fact that man in his evolutionary and developmental past has been both water born and dependent: In effect the rich soft-ground printing on the *chine collé* creates a sense of depth that has the tactile presence of thick fluid through which the forms seem to float.

D.K.

HEALERS

23

Attributed to the First Antwerp Woodcutter (Flemish, active 1485–91)
CHRIST CASTING OUT DEMONS, 1487

From Ludolphus of Saxony, *Tboeck vanden Leven ons Heeren Ihesu Christi* (Antwerp: Gerard Leeu, 1487)
Hand-colored woodcut, 9⅝ x 6⅞″ (24.4 x 17.5 cm)
Purchased: SmithKline Beckman Corporation Fund
58-150-1

This remarkably fresh hand-colored woodcut of Christ casting out demons was created by an unknown artist of the late fifteenth century thought to be from Antwerp.[1] The scene is an illustration to a Dutch translation of the *Vita Christi* of Ludolphus of Saxony (1300–1370?) published in Antwerp in 1487.

Because of the miraculous cures documented in the New Testament, Christ was invoked with great regularity to intercede in the healing of disease. Here, as described in Luke 8:26–33, Christ expels the demons who have possessed a madman's soul, not with bleeding, binding, or whipping (common treatments at this time) but by gesture and gentle word. The madman struggles in his terror but is restrained by two other figures (one of whom appears to be wearing a physician's hat). At Christ's command the bestial demons issue forth from his mouth, the exit route most often depicted in such scenes, and fly off, demonstrating by their retreat that the cure has been achieved.

Healing was one of the central and formative acts of Christianity, and the church, with its sympathetic attitude toward the sick and infirm, was one of the most important forces in the care of the ill in Europe, including the establishment of hospitals. On the model of Christ and his disciples, the various holy orders served the community as healers and caretakers in willing consort with physicians, surgeons, and apothecaries.

1. William Martin Conway, *The Woodcutters of the Netherlands in the Fifteenth Century* (1884; reprint, Hildesheim, 1970), pp. 56–57.

D.K.

24

Anonymous (Italian, late fifteenth century)
Possibly after designs by Gentile Bellini (Italian, c. 1429–1507)
PHYSICIAN URINE GAZING, 1493

From Johannes de Ketham, *Fasciculus Medicinae* (Venice: Cesarem Arrivabenum, 1522)
Woodcut, 11⁷⁄₁₆ x 8¼″ (29.1 x 21 cm)
Purchased: SmithKline Beckman Corporation Fund
49-97-3c

Uroscopy, more commonly called urine gazing or water casting, is one of the methods of medical diagnosis used from the time of antiquity to the present day. During the medieval period the practice of uroscopy was so central to the activity of the physician that the distinctive glass urine flask became the emblem of the medical profession and was used for centuries as a signboard device to advertise the physician's office.

The physician would examine the urine for clarity, color, consistency, odor, and taste, and to make his diagnosis, he would refer to a printed urine chart, many of which were available. One included in the same book as this woodcut, the *Fasciculus Medicinae* of

Johannes de Ketham (see nos. 1 and 2), was a round chart with a series of urine flasks, each hand colored to show gradations of color from clear through yellow, red, and finally black; these were accompanied by descriptions of conditions associated with each color of urine. As is clear from this woodcut, the patients did not have to be present; thus they could have the glass flask with its urine sample delivered by messenger.

The artist has taken the format of this woodcut from the frontispiece of Bartholomaeus Montagnana's treatise *Consilia Medica* of 1476, published in Padua after the author's death. Bartholomaeus was the first in a long line of famous professors of medicine from the Montagnana family who taught at Padua for nearly two hundred years. In the *Consilia* he presented over three hundred case histories with documentation and descriptions of symptoms, diagnoses, and treatment. Central to each discussion are the physician's comments on urine casting. The relationship between this woodcut and the frontispiece in the *Consilia*, together with the facts that the illustration immediately preceding this print in the *Fasciculus* is clearly labeled "Petrus de Montagnana" and that the facial types of the two men are similar, suggests that the senior physician with pointing finger in this image is a reference to the most senior member of this venerated family of physicians.

Although urine gazing was a commonly accepted diagnostic technique, it always had its doubters. In Shakespeare's *Henry IV Part II*, Falstaff asks his page who had been sent to carry the urine flask to the physician: "Sirrah, you giant, what says the doctor to my water?" The page answers: "He said, sir, the water itself was a good healthy water; but, for the party that ow'd it, he might have moe diseases than he knew for" (1.2.1–6).

Urinalysis still plays an important role in the preliminary examination of the patient, but it is now joined by numerous other diagnostic tools. The distinctive shape of the urine flask, once the emblem of the physician, remains essentially unchanged from its medieval predecessors in most modern hospitals, an example of the continuity of certain aspects of the physician's practice.

D.K.

25a

Anonymous (German, early sixteenth century)
CAUTERIZING A THIGH WOUND, 1517

From Hans von Gersdorff, *Feldtbuch der Wundartzney* . . . (Strasbourg: Hans Schotten, 1540)
Hand-colored woodcut, 9¾ x 6⅝" (24.8 x 16.9 cm)
Purchased: SmithKline Beckman Corporation Fund
49-97-11c

25b

Anonymous (German, early sixteenth century)
EXTENSION APPARATUS, 1517

From Hans von Gersdorff, *Feldtbuch der Wundartzney* . . . (Strasbourg: Hans Schotten, 1540)
Hand-colored woodcut, 7 1/16 x 10 5/16" (18 x 26.2 cm)
Purchased: SmithKline Beckman Corporation Fund
49-97-11l

These vivid woodcuts from Hans von Gersdorff's noted book on field surgery do not specifically illustrate any part of the text but are better understood as pictorial reports of procedures or indicators of medical practices. Unlike anatomical charts and figures (see nos. 3 and 4a,b), these illustrations are placed securely within a convincing interior space and landscape. The modeling is accomplished with fine parallel lines and crosshatching, both of which are extremely difficult to achieve in the woodcut process, and the addition of hand coloring adds highlights and a spirit that enhance their inherent beauty.

Cautery, the process of burning or searing body tissue, was a method used to stop wounds from bleeding and as a form of antiseptic. The cauterizing agent could be boiling oil, which was poured over or into a wound (especially gunshot wounds, which were believed by some to be poisonous), or an iron cautery tool, which was heated until red-hot and applied directly. *Cauterizing a Thigh Wound* (no. 25a) depicts a surgeon who studiously applies a cautery to the thigh of a wounded soldier; another cautery in the flaming brazier is ready for use. Hanging on the wall in the field surgeon's simple "office" are long-handled cauteries with heads of various shapes to conform to different parts of the body.

The patient's stoic response is misleading because the level of pain associated with cautery is very high. Because of the inflammation caused by cautery, the treatment was often more harmful than the wound, and the Hippocratic aphorism that diseases not curable by iron are curable by fire caused endless disservice to the patient until more humane methods of wound treatment were advanced by the French surgeon Ambroise Paré in the mid-sixteenth century.

Extension Apparatus (no. 25b) depicts the treatment of a fractured leg. The simple wooden bench and ratchet mechanism, easily dismantled and reassembled for use in the field, enabled gradual extension of a broken limb so that the bones could realign. This method was preferable to a sharp manual tug, which could do more harm than good. The soldier in this scene has removed his sword, which rests on the ground, and he sits with his fractured leg strapped into the apparatus. The practitioner slowly turns the ratchet wheel, which steadily pulls the leg until the bone realigns. The bone would then be splinted, and the patient would be free to move again.

D.K.

26

Lucas van Leyden (Dutch, 1489/94–1533) THE SURGEON, 1524

Engraving, 4 9/16 x 2 15/16" (11.6 x 7.5 cm)
Purchased: SmithKline Beckman Corporation Fund
70-191-4

On first appearance this engraving seems to depict a surgeon performing a minor operation on the back of the ear of a discomforted patient. Further study, however, shows that the subject is more complex and that Lucas van Leyden, in a fashion typical of his work, filled his composition with symbols and attributes that would have made the hidden meaning immediately apparent to the sixteenth-century viewer. The elaborate attire of the "surgeon" reveals him as a charlatan, the purse at his side suggesting that his only goal is monetary gain; the tattered and frayed costume of the man depicted disparagingly as seated at his feet identifies him as a simple peasant who becomes particularly ridiculous when the quack cheats him of his money. The stone under his left hand probably refers to the unnecessary procedure he is undergoing—the removal of stones of folly or stupidity from his head.[1] The doctor acts not as a healer but as a deceiver who might produce a stone kept hidden in his hand to show the "success" of the operation.

The fact that the presentation appears so realistic does not mean that this type of quack actually existed, for Lucas often created moralizing images couched in the guise of ordinary scenes that would appear believable and familiar to his public. While seventeenth-century Dutch artists readily found the inspiration for such characters at markets and fairs, where quacks lucratively performed their trade,[2] there is no evidence of the existence of sixteenth-century quacks who operated on people suffering from pains in the head by removing "stones." It has been suggested that the theme of stone operations may have its origin in the displays of such scenes mounted on wagons that were drawn in local processions.[3] This source would have been readily available for Lucas, who is believed to have participated in such events.

Lucas van Leyden, an esteemed printmaker, painter, glass painter, and draftsman, was the first Dutch printmaker to enjoy an international reputation. He is known primarily for his complicated but plausible depictions of figured landscapes and his painterly chiaroscuro. He has been regarded as the originator of the Dutch genre tradition, although most of his scenes of daily life have been shown to have disguised interpretations. Lucas was especially gifted at portraying the psychological aspects of the human condition, and much of the charm of prints like *The Surgeon,* with its insensitive quack and distressed patient, derives from his ability to capture essential qualities of human nature.

1. D. Bax, *Hieronymus Bosch: His Picture Writing Deciphered*, trans. M. A. Bax-Botha (Rotterdam, 1979), pp. 271–75.
2. Peter C. Sutton, *Masters of Seventeenth-Century Dutch Genre Painting* (Philadelphia, 1984), p. 229, cat. no. 59.
3. Bax, *Bosch*, pp. 271–73.

E.J.

27

Hans Weiditz (German, active c. 1500–1536) ON THE PAIN OF TEETH, 1532

From Petrarch, *Trostspiegel in Glück und Unglück* (Frankfort on the Main: Den Christian Egenolffs Erben, 1572)
Woodcut, 11 1/4 x 7 1/4" (28.5 x 18.4 cm)
Purchased: SmithKline Beckman Corporation Fund
58-150-37b

The typical sixteenth-century dentist's "office," recorded by Hans Weiditz in this woodcut, was the simple, bustling outdoor space of an itinerant practitioner. A roughly hewn wooden bench serves as a seat for the patient while the bearded dentist stands behind on a wooden step or beam. On the crudely made table are the dentist's apothecary jars and small flasks, as well as a huge pile of extracted teeth attesting to his past successes. Strings of teeth also decorate the dentist's flamboyant outfit, which helped to draw attention to his presence. The sign sporting the double eagle, emblem of the Holy Roman Empire, advertises the fact that the dentist not only relieves the pain and suffering caused by rotten teeth but also removes lice and fleas and cures stomach ailments.

With a simple pair of pliers or tongs, the dentist pries a tooth loose from the mouth of a peasant woman, who sits stoically with her hands folded. A man at left, pointing to his greatly swollen jaw, awaits his turn. From the size of the waiting crowd, it is obvious that toothaches were a common problem, which extraction usually solved.

Weiditz drew this as one of the illustrations for a German translation of Petrarch's *On the Remedies of Good and Bad Fortune*, a philosophical work that discusses both good fortunes and misfortunes such as loss of senses, disease, pains, and madness, as well as toothache. In his witty, frank style he observed and recorded the nuances and details of daily life in the early sixteenth century.

D.K.

28a

Anonymous (Polish, sixteenth century)
COLLECTING HERBS FOR MEDICINE, 1534

From Stefan Falimirz, *O ziołach i o moczy ich . . .* (Crakow: Florian Ungler, 1534)
Woodcut, 4 7/16 x 5" (11.3 x 12.7 cm) (trimmed)
Purchased: SmithKline Beckman Corporation Fund
69-190-31

28b

Anonymous (Polish, sixteenth century)
COOKING HERBS FOR MEDICINE, 1534

From Stefan Falimirz, *O ziołach i o moczy ich . . .* (Crakow: Florian Ungler, 1534)
Woodcut, 5 x 4 7/16" (12.7 x 11.3 cm) (trimmed)
Purchased: SmithKline Beckman Corporation Fund
69-190-30

28c

Anonymous (Polish, sixteenth century)
ADMINISTERING MEDICINAL HERBS, 1534

From Stefan Falimirz, *O ziołach i o moczy ich . . .* (Crakow: Florian Ungler, 1534)
Woodcut, 6 3/16 x 4 7/16" (15.8 x 11.3 cm) (trimmed)
Purchased: SmithKline Beckman Corporation Fund
69-190-29

Since earliest times plants have provided most of humanity's medicinal remedies, and the foundation of the modern pharmacopoeia is firmly based on the knowledge of herbs, trees, and plants and their flowers and fruits. Even today many medications are simply refinements or chemical translations of earlier natural remedies.

During the medieval period the cultivation of herbs was primarily the domain of monks and nuns, who not only grew and harvested these plants but also distilled them and prepared medications. An herb, or physic, garden was part of every cloister and monastery. These three plates showing the gathering, preparing, and administering of herbs within a convent appeared in an early Polish herbal published in Crakow in 1534. Compiled by Stefan Falimirz from contemporary botanical works printed in Poland that drew also on ancient and medieval texts, this herbal is one of the oldest pharmaceutical and therapeutic works printed in Polish,[1] and contains 254 chapters describing medicinal plants and their remedial powers. The book is heavily illustrated with woodcuts both copied from earlier works and originally produced for this volume, most likely by unknown Crakow artists.[2] In his dedication Falimirz praised the publisher Florian Ungler for "lavishing great care on the graphic aspect of the work" and for sparing no cost in "adorning the book with wonderful images."[3]

In the first of these three woodcuts (no. 28a), a nun gathers herbs from the physic garden within the cloister walls. To either side of her are the figures of Saints Cosmas and Damian, dressed in handsome robes. Cosmas, patron saint of physicians, gazes at a urine flask, while Damian, patron of apothecaries, holds an apothecary jar, or beaker. In the second plate (no. 28b), the nun with the bundle of herbs on her back and a basket of herbs in her hand enters the cloister kitchen—an alembic, or distilling, plant of the simplest variety, where the herb crops are being converted into medicinal potions and liquors. The third scene (no. 28c) is a hospital room or cell in a cloister, where a sick man lies listlessly in bed while one of the nuns administers medicine by spoon. At the head of the bed two physicians consult over a flask containing the sick man's urine. The box with its circular opening is a simple commode.

1. See Jan Szostak, "Autorzy pierwszych zielników polskich—Stefan Falimirz, Hieronim Spiczyński i Marcin Siennik," *Archiwum Historii Medycyny*, vol. 40 (1977), p. 277.
2. See January Kołodziejczyk, "W poszukiwaniu źródeł do botanicznej ksiegi herbarza Stefana Falimirza," *Archiwum Historii Medycyny*, vol. 20 (1957), pp. 35–36.
3. Quoted in ibid., p. 43. Translation of these quotations and the two articles cited above by Lindsay F. Watton III, Department of Slavic Languages, University of Pennsylvania, Philadelphia.

D.K.

29

Anonymous, possibly by François (Jean) Jollat (French, active 1502–50)
After Francesco de' Rossi, known as Cecco di Salviati (Italian, 1510–1563)
MANUAL REDUCTION OF A DISLOCATED SHOULDER, 1544

From Guido Guidi, *Opera Varia. Omnibus Medicinae Studiosis Utilissima . . .* (Lyons: Ioannem Veyrat, 1599), a cancel title for *Chirurgia é Graeco in Latinum Conversa* (Paris: Pierre Gaultier, 1544)
Woodcut, 13 7/16 x 9 1/8" (34.1 x 23.2 cm)
Purchased: SmithKline Beckman Corporation Fund
68-25-80

This woodcut is from a book on various surgical techniques, mostly dealing with bone fractures and dislocations, published in Paris in 1544. The text for the publication was a new Latin translation of a much older Greek manuscript, which had been purchased in 1492 for the great Florentine patron of art and literature Lorenzo de' Medici and is now in the Biblioteca Laurenziana in Florence.[1] This illustrated manuscript consisted of a compilation of ancient texts, dating to the fifth century B.C., that had been put together in the ninth or early tenth century A.D. by a Byzantine physician, one Nicetas, possibly at the request of the Byzantine emperor Constantine Porphyrogenitus. It contained six works attributed to Hippocrates, the Father of Medicine (including one on bone dislocation); one by Galen, the Eastern-born physician who worked in Rome in the second century A.D. (on techniques of bandaging), along with Galen's commentaries on Hippocrates; and two by the fourth-century A.D. Byzantine medical writer Oribasius, one on knots and harnesses for immobilizing limbs and one on machines for the adjustment of bones and joints. The present print illustrates one such apparatus.

At some point in the early sixteenth century it was decided (and it is not known by whom, where, or for what purpose) to publish a new Latin version of the manuscript with an original commentary by Guido Guidi (Latinized, Vidus Vidius) with illustrations.[2] The part played by Guido Guidi in this entrepreneurial enterprise remains obscure and is shrouded in the elaborate patronage structures of the day. Guido, a Florentine by birth and the grandson of the painter Domenico Ghirlandaio, had been working in Rome when he was summoned to the Collège de France in Paris to hold the first royal chair of surgery established there by Francis I. It is known that while there he shared living quarters with Benvenuto Cellini, who praised him as the "most cultivated, most affectionate, and the most companionable man of worth" he had ever known.[3]

The Byzantine manuscript had contained contemporary illuminations, possibly derived from classical prototypes. At some point in the late 1530s or early 1540s, two new sets of drawings were made to accompany two versions of the manuscript, one in Latin and one in Greek, which Guido was to carry with him when he journeyed to France in May 1542.[4] These new drawings, done in ink and wash and in the then-fashionable Italian Mannerist style, were based on the Nicetas illuminations and apparently as well on another set of diagrams that describe the machinery for the treatment of dislocations, which were drawn by John Santorinos of Rhodes, a sixteenth-century physician working in Rome.[5] The woodcut illustrations for the *Chirurgia* are based on the illustrations in the Latin manuscript. There has been some controversy over the authorship of this splendid set of drawings, and in some of the literature the artist is given as the Bolognese-born Primaticcio. Recent scholarship, however, gives the credit to the Florentine Mannerist artist Francesco de' Rossi, known as Cecco di Salviati.[6]

This print shows a vivid and dramatic enactment of the manual reduction of a dislocated shoulder.[7] It illustrates a section of the Oribasius text dealing with recommended treatments for broken bones and dislocated joints. Guido suggests the methods that he followed: "In the interpretations of these machines I was keen not only to understand what was written but also to depict and to make models in wood so that I can give a better idea of them than by description."[8] The print shows the apparatus described by Oribasius and its utilization by the surgeon (at right), his assistant (at left), and the hapless patient in the middle. The texts on treatment of dislocation from Hippocrates on stress the need to minimize violence in these kinds of operations. In terms of actual treatment, one cannot resist quoting C. E. Kellett: "It is precisely because of these particular illustrations which show so eloquently how not to effect a reduction, that this book has achieved its renown."[9]

1. MS. LXXIV, 7.
2. C. E. Kellett, "The Chirurgia of Vidus Vidius, 1544, An Occasional Lecture, May, 1959," in C. E. Kellett, *Mannerism and Medical Illustration (Lectures on the Iconography of the "Chirurgia" of Vidus Vidius, "De Dissectione" of Estienne Rivière, Given at UCLA, October 1961)* (Los Angeles, 1961), n.p.
3. Benvenuto Cellini, *The Life of Benvenuto Cellini Written by Himself*, ed. and trans. John Addington Symonds (New York, 1906), vol. 2, p. 146.
4. The best account of the *Chirurgia's* complicated history is in Michael Hirst, "Salviati illustrateur de Vidus Vidius," *Revue de L'Art*, no. 6 (1969), pp. 19–28.
5. The manuscripts containing the two sets of Mannerist drawings and the Santorinos diagrams are in the Bibliothèque Nationale, Paris, MSS. Lat. 6866, Gk. 2247, Gk. 2248.
6. By Hirst ("Salviati"), who arrived at his opinion independently of the earlier work by C. E. Kellett, "The School of Salviati and the Illustrations to the Chirurgia of Vidus Vidius," *Medical History*, vol. 2 (1958), pp. 264–68.
7. The preparatory drawing for the print is folio 314, verso, of MS. Lat. 6866 cited in n. 5 above. There is another drawing of almost identical composition, now in the collection of Her Majesty Queen Elizabeth II at Windsor Castle, that Hirst considers to be an earlier version of the Paris sheet (Hirst, "Salviati," pp. 26, 27, fig. 19).
8. Translated and quoted in W. Brockbank, "Three Manuscript Precursors of Vidius's Chirurgia," *Medical History*, vol. 2 (1958), pp. 191–94.
9. Kellett, "Chirurgia of 1544," n.p.

M.C.

30a

Anonymous (Dutch, late sixteenth century) After Hendrik Goltzius (Dutch, 1558–1617) THE PHYSICIAN AS GOD, 1587

From "The Medical Professions," 1587
Engraving with woodcut inscription, 7 15/16 x 8 7/8" (20.1 x 22.5 cm)
Anonymous gift
59-6-6

30b

Anonymous (Dutch, late sixteenth century) After Hendrik Goltzius (Dutch, 1558–1617) THE PHYSICIAN AS ANGEL, 1587

From "The Medical Professions," 1587
Engraving with woodcut inscription, 7 15/16 x 8 15/16" (20.1 x 22.6 cm)
Anonymous gift
59-6-7

30c

Anonymous (Dutch, late sixteenth century)
After Hendrik Goltzius (Dutch, 1558–1617)
THE PHYSICIAN AS MAN, 1587

From "The Medical Professions," 1587
Engraving with woodcut inscription, 8 x 9⅛" (20.3 x 23.1 cm)
Anonymous gift
59-6-8

30d

Anonymous (Dutch, late sixteenth century)
After Hendrik Goltzius (Dutch, 1558–1617)
THE PHYSICIAN AS DEVIL, 1587

From "The Medical Professions," 1587
Engraving with woodcut inscription, 8 x 9" (20.3 x 22.9 cm)
Anonymous gift
59-6-9

The series of four prints known as "The Medical Professions" was published by Hendrik Goltzius at Haarlem in 1587. Engraved by one of Goltzius's pupils after his designs, the series traces the changes in a patient's attitude toward his doctor as he progresses from grave illness back to health, a transition through which Goltzius had passed many times (see no. 10). In the central foreground of each print an allegorical figure of the physician—as god, angel, man, and finally the devil—stands on a platform with his instrument case strapped to his waist. On the platform, to either side of the physician, are various tools and books used by the medical professions. Background vignettes show the patient with various attendants as well as intimate glimpses of contemporary medical and surgical practices.

In the first engraving (no. 30a) the physician is viewed by the gravely ill patient as divine, capable of miraculous intervention on his behalf. The Christ-like, haloed doctor studies the urine flask in his right hand and holds an unguent jar in his left. In the second print (no. 30b) the crisis has passed, and the patient, having responded to the treatment, now sees his physician as an angel—still powerful but not quite divine. In the third engraving (no. 30c) the sick man has largely regained his health, and the physician is presented as a mere man, as the interaction between patient and doctor is more one of equals. In the final print (no. 30d), with the patient having completely recovered, the physician is depicted as the devil, for he has come to collect his fee. In the caption the wise doctor is cautioned to choose his patients carefully and to collect his fee during treatment, both difficult tasks.

D.K.

31a

Abraham Bosse (French, 1602–1676)
THE PURGE, c. 1635

From "The Trades," c. 1635
Etching, 10½ x 13³⁄₁₆" (26.7 x 33.5 cm) (trimmed)
Acquired by exchange
61-191-11

31b

Abraham Bosse (French, 1602–1676)
BLOODLETTING, c. 1635

From "The Trades," c. 1635
Etching, 9⁵⁄₁₆ x 12⁷⁄₁₆" (23.7 x 31.6 cm) (trimmed)
Purchased: SmithKline Beckman Corporation Fund
49-97-18

Bleeding and purging, two of the most common therapeutic procedures in the repertory of the seventeenth-century physician—albeit of questionable efficacy—are depicted in these scenes from a series of etchings by Abraham Bosse on "The Trades." An elegantly dressed physician attends his wealthy patient, and as much information is conveyed about the details and attitudes of the grand style of Parisian life as about the physician and his medical procedures. Bosse, a student of Jacques Callot and a prolific etcher of religious, historical, allegorical, and naturalist subjects—as well as views of contemporary life—inherited his master's attention to the specifics of the everyday world (see also no. 91); in "The Trades" he captured with a cutting edge, tart humor, and sexual inuendo worthy of Molière the city's artisans and professionals at their work.

Each etching is captioned with verses that present a dialogue for the *mise en scène*. In *The Purge* (no. 31a), the physician approaches the bed of a patient suffering from a fever, telling her that with the syringe he holds in his hand, he will gently quench the fever and refresh her. Explaining that her mistress is very modest and cannot suffer his approach, the maid offers to give the enema. The patient chides them for making so much noise in light of the mysterious ailment that forces her to submit to the purge, a treatment she fears will not cure her. Finally, the chambermaid, who carries in a commode, complains that she wants to leave before the physician gives the enema because it will be her task to clean the chamberpot.

In *Bloodletting* (no. 31b), the physician applies a tourniquet to the arm of the patient, who says:

> *I'll be brave, puncture with confidence. . . . How phlebotomy purifies the spirits and cleanses the blood of great putrefaction! Oh gods, the gentle hand, the agreeable puncture! . . . Above all remedies I value bloodletting. . . . I shall endure as much as you may wish to do.*

On the table at right are the physician's tools used to open the vein while the attendant at left holds a graduated bowl in which to catch the blood.

D.K.

32

Rembrandt Harmensz. van Rijn (Dutch, 1606–1669)
THE JEWISH PHYSICIAN EPHRAIM BONUS, 1647

Etching, drypoint, and engraving (ii/ii), 9½ x 7" (24.1 x 17.8 cm)
Purchased: SmithKline Beckman Corporation Fund
49-97-6

In this portrait of a highly respected and beloved clinician, Dr. Ephraim Bonus, Rembrandt presented an image of the ideal physician: intelligent, noble, and humane. Bonus (Bueno) was a Portuguese Jew who had immigrated to Holland and practiced medicine in Amsterdam. Not only his astuteness in diagnosis but also his compassion and character endeared him to the inhabitants of that city, of which he became a burgher in 1651. A writer also, Bonus supported the publishing firm of Samuel Manasseh Ben Israel, through whom he may have met Rembrandt.

This etching is a brilliant impression that demonstrates the subtle treatment of darks and lights and psychological presence characteristic of Rembrandt's finest portraits. There is no idealization of appearance, and Bonus is not made handsome or elegant. He is shown in a simple space punctuated only by the sturdy banister upon which he rests his hand. Rembrandt highlighted the intelligent and compassionate face and the gentle, stubby hand against the darkened ground, emphasizing both mind and hand, the primary tools of a good clinician.

D.K.

33

Giuseppe Maria Mitelli (Italian, 1634–1718) After Annibale Carracci (Italian, 1560–1609)
CHARLATAN ON HIS STAGE, HOLDING A SNAKE, 1660

From *Di Bologna l'arti per via d'Anibal Caraci [Le Arti di Bologna]* (Rome: Gio. Iacomo Rossi, 1660)
Etching, 11³⁄₁₆ x 7¾" (28.4 x 19.7 cm)
Purchased: SmithKline Beckman Corporation Fund
58-150-33(25)

This etching, along with others in the same series, is derived from the famous set of drawings of Bolognese *mestieri ambulanti* (street trades) or *gridi di piazza* (cries of the piazza) done by Annibale Carracci before he moved to Rome in 1595. These drawings, known today by the various prints made after them, occupy an important place in the history of Italian Baroque art, as they furnish concrete evidence of the new interest displayed by seventeenth-century artists in recording aspects of daily life. Aside from this print the series includes representations of the street sweeper, the fruit seller, the peddler of rosaries and holy images, the well cleaner, and others.[1]

This print shows a quack doctor practicing his "art" on a makeshift stage in the public square, attended by an audience of the gullible. The figure of the doctor is easily recognizable by his spectacles (a convention denoting a man of learning), the snake or eel that he dangles (a snake-oil remedy?), the assortment of amulets or religious medals draped over his improvised table that undoubtedly have magical properties, and the vials of medicine on the table. The inscription below the print tells us that the doctor is exerting his "privilege of fooling the world."

It is always difficult to assess the amount of literal truth in an image such as this one of the charlatan doctor. The tradition of representing the trades was an old one, tracing its roots back to the medieval portrayals of the Labors of the Months or even the Dance of Death (see no. 96), in which people from all walks of life are shown facing the eventuality of death. The tradition found further expression in popular prints of the sixteenth and seventeenth centuries that must have been known to the artists themselves.[2]

Although Mitelli tended toward caricature in his treatment of the subjects, the fact that the original Carracci drawings were actually done from life is attested by the account of the seventeenth-century biographer of the Bolognese artists, Count Malvasia. He wrote that Annibale, to relax from the arduous task of producing major paintings, took to the streets with his drawing utensils and made sketches of the faces and figures of tradesmen who went about the city of Bologna making and selling various items.[3]

1. See Franca Varignana, *Le collezioni d'arte della Cassa di Risparmio in Bologna: Le incisioni,* vol. 1, *Giuseppe Maria Mitelli* (Bologna, 1978), pp. 205–20, nos. 1–41.
2. The literature on the popular tradition in northern Italy is considerable. For a discussion of Mitelli's roots in this tradition, see Giorgio Concetti, "Pace, pace non piu guerra: Le stampe di G. M. Mitelli e l'opinione publica bolognese alle fine del secolo XVII," *Strenna storica Bolognese*, vol. 11 (1961), pp. 111–31.
3. Carlo Cesare Malvasia, *Felsina pittrice; vite de' pittori bolognesi* (Bologna, 1841), vol. 1, pp. 335–36.

M.C.

34a

Cornelis Dusart (Dutch, 1660–1704)
THE VILLAGE SURGEON, 1695

Etching, 10¼ x 7¹⁄₁₆" (26 x 18 cm)
Charles M. Lea Collection
28-42-1270

34b

Cornelis Dusart (Dutch, 1660–1704)
THE CUPPER (THE LEECH WOMAN), 1695

Etching, 10 3/16 x 7 1/16" (25.8 x 18 cm)
Purchased: SmithKline Beckman Corporation Fund
71-116-7

Cornelis Dusart was a keen recorder of scenes of seventeenth-century Dutch peasants, and his spirited prints demonstrate a variety of aspects of everyday life in his native Haarlem. In these etchings Dusart turned his attention and sharp wit to the surgeon and cupper, the health practitioners used most often by villagers. Despite their obvious humor, these satirical views provide insights into the tools and procedures of local healers.

For all the scientific advances made in the Dutch universities, the practice of medicine for the general population in the seventeenth century remained poor, much the same as it had been for centuries. The village surgeon, who served as general surgeon, barber, and dentist, is shown performing a minor operation on a patient's arm (no. 34a). The chair with its tilted back allows the patient to recline, while the surgeon, with a lancet tucked into his cap and a probe in hand, goes about his work in front of the window, which provides the only light for his activities. Strapped to his belt is a case for his lancets and scalpels, making them easily accessible—although probably not very sanitary.

The surgeon's office is complete with the tools of his trade: instruments, mortars and pestles, ointment jar, distillation flask, and diagrams. On the window sill and adjacent chest, which serve as an instrument and supply table, are the familiar raffia case with its lid hanging open to reveal the urine flask inside; an oil jar, which probably contained medicinal unguent; a barber's bleeding bowl with a semicircular notch, which allowed it to be brought close to the neck or limb; and a roll of cloth for dressings. On the window jamb hangs an assortment of dental pliers and levers. Suspended from the ceiling is a stuffed reptile (an armadillo?), which, like the skull on the shelf above, is most likely a *vanitas* motif, a reminder of the transience of life.

The Cupper (no. 34b) is another view of seventeenth-century village therapy, this type almost always delivered by women. This "office" is even less elegant than the surgeon's and the scene is more explicitly comic. The cupper is shown busily applying a cup to the foot of the patient, a treatment believed to cure female disorders, gout, migraine, and sciatica.[1] The cupper wears spectacles and a funnel for a hat, a combination suggesting that Dusart considers her an empty-headed fool. Tacked to the mantle is her bogus certificate as a master cupper.

The ludicrous male assistant, who is about to lose his trousers, stands between cupper and patient sharpening a scarificator, which would be used to make slight incisions or scratches so that the blood would be collected when the cup was applied. On his head is the raffia basket ordinarily used to carry a urine flask (a clear indication of what was thought to be in his head) and tucked into his low-slung belt is an enema syringe. An inscription beneath the scene underscores its comic quality: "'You set out the cups,' said fat Piet to Trijn.[2] . . . 'In the meantime, I'll sharpen the files. It will cure her completely, and in case she faints and neither the ribbon nor wine helps, I will speedily give her an enema with my syringe!'"

The ribbon, which is tied to the back of the chair, alludes to a seventeenth-century folk technique commonly used to determine pregnancy. The woman's ribbon would be burned and her response to the smell of the smoke would indicate whether she was pregnant.[3] In this case the smell of burning fabric was expected to revive the woman from her faint. This misapplication of a pregnancy test is consistent with Dusart's view of these figures as objects of ridicule.

1. See Laura K. Manuelidis, "Kopster: An Etching by Cornelius Dusart (1660–1704)," *Journal of the History of Medicine and Allied Sciences*, vol. 22 (January 1967), p. 82.
2. These are characters from the Dutch comic theater; translation by Ella Schaap, Curatorial Associate, Philadelphia Museum of Art.
3. See Peter C. Sutton, "The Life and Art of Jan Steen," *Philadelphia Museum of Art Bulletin*, vol. 78, nos. 337–38 (Winter 1982–Spring 1983), p. 24 n. 10.

D.K.

35

Pier Leone Ghezzi (Italian, 1674–1755)
CARICATURE OF A DOCTOR HOLDING AN ENEMA SYRINGE, 1753

Brown ink over traces of black chalk on light buff laid paper, 12 3/4 x 8 3/4" (32.4 x 22.2 cm)
Purchased: SmithKline Beckman Corporation Fund
1978-62-1

Pier Leone Ghezzi has been described as the most engaging artistic personality in Rome during the first half of the eighteenth century. Painter, antiquarian, picture dealer, amateur musician, and dabbler in medicine and anatomy, he was a central figure in Rome's cultivated circles and held the official titles of director of the papal tapestry manufactory and painter of the Apostolic Chamber, after 1714.[1] Although his professional activities were varied during his long career, he is especially known today for his ink caricatures, which have survived in great numbers. Often dated and almost always identifying the subject by name, or at least by occupation, these record the activities of all levels of society of eighteenth-century Rome, from members of the papal court, nobles, families and friends of patrons, civil servants, and clergymen to artists, foreigners, tourists, and people of the city, documenting local personalities over the entire first half of the eighteenth century. This sheet is dated near the end of the artist's life, when he was nearly eighty years old.

The long inscription at the bottom of the sheet, in the artist's own hand, identifies the sitter as a doctor named Romanelli ("the nephew of Dr. Romanelli, who is also a doctor himself"). The inscription suggests that one or both Romanellis practiced medicine at an abbey belonging to the Albani family, which produced Cardinal Giovanni Francesco Albani, later Pope Clement XI (1700–1721), and Cardinal Alessandro Albani (1692–1779), antiquarian, collector, and patron of Johann Winckelmann and Anton Raphael Mengs, who were important patrons for Ghezzi as well.[2] Romanelli's employer was Cardinal Giovanni Francesco Albani (1720–1803), nephew of Cardinal Alessandro. The younger Romanelli, according to the inscription, came to Rome on May 15, 1753, and was drawn by the septuagenarian Ghezzi nine days later. Ghezzi's caricature exaggerates the eccentricities of the doctor's figure and features, presenting him next to an uncovered commode with an imposing enema syringe in hand.

1. See Edgar Peters Bowron in Ulrich W. Hiesinger and Ann Percy, eds., *A Scholar Collects: Selections from the Anthony Morris Clark Bequest* (Philadelphia, 1980), pp. 23–26, nos. 12–14.
2. Anthony M. Clark, "Pier Leone Ghezzi's Portraits," *Paragone*, vol. 14, no. 165 (September 1963), pp. 11–21.

A.P./D.K.

36

Thomas Rowlandson (English, 1756–1827) THE AMPUTATION, 1785

Hand-colored etching, aquatint, and stipple etching, 10⅜ x 14⅝" (26.4 x 37.1 cm) (trimmed)
Purchased: SmithKline Beckman Corporation Fund
1982-82-1

Thomas Rowlandson, one of Britain's greatest draftsmen and caricaturists, often occupied himself with medical subjects (see nos. 17 and 78). His work includes many prints and drawings of doctors and surgeons, fashionable quacks and apothecaries, and patients being operated on, often with disastrous results.[1]

In this relatively early work,[2] Rowlandson concentrates on a group of overzealous surgeons performing an amputation on a patient, whose right leg, about to be sawn off, appears to be perfectly healthy. The learned men, bewigged and bespectacled, have tied their patient to a chair; as he screams in pain and terror, the surgeons, ignoring his suffering, draw closer to get a better view of the gruesome operation. The man on the left is ready with the wooden leg, which will soon be needed.

Rowlandson drives home his satiric point by using a dissecting room as the setting for the scene. The room is littered with skeletons, and behind the surgeons, a corpse is partly visible. Clearly, at least in Rowlandson's opinion, these doctors are more concerned with impressing each other than they are with the comfort and well-being of any individual patient. The "List of Examined and Approved Surgeons" on the wall, which includes names such as Doctor Peter Putrid and Cristopher Cutgutt, is further proof of Rowlandson's lack of respect for the medical profession.

1. See John Riely, *Rowlandson Drawings from the Paul Mellon Collection* (New Haven, 1977), p. 85, no. 115.
2. This impression is clearly dated 1785. According to Joseph Grego (*Rowlandson, the Caricaturist*, vol. 1 [London, 1879], p. 107, and vol. 2 [London, 1880], pp. 389, 394), this print was first published in 1783 and reissued in 1793.

D.K./K.R.

37

Giovanni Domenico Tiepolo (Italian, 1727–1804) ITINERANT DENTIST TREATING A PATIENT, WITH SEVERAL OBSERVERS, possibly c. 1790

Brown ink and gray and brown washes over traces of black chalk on off-white antique laid paper, 14⅝ x 19¹³⁄₁₆" (37.2 x 50.3 cm)
Purchased: SmithKline Beckman Corporation Fund
1981-63-1

Giovanni Domenico Tiepolo was the pupil, chief studio assistant, and principal collaborator of his famous father, Giovanni Battista, although he was by no means a simple imitator of his father's manner. Returning to Venice from Madrid after his father's death there in 1770, he became the major history painter in the old-fashioned grand manner, although he painted less and less after the 1780s. His particular contributions to the family studio production—and, in fact, to Venetian painting of the period—were his genre scenes drawn from local contemporary life, which he represented with unique and captivating charm. Especially appealing are his numerous ink and wash drawings of these subjects, such as this sheet.

Tiepolo's depictions include country scenes with peasants and Gypsies, glimpses of aristocratic pursuits and entertainments, and vignettes of everyday life in Venice,[1] such as this scene of a street crowd observing the discomfort of a patient treated by an itinerant dentist on an open-air platform, with an attendant dressed in *commedia dell'arte* costume. A number of local genre sheets by Tiepolo bear the date 1791,[2] and it is likely that this undated work belongs to about that time. Certainly it is similar in manner to at least three drawings dated that year;[3] Tiepolo treated the subject in another, differently composed drawing[4] and in several paintings, the best known of which seems to predate the early 1760s.[5]

The kind of dental treatment depicted in this drawing was not the only relief available for sufferers in the 1790s. Educated, professional practitioners of dentistry and dental surgery, capable of treating diseases of the gums and teeth, correcting irregularities, and filling, extracting, replacing, or transplanting teeth, existed; there was also a flourishing literature in the field.[6] In the hierarchy of contemporary dental professionalism, this scene reflects the lowest order, the itinerant tooth puller who set up shop in a public square, fair, or marketplace, often on a platform, embellished with signs, music makers, or elaborate costumes to attract customers.[7] Such mountebanks presented themselves as dentists, barbers, leechers, alchemists, or purveyors of remedies.[8]

Here the tooth puller, seated on his makeshift public platform, treats a patient who raises one hand in supplication as the other holds a cloth, probably as protection from the profuse bleeding of the extraction. The three peasant women at right patiently watch his work, with the woman nearest the platform holding a cloth to her cheek as though to suggest she will be the next patient.

That the "dentist" here is essentially a quack is demonstrated by three inscriptions of 1765 and 1779 related to Tiepolo's painted versions of the subject in the Louvre in Paris and in a private collection in Rome. One refers to the quack's platform set up in a piazza, with one charlatan pulling teeth and the other dispensing medicine; the second complains, "Now with the voice, now with the hand, the charlatan extracts either money or teeth"; the third laments the gullibility of the populace taken advantage of by the quacks out for profit.[9]

1. James Byam Shaw, *The Drawings of Domenico Tiepolo* (Boston, 1962), pp. 48–49.
2. See, for example, ibid., p. 47 and pls. 70, 72–73, 75.
3. See Jacob Bean and Felice Stampfle, *Drawings from New York Collections III: The Eighteenth Century in Italy* (New York, 1971), pls. 260–61; and Adriano Mariuz, *Giandomenico Tiepolo* (Venice, 1971), fig. 27.
4. Byam Shaw, *Tiepolo*, pl. 66.
5. Mariuz, *Tiepolo*, pl. 85.
6. See Bernhard Wolf Weinberger, *An Introduction to the History of Dentistry* (Saint Louis, 1948), vol. 1, pp. 297–388; and Vincenzo Guerini, *A History of Dentistry from the Most Ancient Times until the End of the Eighteenth Century* (Philadelphia, 1909), pp. 255–348.
7. See Arthur Ward Lufkin, *A History of Dentistry* (Philadelphia, 1938), pp. 86–88; and J.-Léonard André-Bonnet, *Histoire générale de la chirurgie dentaire* (Lyons, 1955), pp. 126ff.
8. Weinberger, *History of Dentistry*, vol. 1, pp. 297–98.
9. Quoted in Mariuz, *Tiepolo*, pp. 131, 135.

A.P./D.K.

38

Pierre-Alexandre Wille (French, 1748–1837) ITINERANT DENTIST WITH HIS PATIENT AND TWO OBSERVERS, 1803

Brown ink and colored washes over traces of black chalk on cream wove paper, 13 1/16 x 9 1/4" (33.2 x 23.5 cm)
Purchased: SmithKline Beckman Corporation Fund
1984-81-1

Pierre-Alexandre Wille was the son of the German artist Johann Georg Wille, who lived in Paris from 1736 until his death in 1808 and was one of the important reproductive engravers of the time. Accepted into the Académie Royale de Peinture et de Sculpture in 1774 as a genre painter, Pierre-Alexandre exhibited in all the salons from 1775 to 1787. A painter, draftsman, and engraver, he ended his life in poverty, strapped by the expenses of maintaining his wife in the insane asylum at Charenton.[1]

This sheet is consistent in type with the artist's specialty in genre subjects and similar to one of the few published examples of his ink drawings, a study of *Three Revolutionaries* dated 1793.[2] The "dentist" is identified by the pulled tooth and the dental forceps on the table and by the patient clutching his swollen jaw. His flamboyant hat, his obvious touting of a remedy (possibly laudanum, applied topically at that time in Europe to ease the pain of extraction), and the rapt expressions of the boorish onlookers identify the subject as an itinerant or charlatan, rather than an educated professional.

The man in the lower left corner holding his apparently painful, distorted face glances out as though questioning the promises of the dentist, although his expression may not be one of question but of implication. In his famous dental treatise of 1728, Pierre Fauchard described the itinerant dentist's performance:

> *A man, bribed in advance, appears when the dentist calls for those with a toothache to come forward, pay their pennies, and be cured. This shill, having inserted a previously extracted tooth into his mouth along with a bloody hen's membrane, then sits for the dentist, and before an awed crowd spits out the large, bloodied tooth as testimony of this painless "extraction."*[3]

1. See Louis Hautecoeur, "Pierre-Alexandre Wille le fils (1748–1821?)," *Archives de l'art français*, n.s., vol. 7 (1913), pp. 440–66; and Colin Clark, "Pierre-Alexandre Wille: The Later Years," *Master Drawings*, vol. 18, no. 3 (Autumn 1980), p. 269.
2. K. E. Maison, "Pierre-Alexandre Wille and the French Revolution," *Master Drawings*, vol. 10, no. 1 (Spring 1972), pl. 35.
3. Pierre Fauchard, *Le Chirurgien dentiste; ou, traité des dents . . .* (Paris, 1728), p. 17.

A.P./D.K.

39

Henry Alken (English, 1785–1851)
CALVES' HEADS AND BRAINS, OR A PHRENOLOGICAL LECTURE, 1826

Hand-colored soft-ground etching, etching, and engraving,
9¾ x 12¾" (24.8 x 32.4 cm)
Purchased: SmithKline Beckman Corporation Fund
1984-12-1

The sporting painter and engraver Henry Alken here turns his attention to the fashionable "science" of phrenology.[1] Extremely popular during the 1820s, phrenology was the study of an individual's mental faculties—personality, character, talents—through an examination of the lumps, ridges, shape, and size of his cranium. This theory was based on the work of Franz Joseph Gall (1758–1828) and popularized in Britain by his student Johann Kaspar Spurzheim (1776–1832), who made a lecture tour of England between 1813 and 1817.[2]

Alken's print is a satire on just such a lecture. A fashionably dressed audience, displaying an enormous variety of cranial shapes and facial expressions, listens, enthralled by the speaker's explanations. The lecturer himself, who has torn his wig from his head to make a point, has a skull riddled with an amazing variety of cranial lumps and bumps. Busts of great men (including, of course, Gall and Spurzheim) adorn the lecture room, together with busts whose skulls illustrate general phrenological characteristics of human qualities such as "Slyness," "Pride," "Sleepiness," and "Consequence."

Alken's satirical view of phrenology is further emphasized by the pictures on the wall above the phrenological advertisements and illustrations. From left to right are portrayed "Bumps" (two boxers battering each other), "Life's a Bumper" (a man drinking a bumper, or full glass, of wine), and an actor in the role of a character named Tony Lumpkin. Alken's finishing touch is his "signature," which says that the image was drawn by J. Lump and engraved by L. Bump.

1. This print is unsigned, but there is an impression in the British Museum, London, attributed to Alken.
2. Victoria and Albert Museum, London, *English Caricature: 1620 to the Present* (1984), pp. 38–39.

K.R./D.K.

40

Honoré Daumier (French, 1808–1879)
THE PHYSICIAN: WHY THE DEVIL! ARE ALL MY PATIENTS DEPARTING THIS WAY? . . . , 1833

Published in *Le Charivari*, August 19, 1833
Lithograph, 11⁵⁄₁₆ x 8" (28.7 x 20.3 cm)
Gift of Carl Zigrosser
68-162-20

The French painter, sculptor, and printmaker Honoré Daumier, well known for his political caricatures, became interested in developing new themes for his illustrations for the leftist Parisian newspaper *Le Charivari*, with which he was involved from its founding in 1832. His concern with the plight of the contemporary physician was one of these themes, and a subject to which he would return frequently during his career.

This scene depicts a middle-aged physician, seated at his desk, under the gaze of a bust of Hippocrates. This dejected, melancholy figure, who holds a handkerchief as though he has been crying, is surrounded by images running through his mind that cause him to lament: "Why the devil! Are all my patients departing this way? . . . I do my best to bleed them, purge them, and drug them . . . I don't understand anything about it!"

The skeletal figure of Death, carrying a scythe above the physician's head, leads a grim procession of dead Parisians that rises from the floor. Some of the dead have already been placed in coffins made by the ghoulish carpenters who work on the desk; others are being carried off by underworld assistants to Satan. Even the gendarme seems to be allied with the devil as he walks along with the bereaved family members. Significantly, under the physician's chair a man covering his face in grief is dressed as a worker wearing a nightcap.

The inadequacy of the physician in the face of widespread disease was commonly felt in the early 1830s in Paris, its slums overcrowded with the influx of workers seeking jobs in the newly industrialized French capital. The dangers of epidemics in such neighborhoods were enormous, and statistical studies by public health officials demonstrated that the high adult and infant mortality was caused by inadequate sewage systems and unsanitary, crowded housing. These studies also showed that survival rates from the diseases then rampant were 70 percent lower in the poor districts than in the city's wealthy *arrondissements;* cholera epidemics often killed over 60 percent of the workers in the industrial suburbs. In this lithograph Daumier is warning that physicians would remain powerless to alter this grim picture of death and poverty unless government policies were changed to improve the economic and public health conditions in French cities.

A.S.

41a

Charles Maurin (French, 1856–1914) Study for SERUM THERAPY, 1895

Graphite on architects' linen, 31⁹⁄₁₆ x 40⅜" (80.2 x 102.6 cm) (irregular)
Purchased: SmithKline Beckman Corporation Fund
1984-19-2

41b

Charles Maurin (French, 1856–1914) SERUM THERAPY, c. 1896

Etching and drypoint, 13⅝ x 15⁹⁄₁₆" (34.6 x 39.6 cm)
Purchased: SmithKline Beckman Corporation Fund
1984-19-1

Diphtheria, an acute contagious disease with a high mortality rate, usually strikes pre-school-age children. Before immunization, it was a common and dreaded threat, at times reaching epidemic proportions. The subject of this drawing and etching is the discovery and successful application of a serum treatment against the often fatal illness.

Between 1888 and 1890 one of the pioneers of medical bacteriology, Pierre-Paul-Emil Roux and his assistant Alexandre Yersin, working on the basis of discoveries about innoculation by the Prussian army surgeon Emil von Behring, isolated diphtheria bacteria. In 1892 and 1893 Roux and another assistant, Louis Martin, developed a method of injecting horses with diphtheria toxin to obtain from their blood an antitoxin serum that could be used in treating humans with the disease.[1] Between February 1 and July 24, 1894, Roux treated three hundred children with diphtheria at the Hôpital des Enfants-Malades in Paris with this serum, reducing their mortality rate from 50 to 26 percent.[2] In September 1894 he presented the results of his experiments to the Tenth International Hygienic Congress in Budapest.[3] The next year the lesser known French painter and printmaker Charles Maurin produced one of his more important works in honor of Roux's achievement, a painting entitled *Serum Therapy* (Musée des Hospices Civils, Lyons). This drawing (no. 41a) is his preliminary study for that painting.

Maurin was born and grew up in Le Puy (Haute-Loire). At the age of nineteen he won a local competition enabling him to study in Paris, where he attended the Académie Julian. In the 1880s and 1890s he exhibited in various salons; his primary commissions were portraits, although he also did history paintings, allegories, and architectural decorations and was a productive printmaker.[4]

Maurin's painting *Serum Therapy* is similar in size to the drawing. The artist also made an etching of the subject, of which the Museum owns an impression (no. 41b). The etching, another impression of which bears a manuscript dedication dated 1896,[5] follows the painting in all details, whereas the drawing has different heads on some of the bodies, suggesting that the drawing was done before the painting but the etching after it.

Most of the heads are portraits, and the central, seated figure, hatless in the etching and the painting, is Roux.[6] Above Roux, facing the immunized horse from whose blood the serum would be drawn, are the two assistants, Yersin and Martin. Reclining on the ground below the horse is another bacteriologist, André Chantemesse, with his wife facing him. The patron who presumably commissioned the painting, Henri Laurent, is seen bust-length with folded arms at the left; facing him in the print is an unknown man, and to his right a friend of Maurin, Jean Richepin, stares at him. Richepin was the author of the little poem in homage to Roux that appears at the bottom of the print:

> *Smiles of children cured,*
> *Festive sparks in the mothers' eyes that weep*
> *no more,*
> *Songs of all our birds saved from the birdcatchers,*
> *Be the diamonds, the laurels, and the flowers of*
> *which his crown will be made.*[7]

Members of the Laurent and Richepin families account for other portrait heads. The long-haired woman behind Laurent, holding a baby and being forcibly repelled by another woman, is presumably the figure of Death. The domed structure in the background to the left of center suggests the celebrated Cathedral of the Sacred Heart in Paris, symbol of salvation from national calamities such as invasions, revolutions, or epidemics.

Maurin drew a number of studies for individual heads and other elements in the composition of the painting.[8] His composition, peopled with dignified men, healthy children, and protective mothers, exudes a spirit of triumphant celebration to herald the important breakthroughs in the fight against a major child-killing disease.

1. H. Gillet, *La Pratique de la sérothérapie et les traitements nouveaux de la diphtérie* (Paris, 1895), pp. 18–24, 32–64.
2. Raoul Bayeux, *La Diphtérie depuis arétée le cappadocien jusqu'en 1894 avec les résultats statistiques de la sérumthérapie . . .* (Paris, 1899), pp. 106–9.
3. Address partially quoted in ibid., pp. 105–11. See also Arthur L. Bloomfield, *A Bibliography of Internal Medicine: Communicable Diseases* (Chicago, 1958), pp. 256–57, 260–61.
4. See Roger Gounot, *Charles Maurin, 1856–1914* (Puy, 1978).
5. Ibid., p. 43, no. 93D.
6. Ibid., pp. 46–47, no. 108D.
7. Translation by Suzanne G. Lindsay.
8. Gounot, *Maurin,* nos. 21D, 23D–26D, 33D.

A.P./D.K.

42
James Ensor (Belgian, 1860–1949)
THE BAD DOCTORS, 1895

Etching, 7 1/16 x 9 15/16" (17.9 x 25.2 cm)
Purchased: SmithKline Beckman Corporation Fund
68-166-1

During his early years in Ostend, the Belgian seaside resort where his family operated a small souvenir shop, James Ensor was encouraged to paint small land- and seascapes that could be sold to visitors. In the 1880s, after attending art school, he began to depict scenes of lower-class life. From these early images of beggars and drunkards Ensor developed a commitment to the social purposes of art, an approach he shared with contemporaries such as van Gogh.

The Bad Doctors is a satirical print that has its origin in the popular images of ill-trained healers taking advantage of their patients. Seventeenth-century Flemish and Dutch prints were models for Ensor, and he may have also seen Hogarth's and Rowlandson's (see no. 36) caricatures of greedy and incompetent doctors.

In this print the patient held down by a noose is portrayed as the helpless victim. He will soon be claimed by Death, who stands near the door in his tattered cloak. The three doctors in the center work with the complicity of the patient's aproned "friend," who reaches into a doctor's pocket, apparently to get a share of the fee.

One doctor has removed the patient's backbone, another has purged him, and the third has either given him a pitcher of medication or tapped his abdomen to remove fluids. Their surgical instruments are a carpenter's saw, corkscrew, and butcher knife. As the physicians perform what seems to be a Dance of the Dead (see no. 96), their legs have become entwined in the rope of bones that stretches from the belly of the patient. An additional gruesome touch is found in the basket containing some of the patient's innards.

Ensor provides further comment on these doctors' attitudes toward their patients by the inscriptions on the pages lying in the foreground: "Woman X croaked at seven o'clock. Received one thousand francs. To send Z [perhaps for an unpaid bill]. Nothing received. I left a sponge in the abdomen. Peritonitis resulted."

A.S.

43
Max Beckmann (German, 1884–1950)
THE LARGE OPERATION, 1914

From *Gesichter* (Munich: R. Piper, 1919)
Drypoint, 11 11/16 x 17 11/16" (29.7 x 44.9 cm)
Purchased: SmithKline Beckman Corporation Fund
70-191-6

Max Beckmann remains a solitary figure within the movement known as German Expressionism. His personal vision combined with rigorous objectivity to produce a vast body of prints, drawings, paintings, and sculpture that express his view of the spectacle of human worth and the absurd folly of the world around him.

With the onset of World War I in 1914, Beckmann, rather than bear arms, volunteered as a medical corpsman in East Prussia. At this early date the artist shared the German enthusiasm for the war, but as the bloody, inhuman events unfolded the experience would leave indelible marks on a man already attuned to the macabre side of humanity. Finding himself increasingly exposed to the awesome power of war as he "shared the experience of frightful things" and "died with the dying several times,"[1] Beckmann began to create his powerful images of man in a world that had slipped inexorably into chaos.

Beckmann produced several prints during 1914 that present his views of the war: the soldiers, brothels, maneuvers, and medical scenes. *The Large Operation*, published in the portfolio *Gesichter* in 1919, is drawn from the vantage point of a fly on the wall in a crowded operating room of a German surgical station. Able, in the first year of the war, to find "deep lines of beauty"[2] even in the harsh realities of pain and suffering, here Beckmann has scratched the stark white paper with rapid, sharp, angular lines to record the tense activity and mood of the scene.

Under bright illumination a surgeon prepares to operate on the exposed body stretched in front of him as the nurses bustle around the crowded room. Even before this surgery has begun one more war-ravaged figure is being carried in on a litter, and behind him yet another draped patient lies awaiting attention. The impact of the scene is enhanced by the inclusion, at the back right, of a face (bearing a striking resemblance to the artist) that peers over the shoulder of the surgeon. Early in the war Beckmann experienced a wide range of emotions—horror, fascination, even exhilaration—in response to the vast drama and scale of the destruction he witnessed, a conflict of reactions that was to surface in his drawings and etchings. It was in fact this conflict that contributed to the physical and emotional breakdown that finally wrenched Beckmann from the immediate devastation of the war if not from its images (see no. 83).

1. Beckmann, translated and quoted in Carla Schulz-Hoffmann and Judith C. Weiss, eds., *Max Beckmann: Retrospective* (Saint Louis, 1984), p. 71.
2. Beckmann, translated and quoted in ibid.

D.K.

44

George Bellows (American, 1882–1925)
BASE HOSPITAL (second version), 1918

From "War Series," 1918
Lithograph, 17⅝ x 13⁹⁄₁₆" (44.7 x 34.4 cm)
Purchased: SmithKline Beckman Corporation Fund
1980-52-1

This lithograph, George Bellows's second version of *Base Hospital*, is the first in his "War Series." It depicts a dressing station for wounded soldiers in an American base hospital in Europe during World War I. A number of the great cathedrals of France had been transformed into hospitals complete with enormous wards, infirmaries, and operating rooms. Yet the enormous scale of the architecture shown in this print in no way dwarfs the stature of the surgeon and his team, who prepare to operate on the draped body of the soldier lying on a makeshift table.

In whites, the sharply lit surgeon seems to be caught in the tense moment of contemplation. The male nurse stands by with towels or drapes and a covered container, which may hold sterilized instruments. Around them stands a group of figures—monks, doctors, assistants—whose presence gives human scale to the vast space. The strange, faceless figure at the back, silhouetted against the bright cathedral nave, seems to hover like the very presence of Death—the dark counterpart to the light of the surgeon.

Bellows, a popular illustrator and lithographer, was not in Europe during World War I, and, according to the artist, this image was based on photographic materials rather than direct observation. It grew out of the artist's reactions to the Bryce Committee's "Report on Deliberate Slaughter of Belgian Non-Combatants," which filled three pages of the *New York Times* when it was printed in 1915. The body of the report, a propagandistic document designed to incite the American public's outrage, was a gruesomely detailed eyewitness description of atrocities against civilians. Having been published almost immediately after the sinking of the *Lusitania*, the report had great impact in America as feelings against the Germans grew stronger. Bellows is said to have referred to the prints of the "War Series" as "hallucinations," a quality that registers here with great impact.

D.K.

45

John Sloan (American, 1871–1951)
X-RAYS, 1926

Etching and aquatint (ii/ii), 9¾ x 7¹⁵⁄₁₆" (24.8 x 20.1 cm)
Purchased: Katharine Levin Farrell Fund and funds contributed by Lessing J. Rosenwald
56-35-137

X-Rays, or more accurately *Fluoroscope*, as it was also called, had still another witty title by which John Sloan referred to it: *Department of the Interior*. This amusing etching documents the experience of fluoroscopy from the artist's point of view as a patient. Sloan had considerable internal trouble and underwent various diagnostic tests in an effort to find the cause of his problem. Here, he stands behind the fluoroscope screen holding a half-empty beaker of barium while physicians confer and stare at the eerily lit screen to watch the progress of the chalky opaque material in its course through his digestive tract. The sour expression on Sloan's face, familiar to anyone who has ever taken barium, is a humorous foil to the animated gestures of the physicians, who wear goggles to protect their eyes from the harsh light of the screen while unknowingly exposing themselves and the patient to high levels of radiation. The accuracy of the scene has been manipulated somewhat to reinforce the darkened drama: Goggles were necessary to view the screen only when the room lights were on and were not worn when the lights were turned down and the screen lit up.

The charm of this print lies in its ability to capture the quality of the moment—the patient's passive stance and the physicians' aggressive, hunched postures. With one hand on the machine the doctor brings the screen into focus on Sloan's interior, searching for the cause of his problems. The strange light from the fluoroscope casts bright highlights on the two physicians but sheds little light on the patient, who remains in semidarkness on the other side. Many have experienced this feeling of being in the dark while their physicians knowingly see the light, almost unaware of the patient who stands beyond the vital part on which they focus.

D.K.

46a

W. Eugene Smith (American, 1918–1978)
DR. CERIANI MAKING A HOUSE CALL, 1948

From "Country Doctor," 1948
Gelatin silver print, 19⅜ x 23⁷⁄₁₆" (49.2 x 59.5 cm)
Purchased: SmithKline Beckman Corporation Fund
1981-13-1

46b

W. Eugene Smith (American, 1918–1978)
DR. CERIANI AND PATIENT, 1948

From "Country Doctor," 1948
Gelatin silver print, 10⁹⁄₁₆ x 13½" (26.8 x 34.3 cm)
Purchased: SmithKline Beckman Corporation Fund
1984-55-1

W. Eugene Smith's stirring photographic essays go beyond straightforward documentation to present compassionate, insightful, visual discourses on the people, places, and events of his time. By the age of eighteen Smith had already formulated the principles of photography that would guide his career, as he wrote to his mother:

> *My station in life is to capture the action of life, the life of the world, its humor, its tragedies, in other words, life as it is. A true picture, unposed and real. . . . If I am shooting a beggar, I want the distress in his eyes, if a steel factory I want the symbol of strength and power that is there. . . . I want [my pictures] to be symbolic of something. . . . I realize that this is a pitiful effort to explain my philosophy of photography, but it is out of this haze that the fulfilling of my ambition will be.*[1]

His dedication to portraying his subjects truthfully and as powerfully as possible has made his work the standard of excellence against which all photojournalism is now measured (see nos. 47, 48, 66, 71, 85, and 92).

Smith's energy, enthusiasm, and passion for photography, as well as his extraordinary talent, established his career at a moment when the need for photojournalism was expanding dramatically. Successful magazines such as *Newsweek* (for which he began to work in 1937), *Time*, *Fortune*, and *Life* were constantly competing for photographs to fill their pages, which were attracting an ever-increasing audience. Smith pursued his ideals with unwavering energy, producing photo-essays that expanded the public's awareness of the subjects as well as of his chosen medium.

In 1947 Smith began to work for *Life*; in 1948 he was sent to a small town, Kremmling, Colorado, to photograph Dr. Ernest Ceriani, a country doctor. Over a period of weeks Smith captured the pace, pressure, and minute details of Dr. Ceriani's life. Selected from the twenty-eight photographs published in the "Country Doctor" essay, *Dr. Ceriani Making a House Call* and *Dr. Ceriani and Patient* record two moments in the life of the doctor but convey with startling power the humanitarian aspects of the unheralded rural physician.

Under a sky heavy with rain clouds the solitary figure of the country doctor, black bag in hand, strides forward to make a house call (no. 46a). By dropping the camera near to ground level and shooting up, Smith was able to include a broad swath of clouds and landscape as a backdrop. The lowered perspective sets the physician's slight frame high on the horizon so that he is sharply defined against the sky, his figure echoed by the simple vertical accent of the picket fence. The open space implies the vast distances over which he must travel every day to meet the needs of his community.

In contrast the second photograph focuses on the doctor's simple office and the gentle, unhurried attention he pays to his young patient (no. 46b). The camera, held at the level of the examining table, was brought in tight to the action centered on the young boy and framed with figures of mother and doctor. This is a touching view of a simple human activity and the intense bond that unites mother, son, and physician.

1. Quoted in William S. Johnson, ed., *W. Eugene Smith: Master of the Photographic Essay* (Millerton, N.Y., 1981), p. 6.

D.K.

47

W. Eugene Smith (American, 1918–1978) MAUDE CALLEN, 1951

From "Nurse Midwife," 1951
Gelatin silver print, 10⅜ x 13 7/16" (26.3 x 34.1 cm)
Purchased: SmithKline Beckman Corporation Fund
1982-35-7

Because of the success of his "Country Doctor" series in 1948 (see nos. 46a,b), *Life* sent W. Eugene Smith to Pineville, South Carolina, in 1951 to produce a photo-essay on the life of Maude Callen, a licensed nurse-midwife and public-health nurse. Accompanying this extraordinary woman through her arduous daily activities as she attended to the health and social welfare needs of a widely scattered constituency of rural poor, Smith recorded the courage and compassion as well as the many skills of a woman who was not only a nurse to her patients but also a teacher, adviser, and model for her community.

Smith made himself and his camera as inconspicuous as possible—then a rather new approach to photography—thus giving the viewer the perspective of a participant in this dense scene crammed with objects, textures, patterns, and people. Maude Callen sits pensively with hand on chin seeming to await an answer from the pregnant woman, or perhaps contemplating her next question or simply pondering the weighty responsibilities of the delivery ahead. The thirty photographs from the "Nurse Midwife" essay that *Life* published in December 1951 (see also no. 92), which documented how this conscientious woman brought health care to great numbers despite her poor facilities, spurred so many unsolicited gifts from readers that sufficient funds became available for her to build a well-equipped clinic. This is a moving example of how an artist's work can help change the world.

D.K.

48

W. Eugene Smith (American, 1918–1978)
ALBERT SCHWEITZER, 1954

From "A Man of Mercy," 1954
Gelatin silver print, 9⁹⁄₁₆ x 13⁷⁄₁₆" (24.3 x 34.1 cm)
Purchased: SmithKline Beckman Corporation Fund
1978-146-1

Following W. Eugene Smith's "Country Doctor" (nos. 46a,b) and "Nurse Midwife" (nos. 47 and 92) series, in 1954 *Life* sent him to West Africa for another photo-essay on a healer: Albert Schweitzer and his medical compound in Lambaréné. This story dealt not with an unknown doctor or nurse as before but with a figure already larger than life and, as a Nobel Prize winner, familiar to the public. Smith spent months producing an enormous number of photographs, which convey the qualities of the man and the complex fabric of the medical compound he had built (see also nos. 66 and 85). Rather than focusing on Schweitzer as the great doctor, this photograph presents him as one character in a quiet drama; photographed from a point of intimacy, it makes the camera and therefore the viewer almost participants in the calm discussion between patient and physician.

In the June 1948 issue of *Photo News* Smith expressed his strong feelings on the responsibility of the artist to present his subject honestly, a statement that also reflects difficulties he had encountered with publishers whose concerns were more often directed toward the appearance than the reality of the subject:

> *Photography is a potent medium of expression. Properly used it is a great power for betterment and understanding. Misused, it has and will fire much trouble. . . . The photographer must bear the responsibility for his work and its effect.*[1]

In "A Man of Mercy," *Life* chose to publish twenty-five photographs that focused on Schweitzer as a person from Smith's much larger photo-essay. But Smith keenly felt the need for the public to understand the totality of Lambaréné, an entire community in which this compassionate but realistic doctor was only one, albeit the major, figure. Because his passionate commitment to the truth as he perceived it was no longer compatible with *Life's* limited needs, he resigned his position before the series was published. His essay of almost 250 images from Lambaréné, which Smith called "Dr. Schweitzer, An African Place," has never been published in its entirety.

1. Quoted in William S. Johnson, ed., *W. Eugene Smith: Master of the Photographic Essay* (Millerton, N.Y., 1981), p. 41.

D.K.

DISEASE, DISABILITY, AND MADNESS

49

Israhel van Meckenem (German, c. 1445–1503)
SAINT ELIZABETH OF THURINGIA, c. 1475–80

Engraving (i/ii), 6⅛ x 4¹⁄₁₆" (15.5 x 10.3 cm) (trimmed)
Purchased: SmithKline Beckman Corporation Fund
1984-53-1

As a patron of beggars, the thirteenth-century Hungarian Saint Elizabeth is usually represented with a beggar or a cripple. Here, however, Israhel van Meckenem centered his attention on another aspect of her legend, that of the leper. One day, according to legend, Elizabeth met a leper and, taking pity on his sorry state, brought him home and put him to rest in her own bed. Accused by her husband of sharing her bed with a vile stranger, she was vindicated when he tore back the bedclothes to reveal not the leper but a vision of Christ. In this engraving Saint Elizabeth stands shielding a leper, whom van Meckenem rendered with the eroded, flattened physiognomy typical of this dread disease. The bell, an ever-present companion of the leper used to warn of his approach, and the crutch and wooden kneelers made necessary by the crippling effects of the disease, convey the horrors of leprosy.

In biblical times, according to the earliest known reference to leprosy (Leviticus 13:45,46), lepers were required to live outside the community, wearing rags and calling aloud to warn of their approach. In Europe during the Middle Ages, lepers were isolated in leper houses, or lazar houses.

The work of van Meckenem exemplifies the developing art of copper engraving in Germany during the second half of the fifteenth century. Often drawing upon the art of Dürer, as in this case, or of Master E. S. (under whom van Meckenem may have studied engraving), his works are beautiful in composition as well as in style and often very inventive in their handling of traditional themes.

D.K.

50

Hans Burgkmair (German, 1473–1531)
After Mathis Miller (German, active early sixteenth-century)
CHILD WITH THREE LEGS, 1516

Woodcut, 7¹¹⁄₁₆ x 6¹³⁄₁₆" (19.5 x 17.3 cm) (trimmed)
Purchased: SmithKline Beckman Corporation Fund
1982-42-1

Hans Burgkmair lived in Augsburg and worked as one of the artists who created hundreds of woodcuts primarily to record life at the imperial court of Maximilian I, emperor of the Holy Roman Empire from 1493 to 1519. During Burgkmair's lifetime the phenomenon of *Prodigienbeliefs* (monstrous beliefs) was deeply rooted in Germany: The appearance in the sky of a comet or meteorite, for example, was interpreted as a sign or warning of things to come. Unusual, misformed births were likewise looked on as portents, and the news of any such event was published and circulated as broadsides and in pamphlets.[1] Because they were meant to function as do today's newspapers, these publications were not considered valuable and were rarely kept, which explains the rarity of such prints.

In this woodcut, fascinating for its accuracy of observation and naturalism, the strange three-legged child is rendered twice, shown sitting up and again asleep. The female child was born on April 8, 1516, disfigured with an extra leg, penis, and swollen stomach; it is not known how long she survived. According to the text, Mathis Miller made the drawing of the child after which Burgkmair executed this woodcut. The coat of arms is that of Count Montfort-Tettnang, the ruler of Tettnang, a town near Miller's birthplace of Lindau.

1. Karl Sudhoff, "Deutsche medizinische Inkunabeln," *Studien zur Geschichte der Medizin* (Leipzig, 1908), vol. 2; Eugen Holländer, *Wunder, Wundergeburt und Wundergestalt* (Stuttgart, 1921), pp. 61–83.

D.K.

51

Hieronymus Cock (Flemish, c. 1520–1570)
After Hieronymus Bosch (Dutch, c. 1450–1516)
BEGGARS, mid-sixteenth century

Engraving (i/ii), 11¾ x 8¹¹⁄₁₆" (29.8 x 22.1 cm)
Purchased: SmithKline Beckman Corporation Fund
1983-32-1

Thirty-one cripples with various deformities (legs that are uneven, wasted, withered, stumped, or clubbed; people with spinal deformities who cannot stand) are shown with their rather ingenious prostheses of wooden legs, crutches, small stools, and frames for "walking." Bowls for begging are apparent, as the lame were usually professional beggars; unless they were wealthy there were few other choices for them. They most often solicited funds by providing entertainment. Some of the beggars shown here wear the costumes of fools; others carry musical instruments: Lutes (common and easily portable) are visible, and a kind of hurdy-gurdy and even a harp are carried on their backs.

This print was based on a drawing by Hieronymus Bosch now in the Albertina, Vienna,[1] and was published at the shop of the Flemish artist Hieronymus Cock, Quatre Vents, in the mid-sixteenth century. As Cock was born after the death of Bosch, the drawing was obviously not made for this print, nor does it seem to have been used for any of Bosch's paintings. However, another drawing of the same subject, in the Cabinet des Estampes de la Bibliothèque Royale, Brussels, with the figures more sensitively and even sympathetically drawn, reveals Bosch's continued interest in this theme.

1. Timothy A. Riggs, *Hieronymus Cock: Printmaker and Publisher* (New York, 1977), p. 316, no. 19.

F.F.H.

52

Claes Jansz. Visscher the Younger (Dutch, 1586–1652)
PROCESSION OF LEPERS ON COPPER MONDAY, 1608

Etching, 6¾ x 8⅞" (17.1 x 22.5 cm) (trimmed)
Purchased: SmithKline Beckman Corporation Fund
1983-73-1

The first Monday after the first Sunday following Epiphany, or Twelfth Night, was known in the Low Countries as Copper Monday, and each locality had its own celebrations and traditions.[1] In Amsterdam it was the day on which the lepers who lived in the refuge house were allowed to march through the streets of the city, as shown in this etching of the *Procession of Lepers on Copper Monday* by Claes Jansz. Visscher the Younger. Copper Monday was also the feast day of the sawmillers' or carpenters' guild as well as the day on which members of the printers' guild delivered their calendars and offered some of the coins (coppers) collected to support the city's leper house. The practice of marching through Amsterdam was forbidden in 1604, and Visscher's print of 1608 thus actually harkens back to a time when lepers were allowed to move freely through the city to collect alms.[2]

The verse beneath the print explains some of the complicated scene:

> *The sick ones are made glad*
> *When they see the copper time*
> *'Cause they make money in the can [alms box]*
> *Then they beat upon the drum.*
> *With their clappers they go on beating*
> *Playing also with the* janneman.[3]

Visscher presents a group of "sick ones," as lepers were known in Dutch slang, of all ages, in their distinctive short cloaks and brimmed hats with white bands, as they move from door to door collecting alms and offering thanks and good wishes for the new year. The boy near the door extends the Lazarus *klapper,* which made a distinctive sound and had a hollowed area into which alms could be dropped. In 1595 a decree, seeking to eliminate imposter beggars, mandated the inspection and certification of all lepers, to whom certificates and clappers were subsequently issued. The clapper warned of the leper's approach and often bore the coat of arms of the town of authorization to ensure that lepers did not travel and that each town bore responsibility for its own sick.[4] The *janneman,* the platform with charming wooden dancing dolls held aloft and operated by pulling the strings below, was the symbol of the carpenters' guild, whose members shared this festival day and supported the lepers in their annual endeavor.

Visscher, born in Amsterdam, was a printmaker, printer, and printseller active during the first half of the seventeenth century. Influenced by the tradition of Pieter Brueghel the Elder, his oeuvre is divided between prints after the work of others such as David Vinckboons and original prints such as this very fine and rare example.

1. J. H. Kruizinga discusses the history and customs of Copper Monday in "Herinneringen aan Koppermaandag," *Maanblad Ons Amsterdam*, vol. 6, no. 1 (1954), pp. 2–5.
2. *The Parade of Lepers on Copper Monday in 1604*, a painting of 1633 by Adriaen van Nieulandt in the Amsterdams Historisch Museum, deals with the last procession.
3. Translation by Marjorie Lee Hendrix, Assistant Curator of Drawings, The J. Paul Getty Museum, Malibu.
4. Linda A. Stone-Ferrier, *Dutch Prints of Daily Life: Mirrors of Life or Masks of Morals?* (Lawrence, Kans., 1983), p. 120, no. 29.

D.K.

53
Stefano della Bella (Italian, 1610–1664)
PLAGUE, c. 1648

From "The Five Deaths," c. 1648
Etching (iii/iii), 7³⁄₁₆ x 5⁷⁄₈" (18.3 x 14.9 cm)
Purchased: SmithKline Beckman Corporation Fund
68-215-24

In this etching from Stefano della Bella's series of allegories "The Five Deaths," Death in the image of a skeleton wearing a winding cloth tied around his head and draped over his torso carries a dead child across the field. A second figure of Death with another child runs, his mouth gaping open in a scream that invokes numerous Renaissance and Baroque images of mothers screaming in vain to protect their infants from slaughter during the Massacre of the Innocents at the time of Christ's birth.

The setting is in fact an accurate depiction of the Cemetery of the Innocents in Paris, with the Church of the Innocents at left.[1] The distant landscape itself yields to the silent burial and caring for the dead and dying, as is seen in the funeral procession at right. Throughout the plague of Paris the entire walled cemetery was virtually one grave. There "bodies rotted quickly, and skulls and bones were then moved to open cribs over the arcades around the walls. The pebbles in this earth were teeth."[2]

Born in Florence, della Bella was active in the service of the Medici in his native city as well as in Rome. He is one of the most admired of all seventeenth-century printmakers and draftsmen. Many of his subjects were land- and seascapes, genre scenes, and contemporary events such as battles and court festivals and ceremonies; he also designed ornamental motifs and decorative objects as well as costumes.

1. See Alexandre de Vesme and Phyllis Dearborn Massar, *Stefano della Bella: Catalogue Raisonné* (New York, 1971), vol. 1, p. 66, no. 88.
2. Phyllis Dearborn Massar, *Presenting Stefano della Bella: Seventeenth-Century Printmaker* (New York, 1971), p. 126.

D.K./F.F.H.

54
Lorenzo Baldissera Tiepolo (Italian, 1736–before 1776)
After Giovanni Battista Tiepolo (Italian, 1696–1770)
SAINT THECLA PRAYING FOR THE END OF THE PLAGUE IN THE CITY OF ESTE, c. 1759

Etching (ii/ii), 27¹³⁄₁₆ x 15⁷⁄₈" (70.6 x 40.3 cm)
Purchased: SmithKline Beckman Corporation Fund
1982-83-1

This handsome etching is by the Venetian artist Lorenzo Baldissera Tiepolo, who during his short lifetime executed only ten prints, nine (including this image) after paintings by his father, Giovanni Battista. This print is derived from one of Giovanni Battista's altarpieces, commissioned by the city of Este, near Padua, in 1758 and erected on the high altar of the cathedral on Christmas Eve of 1759, to commemorate the end of the plague in that city more than a century before, in 1630.[1]

Saints or martyrs who had survived the wrath of earthly trials or who had acted as great healers during their lives or, miraculously, after their deaths were often invoked as intercessors on behalf of the people. Saint Thecla, a first-century martyr whose reputation as a healer was so great that physicians were said to have been jealous of her and arranged to have her killed, was undoubtedly chosen as Este's intercessor in the seventeenth century, and as the subject of the altarpiece in the eighteenth century, because the cathedral had been dedicated to her six centuries before.[2]

Saint Thecla is presented at right, kneeling in prayer, imploring God to bring an end to the plague. At the upper left of the print the figure of God the Father descends from the heavens surrounded by angels, cherubs, and an aura of divine light to answer her prayers and drive the demon of the evil plague into a hasty retreat. The allegorical figure of the plague flies off toward the right, out of the city, in response to the gestures of the Eternal Father and His assistants.

The human drama is intensified by the presence in the left foreground of a small child clinging to the body of its dead mother. Just in front of these, Tiepolo created a dark horizontal band of rich, deep black etching in which the edges of coffins and litters protrude upward, implying that the area outside the city walls, upon which this scene takes place, is literally piled high with the debris of death. In the background lies the city of Este and before it, secondary, reinforcing scenes of figures carrying away the dead.

1. See Antonio Morassi, *G. B. Tiepolo: His Life and Work* (London, 1955), p. 149, no. 75.
2. For the life of Saint Thecla, see Herbert Thurston and Donald Attwater, *Butler's Lives of the Saints* (New York, 1956), vol. 3, pp. 623–25 (September 23); and Antonio Morassi, *A Complete Catalogue of the Paintings of G. B. Tiepolo* (London, 1962), p. 12.

D.K./F.F.H.

55

Benjamin West (American, active England, 1738–1820)

THE BLIND BELISARIUS LED BY A BOY, 1784

Brown ink and brown and pale blue washes with stylus lines on buff laid paper, 17³⁄₁₆ x 19½" (43.6 x 49.5 cm)
Purchased: SmithKline Beckman Corporation Fund
66-9-1

Although the famous Roman general Belisarius (c. 505–565) was a historical figure, the often-depicted subject of his wandering as a blind beggar through Constantinople because of his unjust imprisonment by the emperor Justinian appears to be a later fiction. This romantic legend was taken up by a French writer and historiographer, Jean-François Marmontel, in a novelette entitled *Bélisaire*. Published in 1767, Marmontel's work was the source for several late-eighteenth-century French painters' versions of the subject as well as for the drawing by Benjamin West shown here.[1]

Belisarius as a blind mendicant accompanied by a boy is the subject of Jacques-Louis David's well-known painting of 1781 (Musée des Beaux-Arts, Lille), a smaller version of which was completed in 1784 (Louvre, Paris), the same year as this drawing by West. In its restrained formality West's simpler composition, with its pair of figures arranged, friezelike, parallel to the plane of the picture, is as neoclassical as David's painting. Yet the American artist's attention to the quality of human movement that conveys a state of blindness is of much greater veracity than the Frenchman's observation of that subject. Belisarius's turned head, cautious step, tentatively outstretched hand, and discomfiture of expression all suggest not only blindness but also the sudden loss of vision by an elderly adult, translated with great credibility into hesitatingly compensatory movements.

West was the first native American artist to study abroad and achieve a wide international reputation. Born in Springfield, Pennsylvania, at the age of twenty-one he traveled to Italy, where he came into contact with the neoclassical style. In 1763 West moved permanently to London, where he launched a stellar career, becoming a charter member of the Royal Academy in 1768, historical painter to the king in 1772, and president of the Royal Academy almost uninterruptedly from 1792 until his death in 1820.[2] He was a dedicated history painter in a time and place in which it was not easy to earn a living in that profession, producing numerous heroic compositions from the Bible, ancient and modern history, and classical mythology.

In the contemporary biography of West by John Galt, four Belisarius subjects are listed.[3] It is not known, however, if this drawing is related to a painting. West produced copious quantities of drawings during his long career, including numerous ink or chalk figural and compositional studies for his various paintings, works ranging from thumbnail sketches to highly finished sheets such as this. His style of draftsmanship varies a great deal and reflects numerous influences from both contemporary and earlier artists. This drawing is done in a graceful and lyrical manner that probably was in part inspired by the draftsmanship of the seventeenth-century Bolognese artist Giovanni Francesco Barbieri, known as Il Guercino (see no. 93).

1. See Frederick Cummings, Allen Staley, and Robert Rosenblum, *Romantic Art in Britain: Paintings and Drawings 1760–1860* (Philadelphia, 1968), pp. 99–100, no. 50.
2. See Philadelphia Museum of Art, *Philadelphia: Three Centuries of American Art* (April 11–October 10, 1976), p. 69.
3. Two small pictures of Belisarius and the boy and two drawings of Belisarius and his family are cited; one of the former is presumably the small painting *Belisarius and the Boy* dated 1802 in the Detroit Institute of Arts. See John Galt, *The Life of Benjamin West (1816–1820)* (1820; reprint, Gainesville, Fla., 1960), vol. 2, pp. 224, 226–27, 234. For more on West's Belisarius themes, see Ruth S. Kraemer, *Drawings by Benjamin West and His Son Raphael Lamar West* (New York, 1975), pp. 40–42, no. 67.

A.P./D.K.

56

George Cruikshank (English, 1792–1878)

THE CHOLIC, 1819

Hand-colored etching (i/ii), 8⅛ x 10⅛" (20.7 x 25.7 cm) (trimmed)
Purchased: SmithKline Beckman Corporation Fund
1983-96-1

The son of Isaac Cruikshank, an outstanding caricaturist in his own right, George Cruikshank was one of the most masterful and prolific illustrators of the nineteenth century. He lived a long life; his early work, political and satirical caricatures such as the one shown here, gave way to his increasing interest in book illustration, and he is perhaps best known for his later illustrations of Dickens's writings.

The Cholic shows a fashionably dressed woman, at home on her fashionable Regency sofa, suffering from a fashionable stomach upset, probably brought on by overindulgence in food and drink. Her extreme slimness is contrasted to the Rubensian amplitude of the woman comfortably downing a glass of wine in the picture above the sofa. Small demonic figures in the form of animals torture the woman with arrows, knives, and pitchforks; one with a needle and thread personifies the uncomfortable feeling of having a stitch in one's side. *The Cholic* was published together with a companion print, *The Headache,* which shows a man being attacked by a similar group of tiny demons.

Like much of Cruikshank's early work, *The Cholic* shows the influence of James Gillray, one of the leading political caricaturists of the preceding decades. Cruikshank here displays the same propensity for grotesque distortion of the human body and the same fascination with overindulgence in food and drink as a metaphor for human folly.

K.R./D.K.

57

Jean-Louis-André-Théodore Géricault (French, 1791–1824)

A PARALEYTIC WOMAN, 1821

From *Various Subjects Drawn from Life and on Stone* (London: Rodwell & Martin, 1821)
Lithograph, 9 9/16 x 12 7/16" (24.3 x 31.6 cm)
Purchased: SmithKline Beckman Corporation Fund
1982-117-1

In 1820–21 the French painter Théodore Géricault was in England, where he set about producing a series of lithographs that recorded his impressions of London life. These carefully observed scenes, which present an almost matter-of-fact view of the common people who were drawn to the streets of early nineteenth-century London, are not tempered in the least with sentiment or ennobled with the heroism of his earlier paintings.

In this powerful print, Géricault recorded the isolated existence of a person suffering from paralysis. Wrapped in her cloak, the paralytic woman, with an expression speaking of hopelessness, sits slumped in a heavy wooden wheelchair with large wheels. The unkempt porter stops to rest from the task of dragging this huge burden, leaning back on the chair for support, the leather harness slackened over his shoulders. In contrast, a young girl recoils from the sight and an elegant carriage effortlessly moves through the London streets, carrying its riders in comfort and privacy. With exquisite attention to simple detail, the scene suggests the lack of sympathy and public response to disabilities as well as the simple technology available to compensate for the patient's immobility. Because of the lack of commercial success of this particular lithograph, the stone was erased in 1821 before very many impressions were made.

It is not surprising that Géricault was interested in depicting the treatment of the ill in London. A few years before he went to England he had become a close friend of several Parisian physicians. He had received their permission to study corpses in a hospital morgue in order to enhance the realism of his large painting showing the dead victims of a shipwreck, *The Raft of the Medusa* (Louvre, Paris). After his return from England he painted several portraits of insane patients for a Paris physician, who used the pictures in his medical lectures on the physiognomy of the mentally ill.

D.K.

58

Louis-Léopold Boilly (French, 1761–1845)

THE BLIND, 1825

From "The Collection of Grimaces," 1823–28
Hand-colored lithograph, 10 7/16 x 7 5/16" (26.5 x 18.6 cm)
Purchased: SmithKline Beckman Corporation Fund
1978-25-2

An extremely prolific artist, Louis-Léopold Boilly is best known for his meticulously painted scenes of Parisian life. His series "The Collection of Grimaces" is a group of about one hundred lithographs representing different kinds of facial expressions. This series, which became extremely popular, has been compared to Balzac's *Comédie humaine* and Daumier's caricatures.[1]

In *The Blind* Boilly concentrates on the particular facial contortions of those trying to communicate with an audience they cannot see. The artist's depiction of blind men who earn their living as musicians is a variation on the theme of The Senses. It suggests that although these men are deprived of one sense, their other senses may have compensated for the loss by becoming more acute. The great interest in facial expression or physiognomy was seriously pursued during the late eighteenth and nineteenth centuries by Johann Caspar Lavater in his *Essays on Physiognomy*, published in English in 1789, and Sir Charles Bell in *The Anatomy and Philosophy of Expression, as Connected with the Fine Arts*, first published in 1806.

1. A. Mabille de Poncheville, *Boilly* (Paris, 1931), pp. 135–36.

K.R./D.K.

59

Utagawa Yoshitsuya, known as Ichieisai (Japanese, 1822–1866)

PROTECTION FROM THE MEASLES EPIDEMIC, 1862

Color woodcut, 14 7/16 x 9 3/4" (36.7 x 24.8 cm)
Purchased: SmithKline Beckman Corporation Fund
1978-87-1

The usual association of Japanese wood-block prints is with the great tradition of elegantly refined scenes of courtly life or urbane pastimes. The woodcut, however, served a far broader spectrum of purposes and functions, as demonstrated by this print, which was published as a charm or token against measles. The text explains its use: "By displaying this, both wealthy families and poor ones, too, can protect themselves—demons, get out!"[1]

For a small sum any household could purchase this print and, by displaying it, invoke the mythical figure Shoki to chase away the demons of measles. Shoki, or Chung K'uei in Chinese, was frequently represented in the popular arts of both China and Japan. He was originally a legendary figure of T'ang dynasty China and was said to have appeared in a dream to an eighth-century emperor to promise protection against the demons of disease. His powers are here invoked against the demons that caused measles, a disease that had destroyed so many children in families of all levels of society across Japan.

Shoki, with sword and saber, dominates the foreground of the brightly colored print. His identity is established by his Chinese official's costume and by the hair that radiates like a lion's mane from his head. In the upper left, the two measles demons taunt and jeer but seem ready to retreat in the face of the powerful Shoki.

The measles epidemic of 1862, the year of this print, was possibly brought by Westerners traveling to Japan from America and Europe, where measles was also causing great suffering. The opening of Yokohama to world trade as a result of Commodore Matthew C. Perry's expedition in 1853 ended Japan's two hundred years of self-imposed isolation from the Western world. The treaty that resulted from Perry's visit gave Western nations permission to use the village of Yokohama in Edo Bay as a primary trade center. Despite the Japanese governmental restrictions on trade and free travel, Yokohama flourished and the contact between Japan and the West grew apace.

1. Translation by Sarah Thompson, Columbia University, New York.

D.K.

60
George John Pinwell (English, 1842–1875) DEATH'S DISPENSARY, c. 1866

Graphite on light buff wove paper, 7 15/16 x 6 5/16" (20.2 x 16.1 cm)
Purchased: SmithKline Beckman Corporation Fund
1984-17-1

This powerful drawing by the wood engraver and watercolorist George John Pinwell was a preparatory sketch for an illustration published in the English magazine *Fun* during the outbreak of cholera in London in 1866, when the disease was once again ravaging Great Britain.

European doctors had taken little notice of cholera until an epidemic occurred in India in 1817. After spreading over British India and then into Asia Minor and Russia, the disease moved slowly but devastatingly west across the Continent; by the early 1830s cholera had swept through northern and central Europe and into England. As the disease reappeared in a series of epidemics, English physicians began to unravel the mechanisms by which cholera was transmitted. In 1832, the year of a massive outbreak in London, John Parkin first suggested the water-borne nature of the disease.[1] Civic authorities, however, disagreed, continuing to believe that miasmas were the source of contagion. In 1844 another physician, John Snow, also expressed the opinion that the disease was contracted through drinking water, and in 1849 published an article that presented a large body of data correlating numerous outbreaks of cholera with specific local water supplies.[2] In 1854, amidst another explosion of cholera in London, Snow convinced the vestrymen of the most severely affected parish to remove the handle of the now-infamous Broad Street waterpump, a move that dramatically halted the spread of the disease. In the years that followed, greater emphasis was placed on public sanitary control as a means of fighting the illness.

Pinwell's image, which shows a skeletal figure of Cholera working the handle of a pump and thus dispensing the disease to all who imbibed the contaminated water, conveys the horror of the realization that parts of the population in 1866 might have still been unwittingly exposing themselves to destruction.

1. Leslie T. Morton, *Garrison and Morton's Medical Bibliography*, 2d rev. ed. (New York, 1965), p. 446.
2. John Snow, "On the Pathology and Mode of Communication of Cholera," *The London Medical Gazette*, vol. 9 (1849), pp. 730–32, 745–52, 923–29.

D.K.

61
Eadweard Muybridge (American, born England, 1830–1904) SPASTIC WALKING, 1885

From Eadweard Muybridge, *Animal Locomotion: An Electro-Photographic Investigation of Consecutive Phases of Animal Movements* (Philadelphia: University of Pennsylvania, 1887)
Collotype, 8 1/4 x 14 1/8" (20.9 x 36 cm)
Gift of the City of Philadelphia Trade & Convention Center, Department of Commerce
62-135-242

In 1883 the University of Pennsylvania sponsored an extensive series of studies of the movement of humans and animals by the photographer Eadweard Muybridge. Previously acclaimed for his photographs that for the first time caught the successive stages of the horse running and proved that all four hooves leave the ground at one time, Muybridge hoped to expand his exploration of human and animal locomotion to capture the narrative element of everyday action, "accurately recording the successive attitudes, oscillations and movements of the human body—in health and disease."[1]

The goal of this photographic investigation was to publish an atlas that would provide realistic and scientific information about motion, eventually issued as *Animal Locomotion* in 1887 with a total of 781 plates. In 1884 Muybridge set up an open-air studio in the courtyard of the university's veterinary hospital and school, which was temporarily enclosed by a high fence for privacy. There he produced a series of photographs of healthy male and female subjects engaged in a wide variety of endeavors, mostly photographed in the nude. A newly developed, more sensitive dry-plate technique replaced the wet plates that Muybridge had used for his earlier photographic work, and he had developed a portable camera with thirteen lenses that could produce twelve images on a single dry plate (the thirteenth lens was for focusing and viewing). These cameras were situated in front of, beside, and behind the subject to render a series of three photographic sequences of movement for each study.

During the summer of 1885 Muybridge was assisted in his studies of the movements of diseased human bodies by Francis X. Dercum, Instructor of Nervous Diseases at the university,[2] who, with his fellow physicians, arranged for patients from the university hospital to be photographed. Within the hospital grounds, Muybridge set up another studio, similar to that constructed earlier at the veterinary hospital, and produced a large group of studies. In all, some twenty of the final plates of *Animal Locomotion* were of these patients with abnormal movements.

The plate *Spastic Walking* records with remarkable clarity both the gait and posture of the subject, who appears to suffer from chorea (note the rotating movements of the head and the turned-out extension of the arms). By combining the careful study of these sequential photographs with other research,[3] Dercum hoped to better understand the neurological process as it is transmitted to the muscles and perhaps unravel the mystery of diseases such as chorea, epilepsy, and multiple sclerosis.

The Muybridge work on abnormal locomotion was not only the first motion photography of neurological patients but also the first scientific study of abnormal gaits. These early studies were the beginning of a sequence of physician-artist relationships at the University of Pennsylvania dedicated to the documentation of abnormal gait and neurological disease that continued through the 1930s.[4]

1. From Muybridge's "Proposal to the Trustees of the University of Pennsylvania," 1883, Muybridge Papers, Archives, University of Pennsylvania, Philadelphia.
2. Lawrence C. McHenry, Jr., M.D., Professor of Neurology, Bowman Gray School of Medicine, Wake Forest University, Winston-Salem, North Carolina, offered valuable insights into this subject. Dr. McHenry is presently preparing a study of the relationship between Dercum and Muybridge.
3. Among Dercum's publications on his work with Muybridge is "A Study of Some Normal and Abnormal Movements Photographed by Muybridge," in Eadweard Muybridge, *Animal Locomotion: The Muybridge Work at the University of Pennsylvania* (1888; reprint, New York, 1973), pp. 103–33.
4. Linda Cowell is researching this ongoing work in the motion studies of neurological patients at the University of Pennsylvania begun by Muybridge and Dercum.

D.K.

62
Edvard Munch (Norwegian, 1863–1944)
THE SICK CHILD, 1894

Drypoint (v/v/c), 15³⁄₁₆ x 11⁷⁄₁₆" (38.6 x 29 cm)
Purchased: SmithKline Beckman Corporation Fund
49-97-38

Edvard Munch, the foremost artist in Scandinavian history, is often referred to as the father of German Expressionism. His powerful, emotional works, based often on his own experiences (see nos. 112 and 113), touch a chord of psychological anxiety in nearly every viewer. For this moving drypoint of a young girl dying of consumption, or tuberculosis, Munch drew upon vivid, haunting memories of his youth. The disease, which reached epidemic proportions in the nineteenth century, was to claim first his mother and then his younger sister.

In *The Sick Child* Munch portrayed the pallor and transparency of the skin, the fever, and the physical weakness so characteristic of pulmonary tuberculosis. The physical symptoms are combined with psychological and emotional elements to convey the intensity of the destructive force of the disease. The young girl's weakened condition is suggested by the aureole of white bed linens and pillows around her, which barely seem to yield under the weight of her frail body. The realization of the ultimate end of the disease seems to weigh far more heavily upon the bowed, darkened form of the grieving woman, who helplessly clutches the child's small hand, than upon the child herself, who stares into a veil of darkness. The dark, foreboding presence at left is an appropriate metaphor for this vicious destroyer.

Like a dream world, a faint landscape is shown below this touching scene, a landscape without figures, which may imply the quiet realm of eternal rest or an idealized worldly setting now lost.

D.K.

63
Eugène-Samuel Grasset (French, born Switzerland, 1841–1917)
MORPHINOMANIAC, 1897

From *L'Album des peintres-graveurs* (Paris: Ambroise Vollard, 1897)
Color lithograph, 16⁵⁄₁₆ x 12⅜" (41.4 x 31.4 cm)
Purchased: SmithKline Beckman Corporation Fund
1983-99-1

The brutal frankness of this strangely beautiful and haunting lithograph by Eugène-Samuel Grasset conveys the intensity and horror of drug addiction. In strong, acrid colors pressed tight to the picture plane

Grasset depicts the awful desperation of the addict with such a brutal sense of immediacy that the print remains as potent today as it must have been when it was created nearly ninety years ago.

The young woman with dark, serpentlike hair literally fills the surface of the print. Her frightful expression and action are grim statements of morphine addiction, which by the late nineteenth century had invaded all classes of French society. Discovered by the German pharmacist Friedrich Wilhelm Sertürner in 1817, morphine was prescribed with abandon until its destructive addictive power was realized.

Published by the Parisian dealer Ambroise Vollard in an album that included prints by Bonnard, Cézanne, Maurin, Redon, and Toulouse-Lautrec, among others, *Morphinomaniac* is an example of the decorative style of Grasset, who provided designs for furniture, fabrics, glass, and other objects as well as for prints and posters.

D.K.

64

Max Klinger (German, 1857–1920) THE PLAGUE, 1903

From "On Death, Part II," 1898–1909
Etching and drypoint, 16 13/16 x 13 1/4" (42.7 x 33.6 cm)
Purchased: SmithKline Beckman Corporation Fund
1980-51-1

The paintings, sculpture, and graphics of the Symbolist artist Max Klinger (see also no. 109) are imbued with themes of personal anxiety, sublimated sexuality, and romantic fantasy. His work, which explored the powerful dark side of man's mind, had great influence on a number of twentieth-century artists, and he has been recognized as an important precursor of Surrealism.

This plate, *The Plague*, is the third in the cycle entitled "On Death, Part II," to which Klinger devoted more time than any other series of prints. Unlike the plates in the cycle "On Death, Part I" of 1889, which deal with the physical reality of unexpected death, the later cycle approaches death as a symbolic phenomenon. *The Plague* was created not as a representation of one particular epidemic but of the emotion-laden idea of plague in its most basic sense as a mass destroyer, a contagion spread from man to man.

The scene is a hospital ward whose beds are filled with those in a state of physical decay and psychological disarray. A sudden, strong gust of wind forces open the windows, violently whipping the curtains aside. With the wind comes a flock of crows, large, threatening birds who feed on carrion, the putrefying flesh of corpses. Laughing their hideous, taunting calls, they perch menacingly on the foot of one bed or fly through the heavy air of the ward, waiting for death to take the victims of the plague. The crows and wind appear as metaphors for the plagues that have swept across continents leaving suffering and death in their wake, indifferent to the pleas and prayers of man.[1] Using etching and drypoint with remarkable deftness, Klinger created a palpable sense of the dark power of disease, and in the form of the nun's brandished rosary and the patients' fervent prayer before the cross, symbolized the inefficacy of religion to combat it.

1. See J. Kirk T. Varnedoe and Elizabeth Streicher, *Graphic Works of Max Klinger* (New York, 1977), p. 90, no. 73.

D.K.

65

August Sander (German, 1876–1964) CHILDREN IN A HOME FOR THE BLIND, DUREN, 1930

From "Man of the Twentieth Century"
Gelatin silver print, 11 7/8 x 9" (30.2 x 22.9 cm)
Purchased: SmithKline Beckman Corporation Fund
1980-97-1

Born in a German farming and mining community near Cologne, August Sander, like his father, was apprenticed to the mines at an early age. One day a mine foreman assigned Sander to guide a landscape photographer around the area, and it is to this chance encounter that Sander attributed his lifelong fascination with photography. In 1910, traveling on his bicycle, he began to photograph farmers and tradesmen of Germany's Westerwald region. It was at this time that he conceived the idea for his lifelong project, "Man of the Twentieth Century," in which he set out to produce a photographic portrait of the German people. Toward this end, after World War I Sander expanded the original Westerwald project to include archetypes from all walks of German life, which he organized in a pyramidal hierarchy, placing artists and intellectuals at the top and the disabled, ill, and insane at the bottom.

As chronicler of the Weimar Republic, the tumultuous period in his nation's history between the fall of Kaiser Wilhelm and the rise of Adolph Hitler, Sander was not interested in pursuing the traditional role of photographic portraiture but rather sought to find subjects who filled a specific place in society and yet also manifested the quality of the individual. His sitters face the camera in a direct, unpretentious manner, aware of their own projected presence and that of the photographer. Often set against a background of familiar surroundings, his photographs thus document the German environment as well as the people.

Like the other portraits in the series, this gentle image of two children in a home for the blind in Düren conveys with untouched honesty the subjects' character and the quality of their lives. "More than anything else," Sander stated, "physiognomy means an understanding of human nature. . . . We can read in [someone's] face whether he is happy or troubled, for life unavoidably leaves its trace there."[1] The disabled, although among those at the bottom of Sander's social hierarchy, were as much a part of his Germany as the healthy, and he allowed his records of their faces to speak for that portion of all levels of the society that experiences illness or disability.

1. Translated and quoted in Beaumont Newhall and Robert Kramer, *August Sander: Photographs of an Epoch, 1904–1959* (Millerton, N.Y., 1980), p. 40.

D.K.

66

W. Eugene Smith (American, 1918–1978)
LEPROSY, 1954

From "A Man of Mercy," 1954
Gelatin silver print, 10 7/16 x 13 7/16" (26.5 x 34.1 cm)
Purchased: SmithKline Beckman Corporation Fund
1978-95-4

When W. Eugene Smith returned to the United States after several months in Lambaréné in West Africa (see nos. 48 and 85), he promised Albert Schweitzer that he would not produce yet another story of hero worship. For Smith, Schweitzer alone was not the story of Lambaréné but part of the larger context of the medical compound. Smith, in his discussion of his photo-essay, related: "The visitor, unprepared, will even have difficulty in trying to determine the nature of the place. . . . It is of a wisdom, a philosophy, a total meaning uniquely its own."[1]

This photograph of a man suffering from leprosy presents with clarity and directness the harsh reality of a disease long associated with the Middle Ages but still very much a part of the twentieth century. A chronic bacterial disease that primarily affects the peripheral nervous system and the skin, it is crippling and deforming, but can be cured if medication is made available.

1. W. Eugene Smith, *W. Eugene Smith: His Photographs and Notes* (New York, 1969), n.p.

D.K.

67a

Larry Clark (American, born 1943)
UNTITLED, 1963–70

From "Tulsa," 1963–70
Gelatin silver print, 11 15/16 x 8" (30.3 x 20.3 cm)
On extended loan from Milton J. Green

67b

Larry Clark (American, born 1943)
UNTITLED, 1963–70

From "Tulsa," 1963–70
Gelatin silver print, 12 1/4 x 8 1/16" (31.1 x 20.5 cm)
On extended loan from Milton J. Green

These photographs bring forward an uncompromising view of Larry Clark's own experiences with the drug subculture of the 1960s. Taken in Tulsa between 1963 and 1970, they convey with great intensity the involvement of young people with the violence of the drug scene. Identifying himself as participant as well as observer, Clark made photographs that are neither moralizing nor journalistic but convey a sense of extended autobiography in their brutal, visceral narrative. The wrenching views of the young addict who injects heroin into his veins (no. 67a) and experiences the violent rush associated with the collision of heroin and blood (no. 67b) strike a sharp note of warning. Clark's photographs force the viewer to focus on the horrifying reality of the drug epidemic in society today. They show drug use functioning as a social mechanism within the teenage community, which paradoxically brings about the isolation of the individual.

D.K.

68

Diane Arbus (American, 1923–1971)
RUSSIAN MIDGET FRIENDS IN A LIVING ROOM ON 100TH STREET, NEW YORK CITY, 1963

Gelatin silver print, 8 9/16 x 8 3/8" (21.7 x 21.2 cm)
Purchased: SmithKline Beckman Corporation Fund
1984-49-2

Diane Arbus developed her photographic technique in the late 1940s and 1950s during the same period that she was working in fashion photography in association with her husband, Allan. After studying with the photographer Lisette Model, she began to work in a more personal and powerful style during the late 1950s. In 1967 her photographs were included with those of Lee Friedlander and Garry Winogrand in the "New Documents" exhibition at the Museum of

Modern Art in New York, which established her reputation and thrust her into the forefront of modern photography.

Arbus was fascinated by what she called "freaks," those who were not average in size, appearance, or behavior, those who lived on the periphery of society. Fixing on that quality that made each of her subjects "different," she pursued them in their own situations (as had August Sander in Germany before her; see no. 65), expanding their portraits to include their surroundings, thus emphasizing both their differences from and striking similarities to what is considered normal.

In this photograph of three midgets in the living room of a New York apartment, each sits forward on the edge of the seat, looking into the camera. It was about this time that Diane Arbus switched to a twin-lens reflex camera, which she would hold at waist height. This allowed her to continue a dialogue with her sitters, unencumbered by the barrier of the camera, and in this instance put the camera at eye level with her subjects. The photograph is not in itself about size, for the chairs in which they sit are scaled to the diminutive stature of the sitters, but about the intimacy and richness of this Lilliputian world—a world where the photographer herself was out of scale.

D.K.

69
Diane Arbus (American, 1923–1971)
JEWISH GIANT AT HOME WITH HIS PARENTS IN THE BRONX, 1970

Gelatin silver print, 14⅞ x 14¾" (37.8 x 37.5 cm)
Purchased: SmithKline Beckman Corporation Fund
1984-49-3

Diane Arbus was very sensitive to the strange effects of fate, explaining her fascination for her unusual subjects in one of her most often quoted statements: "Most people go through life dreading they'll have a traumatic experience. Freaks were born with their trauma. They've already passed their test in life. They're aristocrats."[1] Photographed with his parents in their Bronx, New York, apartment is the man known as the Jewish Giant, who towers over his parents and the interior setting like a Gulliver in Lilliput. The subject of the photograph becomes one of the dramatic differences of scale. Arbus said she found "a quality of legend about freaks. Like a person in a fairy tale who stops you and demands that you answer a riddle."[2] The giant is, like the midgets in their own home (see no. 68), a product of genetic poker.

1. Quoted in Aperture, *Diane Arbus* (Millerton, N.Y., 1972), p. 3.
2. Quoted in ibid.

D.K.

70
Diane Arbus (American, 1923–1971)
UNTITLED (6), 1970–71

Gelatin silver print, 15⅞ x 15⅜" (40.3 x 39 cm)
Purchased: SmithKline Beckman Corporation Fund
1984-49-1

R. D. Laing's controversial works on mental illness, among them *The Divided Self*, published in 1969, intrigued Diane Arbus. She was fascinated by his insights into the ways society defines and compartmentalizes normalcy, freaks, sanity, and insanity—an idea she had been exploring with her camera. In 1968 she wrote to Peter Crookston, then deputy editor of the *London Sunday Times Magazine*: "I am . . . trying to get to cheerful retarded adults, morons, idiots, imbeciles . . . they are clearly defined."[1] The next year she began a series of photographic studies of patients in institutions for the mentally retarded, one of which was this photograph of three young women afflicted with Down's syndrome. Exploring not the illness but the interior portraits that determine their appearance and behavior, Arbus has shown three unique individuals who revel in the warmth of the sun, the freshness of the air, and the pleasure of being outdoors. Arbus confided: "My favorite thing is to go where I've never been,"[2] and through her photographs she takes the viewer with her.

1. Letter copyright © Estate of Diane Arbus.
2. Quoted in Aperture, *Diane Arbus* (Millerton, N.Y., 1972), p. 1.

D.K.

71
W. Eugene Smith (American, 1918–1978)
TOMOKO IN BATH, 1972–75

From "Minamata," 1972–75
Gelatin silver print, 8$\frac{7}{16}$ x 13¼" (21.4 x 33.6 cm)
Purchased: SmithKline Beckman Corporation Fund
1979-144-5

When W. Eugene Smith and his wife Aileen accompanied his major retrospective exhibition to Japan in 1971, they were contacted by, and subsequently joined, an activist group concerned with the longstanding problems of industrial pollution in the small city of Minamata on Kyūshū, Japan's southernmost island. For years a mysterious disease had afflicted the population of Minamata, crippling many, killing some, and threatening all. Gradually, it became apparent that mercury being dumped into the waters of Minamata and consumed by the local fish, a staple of the diet, was the cause of the widespread poisoning of the population, and a local factory of the Chisso Corporation, the source of the pollutant. This "strange disease," as the population called it, "conjured such fears of contagion that the victims and those close to them became outcasts, stigmatized and degraded, frequently even in their own eyes."[1]

From 1972 to 1975 the Smiths lived and worked in Minamata, documenting the tragic lives of the victims of Chisso-Minamata Disease. This extraordinary portrait is of Tomoko Uemura, a child who was poisoned *in utero* by the mercury. Even in an apparently healthy mother, the mercury penetrated the placenta to reach the fetus and begin its devastating destruction; Tomoko's nervous system never properly developed because mercury destroyed the fetal brain tissue. This photograph portrays not only the unfortunate child but also the disease itself and the tender care and devotion of the parents whom Tomoko may or may not know.

1. W. Eugene Smith and Aileen M. Smith, *Minamata* (New York, 1975), p. 11.

D.K.

72a–b

Eugene Richards (American, born 1944)
a: DOROTHEA, AFTER THE DISCOVERY OF A LUMP, 1978; b: DOROTHEA'S BIOPSY, 1978

From "Exploding into Life," 1978–79
Gelatin silver prints, a and b: 17 13/16 x 11 15/16" (45.3 x 30.4 cm)
Purchased: SmithKline Beckman Corporation Fund
1984-161-3,2

72c–d

Eugene Richards (American, born 1944)
c: DOROTHEA AND I, 1978; d: DOROTHEA'S FIRST MILE RUN, MAINE, 1979

From "Exploding into Life," 1978–79
Gelatin silver prints; c: 12 5/16 x 18 1/8" (31.2 x 46 cm), d: 12 x 17 15/16" (30.5 x 45.5 cm)
Purchased: SmithKline Beckman Corporation Fund
1984-161-1,4

In his photo-essays Eugene Richards has confronted difficult and controversial subjects, including the protest of nuclear war and the conduct of hospital emergency-room personnel. In this group of photographs and the attendant diary script from the series "Exploding into Life," he joined with the late Dorothea Lynch, a poet, social worker, newspaper correspondent, and magazine writer, in documenting a disease that has become the modern plague: cancer.

Both images and words seek to make understandable the physical and psychological changes through which Dorothea passed in her desperate fight against the cancer cells that were "exploding into life" within her body. The series follows Dorothea's diagnosis, surgery, chemotherapy, and road back to "normal" life. The intensely personal text expresses her fears and anguish as well as her new awareness of life.

Susan Sontag has observed that in advanced industrial societies it is often difficult to come to terms with the diseases that are associated with death, "that disease widely considered a synonym for death is experienced as something to hide."[1] Because the name conjures up such fear, there is almost a taboo about discussing cancer. Such taboos, however, only serve to reinforce cancer patients' feelings of isolation—one of their greatest personal pains. Richards and Lynch broke the longstanding taboo and dealt directly with this forbidden subject through powerful photographs and intense prose, piercing some of the isolation and lifting the veil from the unspeakable to reveal the process of this disease in its human aspects.

1. Susan Sontag, *Illness as Metaphor* (New York, 1978), p. 8.

D.K.

73

Martin Schongauer (German, c. 1450–1491)
THE TRIBULATIONS OF SAINT ANTHONY, c. 1470–75

Engraving (ii/ii), 12 1/4 x 9 1/16" (31.1 x 23 cm) (trimmed)
The W. P. Wilstach Collection
W'50-4-9

The legend of Saint Anthony, which was popularized in literature in the thirteenth century, featured as one of its best-known scenes the tribulations of this early Christian ascetic. Born in Egypt in the middle of the third century A.D. to wealthy parents, upon their death Anthony distributed his inheritance among the poor and retired to the desert to lead a pious life. He, like other religious hermits, was subject to frightening hallucinations that he interpreted as demonic temptations. In this enduring image of madness, Martin Schongauer has captured the saint's resistance through inner faith to the torment of a wild phantasmagoria of grotesque demons. His ability to resist these evil forces of the devil made Saint Anthony an example for those seeking salvation or plagued by sin and temptation.

The height of Anthony's representation in artistic works came in the fifteenth century through his role as a patron saint of plague victims and the spread of the hospital order that bears his name. This order was primarily devoted to the care of those suffering from Saint Anthony's Fire, an inflammatory or gangrenous skin disease. As the number of their hospitals reached a peak in the fifteenth century, worship of the saint moved from its previous monastic center into the realm of popular culture.

Artistic depictions of the Tribulations of Saint Anthony generally represent his temptations as either seductive or, as here, diabolic. The latter interpretation is in turn either pictured as a terrestrial event (see no. 76) or, as in Schongauer's print, an aerial confrontation (see no. 74). In this engraving the saint, considered the founder of monasticism, is identified by his characteristic cowl, cloak, girdle book, and tau-handled staff. He is shown at the point in his ascent to heaven when he was arrested by satanic creatures who tormented him by recounting all his sins. The demons are, however, ultimately silenced, for Anthony's earlier struggles against temptation had assured him of the grace of God, which surely accounts for Schongauer's rather passive portrayal of the besieged saint.

Schongauer, renowned in his own time as a painter, is best remembered today for his exquisite engravings in the goldsmith tradition that were widely circulated and copied for their technical and stylistic innovations. His fame is best attested to by the fact that Albrecht Dürer sought him out as a teacher, only to find that Schongauer had died by the time the younger artist reached his town of Colmar. This particular print inspired Dürer as well as Matthias Grünewald and Michelangelo to create similar works.

E.J./D.K.

74
Lucas Cranach the Elder (German, 1472–1553)
THE TRIBULATIONS OF SAINT ANTHONY, 1506

Woodcut (ii/ii), 16 x 11" (40.7 x 28 cm)
Purchased: Thomas Skelton Harrison Fund
71-238-1

Lucas Cranach the Elder's debt to Martin Schongauer's earlier portrayal of the theme of the Tribulations of Saint Anthony (see no. 73) is apparent in his depictions of the demonic creatures of sin and temptation who claw and grab at the airborne saint. There are, however, notable differences between the two prints. In Cranach's version Saint Anthony is slightly more demonstrative and involved in the action that swirls around him, creating a graphic portrayal of hallucinatory madness. The demonic beings are even more imaginatively conceived in strange combinations of natural forms. Furthermore, Cranach's use of a fully developed landscape, reminiscent of the Danube School of landscape painting, seems to reflect the Humanist interest in the relationship between man and nature; the same type of landscapes embellishes his portraits and paintings of saints of the period, which have been shown to reveal his concern with the interconnection of all forces in nature and the world.[1]

This landscape addition also gives a new dimension to Cranach's interpretation of Saint Anthony. It has been suggested that the town seen in the distance in this woodcut is the artist's native city of Kronach.[2] By incorporating a local setting into his print, Cranach has turned the story into a contemporary event, thus making it more applicable to the viewer's own life. In the late fifteenth and early sixteenth centuries, when Europe was undergoing a series of social and religious upheavals, the worship of saints as examples of moral probity proliferated. Cranach's depiction of Saint Anthony's resistance to the torments around him may reflect the artist's view of contemporary man's need to battle aggressively the demons that threatened the order of society.

Cranach was a prolific printmaker and painter who worked primarily for the court of the Saxon elector in Wittenberg between 1504 and 1520. A close friend of Martin Luther, he published numerous works related to the Protestant Reformation.

1. James Snyder, *Northern Renaissance Art* (New York, 1985), pp. 370–71.
2. Jakob Rosenberg, "Lucas Cranach the Elder: A Critical Appreciation," *Record of the Art Museum: Princeton University*, vol. 28, no. 1 (1969), p. 29.

E.J./D.K.

75
Albrecht Dürer (German, 1471–1528)
MELENCOLIA I, 1514

Engraving (ii/ii, e), 9½ x 7$\frac{5}{16}$" (24.1 x 18.5 cm) (trimmed)
Purchased: Lisa Norris Elkins Fund
51-96-5

The theme of melancholy has been taken up by numerous artists but rarely with both the aesthetic refinement and iconographic complexity of Albrecht Dürer's *Melencolia I*. Dürer's engraving has been seriously studied by several generations of thinkers and scholars and yet, like the condition itself, it still maintains an aspect of aloof isolation and secrecy. Dürer left some notation on the iconography of this remarkable image, which helps to unravel the meaning but does not explicate it completely.[1]

The Humanists of Dürer's time were particularly interested in the study of the human temperaments, a subject that drew on both ancient and medieval thought. It was Hippocrates who during the fifth century B.C. firmly established the humoral theory, which conceives of the human body as consisting of four humors, or fluids: blood, phlegm, yellow bile, and black bile. Health was perceived as being dependent upon the equilibrium of these four fluids, and they became the determinants of man's temperament. Thus the preponderance of blood was thought to make one sanguine; phlegm, phlegmatic; yellow bile, choleric; and black bile, melancholic. During the Middle Ages the humoral theory was conjoined with astrology as man's temperament, interests, and talents were believed to be determined by a particular planet.[2] Melancholy, with its determining planet Saturn, long intrigued philosophers and physicians, who believed in two distinct types; they saw a positive melancholy of the artist's divinely inspired creativity and a negative melancholy of deep despair.

Dürer's remarkably complicated engraving epitomizes the twin aspects of melancholy. The winged figure of Melancholy, with the dramatically darkened countenance considered characteristic of melancholics, sits in an archetypical pose, head in hand. Her purse, signifying wealth, and the keys tied to her waist, denoting power, hang useless at her side, demonstrating that neither wealth nor power can overcome the most feared of the four humors. The figure is crowned by a wreath of *Levisticum officinalis koch,* a plant recommended in the sixteenth century as a palliative for excessive melancholy, but even the strongest available medicine offers no relief.[3]

Other symbols in the engraving reinforce the meaning. Set in the wall of the building is a type of magic square known as a Jupiter square, thought to attract the influence of Jupiter, a positive counter to the influence of Saturn and thus melancholy. Lying unused around the central figure are various tools and instruments, symbols of the arts and sciences, particularly geometry, included because artists and men of science were considered susceptible to melancholy,[4] especially its creative dimension.

The sleeping dog is yet another traditional symbol of the dark side of melancholy, for curled up tightly into an almost perfect ellipse it serves as a reminder of the inward-turned eye of despair. It has been suggested that the bat whose outstretched wings bear the title of the work is also a symbol of despair, as it flees from the rainbow and comet, sources of light in the darkened sky.[5] Yet Dürer's image is not solely a negative or hopeless one, for the bat seems to fly off not only in response to the light of the rainbow and comet but also because of the sharp, raking light cast from the right. This, like the continuity represented by the sphere, suggests a gradual passage from darkness into light, just as the slowly turning earth moves from night into day.

1. See Erwin Panofsky, *Albrecht Dürer*, 2d rev. ed. (Princeton, 1945), vol. 1, pp. 156–71.
2. In his *De Triplici Vita* of 1489, the Florentine physician and Platonic philosopher Marsilio Ficino discussed the relationships among medicine, astrology, and philosophy and clearly outlined the classical view of divine inspiration and despair as the twin aspects of melancholy. While studying in Italy, Dürer's close friend Willie Pirkheimer sent to Nuremberg a copy of Ficino's treatise, which the learned Dürer would likely have read.
3. Panofsky, *Dürer*, p. 158.
4. Ibid., p. 160.
5. Konrad Hoffmann, "Dürer's 'Melencolia,'" *The Print Collector's Newsletter*, vol. 9, no. 2 (May–June 1978), pp. 33–35.

D.K.

76

Jacques Callot (French, 1592–1635)
THE TRIBULATIONS OF SAINT ANTHONY (second version), 1635

Etching (iv/v), 14 x 18⅛" (35.6 x 46 cm) (trimmed)
Charles M. Lea Collection
28-42-791

Like Martin Schongauer (see no. 73) and Lucas Cranach the Elder before him (see no. 74), Jacques Callot produced an image of Saint Anthony that may be interpreted as a view of a man driven mad by his battles with the forces of evil around him. Callot's grand etching may in fact specifically have been occasioned by the torments of the plagues that ravaged the artist's region of Lorraine in the 1630s, for Saint Anthony was a patron saint of plague victims.[1] A world in torment is aptly conveyed by Callot's dramatic scene, inspired by contemporary theatrical depictions of hell, for the saint appears as only a small, resisting force against a fantastic world of wild monsters and frenzied activity. This print, with satanic forces dressed in military attire, may also be interpreted as a response to the torment Callot perceived around him in the random destruction and rampant suffering caused by the aftermath of the religious wars that had ravaged his homeland, inflicting misery on all levels of society. Particularly devastating were the typhus, smallpox, syphilis, and plague carried by the soldiers.

This is Callot's second of two versions of the subject. While the first was a denunciation of worldly indulgence, this emphasizes the torments of hell and sin.[2] As the inscription below makes clear, the saint is an example of one who is steadfast in the face of the tribulations that threaten to engulf him:

> *Nothing mortal inspires you, nor do alluring Joys move your heart; neither Love breaks it nor death frightens. The mind fixed on heaven and restoring its strength from the Source, endures on earth the battles, which he derides, in the upper air.*[3]

The inscription also speaks of the creatures of the lower world of darkness that battle the forces of light or good for dominance of the hermitage to which Anthony has retreated: "Shapeless spectres, monsters stabled in obscure hiding places, broke out of their lower world and in close marching order profane the world and light with deadly poisons."[4]

Religion was a significant part of life in Callot's seventeenth-century Lorraine, and images of saints played an important role in man's struggle for salvation. This fantastic vision, in the tradition of Bosch and Brueghel, aptly conveys the nightmarish depths of Saint Anthony's existence and by extension the raging battle facing all mankind.

Callot was one of the greatest and most prolific printmakers, having produced over fifteen hundred plates. He is known for two technical innovations that transformed copper etching. The first was to replace the waxy etching ground with a tough varnish adapted from musical instruments. This ensured that the acid would bite only the exposed parts of the plate. His second innovation was the development of the *echoppé,* an etching tool that could vary the line from thick to thin.

1. H. Diane Russell, *Jacques Callot: Prints & Related Drawings* (Washington, D.C., 1975), p. 160.
2. Ibid., p. 159.
3. Translated and quoted in ibid., p. 178, no. 139.
4. Translated and quoted in ibid.

E.J./D.K.

77
William Hogarth (English, 1697–1764) IN BETHLEHEM HOSPITAL (BEDLAM), 1735, reworked 1763

From "A Rake's Progress," 1735
Engraving and etching (iii/iii), 14¹⁄₁₆ x 16¼" (35.7 x 41.3 cm)
Gift of Boies Penrose
40-11-20

William Hogarth often presented his themes in a series of engravings, which, because of their relatively low cost, allowed him to reach a wider audience (see also no. 15). Since Hogarth's works were so popular, they were often copied and sold by other printmakers without his consent; he was instrumental in securing passage of the Engravers' Act in 1735, which helped prevent such piracy.

"A Rake's Progress," a series of eight engravings, was the first work Hogarth published after the copyright law took effect. As was sometimes his custom, he took the compositions of the engravings directly from a series of canvases he had painted (now in Sir John Soane's Museum, London). "A Rake's Progress" tells the story of Tom Rakewell, a young man of little moral fiber, who inherits a fortune and later loses it through carelessness, greed, and the predatory schemes of others. At last, as shown here, Rakewell goes insane and is sent to a madhouse, probably London's Bethlehem Hospital, known as Bedlam, where penniless madmen were confined.

Hogarth's print shows the hospital corridor onto which the individual cells opened. Stretched out on the floor, Rakewell is being manacled by an attendant. Sarah Young, a girl whom Tom had earlier mistreated and then abandoned, is beside him. Most of the hospital's other inmates are suffering from delusions made graphically clear by Hogarth. The man in the cell on the left is suffering from extreme religious fervor; face and body contorted, he prays to a cross made of straw. Images inscribed with the names of Saints Clement, Athanatius, and Lawrance adorn his wall. The man in the adjacent cell, wearing a straw crown, thinks he is king. The lunatic behind the door, drawing diagrams on the wall, is calculating longitudes. In front of him, the man peering through the "telescope" fancies himself an astronomer. In the center of the composition is a mad tailor holding a tape measure. A mad musician is beside the staircase, on which are a man who thinks he is the pope and a man who suffers from extreme melancholy, or depression. The inscription on the handrail, "Charming Betty Careless"—the name of a well-known prostitute with whom this poor melancholic man evidently has fallen in love—provides the key to the cause of his depression. The collar or bandage around his neck indicates that he has tried to hang himself.

Hogarth also included two fashionably dressed visitors who have come to gawk at the madmen, a popular recreation for mid-eighteenth-century Londoners. As the mad king urinates on the wall of his cell, one young woman hides her head behind her fan as the other stares at him over her friend's shoulder.

Although first engraved in 1735, the print displayed here was reworked in 1763. Hogarth changed several details: With neckbands added, the attendant leaning over Tom is now a clergyman and a medallion inscribed "Britannia 1763" is on the wall between the cells. With this addition, Hogarth seems to have suggested that in 1763 all of Britain was as mad as those confined to Bedlam.[1]

1. Ronald Paulson, *Hogarth's Graphic Works* (New Haven, 1965), vol. 1, p. 169, no. 139.

K.R./D.K.

78
Thomas Rowlandson (English, 1756–1827) After James Dunthorne (English, 1730–1815) THE HYPOCHONDRIAC, 1788

Hand-colored etching, 16⁷⁄₁₆ x 22¾" (41.7 x 57.8 cm)
Purchased: SmithKline Beckman Corporation Fund
69-190-54

Etched by Thomas Rowlandson (see also nos. 17 and 36), this composition is the invention of James Dunthorne, an amateur artist.[1] Amateurs such as Dunthorne often suggested ideas for satirical caricatures to professional artists, who were sometimes paid to improve and etch their designs.[2]

This bizarre print is distinguished by its graphic personification of mental illness. The hypochondriac, presumably so named because his malady is not physical, sits huddled in a chair, his arms clutching each other inside the sleeves of his long robe. He is unshaven and his hair is uncombed and unpowdered. His suicidal thoughts are vividly embodied in the creatures before him. A corpse in a clinging shroud offers him a choice of rope or pistol while a skeleton of

Death aims its arrow at his breast. A goblin holds out a cup of poison and a tormented man demonstrates throat cutting. Amid other phantoms, specters, and madmen, a ghostly hearse appears.

The right side of the print presents a complete contrast to the hypochondriac's terrifying visions. The well-fed doctor, who seems to be in the act of shaking his head and admitting that nothing can be done for the patient, is attended by a robustly healthy parlormaid. The table beside her is littered with ineffective medicines and prescriptions. Even the paintings on the walls carry a message: The calm, idyllic landscapes represent a state of mind that the tormented hypochondriac can never attain.

1. Joseph Grego, *Rowlandson, the Caricaturist*, vol. 1 (London, 1879), p. 314.
2. Victoria and Albert Museum, London, *English Caricature: 1620 to the Present* (1984), p. 68.

K.R./D.K.

79

Francisco José de Goya y Lucientes (Spanish, 1746–1828)

THE SLEEP OF REASON PRODUCES MONSTERS, 1797–98

From *Los Caprichos* (Madrid, 1799)
Etching and aquatint, 8⁷⁄₁₆ x 5¹⁵⁄₁₆" (21.4 x 15 cm)
Purchased: SmithKline Beckman Corporation Fund
49-97-9

Los Caprichos was etched by the Spanish artist Francisco José de Goya y Lucientes between 1797 and 1798, when the oppressive Inquisition still held power in his country. The eighty plates of the series express Goya's cynical, rational commentary on the state of Spanish society in particular and of mankind in general during the final years of the eighteenth century. Focusing on the various manifestations of human frailty, the artist presented a sequence of social archetypes—including greed, gluttony, cruelty, lust, pride, and vanity—that he believed pushed man's behavior to the depths of insanity and inhumanity.

The Sleep of Reason Produces Monsters is a self-portrait of Goya collapsed in sleep over his drawing table, surrounded by the grainy darkness of the aquatint and haunted by bats and owls, symbols of darkness, folly, and stupidity.[1] An owl that has alighted on the desk holds the artist's crayon in its claw and stares at the sleeping artist as though to goad him into registering his nightmarish images or to challenge the work already done. The black cat, another stealthy, nocturnal creature, sits near the artist's chair, closing the sleeping figure in from the right. The significance of the print's title, which appears on the front of the desk, is amplified by the commentary on the image, attributed to Goya, that reads: "Fantasy abandoned by reason produces impossible monsters: united with her, she is the mother of all the arts and the source of their wonders."[2] It thus appears that Goya, like Dürer before him (see no. 75), used his image to explore the relationship between the two types of melancholy—the creative and the destructive—that are twin aspects of the artistic human mind.

This image was apparently originally designed to be the frontispiece to the series of scenes of fantasy that Goya intended to publish as "Sueños." In that earlier project, which was a source for *Los Caprichos*, Goya explored the function of dreams in man's search for the truth. The ink drawing for this etching, now in the Prado in Madrid, includes a halo of light from the upper left that appears to repel the bats and owls, denizens of the darkness. An inscription on the drawing adds to an understanding of the image: "The author dreaming. His one intention is to banish harmful beliefs commonly held and with this work of *caprichos* to perpetuate the solid testimony of truth."[3] When *Los Caprichos* was published in 1799, a more conventional self-portrait was used as the frontispiece, and *The Sleep of Reason* became plate forty-three in the series.

1. Eleanor A. Sayre, *The Changing Image: Prints by Francisco Goya* (Boston, 1974), p. 100.
2. Translated and quoted in Tomás Harris, *Goya: Engravings and Lithographs* (Oxford, 1964), vol. 1, p. 101.
3. Translated and quoted in Sayre, *Changing Image*, p. 100.

D.K.

80

Ambroise Tardieu (French, 1788–1841)

MANIA SUCCEEDED BY DEMENTIA, 1838

From Jean-Etienne-Dominique Esquirol, *Des Maladies mentales considérées sous les rapports médical, hygiénique et médico-légal*, vol. 2 (Paris: J.-B. Baillière, 1838)
Etching, stipple etching, and engraving, 6 x 3¹¹⁄₁₆" (15.2 x 9.4 cm)
Purchased: SmithKline Beckman Corporation Fund
68-109-4b

Philippe Pinel, a respected Paris physician, was appointed chief physician to the Bicêtre and Salpêtrière hospitals during the French Revolution. Despite a general awareness of the harsh treatment of the insane, he was shocked by the conditions he discovered there. He found many patients in chains, some having been so for years; others were beaten and whipped regularly, and still others were all but starved. Pinel insisted on humane treatment for all patients, no matter how recalcitrant, and increased the numbers of specially selected physicians to treat them. Having devoted the rest of his life to the insane, he was one of the most influential reformers of the archaic system for the care of mental deviants in France, and his teachings and writings had an impact on the treatment of the insane throughout Europe, Great Britain, and America.

Pinel's most outstanding student was Jean-Etienne-Dominique Esquirol, who so closely followed his teacher's approach that the work of the two is sometimes inseparable. Like Pinel, Esquirol did not attempt to analyze mental illness from a predetermined philosophical perspective but made great effort to observe his patients and record their actions and appearances in order to describe and classify the various kinds of insanity he encountered in clinical practice. Esquirol developed and applied new terms to certain patterns of behavior in order to clarify and differentiate them. "Hallucination" was used to distinguish one type of episode from illusion, and "monomania" was used to describe an illness pattern that anticipated the modern view of schizophrenia. Esquirol was the first to apply statistical methods to his clinical studies, compiling tables included in the text, which are enlightening today both in their method and their information. Esquirol succeeded Pinel as chief physician at La Salpêtrière in 1810 and was the first physician to lecture formally on psychiatry within that system. In 1817 he began a series of lectures on the treatment of the insane, exposing abuses in French asylums, which generated a government-appointed commission to study the problem. He continued to press for greater reforms in the regimen and housing of mental patients and gained support for his humanitarian movement by lecturing throughout Europe.

One of Esquirol's major contributions to the field of psychiatry was his landmark study of mental illness published in 1838 and illustrated with prints by Ambroise Tardieu. The plates in this first atlas of psychiatric physiognomy comprise portraits of Esquirol's patients executed in a factual, striking manner. The documentation of the appearance of patients during acute episodes of insanity in conjunction with descriptions of the progress of their case histories offered a very important tool for assessing and identifying psychopathology. As Esquirol himself wrote, this method of study offered valuable insights into the treatment of the insane, for "their physiognomy carries the imprint of their sadness . . . ."[1]

Mania Succeeded by Dementia is a powerful image of madness. The attendant case history describes the patient as a twenty-seven-year-old Swiss soldier admitted to the Charenton asylum in November 1827. According to Esquirol, the episode of madness occurred shortly after the soldier had had a dispute with his officers that led to his demotion. In the initial stage, "his delirium was general, he talked constantly, indulged in wild actions, ripped up and broke everything he could lay hands on." Later he became withdrawn, incoherent, then almost mute. "He spent a large part of each day crouching in an armchair, head sunk on his chest, eyes dull, but with a fixed stare."[2] The sense of isolation and withdrawal is sharply conveyed in this print, whose starkness of line and space present not just the appearance but the mood of the madman.

1. Jean-Etienne-Dominique Esquirol, *Des Maladies mentales considérées sous les rapports médical, hygiénique et médico-légal* (Paris: J.-B. Baillière, 1838), vol. 1, p. 17.
2. Ibid., vol. 2, p. 229.

D.K.

81

Hugh Welch Diamond (English, 1809–1886)
FEMALE PATIENT, SURREY COUNTY LUNATIC ASYLUM, c. 1850

Albumen print, 7 x 5³⁄₁₆" (17.6 x 13.1 cm)
Purchased: SmithKline Beckman Corporation Fund
1984-93-1

This photograph conveys the melancholic isolation of a depressed patient housed at the Female Department of the Surrey County Lunatic Asylum in England in the mid-nineteenth century. With her hands folded in her lap, the woman sits for her portrait in front of a dramatically lit curtained background. Her unfocused stare and despondent expression speak not of violent disturbance but perhaps of the very same melancholic state upon which Dürer had focused his attention almost three and one-half centuries earlier (see no. 75). This early albumen photograph was one of a series of portraits of female patients exhibited by Dr. Hugh Welch Diamond under the general title "Types of Insanity," which received much favorable notice at the first exhibition of photography at the Society of Arts in 1852 in London and which then traveled throughout Britain.

After distinguishing himself as a physician during the outbreak of cholera in London in 1832, Diamond turned his attention to the problem of mental disease, which he studied at Bethlehem Hospital in London. In 1848 Diamond was appointed superintendent of the Female Department of the Surrey County Lunatic Asylum. Having experimented with the photographic process for some years, Diamond began to document the appearance of the various types of mental disease that his patients manifested. In 1856 he presented a paper before the Royal Society on the application of photography in the practice of psychiatry.[1] In this paper Diamond outlined the important function of photography in the treatment of the mentally ill. Such photographs would record the physical appearance of mental illness for study; they could also be used to assist in the treatment of the patient by giving an accurate image of various mental states and to record appearances for comparison and identification in case of future episodes of illness. Photography, which was revered in England as the ultimate medium for realistic portrayal, is here coupled with the study of the physiognomy of insanity to produce one of the earliest examples of the clinical psychiatric photograph.

1. "On the Application of Photography to the Physiognomic and Mental Phenomena of Insanity," reprinted in Sander L. Gilman, *The Face of Madness: Hugh W. Diamond and the Origin of Psychiatric Photography* (Secaucus, N.J., 1977), pp. 17–24.

D.K.

82

Désiré Magloire Bourneville (French, active late nineteenth century) and Paul Regnard (French, active late nineteenth century) TERMINAL STAGE: MELANCHOLIA, 1877

From Désiré Magloire Bourneville and Paul Regnard, *Iconographie photographique de La Salpêtrière,* vol. 1 (Paris: Bureaux du Progrès Médical & V. Adrien Delahay & Cie, 1877)
Albumen print, 2⅜ x 3¹¹⁄₁₆" (6 x 9.3 cm)
Purchased: SmithKline Beckman Corporation Fund
71-116-2a

Between 1875 and 1877 Désiré Magloire Bourneville and Paul Regnard worked in the Parisian hospital La Salpêtrière under the direction of Jean Martin Charcot, a pioneer in psychiatric medicine and one of the greatest neurologists of his time, to document with words and photographs the condition of hysterical epilepsy. At Charcot's request Bourneville, the photographer, and Regnard, the doctor, attempted to capture not only the physiognomy of the deranged but also the process of their disease in its various stages and forms. *Terminal Stage: Melancholia* is one of the one hundred photographs published in their book, which was intended to serve the physician and student of neurology.

The success of their first project within the medical community was such that Bourneville and Regnard, with great support from Charcot, continued to document the case histories of the patients at La Salpêtrière. A photographic darkroom was built for their use next to Charcot's laboratory at the hospital, and until 1918 they published a series of albums containing written descriptions of disease and methods of treatment accompanied by an impressive group of documentary photographs.

D.K.

83

Max Beckmann (German, 1884–1950) THE MADHOUSE, 1918

From *Gesichter* (Munich: R. Piper, 1919)
Drypoint, 10¼ x 12⅛" (26 x 30.8 cm)
Purchased: SmithKline Beckman Corporation Fund
1983-93-1

In 1914, volunteering as a medic rather than bearing arms during World War I, Max Beckmann found himself confronting both his fascination with the immense drama of the conflict and his horror at its destructiveness (see no. 43). This print from the portfolio *Gesichter* reflects the emotional price that many, including the artist, paid for the war. As the war dragged on and Beckmann was transferred to the battlefront in Belgium, his letters and images began to convey more of the horror and less of the enthusiasm felt in the early years of the fighting. Trying to describe the nightmarish intensity of the front and his personal emotional crisis in the face of the hellishness he witnessed, in September 1915 he wrote, "For me every day is a struggle. And indeed a struggle with myself and with the bad dreams that whir around my head like gnats."[1] Sometime in late 1915 or 1916, Beckmann, suffering from physical and emotional exhaustion, was sent to Frankfort to recover. Perhaps it was his own experience with war's frightening power to devastate the mind that makes his image of *The Madhouse* so powerful.

Using drypoint to scratch out the strange interior of the madhouse, Beckmann created a densely packed, claustrophobic space. The inmates, despite their proximity within the oppressive room, do not interact. They are isolated from each other by the madness that brings them together. To reinforce this isolation, Beckmann rendered the figures in varying proportions, as if to imply their existence on vastly different planes of emotional space.

The intense power of the gestures and expressions of the characters in this scene is the one point of contact with their individual reality, for their emotional pain is recognizable if not familiar. For Beckmann the madness within this room seems to serve as a mirror of the upheaval in Germany late in the war. The frightening drama of the mad people, each lost in a personal hell, may be seen as a metaphor for the drama of a nation that had reached the brink of rational behavior and seemed to be plummeting into the void.

1. Translated and quoted in Carla Schulz-Hoffmann and Judith C. Weiss, eds., *Max Beckmann: Retrospective* (Saint Louis, 1984), p. 76.

D.K.

84

Robert Riggs (American, 1896–1970)
PSYCHOPATHIC WARD, 1940

Lithograph, 14⁵⁄₁₆ x 18⅞" (36.3 x 47.9 cm)
Gift of R. Sturgis Ingersoll
46-80-8

In 1939 the American lithographer and commercial illustrator Robert Riggs, having established his reputation as a fine artist with dramatically designed and meticulously detailed lithographs of the circus and the boxing ring, told an interviewer that he hoped "someday to exploit the artistic potentialities of hospitals, prisons, docks and madhouses."[1] In 1940 the Philadelphia pharmaceutical corporation of Smith, Kline and French provided the opportunity to complete part of that plan when it commissioned Riggs, through the advertising firm N. W. Ayer & Son, to execute a set of four lithographs on the themes of contemporary medical practice and the care of the insane.[2]

Riggs, a Germantown resident, visited the Philadelphia State Hospital for the Mentally Ill, called Byberry, in nearby northeast Philadelphia, to make sketches, a practice he followed in all his work, and *Psychopathic Ward* probably was completed by the end of 1940. Technically the print is a superb example of the artist's method of creating an image by making thousands of densely packed, microscopic scratches with a razor blade into a layer of greasy tusche spread over the stone's surface.

Psychopathic Ward is one of Riggs's most disturbing works and justly his most famous. (To be clinically correct, the title should be "Psychotic Ward," since "psychopathic" suggests a criminal mentality and "psychotic," mental illness.) Although too many figures are unrealistically crowded into the same room, the sufferings of psychotic patients, most of whom are tormented by voices only they can hear, are rendered with clinical exactitude. Before such patients could be sedated with Thorazine, a drug developed and made available by Smith, Kline and French in 1954, the treatment of psychoses included the use of a variety of barbiturates, electric shock therapy, insulin shock therapy, and prefrontal lobotomy.[3] Riggs's print, reproduced and circulated to physicians by the pharmaceutical company, seems both a plea for and prediction of progress in this branch of medicine.

1. Quoted in Grover Bacon Smith, "Not for Art's Sake," *Coronet* (January 1939), p. 52.
2. Warren Blair, Director of Design, SmithKline Beckman Corporation, to author, October 9, 1980.
3. Interview with Dr. Karl Salus, a psychiatrist who practiced at Byberry in the mid-1940s, March 1985.

B.B.

The intensity of emotions of the patients compelled Robert Riggs to sketch the living nightmare of the asylum. In 1940 Byberry was a model of modern mental-health care, yet the scene depicted does not speak of a particular time. The number 12—the ward number—is on the back of the inmates' simple hospital shifts. Their individuality is not important; rather, they are identified by psychological status, general severity of their illness, and hospital location. Displaying complete withdrawal to physical violence, the women act out a drama repeated thousands of times each day in asylums across three continents. The frenzy of the inmates who scream and pace, expose their bodies, and attack each other sets the mood of disorder and anxiety that radiates from the print, made immediate for the viewer by the newspaperlike quality of observed reality that keeps it from slipping into the extremes of fiction.

D.K.

85

W. Eugene Smith (American, 1918–1978)
INSANE COMPOUND, LAMBARENE, 1954

From "A Man of Mercy," 1954
Gelatin silver print, 9 x 13½" (22.9 x 34.3 cm)
Purchased: SmithKline Beckman Corporation Fund
70-33-2

The power of a truly brilliant image is clearly exemplified by W. Eugene Smith's extraordinary photograph of the insane compound in Lambaréné, West Africa, from his photo-essay "A Man of Mercy" (see nos. 48 and 66) in the rough textures of the natural wooden planks, the simplicity of the common hardware, and the hands clinging to a crossbar of the window. This is not a clinical case history of one of the patients, but the reality of a human being psychologically and physically separated from his community.

An isolated observation devoid of idealization or social criticism, this image beautifully expresses Smith's faith in the photograph, as he later explained:

> *Photography is a small voice, at best, but sometimes—just sometimes—one photograph or a group of them can lure our senses into awareness. Much depends upon the viewer; in some, photographs can summon enough emotion to be a catalyst to thought. Someone—or perhaps many—among us may be influenced to heed reason, to find a way to right that which is wrong, and may even be inspired to the dedication needed to search for the cure to an illness. The rest of us may perhaps feel a greater sense of understanding and compassion for those whose lives are alien to our own. Photography is a small voice. I believe in it. If it is well-conceived, it sometimes works.*[1]

In Lambaréné the insane were separated only during severe episodes that could conceivably be dangerous to either the patient or the community. But even when separated physically, they were still visited by friends and family and, as soon as possible, were returned to their homes. Just as the photograph indicates, this "compound" was a temporary space, and like the rest of the hospital it was integrated into the very fabric of the village.

1. Quoted in William S. Johnson, ed., *W. Eugene Smith: Master of the Photographic Essay* (Millerton, N.Y., 1981), p. 153.

D.K.

86a

Raymond Depardon (French, born 1942)
UNTITLED, 1977–79

From "Insane Asylums in Italy," 1977–79
Gelatin silver print, 9 7/16 x 14 1/4" (24 x 36.2 cm)
Purchased: SmithKline Beckman Corporation Fund
1983-30-10

86b

Raymond Depardon (French, born 1942)
UNTITLED, 1977–79

From "Insane Asylums in Italy," 1977–79
Gelatin silver print, 9 9/16 x 14 3/16" (24.4 x.36 cm)
Purchased: SmithKline Beckman Corporation Fund
1983-30-11

In 1977 the French photojournalist Raymond Depardon came across a newspaper article reporting on the alternative psychiatry movement in Italy aimed at emptying mental institutions and reintegrating patients into society.[1] Intrigued by reports of this development in psychiatric care, he decided to attend a conference on the subject to be held at the mental hospital in Trieste, where he hoped to photograph the results of these experiments. Depardon was impressed with the success of the public program, which not only situated the patients in small groups throughout the city but also provided for their future care. While on the grounds of the hospital, he wandered by accident into a ward of patients too seriously ill to be included in the community placement program and was confronted with a "traditional nineteenth-century nightmare. Everything was out of the myth of the madhouse."[2] After securing permission from the director, he immediately began to photograph the patients.

Over the next three years, living and working in asylums in Trieste, Venice, Perugia, Turin, Arezzo, and Naples, Depardon dedicated himself to photographing not the mental-health care revolution that had originally intrigued him but the residue. He was attracted to "the survival of a world that must have once been everywhere."[3] Inside the asylums the patients were treated mainly by electroshock and massive doses of tranquilizers, or they were physically restrained simply to keep them in order. With his powerful photographs, Depardon sought to demonstrate the need for a more progressive approach to the treatment of patients in mental institutions. His haunting studies of this frightening aspect of the human condition, the mind under siege, need no words to assist in conveying their powerful message.

1. See Lauren Shakely, "Asylum," *Aperture*, no. 89 (1982), pp. 10–23.
2. Depardon, quoted in ibid., p. 12.
3. Depardon, quoted in ibid.

D.K.

87

Richard Bosman (American, born 1944)
SUICIDE, 1980–81

Color woodcut, 13 3/16 x 27 9/16" (33.5 x 70 cm)
Purchased: SmithKline Beckman Corporation Fund
1982-115-1

The raucous color, active surfaces, and intense, emotional subject matter of much of Richard Bosman's work underscore his exploration of raw, personal anxiety. His figurative subjects are derived in part from Asian comic books, which utilize stereotypic images and simple narrative. In this print the tensions of modern life, technology, and the impersonality of urban living are at last released by the single violent gesture of self-destruction registered with great chromatic intensity.

Using a large sheet of plywood, the artist created a powerful and aggressive woodcut image that focuses on a scene of personal disaster. Below a garish orange moon the suicide holds a gun to his head, isolated against the flame-licked city skyline. For Bosman the city—distant and schematic—is the setting in which violence at its most primitive level is acted out.[1] The surface of the wood is attacked with harsh, jagged, expressive cuts that read like wounds reinforcing the powerful emotional image. Even the flecks of the *tairei* red paper on which the woodcut is printed are drawn into the narrative, like exploding fragments or drifting debris.

Bosman's awful drama is partly a plea for a more caring society, where those oppressed by life can seek and find help rather than be driven to self-destruction. But it is also a sharp comment on the frighteningly real fact that everyday contemporary life willingly embraces violence: Car wrecks, murders, drownings, disasters, and urban crime are popularized and clichéd in newspapers, comics, films, and television. Here Bosman focuses not on the society or perpetrator of the violence but on its unfortunate victim. Unlike many of his "psychodramas" in which he shows both victim and implied villain, this print portrays a private act in which the central figure is both victim and attacker. The suicide act, typically hidden from view and discovered only after the fact, is here played out before one's horrified yet fascinated eyes.

1. See Jeanne Siegel, "Richard Bosman: Stories of Violence," *Arts Magazine*, vol. 57, no. 8 (April 1983), pp. 126–28.

D.K.

THE CYCLE OF LIFE

88

Albrecht Dürer (German, 1471–1528)

BIRTH OF THE VIRGIN, c. 1503–4

From "The Life of the Virgin," 1502–10
Woodcut (b/b), 11 11/16 x 8 3/16" (29.7 x 20.8 cm)
Gift of Lessing J. Rosenwald
50-8-5

Albrecht Dürer often placed his religious narratives in settings that reflected the attitudes and activities of his time, and *Birth of the Virgin*, a beautiful and well-known print, is both a depiction of a New Testament story and a vivid delineation of a contemporary birthing event. This bustling image is one of nineteen woodcuts from the series "The Life of the Virgin" that Dürer published in book form in 1511.

Dürer has chosen to present not a sequential narrative of consecutive events but rather a series of simultaneous actions. There is a pleasant aura surrounding this representation of the beginning of life, and one suspects that such a scene was typical of the activities accompanying childbirth at the time. The angel above swings a smoking censer to focus attention on the main scene under the canopy at the distant right, where Anne rests wearily after having given birth to Mary. She is attended by a midwife, denoted by the knife and surgical kit, and a woman offering nourishment. At the side of the bed another woman rests, her collapsed posture suggesting she has assisted in the exhausting event. In the foreground the newborn is being washed as a young woman delivers a simple cradle. Groups of women chatting, drinking, and playing with a young child complete the scene.

The picturesque details of the setting, such as the towel, candelabrum, washtub, and basket, provide records of the domestic interiors of the period. The space itself, with the high ceiling and decorative archway, is probably an elaboration of contemporary sixteenth-century domestic architecture. Dürer used such inventive evocations of space throughout this series as a format for the study of linear perspective.[1] The woodcutter's ability to meet unusual technical demands is demonstrated by the abundance of exquisite textural details in the broad areas of stone, wooden surfaces, and fabrics that add an exciting surface to the print.

A preliminary ink study for the woodcut in the Kupferstichkabinett in West Berlin contains the principal elements of the print, but in the drawing the bed fills the space and the washing of the infant is the central action.

1. Museum of Fine Arts, Boston, *Albrecht Dürer: Master Printmaker* (November 17, 1971–January 16, 1972), p. xx.

D.K./E.J.

89

Anonymous (Swiss, early sixteenth century)

CAESAREAN BIRTH, c. 1506

Woodcut, 7 13/16 x 5 15/16" (19.9 x 15.1 cm)
Purchased: SmithKline Beckman Corporation Fund
71-54-2

This simple, early sixteenth-century woodcut, which is from a medical text thought to have been published in Basel around 1506, documents the procedure known as a Caesarean section, the surgical delivery of a baby by cutting through the woman's abdominal and uterine walls. Here the mother lies in bed with the linens pulled back to reveal the gaping incision through which the child, now wrapped in swaddling, was removed. The placement of the incision in the center of the woman's abdomen is not typical in depictions of this form of childbirth, for in medieval and Renaissance manuscripts and printed illustrations the curved cut is most often on the left side of the body.

Sixteenth-century depictions of childbirth are generally of two types: images with a series of consecutive scenes that describe the various stages of the birth process, or representations of lying-in rooms at a specific moment of the birth, as shown here.[1] In this woodcut, however, the austere interior of the room with its skewed perspective and tilted bed gives but a very generalized view of the event.

The Caesarean procedure, which takes its name from the way in which Julius Caesar is said to have been delivered,[2] has been practiced for centuries in both East and West. Ancient legends tell of surgical births, although there is no mention of this method of childbirth in the writings of Hippocrates from the fifth century B.C. One of the earliest written references to this surgery is found in the Talmud, the body of Jewish civil and religious law codified between the second and sixth centuries A.D. The operation is also described in the extraordinary *Sushruta Saṃhitā*, the Indian encyclopedic surgical and medical compendium written well before the eighth century A.D.[3]

1. Robert Herrlinger, *History of Medical Illustration from Antiquity to A.D. 1600* (Nijkerk, The Netherlands, 1970), pp. 150–52.
2. It has also been suggested that the term derived from a law of the Caesars that a woman who died in advanced pregnancy should be promptly operated upon to remove and perhaps save the fetus. See Arturo Castiglioni, *A History of Medicine*, ed. and trans. E. B. Krumbhaar, 2d ed., rev. and enl. (New York, 1947), p. 854.
3. Leo M. Zimmerman and Ilza Veith, *Great Ideas in the History of Surgery*, 2d rev. ed. (New York, 1967), p. 63.

D.K.

90

Jost Amman (Swiss, active Germany, 1539–1591)

CHILDBIRTH, 1580

From Jacob Rueff, *De Conceptu et Generatione Hominis . . .* (Frankfort on the Main: Sigismundi Feyerabendius, 1580)
Woodcut, 7 11/16 x 5 7/8" (19.5 x 14.9 cm)
Purchased: SmithKline Beckman Corporation Fund
49-97-12a

This woodcut is one of seventy-four illustrations done by the Swiss-born artist Jost Amman for a book by Jacob Rueff primarily on obstetrical practices but also rich in information on the habits, dress, and customs of women in sixteenth-century Germany. This animated scene, which shows a woman about to deliver seated on a birthing stool and attended by a midwife and two women giving aid and comfort, is one of the most vivid depictions of an actual childbirth in early obstetrical literature. On the table are earthy details such as a stein and an empty plate, evidence of recent nourishment for the laboring mother, and scissors and string for cutting and tying the cord. In the background, in an imaginary addition, two astrologers plot the newborn's horoscope.

The first edition of Rueff's text, published in Zurich in 1554, had contained illustrations as well, but by a different artist and in a somewhat more archaic style. Two later editions of the text with the new illustrations by Amman were published in Frankfort in 1580. The first of these, in German, bore the homely title *Hebammen Buch* (Midwife's Handbook). The title goes on to assert that from the book one could learn the secrets of the female sex and the form of man in the womb. The second edition was distinguished by the more formal Latin title *De Conceptu et Generatione Hominis* (Concerning the Conception and Birth of Man).

In a discussion of the iconography of Amman's illustrations for Rueff's text, K. B. Roberts noted that the first plate, which shows the Fall of Man with Adam, Eve, the Serpent, and the Tree, set the tone for the book's deeper moral implications. Roberts has suggested that

> *sexual activity and hence conception and childbirth are associated with seduction, the Fall and Death: the fruit of the tree of knowledge brings death and suffering into the world. This illustration of the Fall of man, placed at the very beginning of an influential 16th century book on obstetrics, reminded the reader that women, and their babies, faced sorrow and death in childbirth and that this was Eve's fault.*[1]

Amman was one of the most interesting and prolific artists active in late-sixteenth-century Germany. Most of his work centered in Nuremberg, but he provided numerous book illustrations to the active publishing houses in Frankfort as well. He illustrated numerous medical texts, including the *Opus Chyrurgicum* of the enigmatic Doctor Paracelsus, the frontispiece of which is a detailed and realistic depiction of an actual dissection taking place in Nuremberg.[2] Bartsch claimed that Amman did not actually cut his own blocks but rather had a number of skilled craftsmen working after his inventive and distinctive designs.[3] However, the long list of prints ascribed to Amman certainly attests to his wide-ranging curiosity about all aspects of human knowledge.

1. K. B. Roberts, "Illustrations in a Sixteenth-Century Book on Obstetrics," *Canadian Bulletin of Medical History*, vol. 1, no. 2 (Winter 1984), pp. 80–95.
2. Robert Herrlinger, "Die Anatomie des Jost Amman und die Illustration zu Feyerabends Paracelsus-Ausgabe von 1565," *Sudhoffs Archiv für Geschichte der Medizin und der Naturwissenschaften*, vol. 37 (1953), pp. 23–38.
3. Adam Bartsch, *Le Peintre graveur*, vol. 9 (Vienna, 1808), p. 351.

M.C.

91
Abraham Bosse (French, 1602–1676)
CHILDBIRTH, 1633

From "The City Marriage," 1633
Etching, 10¼ x 13¼" (26 x 33.5 cm) (trimmed)
Purchased: SmithKline Beckman Corporation Fund
49-97-13

The numerous scenes of seventeenth-century French life etched by Abraham Bosse are accurate mirrors of the behavior, mores, activities, costumes, and interiors of his time (see also nos. 31a,b).[1] The six prints in the series "The City Marriage," all but the first set in a handsomely appointed bedchamber, follow the marriage relationship from the contract and exchange of vows through the delivery of the first child, its baptism, and visits to the nursing mother. All these scenes and their accompanying verses focus on the role of the woman as wife and mother.

In *Childbirth*, the third of the series, the laboring mother lies prone on a portable birthing table that has been placed near the fireplace for light and warmth. Included in the print are the midwife, several women attendants, and the husband; the latter was rarely depicted in birthing scenes before the seventeenth century.

In the quatrains below the scene, the mother pleads, "Alas, I can no more; the pain possesses me, enfeebling all my senses; my body has given up and there is no help for the pangs I feel." As one of the women who attends her asks for divine support in the childbirth, the midwife reassures the mother, "Madame, have patience, do not cry out so. It is all over; by my faith you are delivered of a fine son," and indeed the baby's head has emerged. At this the relieved husband reassures his wife and coaxes her to relax, saying, "That news comforts me; all my grief has vanished. Keep on, dear heart, take courage, your pain will soon be over."

The simple tool kit always shown strapped around the waist of the sixteenth-century midwife (see no. 90) has been replaced here by a handsome box containing clean linen bandages and most probably a variety of obstetrical instruments. Until the end of the seventeenth century in France it was not physicians or surgeons but rather midwives (and their assistants) who had complete charge during labor and delivery. These women were usually very skillful and quite capable of handling deliveries of both a complicated and uncomplicated nature. In 1609 a very well known French midwife, Louise Bourgeois,[2] who had studied under the surgeon Ambroise Paré, published an important work[3] that included her observations and recommendations on infertility, lying-in, delivery, postpartum difficulties, and problems of the newborn. Toward the end of the seventeenth century—as surgeons were first admitted to normal deliveries, maternity institutes were established, and new midwifery books were published—there was rapid, marked improvement in obstetrical care in France.

1. André Blum, *L'Oeuvre gravé d'Abraham Bosse* (Paris, 1924), p. 5.
2. Arturo Castiglioni, *A History of Medicine*, ed. and trans. E. B. Krumbhaar, 2d ed., rev. and enl. (New York, 1947), pp. 556–57.
3. Louise Bourgeois, *Observations diverses, sur la stérilité, perte de fruict, foecondité, accouchements, et maladies des femmes, et enfants nouveaux-naiz* (Paris, 1609).

D.K.

92
W. Eugene Smith (American, 1918–1978)
MAUDE CALLEN, 1951

From "Nurse Midwife," 1951
Gelatin silver print, 12 13/16 x 9⅞" (32.7 x 25 cm)
Purchased: SmithKline Beckman Corporation Fund
1978-95-15

In this dramatic photograph from the photo-essay "Nurse Midwife" published in *Life* in 1951 (see no. 47), W. Eugene Smith focuses attention on the moment of birth. The energy and potential of the small being cradled in the knowing hands are the center of attention. The midwife and her assistant hold the howling newborn with a sense of scrutiny of the present as well as reverence for the future.

It is the moment just after delivery when the infant is still attached to its mother by the umbilicus yet capable of breathing and taking nourishment on its own. This is its first experience not insulated by the warmth and protection of the uterus. The corner table beyond, covered with fresh newspaper and lit by an oil lamp, holds the few tools used during a normal delivery: the suture to tie off the umbilicus and the knife to sever it, the same tools laid out on the table in Jost Amman's 1580 woodcut (no. 90). Here Smith did not glorify labor; he included only the mother's leg and hand so that her presence is acknowledged but not made central.

D.K.

93

Giovanni Francesco Barbieri, known as Il Guercino (Italian, 1591–1666)
CARICATURE OF AN EMACIATED OLD MAN

Brown ink and brown washes on light buff antique laid paper, 11⅜ x 8¼" (29 x 21 cm)
Purchased: SmithKline Beckman Corporation Fund
1984-77-1

Giovanni Francesco Barbieri, whose nickname Il Guercino derives from his squint or crossed eye or eyes, is one of the most admired of all seventeenth-century draftsmen and painters. Born in the small Emilian town of Cento between Bologna and Ferrara, he matured in the tradition of the important Bolognese painters Annibale, Agostino, and Lodovico Carracci. Guercino's ink-and-wash drawing style is characterized by an expressive, calligraphic line combined with a brilliantly atmospheric use of wash. His many drawings, assiduously collected in his own lifetime,[1] served both as preparatory sketches and studies for his paintings and (rarely) as highly finished sheets, as well as records of contemporary scenes or individual faces, such as this *Caricature of an Emaciated Old Man*.

With great deftness Guercino captured the physical quality of aging. The old man with sunken cheeks has lost his teeth, causing his chin to protrude and his lower lip to rest in front of the upper. The broad, flat chin with the narrowing of the face at the mouth suggests a degeneration of the jaw. Reduced visual acuity may be implied by the simplified rendering of the eye sockets without clear notation of eyes; the result is a furrowed squint, suggesting the visual difficulties of old age associated with cataracts or severe refractive error. The exaggerated quality of the snoutlike nose and the unusually squared jaw may also place the image within the genre of caricature, although the face is very much rooted in observation from life. The fascination with a strange and hauntingly disfigured face is typical of one facet of Guercino's artistic personality, as witnessed by the survival of a number of caricatures and studies of heads in his drawn oeuvre.[2]

1. See Denis Mahon, "Drawings by Guercino in the Casa Gennari," *Apollo*, n.s., vol. 88, no. 81 (November 1968), pp. 346–57.
2. See Diane DeGrazia, *Guercino Drawings in the Art Museum, Princeton University* (Princeton, 1969), no. 34.

D.K./A.P.

94

Nicholas Nixon (American, born 1947)
C. C., BOSTON, 1983

Gelatin silver print, 8 x 9¹⁵⁄₁₆" (20.3 x 25.2 cm)
Purchased: SmithKline Beckman Corporation Fund
1985-17-1

The contemporary American photographer Nicholas Nixon, well known for his Boston-area cityscapes and yearly portraits of his wife and her sisters, has recently produced a group of photographs that emerged from his experiences as a volunteer in an old-age home in Boston. This image of a resident identified only as C. C. is one of the most successful and striking of this series, and brings into focus the interest artists have maintained in the physical transformations wrought by the process of aging (see no. 93).

Nixon's style is one of profound respect for and noninterference with his subject, and here he has deftly used the fine detail of the contact print to convey both the fragility and beautiful delicacy of old age. The medium-range vantage point of the photograph balances the lines of age with other elements of the composition, and provides a framework for empathetic contemplation of the sitter, whose closed eyes and still pose serve as powerful reminders of the closeness of death in extreme old age.

M.Ch./D.K.

95

Master E. S. (German, active c. 1450–67)
TRIUMPH OVER TEMPTATION, c. 1450

From the *Ars Moriendi*, c. 1450
Engraving, 3⁷⁄₁₆ x 2⁹⁄₁₆" (8.7 x 6.5 cm) (trimmed)
Purchased: SmithKline Beckman Corporation Fund
1983-72-1

Illustrated treatises of the *Ars Moriendi*, or the "Art of Dying," appeared during the early fifteenth century and paralleled the increased popularity of the themes of the Danse Macabre (see nos. 96 and 98) and the Apocalypse (see no. 97). It is likely these subjects were taken up in direct response to the waves of plague and other destruction that repeatedly washed over Europe. The irrational patterns of voracious death understandably made the population uneasy, and man became oppressively aware of his mortality. The realization that death was a constant companion and might strike without warning prompted works such as the *Ars Moriendi* that showed one how to prepare for death and take leave of this world properly.

The *Ars Moriendi* portrays the temptations offered by the devil in his efforts to win the soul of a dying man: Infidelity, Despair, Impatience, Vainglory, and

Avarice. In the typical format of this treatise, each temptation was paired with the defenses against it in a series of temptations and triumphs. This engraving by Master E. S., as he is known from the monogram with which he signed his works, is the eleventh and final scene in the series.[1] It demonstrates the triumph over all temptation at the moment of death. A monk offers the dying man the Last Sacrament, placing a lighted candle into his hand. Angels above the bed receive his soul, which issues forth from his mouth in the form of a child, while the enraged demons, having lost their prey, stamp and fume angrily around the foot of his bed.

Master E. S., one of the most accomplished as well as prolific early engravers, apparently based this series of prints on an earlier manuscript illumination,[2] with the intention that they could then be pasted into a copy of the *Ars Moriendi*. The only complete set of these prints is at the Ashmolean Museum, Oxford, which also owns the only other known example of this engraving. Printing from engraved plates probably developed during the second quarter of the fifteenth century as an offshoot of the goldsmith's art of incising designs on metal, and it is no coincidence that this rich, sharp impression conveys the delicacy of the goldsmith's hand.

1. See Alan Shestack, *Master E. S.: Five Hundredth Anniversary Exhibition* (Philadelphia, 1967), nos. 4–14.
2. See F. Saxl, "A Spiritual Encyclopaedia of the Later Middle Ages," *Journal of the Warburg and Courtauld Institutes*, vol. 5 (1942), pp. 82–134.

D.K.

96

Wilhelm Pleydenwurff (German, active 1482/83–died 1494)
After Michel Wolgemut (German, 1434–1519)
IMAGO MORTIS: DANCE OF THE DEAD, 1493

From Hartmann Schedel, *Liber Chronicarum . . . ab Inicio Mundi . . .* (Nuremberg: Anthonius Koberger, 1493)
Woodcut, 7 15/16 x 9 3/16" (20.1 x 23.3 cm)
Gift of Carl Zigrosser
74-179-511

This *imago mortis*, literally "picture of death," is one of many woodcut illustrations found in the early encyclopedia of world history, geography, mythology, and general information commonly called the "Nuremberg Chronicle." Published in 1493 with illustrations drawn by Michel Wolgemut and cut by Wilhelm Pleydenwurff, it chronicles the seven ages of world history from creation to the fifteenth century.

Imago Mortis: Dance of the Dead is from the seventh age of the "Nuremberg Chronicle," which treats the approaching end of the world; it is therefore related to the themes of the Apocalypse (see no. 97) and the *Ars Moriendi* (see no. 95). In a society in which unpredictable pestilence, famine, and war had long exacted a daily toll, a widespread belief developed that the millennium, the end of the world foretold in Revelations, was imminent as the year 1500 approached.

The Dance of the Dead is related to the theme of the Dance of Death, or Danse Macabre (see no. 98), which may have its origins in thirteenth-century French church dramas.[1] Its typical visual format, which became popular in Germany, Italy, England, and France, is believed to be based on a cycle painted in 1424 in the cloister that once surrounded the Church of the Innocents in Paris. In that depiction, living figures, each attended by a figure of Death, march along solemnly;[2] the austere procession proceeds by social hierarchy—from pope and king to astrologer and physician and down to hermit.

By 1493, as seen in this German woodcut, the iconography had changed and figures of living people were no longer included. Whereas the Dance of Death was primarily intended as a social statement showing people from all walks of life confronting their mortality, the Dance of the Dead was an artistic representation of the folklore belief that the dead might rise from their graves at night to dance.[3] In this print energetic skeletons and decaying cadavers wearing burial shrouds merrily dance to the music of a wind instrument. This macabre revelry may be related to the Orchestra of Death, with its music-making skeletons, illustrated in Guyot Marchand's *Danse macabre des hommes*, published in Paris in 1490. This image is one of the few known examples of the Dance of the Dead (as distinguished from the processional Dance of Death). The text on the back of the woodcut praises death as an eternal release from work and an acceptable alternative to the miseries of life.

Unlike other artists of the period, Wolgemut made no apparent attempt at anatomical accuracy, for the skeletons make only the slightest schematic reference to the reality of the human skeletal system. The single bones of leg and arm, the curlicue ribs, and the tubelike pelvis are only the most obvious approximations of actual anatomy. The impact of the print is enhanced by its linear simplifications and animated design, and its creative composition is what might be expected from Wolgemut, the teacher of one of the great printmakers of all time, Albrecht Dürer.

1. Aldred Scott Warthin, *The Physician of the Dance of Death* (1931; reprint, New York, 1977), p. 10.
2. Clifton C. Olds, Ralph G. Williams, and William R. Levin, *Images of Love and Death in Late Medieval and Renaissance Art* (Ann Arbor, 1975), pp. 56–57.
3. Ibid.

D.K.

97

Albrecht Dürer (German, 1471–1528)
THE FOUR HORSEMEN OF THE APOCALYPSE, 1498

From *Apocalipsis* (Nuremberg: Albrecht Dürer, 1498)
Woodcut, 15⁹⁄₁₆ x 11¹⁄₁₆" (39.5 x 28.1 cm)
Purchased: SmithKline Beckman Corporation Fund
1984-51-1

Albrecht Dürer's *Four Horsemen of the Apocalypse* is one of fifteen woodcuts in his series illustrating the Apocalypse, the end of the world and ultimate victory of Christ prophesied in Revelations. In his interpretation, Dürer combines a heightened sense of naturalism with the contemporary experience of living in a world tormented by a widespread belief in the imminency of the millennium (see no. 96). *The Four Horsemen* may in fact be seen as Dürer's visionary conception of the climactic end of the world.[1]

Dürer's Horsemen charge thunderously across the page with a drama matching that described in Revelations 6:1–5, 7, 8:

> *And I saw when the Lamb opened one of the seals, and I heard, as it were the noise of thunder, one of the four beasts saying, Come and see. And I saw, and behold a white horse: and he that sat on him had a bow; and a crown was given unto him: and he went forth conquering, and to conquer. And when he had opened the second seal, I heard the second beast say, Come and see. And there went out another horse that was red: and power was given to him that sat thereon to take peace from the earth, and that they should kill one another: and there was given unto him a great sword. And when he had opened the third seal, I heard the third beast say, Come and see. And I beheld, and lo a black horse; and he that sat on him had a pair of balances in his hand. . . . And when he had opened the fourth seal, I heard the voice of the fourth beast say, Come and see. And I looked, and behold a pale horse: and his name that sat on him was Death, and Hell followed with him. And Power was given unto them over the fourth part of the earth, to kill with sword, and with hunger and with death, and with the beasts of the earth.*

The Four Horsemen are War (with crown and bow and arrow), Strife (with sword), Famine (with scales), and Death, which rides the pale horse of pestilence. They trample the poor and rich alike (note the man with a crown, who has fallen at left). Death is indiscriminate and will, with war, strife, famine, and pestilence, destroy a quarter of the earth's inhabitants.

Interestingly, in the woodcut of the Four Horsemen in Martin Luther's so-called September Bible of 1522,[2] which was so greatly influenced by Dürer as to be considered a version of this print, a more political statement is made: the downtrodden are only the poor.[3] Images of the Four Horsemen made before Dürer's woodcut noticeably lack the magnificence and strength imparted by Dürer and those who followed him. By comparison, the riders depicted in the Bibles printed in Cologne around 1479 and in Strasbourg in 1485 seem to be taking polite country strolls.[4]

The innovations found in Dürer's Apocalypse series include the revolutionary method of his woodcut technique, which achieved a refined, lyrical line; the large scale of the images; and the incorporation of the images with text. Printed on the reverse of each sheet, except the last, are passages from Revelations, although the text is continuous and does not necessarily correspond to the image it faces. The woodcuts were published in German and Latin editions in 1498, with this print coming from the latter.

1. Clifton C. Olds, Ralph G. Williams, and William R. Levin, *Images of Love and Death in Late Medieval and Renaissance Art* (Ann Arbor, 1975), p. 77, no. 36.
2. This work, the reformer's first edition of the New Testament, was illustrated at least in part by Lucas Cranach the Elder or his son Hans or both.
3. Kenneth A. Strand, *Woodcuts to the Apocalypse in Dürer's Time* (Ann Arbor, 1968), p. 40, no. 35; see also p. 37.
4. Ibid., p. 29, nos. 18–19.

F.F.H./D.K.

98

Hans Lützelburger (Swiss, died 1526) After Hans Holbein the Younger (German, 1497/98–1543)
DEATH AND THE PHYSICIAN, c. 1524–26

From Hans Holbein the Younger, *Imagines Mortis* . . . (Lyons: Ioannes & Franciscus Frellonii, 1545)
Woodcut, 5⅝ x 3¹³⁄₁₆" (14.3 x 9.7 cm)
Purchased: SmithKline Beckman Corporation Fund
49-97-16b

Hans Holbein's treatment of the Dance of Death from the *Imagines Mortis* is probably the most celebrated and copied of all dramas of man's mortality (see also no. 96). Despite their diminutive scale, these woodcuts are profoundly powerful. Designed in Basel in the 1520s, the images were first published in 1538 in Lyons and were reused for eleven more publications through 1562.

Holbein had dealt with the theme of the Dance of Death in an earlier innovative work, the "Alphabet of Death," whose initial blocks appeared as early as 1524; however, the blocks for the *Imagines Mortis,* masterfully cut by the woodcarver Hans Lützelburger after Holbein's designs, depart from the established tradition of depicting Death and his victims as a series of dancing or walking couples. Instead, with inventiveness and a witty imagination Holbein shows men and women going about their daily tasks as Death takes them by surprise.

Here the doctor, whose life is spent keeping death at bay, is seen in the familiar space of his study. While his dog sleeps contentedly, the physician reaches to scrutinize the urine flask held out to him by Death. The physician, or urine gazer (see no. 24), may be able to cure the frail old man who stands by the door, but Death has come for the physician himself. The inscription above, "Physician, heal thyself" (Luke 4:23), alludes to this. It is followed by a quatrain, probably written by Gilles Corrozet of Lyons, that "warns the doctor against the sin of pride in his earth-bound knowledge and power among men."[1] This implies that despite the common perception of the power of the physician, his regular contact with the sick may be seen as presaging his own death. Holbein occasionally depicts the victim resisting or pleading with Death; at other times the victim seems oblivious to Death's presence. Here the doctor is a willing and even familiar participant in his inevitable interaction with Death.

Holbein, a prolific and well traveled artist, worked throughout Europe as a painter of portraits and religious subjects and as a designer of stained glass. He trained in the Augsburg shop of his painter-father and died as court painter to King Henry VIII in London.

1. Clifton C. Olds, Ralph G. Williams, and William R. Levin, *Images of Love and Death in Late Medieval and Renaissance Art* (Ann Arbor, 1975), p. 55, no. 14-J.

D.K./F.F.H.

99a

Georg Pencz (German, 1500–1550)
THE TRIUMPH OF DEATH, c. 1540

From "The Six Triumphs of Petrarch," c. 1540
Engraving, 5 15/16 x 8 1/4" (15.1 x 21 cm) (trimmed)
William S. Pilling Collection
33-72-1744

99b

Georg Pencz (German, 1500–1550)
THE TRIUMPH OF ETERNITY, c. 1540

From "The Six Triumphs of Petrarch," c. 1540
Engraving, 5 15/16 x 8 1/4" (15.1 x 21 cm) (trimmed)
William S. Pilling Collection
33-72-1746

The Triumph of Death and *The Triumph of Eternity* are from a series of engravings by Georg Pencz inspired by six poems of the fourteenth-century Italian Humanist poet and writer Francesco Petrarca (Petrarch) known as *The Triumphs,* allegories on the triumphs of Love, Chastity, Fame, Time, Death, and Eternity. Because of their power and elegance they were frequently depicted in fifteenth- and sixteenth-century art.

In Petrarch's view, Death will triumph over Love and Chastity, and Time will triumph over Love and Fame. Only Eternity, the eternal God, is able to triumph over others as well as the entire earthly realm.[1] Although the inscriptions on the engravings, like Petrarch's poems, refer to the glory of God, they are essentially *vanitas* messages intended to remind man that his time on earth is fleeting and that his heavenly reward depends on what he does here (see also nos. 100, 102, and 103).

In *The Triumph of Death* (no. 99a) the figure of Death rides a chariot as he tramples over all, leaving no living being in his wake. A crown and scepter lie fallen in the foreground while a pope and bishop pray in the background. According to the poem, not even the powerful will be spared:

Popes, emperors, and others who had ruled;
Now are they naked, poor, of all bereft.
Where now their riches? Where their honors now?
Where now their gems and scepters, and
their crowns,
Their miters, and the purple they had worn?
Wretched who sets his hope on mortal things—
Yet who does not?—and if he find himself
Deluded at the last, it is but just.[2]

Petrarch composed this poem after the outbreak of the Black Death of 1348, the devastating epidemic that claimed many of his friends and patrons. The second canto of *The Triumph of Death* is famous for the poet's evocation of his love for the dead Laura, also a victim of the plague.

The Triumph of Eternity (no. 99b), the sixth Triumph, is set in a heavenly realm in which the risen Christ stands amid symbols of the Evangelists, surrounded by a company of prophets and a host of trumpeting angels. Christ is thus the ruler of the heavens, but it is Death that triumphs below on earth. The poem admonishes man to place his trust in the Lord, for to "Who keepeth ever His covenant with one who trusts in Him . . . Divine mercies never come too late."[3]

Pencz, a Nuremberg artist who worked in Dürer's shop and painted large-scale portraits, mythological subjects, and biblical scenes, was one of the group of sixteenth-century German artists known as the Little Masters for their skill at executing engravings in very small formats (see also nos. 100 and 101). He produced several series of prints on biblical and classical themes.

1. Francesco Petrarca, *The Triumphs of Petrarch*, trans. Ernest Hatch Wilkins (Chicago, 1962), pp. 109–12.
2. Ibid., p. 56.
3. Ibid., p. 107.

F.F.H./D.K.

100
Hans Sebald Beham (German, 1500–1550)
YOUNG WOMAN ACCOMPANIED BY DEATH AS A JESTER, 1541

Engraving (ii/iii), 3 1/16 x 2" (7.8 x 5.1 cm) (trimmed)
Purchased: SmithKline Beckman Corporation Fund
1983-94-1

This exquisite engraving of 1541 is a *vanitas* image, meant to remind the viewer of the transience of life (see also nos. 99a,b; 102; and 103). Hans Sebald Beham depicted a young woman in elegant dress holding a small bunch of cut flowers, strolling along a garden path. In front of her is a tall lily that, planted in an urn, clearly symbolizes her purity, while behind her the fence post is broken off in a sharp, jagged stump, implying that her life could be cut short at any moment. Although she seems to be lost in a personal reverie, she is not alone, for a skeletal image of Death dressed as a jester accompanies her, his costume a statement on the foolishness of ignoring the presence of death. In one hand he holds an hourglass, the measure of sand in which has nearly run out, thereby implying the imminency of death, and with the other he lasciviously reaches around her waist from behind, perhaps suggesting the temptation of sin, especially lust. The woman is oblivious to the presence of Death. Above the scene, however, is the grim warning: "Death destroys all human beauty." The young woman's beauty itself is a *vanitas*—a fleeting element dependent on time.

Young Woman Accompanied by Death as a Jester appears to be a version of *Young Woman with a Fool,* dated to the preceding year, in which Beham depicted the same woman with a young man (rather than Death) in the jester's costume. Instead of an hourglass he holds flowers and there is no inscription. The theme of Death and a Young Couple, seen in the combination of both prints, may relate to the scourge of syphilis (known to have been introduced through sexual contact), which was spreading through Europe at this time. It is also present in other images of young women and Death and of young couples[1] that Beham executed throughout his career.

One of the most productive graphic artists of his time, Beham concentrated on genre themes and was the head of a Nuremberg group that included his student-brother Barthel and Georg Pencz (see nos. 99a,b). These artists were among those known as the Little Masters because of the small format of their prints (see also no. 101).

1. See R. F. Timken-Zinkann, "Medical Aspects of the Art and Life of Albrecht Dürer (1471–1528)," *Proceedings of the XXIII International Congress of the History of Medicine* (London, 1972), pp. 870–77.

D.K./F.F.H.

101
Heinrich Aldegrever (Trippenmeker) (German, 1502–c. 1560)
THE RICH MAN AND THE DEVIL, 1554

From "The Parable of the Rich Man and Lazarus," 1554
Engraving, 3 1/16 x 4 3/16" (7.8 x 10.6 cm) (trimmed)
Purchased: SmithKline Beckman Corporation Fund
1983-31-1

The Rich Man and the Devil (also known as *The Rich Man Dies*) is one of five engravings from Heinrich Aldegrever's series "The Parable of the Rich Man and Lazarus," which narrates the story told in Luke 16:19–31. The rich man lived a life of luxury; the beggar, full of sores, lay at his gate, asking only to be fed with the crumbs from the rich man's table. In death, however, their situations are reversed, for it is Lazarus who is carried to heaven and comforted in Abraham's bosom and the rich man who is tormented by the flames of hell. The rich man, told by Abraham that he will have no relief, pleads that Lazarus be sent to his brothers on earth as a sign to repent and avoid his fate. But, Abraham says, the revelation they have already been given by Moses and the Prophets should be sufficient warning for them. If they refuse to heed their word, not even a messenger sent from the dead would save them from their fate.

This image shows the rich man lying on his luxurious death bed attended by his friends, family, and clergymen. His wife and two children already grieve, and a funeral procession in the street beyond foretells coming events. Laid out on the small table at the foot of the bed are the now useless tools of the medical profession—the ointment jar, pitcher, and raffia carrier for a urine flask. The devil, weighted down with the rich man's gold and valuables, is preparing to claim his most important possession, his soul.

Aldegrever, who worked in Soest, Westphalia, was one of the leading engravers of the mid-sixteenth century outside Nuremberg. Working in a small format like the other Little Masters (see also nos. 99a,b and 100), he appears to have come into closer contact with the art of the Netherlands than did his Nuremberg contemporaries. He, like the other Little Masters, engraved themes from the Old and New Testaments, but his real fame rests on his dazzling ornamental prints.

F.F.H./D.K.

102

Abraham Bloemaert (Dutch, 1564–1651) PUTTO WITH SKULL, ROSE, AND HOURGLASS, c. 1610

Black ink and blue and gray washes over traces of black chalk, heightened with opaque white watercolor, on light buff laid paper, 3 9/16 x 4 9/16" (9.1 x 11.5 cm)
Purchased: SmithKline Beckman Corporation Fund
1984-15-1

The juxtaposition of a putto with a skull in this drawing by Abraham Bloemaert suggests that this is a *vanitas* image, that is, an image based on themes from Ecclesiastes—"Vanity of vanities; all is vanity" (1:2); "One generation passeth away, and another generation cometh" (1:4); "All is vanity and vexation of the spirit" (1:14)—that lament the futility of life. The hourglass and the cut flower, a rose, also symbolize the brevity of life. The hourglass measures the passing of time and the flower begins to die as soon as it is cut: "As for man, his days are as grass: as a flower of the field, so he flourisheth. For the wind passeth over it, and it is gone" (Psalms 103:15,16).

Examples of these melancholic images of children or young men with skulls or soap bubbles or both, hourglasses, and other symbols of *vanitas* (see no. 103) are common in the works of Bloemaert's contemporaries and predecessors such as Lucas van Leyden and Hendrik Goltzius. While the theme was not new—it can be traced to antiquity—it became more common in the fifteenth and sixteenth centuries because of the severe ravages of death at that time (see also nos. 99a,b and 100).[1]

Bloemaert was a cofounder of the painters' Guild of Saint Luke in Utrecht and teacher of early seventeenth-century Dutch artists such as Hendrik ter Brugghen and Boetius Adam van Bolswert. He was also a prolific draftsman, and well over six hundred of his designs were engraved, etched, or cut in wood by other artists.[2] It is possible that this drawing, with its large forms and crosshatched lines, was also made for a print, although none has yet been associated with it.

1. Horst W. Janson, "The Putto with the Death's Head," *Art Bulletin*, vol. 19 (1937), p. 437.
2. Clifford S. Ackley, *Printmaking in the Age of Rembrandt* (Boston, 1981), p. 33.

F.F.H./D.K.

103

Boetius Adam van Bolswert (Dutch, 1580–1633) After David Vinckboons (Flemish, 1576–1629) ALL-CONQUERING DEATH, 1610

Engraving, 10 15/16 x 14 7/8" (27.8 x 37.8 cm) (trimmed)
Purchased: SmithKline Beckman Corporation Fund
1983-95-1

The overall theme for Boetius Adam van Bolswert's engraving *All-Conquering Death* probably comes from the *Triumphs* of Petrarch (see nos. 99a,b). With the assistance of Father Time (seen at left with his hourglass) and heralding angels, Death confronts all the inhabitants of a walled city as they rush out of its gateway, a triumphal arch. The citizens—king and queen, knights, peasants, and beggars—surge forward armed with sword and spear, club and mallet, stick and spindle, all united in battle against this powerful enemy. Even the physician has armed himself against Death as he raises a urine flask in a threatening gesture. The inscription tells of Death—who is often shown with a scythe but is here a bowman[1]—piercing both men and animals with his arrows. The fact that all the various inhabitants of the town join in combat suggests that Death may here represent an epidemic event such as the plague. What other power could take on an entire population, man and beast alike, destroying them all in one great battle?

The banner carried by the people is emblazoned *Vanitas,* with an image of a *homo bulla,* a putto blowing bubbles, a reminder of the fleeting nature of life: "So the life of man, already ebbing in the newly born, Vanishes like a bubble or like fleeting smoke" (see also no. 102).[2]

Bolswert was a student of Abraham Bloemaert and engraved and published many prints after the work of his teacher and other notable artists of his time. This print is after a painting of the same subject by the Flemish genre painter David Vinckboons in the Museo Nacional de Bellas Artes in Buenos Aires.[3]

1. John B. Knipping, *Iconography of the Counter Reformation in the Netherlands: Heaven on Earth* (Leiden, 1974), vol. 1, p. 81.
2. Translation of the Latin inscription by F. Estius on the bottom of *The Allegory of Transitoriness*, an engraving of a *homo bulla* by Hendrik Goltzius; see Horst W. Janson, "The Putto with the Death's Head," *Art Bulletin*, vol. 19 (1937), p. 447.
3. Knipping, *Iconography*, vol. 1, p. 81. There is also a repetition and a variant of the painting. The print is very rare.

D.K./F.F.H.

104

Jan Lievens (Dutch, 1607–1674) QUARRELING CARD PLAYERS AND DEATH, c. 1635

Etching (iii/iii), 7 15/16 x 10 9/16" (20.2 x 26.8 cm)
Charles M. Lea Collection
28-42-2156

Jan Lievens, one of the most productive and innovative printmakers of seventeenth-century Holland, is best known for his association with Rembrandt between 1625 and 1631 in Leiden, where they were both born and trained. Lievens, unlike Rembrandt, also lived in England and Antwerp for several years. In *Quarreling Card Players and Death*, the low-life nature of the theme, the coarse peasant figure types, and the loose style of etching suggest the influence of Adriaen Brouwer, who was active in Antwerp in the 1630s, and therefore date the etching to the early years of Lievens's stay in that city (1635–44).

The three participants in the quarrel, two peasants and the skeleton Death, assault one another with weapons—a knife, jug, and bone. The inscription beneath the print says that the ancient serpent (Greed?) has arisen to spread hatred and that the quarreling card players will fall together. Their argument, probably caused by cheating and fueled by drinking, can thus only be followed by the triumph of Death, who already wears the laurel wreath of victory.

Although the folly and dangers of drinking and gambling are commonly illustrated in seventeenth-century Dutch paintings and prints, which stress the virtues of moderation, the presence of a full-sized Death figure, so typical of earlier prints (see no. 100), is extremely rare in original work of this later period. Its prototype may be Holbein's treatment of the Dance of Death (see no. 98), which shows everyday characters accosted by a figure of Death.

F.F.H.

105

Attributed to Giovanni David (Italian, 1743–1790) ALLEGORY OF THE DEATH OF AN ARTIST, 1780–90

Ink with colored washes over traces of black chalk on off-white antique laid paper, 13 5/16 x 16½" (33.8 x 41.9 cm)
Purchased: SmithKline Beckman Corporation Fund
1978-62-2

The attribution of this unsigned sheet to the little known artist Giovanni David is based on two inscriptions on the mount to which the drawing is affixed. On the recto an Italian inscription in brown ink in an old hand, possibly contemporary with the drawing, reads: "Allegory composed by him after the illness suffered in Venice in 1780." Unfortunately, the person who composed the allegory is not named. A relatively recent note written in French in black chalk on the verso of the mount tells us that "Giovanni David himself had the plague and did not die of it." From these two scraps of information it may be inferred that the Giovanni David who survived an illness—perhaps the plague—composed the allegory and that this was the Giovanni David who was a painter and printmaker born in Cabella Ligure (between Genoa and Tortona), probably in 1743, and active in Venice and Genoa between about 1775 and his death in 1790.

At present little is known or written about this obscure Ligurian artist, who trained in Rome under one of the major painters in that city during the latter half of the eighteenth century, Domenico Corvi, especially known for his academy drawings.[1] Old dictionaries of artists and engravers' manuals list a few paintings by David in Genoese churches, as well as prints by him after Andrea Mantegna, Jacopo Bellini, Giulio Romano, and Lodovico Carracci. He also engraved or etched his own designs and was important in introducing the aquatint process to Italy, his prints possibly even influencing Goya. The tonal quality of this work is consistent with David's use of aquatint tone to describe shapes, and the figures, composition, and style of the drawing are consistent with those in the few of his prints and one painting that one easily finds reproduced;[2] however, until further research clarifies the nature of his work as a draftsman, the sheet's attribution to David must remain a matter of conjecture.

A stone tomb tops the composition, decorated with a skull and crossbones and beneath it the word *Finis* (end). The end is death. Directly beneath the tomb, water flows from the urn of a classical river-god, becoming the waters of the River Styx, the mythological river of the dead. Charon, ferryman of the Styx, wrestles with a sail, while the winged, bearded figure of Time wraps a shroud over the victim. The victim (an artist) looks on helplessly, while a skeletal, grimacing figure of Death torches his palette and brushes as well as his prints or drawings. Standing over the artist is a sensuous, bare-breasted woman holding a snake that bites its tail, a symbol of eternity; the three old women to the left are the Three Fates, who spin the thread of life. One cuts that thread with a pair of scissors. Beneath the palette is a tomb or plinth with an inscription to the effect that "a single puff of air disperses every effort," a reference to the temporary nature of human life and achievement.

Although this composition has been interpreted as an allegory of the plague in Venice in 1780, no major outbreak of plague struck the city in that year; however, epidemics were a continual problem during the late eighteenth century, as witnessed by civic concern over maintaining modern and functional *lazzaretti* (quarantine shelters or hospitals).[3] Moreover, in contrast to our considerable lack of knowledge about David's artistic career, we are remarkably well informed as to the state of his health in the 1780s: The diagnosis and treatment of his fatal illness in 1788–90 occasioned a minor medical scandal in Genoa and the publication of at least one pamphlet explaining its circumstances.[4] From the latter it is known that David suffered an acute illness, arthritis, and dropsy in 1781; another attack of arthritis, fever, and dropsy in 1785; and a small fever accompanied by symptoms of heart trouble in 1788. No mention of the plague appears. A complicated regimen of pills cured the dropsy and, although it is not clear whether in the end David died of heart or liver problems, his continuing struggle with illness in the 1780s seems to have inspired this allegory of the painter snatched untimely from his labors by the joint efforts of Time and Death.

1. A long but not very informative account of David's career appears in Federigo Alizeri, *Notizie dei professori del disegno in Liguria dalla fondazione dell'Accademia*, vol. 1 (Genoa, 1864), pp. 359–88.
2. See P & D Colnaghi & Co., Ltd., London, *Pictures from the Grand Tour* (November 14–December 16, 1978), nos. 168–74; Claudia Lazzaro, *Eighteenth-Century Italian Prints from the Collection of Mr. and Mrs. Marcus S. Sopher, with Additions from the Stanford University Museum of Art* (Palo Alto, 1980), p. 38, no. 69; and Corrado Maltese et al., *Neoclassicismo: Atti del convegno internazionale promosso dal Comité International d'Histoire de l'Art* (London, 1971), fig. 77.
3. In 1775 the Venetian health officials were concerned about sites for housing the contagious; in 1782 a provisional allocation was made for them at various sites; by 1793 a new *lazzaretto* at Poveglia was in operation, and a special coin was struck celebrating the event (Comune di Venezia, *Venezia e la peste, 1348/1797* [Venice, 1979], pp. 179, 325, 344–45). No mention of a particular plague in 1780 occurs in this source, nor in Noah Webster, *A Brief History of Epidemic and Pestilential Diseases*, vol. 1 (Hartford, 1799), pp. 266–68, or A. Corradi, *Annali delle epidemie occorse in Italia dalle prime memorie fino al 1850*, vol. 5 (Bologna, 1973), p. 602.
4. N. Covercelli, *Dichiarazione del medico Covercelli su la questione mossa dal sig. Cesare Canefri, Dottore di Medicina, Professore d'Istoria Naturale e Chimica nell'Università di Genova intorno la malattia del fu sig. Giovanni David* (Genoa, [1790]). The unfortunate Giovanni David is described as a painter. This source indicates that he traveled to Vienna, France, Holland, and England as well as Venice (p. 7 n. 7).

A.P./F.F.H./D.K.

106

Anonymous (German, seventeenth century) QUARANTINE SIGN, c. 1683

Woodcut, 6$\frac{1}{16}$ x 12$\frac{11}{16}$" (15.4 x 32.2 cm)
Purchased: SmithKline Beckman Corporation Fund
71-116-1

The awesome destruction of plague ravaged Europe repeatedly from the fourteenth to the eighteenth century. In just one epidemic, the Black Death of 1348, some sixty million people were lost to bubonic plague. Panic about the spread of the disease led cities to pass ordinances isolating its victims. Houses found to contain plague were marked with signs warning outsiders to stay away and forcing those within—both plague victims and healthy inhabitants—to remain there. In his history of the Great Plague of London in 1665 Daniel Defoe wrote of the miseries and frustrations suffered by the families who were locked within their plague-marked houses.[1] In London, according to Defoe, a simple red cross and the words "Lord have mercy upon us" were painted on the doors of houses of the diseased.[2]

This quarantine sign, a boldly printed woodcut with two *X*'s and the word *Pest* (plague) inscribed beneath each, was issued in large numbers in Erfurt, Germany, at the height of its plague epidemic around 1683. The city fathers ordered the clear marking with such signs and the vigorous cleaning of every house that had been contaminated.[3]

1. Daniel Defoe, *A Journal of the Plague Year* . . . , ed. G. H. Maynadier (New York, 1907), pp. 53–65.
2. Ibid., p. 49.
3. Martin Sprössig, "Die Erfurter Seuchengeschichte und die moderne Mikrobiologie," pl. 11, in Rektor der Medizinischen Akademie Erfurt, *Festschrifte zum Zehnjährigen Bestehen der Medizinischen Akademie Erfurt*, Beiträge zur Geschichte der Universität Erfurt (1392–1816), vol. 11 (Erfurt, 1964).

D.K.

107

Anonymous (French, seventeenth century) SKULL AND CROSSBONES, seventeenth century

Woodcut, 15¼ x 12$\frac{13}{16}$" (38.8 x 32.5 cm)
Purchased: SmithKline Beckman Corporation Fund
1982-118-1

This coarsely executed print of a skull and crossbones is one of the most direct statements of the power of the arts to convey information about states of human health. It is a simple image that has an immediacy and recognizability as powerful today as they were three hundred years ago.

France, as well as Germany, England, and Italy, was visited by severe epidemics of plague during the seventeenth century. Like the quarantine sign (no. 106), this raw, aggressive, almost violent woodcut printed on heavy paper was probably meant to be affixed to the door of a house contaminated by disease as a warning to keep outsiders from entering. The nefariously grinning skull above the crossed bones was a symbol used on grave monuments of the period and was an obvious warning as well as an admonition. Because plague almost invariably led to death, its visual message was quite clear.

D.K.

108a

Richard Julius Jungtow (German, 1828–after 1851)
After Alfred Rethel (German, 1816–1859)
DEATH AS A FRIEND, c. 1851

Wood engraving, 12 x 10¾" (30.5 x 27.3 cm)
Purchased: SmithKline Beckman Corporation Fund
58-150-20

108b

Gustav Richard Steinbrecher (German, 1828–1887)
After Alfred Rethel (German, 1816–1859)
DEATH AS AN ENEMY (THE FIRST OUTBREAK OF CHOLERA AT A MASKED BALL IN PARIS, 1831), 1851

Wood engraving, 12¼ x 10⅞" (31.1 x 27.6 cm)
Purchased: SmithKline Beckman Corporation Fund
58-150-19

German wood engravings of the Renaissance period were one of the great loves of the painter Alfred Rethel. He sought to revive the medium in the mid-nineteenth century and looked for inspiration to the masters of the German tradition, particularly Hans Holbein the Younger. Holbein had popularized the imagery of the Dance of Death theme (see no. 98), and Rethel produced his own version of the subject in a series of six woodcuts entitled *Auch ein Totentanz, aus dem Jahre 1848* (A Dance of Death of the Year 1848), published in Leipzig in 1849. Other moving images on the theme of death are seen in a series of drawings he made about the same time, two of which were later transferred to wood for publication, *Death as an Enemy* (dated 1851) and *Death as a Friend* (assumed to have been engraved about the same time).

Death as a Friend and *Death as an Enemy* explore two very different perceptions of death. In the first (no. 108a), Death brings eternal rest at the end of a long and good life. Dressed in monk's robes as a fellow pilgrim (with cockleshell, drinking gourd, and sandals), Death signals the end of life for the old man. Sitting tiredly in the bell tower of a great church, humble quarters adorned only by a crucifix, the old man nears the end of a life of piety, indicated by telling details such as the open Bible on the table and the pilgrim's hat and staff nearby. As the sun sets over the landscape beyond, Death tolls the knell as the pilgrim slips into eternity. There is nothing menacing or threatening about the scene—only the quietness of a welcomed end.

In contrast is the gruesome scene of *Death as an Enemy* (no. 108b), inspired by an account of the first appearance of cholera in France written by the German poet Heinrich Heine, an episode that occurred at a masked ball during the mid-Lent celebrations in Paris in 1831. Death stands in a hooded monk's robe in the center of the room, incongruously wearing dancing slippers, his mask dangling from one bony arm as he fiddles away on a large human bone. Around this macabre figure lie the bodies of costumed partygoers, whose evening revels—and lives—have been cut short by this uninvited guest. The musicians steal out of the ballroom, covering their faces and casting fearful glances at the lone figure standing on the ballroom floor—the enemy Death.

D.K.

109

Max Klinger (German, 1857–1920)
CUPID, DEATH, AND THE BEYOND, 1881

From *Intermezzi* (Munich: Theo. Stroefer, 1881)
Etching and aquatint (iii/iii), 7¾ x 16⅝" (19.7 x 42.2 cm)
Purchased: SmithKline Beckman Corporation Fund
1984-18-1

Believing that prints and drawings were particularly well suited for the expression of one's attitudes toward the world, Max Klinger effectively used these mediums to examine the sordid and grotesque that existed in his life and his imagination. In *Cupid, Death, and the Beyond* the artist offers insights into his metaphysical anxiety and personal reality as he renders his own increasing awareness of mortality, death, and the endless hereafter within the exquisite finesse of the printed image. In a moving, modern version of the *vanitas* theme that explores the fleeting quality of life (see also nos. 99a,b; 100; 102; and 103), his anxieties and fears are registered in sharp, etched lines and soft aquatint.

Within an eerie, empty landscape Klinger has staged a race of the three forces that tormented him. Leading the race is Cupid, armed with bow and arrow and astride a winged unicycle, who serves as a symbol of the eroticism that was a strong force in the young artist's life. Death, however, follows close behind, mounted on a clumsy steed with wooden legs and coffin body. Holding the shroudlike reins, he goads his macabre mount with the blade of his scythe. In last place is the strange, composite figure of the Beyond. Vaguely and uncertainly defined, as is the nature of any existence after death, this form rides a horned beast that presses along upon a bed of human hands as ghostlike faces peer out of the billows of the shrouded shape. Like the Symbolist writers who were his contemporaries, Klinger has here brought together in poetic juxtaposition images whose interrelationships offer new insights into the intangible and the unknown.

D.K.

110
James Ensor (Belgian, 1860–1949)
MY PORTRAIT IN THE YEAR 1960, 1888

Hand-colored etching, 2¾ x 4¾" (7 x 12.1 cm)
Purchased with funds given by Derald H. Ruttenberg and Robert A. Hauslohner
72-216-1

James Ensor, the Belgian painter and printmaker, combined an understanding of the tragic mystery of nature with mischievous humor (see also no. 42). For most of his creative life he was obsessed with the specter of death, depicting it in myriad social and personal situations.

Perhaps his most moving image in contemplation of death is the 1888 etching *My Portrait in the Year 1960* (the year of his one-hundredth birthday). The image, with its economy of line and intense sense of plausibility as well as its self-mockery, is a mixture of humor and the macabre: The combination of a reclining skeleton in shoes, a spider, and snails leaves the viewer uneasy. The twenty-eight-year-old artist is contemplating his own death, but at a moment in time distant enough to allow himself and the viewer a hesitant chuckle. His foresight, however, may have been correct; the image could well have been what he looked like in 1960, over a decade after he had died.

Death for Ensor was not a vague threat but a reality as clear and tangible as any aspect of life. Yet Ensor in his art chose to do battle with the inevitable. "I want to live," he said, "to speak for a long time yet to the men of tomorrow. I think of solid copper plates, of inks which cannot be altered, of simple reproductions, of faithful impressions, and therefore I have taken etching as my means of expression."[1] His print indeed remains as a messenger long after his demise.

1. Translated and quoted in Louis Lebeer, *The Prints of James Ensor from the Collection of H. Shickman (Formerly Franck Collection, Antwerp)* (New York, 1971), p. xiv.

D.K.

111
Odilon Redon (French, 1840–1916)
DEATH: MY IRONY SURPASSES ALL OTHERS, 1889

From *A Gustave Flaubert: Six Dessins pour la "Tentation de St.-Antoine"* (Paris, 1889)
Lithograph (proof before letters), 10⁵⁄₁₆ x 7⅝" (26.2 x 19.3 cm)
Purchased: SmithKline Beckman Corporation Fund
1984-20-1

Lithography, which had declined in artistic importance in the mid-nineteenth century because of its application primarily for commercial purposes, gained new significance with the increased use of the medium by artists such as Pissarro, Degas, and Manet. Odilon Redon first used lithography to reproduce his charcoal drawings, but soon found that far from being an unimaginative means of reproduction, it was a medium that, he said, obeyed "the subtlest breath of sensitivity."[1] His fascination with the opportunities offered by this medium was such that between about 1880 and 1900, lithographs, along with black-and-white drawings, were his chief means of expression. Indeed the deep, rich blacks of his lithograph *Death: My Irony Surpasses All Others* speak of sources of shadows and darkness previously only sensed but never truly known. The print reaches into the world beneath and beyond that of everyday vision.

This brilliant, rich impression is a rare artist's proof of the image of Death from a series of six lithographs inspired by the French writer Gustave Flaubert's 1874 drama *La Tentation de Saint-Antoine*, the second of Redon's three series on this subject. The title of the print adds another dimension to the image, for here Death expresses the irony of the unquestionable and the inevitable, which man spends his life either ignoring or fighting.

Literature, particularly that of the French Symbolists such as Stéphane Mallarmé, played a significant part in the career of Redon. His mystical, fantastic images were an important source of inspiration for their writings, and the artist illustrated several of their poems and plays.

1. Translated and quoted in Alfred Werner, *The Graphic Work of Odilon Redon* (New York, 1969), p. x.

D.K.

112
Edvard Munch (Norwegian, 1863–1944)
DEATH AND THE MAIDEN, 1894

Drypoint (ii/ii/b), 12 x 8¾" (30.5 x 22.2 cm)
Purchased: SmithKline Beckman Corporation Fund
1983-36-1

Susan Sontag suggests that "illness is the night-side of life, a more onerous citizenship. Everyone who is born holds dual citizenship, in the kingdom of the well and in the kingdom of the sick."[1] If this is true, the proportion of time spent in each kingdom determines the perceptions of each individual. Edvard Munch was himself a frail, sickly child, and he also witnessed the grave illnesses of those around him (see no. 62). The artist's words attest to these experiences: "Illness, insanity, and death were the black angels that hovered over my cradle and have followed me ever since through my life."[2] Brought up in a rigidly disciplined home by his father, a military physician, Munch suffered from an ever-present anxiety about death and disease and a fear of punishment for moral errors, apparently engendering the difficulties with female relationships that haunt his works.

Death and the Maiden is a convulsive image of both the beginning and end of life, birth and death for Munch being interrelated phenomena separated merely by the transience of a lifetime (see also no. 113). The woman does not recoil but passionately embraces Death (Munch's way of reminding us that by embracing life we court death), and Death responds with an equally aggressive and erotic embrace. The images in the margins complement the interrelated themes of life, love, and death: Spermatozoa swim downward at the sides, assuming embryonic shapes at the bottom, while the center embryo stretches out almost like a corpse.

The rich, raw drypoint is an ideal vehicle for the disturbing image of the two figures. It is difficult to believe that this masterful etching is one of the first of Munch's prints, considered by many his finest medium of expression.[3] Its power of imagery and design and its technique make a remarkable statement.

1. Susan Sontag, *Illness as Metaphor* (New York, 1978), p. 3.
2. Translated and quoted in Sarah G. Epstein, *The Prints of Edvard Munch: Mirror of His Life* (Oberlin, 1983), p. 11.
3. Los Angeles County Museum of Art, *Edvard Munch: Lithographs, Etchings, Woodcuts* (January 28–March 9, 1969), p. x.

D.K.

113
Edvard Munch (Norwegian, 1863–1944)
VISIT OF CONDOLENCE, 1904 (inscribed 1912)

Woodcut, 19½ x 23½" (49.5 x 59.7 cm)
Purchased: SmithKline Beckman Corporation Fund
1980-18-3

Edvard Munch's life made him all too familiar with death and its attendant rituals and the endless sense of loss at the death of a loved one (see no. 62). Here, in this powerful woodcut depicting a visit of condolence, Munch created an image in which the themes of love and death again are joined (see no. 112).

Munch used the grain of the wood with its naturally rhythmic horizontal banding as a foil for the bold, violent cuts into the block, like the harsh intrusion of death on a loving relationship. As in an earlier lithograph, his *Death Chamber* of 1896, the room contains both the deceased and the mourners, but here the mood is dominated by the rushing cuts of the floor and the large, dark shapes of the mourners.

The dead body lies covered on the bed in the back of the room—a large, negative form framed in heavy black ink. Through the door come the visitors offering their condolences, support, and sympathy to the grieving man, but what they find is the stench of death: The little girl and one of the women immediately hold their noses to ward off the strong odor of decay, even though they have barely entered the room. With lowered heads and somber faces the callers reflect the oppressive weight of death. For Munch, love—whether for parent, sibling, or partner—implied vulnerability to feelings of loss, and indeed death was the tragic end to several of his close relationships.

D.K.

114
Erich Heckel (German, 1883–1970)
THE DEAD WOMAN, 1912 (inscribed 1919)

Woodcut (ii/ii), 9 13/16 x 11 11/16" (24.9 x 29.7 cm)
Purchased: SmithKline Beckman Corporation Fund
1983-35-1

As a member of the German Expressionist movement Die Brücke (The Bridge), Erich Heckel sought ties to the German medieval past through the medium of the woodcut. The historic importance of this process in German art and its expressive possibilities were exploited in the raw, emotional power of his work.

The sharp, angular gouges that leave the paper white against areas of heavy black ink create in this print a visually stunning image of psychological states in response to death. The two men, each expressing a stage of grief, sit on the floor of the sickroom in which the woman has died. The man at right, convulsed in grief, his body hunched forward, head in hands, knees tightly pulled to his chest, turns inward in anguish. In contrast the figure at left leans back on his elbows and stares at the pale immobile figure in the bed in wide-eyed disbelief, unwilling to accept the loss.

The two stages of grief—disbelief and the initial pain of loss—are balanced within the black frame of the woodcut. Heckel has presented the emotional torment of those who survive the death of a loved one with an insight of both experience and compassion (see also no. 113).

D.K.

115

Josef Koudelka (Czechoslovakian, born 1938)
JARABINA, 1963

Gelatin silver print, 9 3/16 x 14 1/16" (23.4 x 35.8 cm)
Purchased: The Contemporary Photographers Exhibition Fund
1977-231-1

Between 1962 and 1968 the Czechoslovakian photographer Josef Koudelka followed his fascination with the Gypsies of Slovakia, recording their unique traditions, life style, and appearance. The Slovakian Gypsies have had a long and troubled history but their astounding emotional strength and resiliency as a group have repeatedly drawn them back from the brink of destruction. Attracted at first by the physical beauty of this insulated population of Eastern Europe, Koudelka quickly became fascinated by their history, habits, and rituals.[1]

In this photograph the universal quality of the funeral, the last contact with the corporal presence of the deceased, is captured with a sharpness of vision that intensifies the drama of the moment. The mourners stand like two shadowed walls of a corridor, which recedes sharply from dark to light, stretching from the photographer (or viewer) above the body of the deceased, who lies in a white shroud, to the intensely lit window, which presents no vista of this earthly world. In its movement from dark to light, this corridor seems to imply the passage traditionally believed to be taken by the soul now free to soar into eternal light.

The mourners, young and old, male and female, stand quietly, somberly; while each seems to be contemplating the passing of a life, some glance back toward the camera, reminding us of its presence. This moving photograph conveys the power of the living to embrace the ultimate end.

1. See Josef Koudelka, *Gypsies* (New York, 1975).

D.K.

116

George Tooker (American, born 1920)
THE MIRROR, 1975

Color lithograph, 19 15/16 x 16 1/8" (50.6 x 41 cm)
Purchased: SmithKline Beckman Corporation Fund
1982-116-1

George Tooker is a Vermont painter, active since the late 1940s, whose primary concerns are the psychological aspects and phenomena of day-to-day urban life. Throughout the years that Abstract Expressionism dominated the artistic scene he maintained his position as a figurative painter, but he has never worked as a straightforward realist. His figures seem to move through a psychologically intense limbo of recognizable, common situations, yet they are never simply familiar scenes. His subjects are city people caught in normal situations that are presented with an edge of anxiety reaching toward the seat of man's deepest fears. Drawing on traditional themes, he injects a modern perspective that simultaneously pulls back into history and draws history into the present moment.

The Mirror is a traditional *vanitas* theme applied to the late twentieth century. The woman who admires herself in the mirror and fingers her pearls is Tooker's Venus, the twentieth-century ideal of beauty. But her beauty is temporary, for the face of Death peers over her shoulder at her reflection and at the viewer. The *vanitas* theme, which touches emotional chords of life's transience and unpredictability (see nos. 99a,b; 100; 102; and 103), appears with less frequency in the iconographic vocabulary of the nineteenth and twentieth centuries—perhaps because medicine has reduced the threat of many diseases and increased longevity.

In this lithograph, which follows the composition of a painting of 1962,[1] Tooker has used one light source, reflecting off the mirror's surface, to highlight the faces of the woman and her eventual destroyer. The softly rounded forms so elegantly rendered in this print are reminiscent of the *vanitas* image of Abraham Bloemaert (no. 102) and serve as a reminder that despite today's scientific knowledge, life is fleeting. Tooker has also produced several variations on the *vanitas* theme of youth, old age, beauty, and death in his paintings.[2]

1. Thomas H. Garver, *George Tooker: Paintings 1947–1973* (San Francisco, 1974), pl. 19.
2. Ibid., pls. 17, 22.

D.K.

Glossary of Graphic Terms

Albumen Print

A photograph printed on paper coated with a solution of egg white (albumen) saturated with salt (ammonium or sodium chloride) and floated on a solution of silver nitrate, which combine to produce silver chloride, a light-sensitive silver salt. When the albumen paper is exposed to sunlight under a negative, the light's energy converts the silver salt to metallic silver, thus forming the image. The image becomes gradually visible during exposure and does not require a chemical developing solution. After exposure the print is usually toned with gold to achieve a darker, more pleasing color and to protect the silver image. The print is then stabilized in a bath of hypo (sodium thiosulphate) to remove residual light-sensitive materials and washed in water.

An albumen print is frequently characterized by a minutely crackled surface. These photographs exhibit a wide gradation of either reddish brown or purplish black tones; however, many have faded and yellowed to a narrow tonal scale of tannish brown. Albumen paper, invented by the Frenchman Louis Blanquart-Evrard in 1850 and first commercially available during that decade, produced the most popular nineteenth-century photographic print.

Aquatint

An intaglio, acid-etched printmaking technique used to create a tonal effect. Traditionally, aquatint is produced by evenly dispersing fine granules of resin on a metal plate, fusing them by heat, and etching the plate in acid that attacks the exposed interstices of metal not protected by resin. Image areas that should not be etched are protected by coating the plate with an acid-resistant material in a process known as stopping out; tonal gradations can be achieved by progressively stopping out and re-etching. The resin and acid-resistant material are removed from the plate before printing. During the intaglio printing process, ink remains in the etched intervals to create a granular effect. Because aquatint cannot produce a sharp line, it is often used with etching. The aquatint technique was developed by Jean-Baptiste Le Prince in France around 1768.

Chalk

A dry drawing medium mined from the earth, cut into sticks, and used directly on a paper support. Black and red chalks are amorphous composites of the minerals carbon and hematite, respectively, uniformly diffused with soft clay; white chalk is composed of calcite or steatite. Generally used for drawing by the early sixteenth century, natural chalks were the preferred dry drawing medium until the late eighteenth century, when the supply of high-quality natural chalk dwindled and fabricated chalks, crayons, and graphite became increasingly popular.

Fabricated chalks, or pastels, are powdered pigments bound with a water-soluble material such as gum or glue, rolled into sticks, and dried. Pastels were developed during the sixteenth century and commercially manufactured by the eighteenth. It is often difficult to differentiate between natural and fabricated chalks after they have been applied to a drawing surface.

Chine Collé

The lamination of a thin piece of paper to a heavier sheet as the impression is passed through the printing press. The thin paper is smoother and more receptive to the ink but usually requires the strength offered by the secondary support. Although the process is referred to as *chine collé* because the thin paper used was traditionally thought to be of Chinese origin, the term is broadly used to designate any such laminate. *Chine collé* became a popular printmaking technique in the beginning of the nineteenth century.

Collotype

A photomechanical reproductive process used in conjunction with a photographic negative and printed by a planographic method similar to lithography. To prepare the photomechanical plate, a flat surface such as glass or zinc is evenly coated with light-sensitive bichromated gelatin. The image is produced by exposing the plate to light under a photographic glass positive and then immersing it in cool water that hardens the gelatin coating in the exposed image areas and softens it in the nonimage areas. The plate is then dampened with a water solution and rolled with stiff, oily lithographic ink, which adheres to the hardened gelatin surface of the image areas and is repelled by the moisture-retentive, nonimage areas of softened gelatin. The collotype can be recognized by the inked image's microscopic, reticulated pattern caused by characteristic puckers in the gelatin coating. Developed independently by several men during the late 1860s, the collotype was used for small editions of high-quality reproductions until the middle of the twentieth century, when it was largely replaced by other methods.

Colored Print

An image printed with one ink and then hand colored; distinguished from a color print, which is printed in ink of one or more colors. Most printmaking techniques—

relief, intaglio, or planographic—can produce either colored or color prints. Colored prints are usually hand colored with watercolor over an outline image printed in black ink. Color prints are most often produced by making a separate block, plate, or stone for each color and superimposing them on the paper.

Crayon

A dry drawing medium of powdered pigments mixed with an oily, waxy, or greasy binder and shaped into a stick. The oleaginous binder distinguishes crayon from natural and fabricated chalks, which are more friable. Although several idiosyncratic attempts to produce crayons with various fatty binders have been documented through the ages, a sustained increase in the production and use of crayons for drawing did not occur until the late eighteenth century.

Drypoint

An intaglio printing process in which lines are directly scratched into a copperplate with a sharp metal stylus known as a drypoint needle. As the needle plows through the copper, it throws up a curled ridge of metal, or burr, along each side of the incision. Unlike engraving, in drypoint the excess metal is not scraped off the plate before printing but rather remains to catch a surplus of ink that prints a rich, fuzzy line. The fragile burr is weakened with each pass through the press and can endure only twenty to thirty impressions. Because the rich burr is drastically altered after relatively few impressions, a pure drypoint is rare; however, this process is often used to augment other intaglio techniques.

Engraving

An intaglio printing process in which linear, V-shaped grooves are directly incised into a copperplate with a tool known as a graver or burin. To achieve a clean line, before printing the stray curls of lifted metal are usually removed with a sharp-edged tool known as a scraper. The printed line is characterized by a tapered, pointed end and an angular ridge of ink created by the V-shaped burin.

Engraving as a print form developed from techniques used since antiquity to embellish precious metal objects. The earliest European engraved impressions on paper are believed to have been executed during the 1430s in Germany.

Etching

An intaglio printing process in which linear incisions are created in a metal plate by acid corrosion rather than by direct gouging with a sharp tool, as in drypoint and engraving. The etching process begins by coating the plate, usually copper or zinc, with a thin layer of acid-resistant material called the ground. The etching needle, a pointed steel stylus, is drawn through the ground to expose lines of bare metal, which are then etched in a diluted acid solution that creates furrows below the surface of the metal. Before printing, the ground is cleaned off the plate. The action of acid corrosion produces a printed line with a blunt, rounded end, mounded profile, and irregular outer edges.

Etching as a print form developed in Europe during the first decades of the sixteenth century from techniques used to decorate armor. In the seventeenth century the French artist Jacques Callot popularized the use of the *échoppe,* a tool consisting of a solid cylindrical rod cut at an oblique angle that was used instead of the etching needle to imitate the arched, tapered line typical of engraving.

Gelatin Dry-Plate Negative

A photographic glass-plate negative that is machine-coated with an emulsion of light-sensitive silver bromide suspended in gelatin. The gelatin dry plate is exposed to light in a camera and then immersed in a chemical solution that converts the silver bromide to metallic silver to form the image. The image is stabilized by hypo (sodium thiosulphate), which removes residual light-sensitive materials, and then washed in water.

The collodion wet-plate negative, the forerunner of the gelatin dry plate, required the cumbersome image-producing process of coating, sensitizing, exposing, and chemically treating to be executed while the plate remained moist. In 1877 the English physician Richard L. Maddox developed the more convenient dry-plate negative using a presensitized gelatin emulsion that, once exposed, could be developed later in the darkroom.

Gelatin Silver Print

A photograph printed on paper coated with an emulsion of light-sensitive silver salts, such as silver chloride and silver bromide, suspended in gelatin. The two major types of gelatin silver paper, which form the image in different ways, are printing-out paper and develop-out paper. Printing-out paper is coated with a light-sensitive emulsion that causes the image to become visible gradually during exposure to light under a negative, requiring no chemical development. Develop-out paper, once exposed under a negative, remains blank until it is treated in a chemical solution. In both cases the light-sensitive silver salts are converted to metallic silver as the image is formed. The image must then be stabilized in hypo (sodium thiosulphate) to remove residual light-sensitive materials and washed in water. Gelatin silver prints were introduced around 1880, and have become the most popular photographic medium.

Ink

A liquid drawing medium composed of fine pigment particles or dyes dissolved in gum or glue water and applied to paper with a pen to form lines or with a brush to produce tonal washes. Four basic types of ink were traditionally used for drawing: carbon ink, iron gall ink, bister, and sepia.

The oldest black inks are carbon ink and iron gall ink; carbon ink remains permanently black, whereas iron gall fades to brown with age and often corrodes the paper fibers. Carbon ink, which originated in ancient Egypt and China, was exported from China to Europe, where it was highly esteemed. Medieval treatises contain formulas for both carbon and iron gall ink. The fine black pigment particles used in carbon ink were derived from a variety of materials such as charred wood or burned lamp oil. Iron gall ink was created by a chemical reaction between the tannin in oak tree gallnuts and ferrous sulfate that produces the black ferric gallotannate. Relatively easy to manufacture, this was the most common writing ink, as well as an inexpensive drawing medium used by many old masters.

Two traditional brown drawing inks are bister, a transparent ink of luminous hue, and sepia, an opaque wash. Formulas for bister, extracted from the soluble tars of wood soot, were recorded as early as the fifteenth century. Sepia, a complex nitrogenous organic compound derived from the inky secretion of the cuttlefish or squid, was first mentioned as a drawing medium in the late eighteenth century. The term sepia, when used to identify many brown inks of earlier periods, refers to their brown tone rather than to a genuine sepia ink composition.

Intaglio Process

A printing process that transfers ink from the indentations and incisions in a metal plate to paper. The ink is forced into the recessed areas with a dabber (a leather-covered pad), after which the raised surfaces are either wiped clean or left with a light tone of ink. A piece of paper, dampened for greater flexibility, is placed on the inked plate and passed through a double-roller press at considerable pressure to force the paper into the ink-holding incisions and lift the ink out of the furrows to form raised lines on the surface of the sheet. The great pressure of the press produces the hallmark of the intaglio process, the plate mark, an embossed demarcation in the paper created by the force of the roller on the edge of the plate. Engravings, etchings, soft-ground etchings, stipple etchings, drypoints, aquatints, and mezzotints are among the most common intaglio processes.

Laid Paper

Paper distinguished by a pattern of linear impressions cast into the paper fibers during sheet formation (see Wove Paper). Paper is produced by dipping a sievelike screen, known as a mold and deckle, into a slurry of macerated fibers to form a fibrous, webbed sheet. The mold is constructed of metal wires attached at all edges to a wooden frame; the deckle is a wooden strainer that fits over the mold to prevent the liquid slurry from flowing off the edges of the screen. The laid mold screen consists of many fine, closely spaced parallel laid wires secured by chain wires to perpendicular wooden crossbeams at 1″ to 1½″ intervals. The moist web of fibers resting on the screen results in a corresponding pattern of thin lines visible in raking and transmitted light once the sheet is dry.

European papermaking evolved from a Chinese invention, traditionally attributed to T'sai Lun in A.D. 105, which spread westward along the silk route and into the Iberian Peninsula by the eleventh century. Around 1750 an improvement in the European mold made possible the production of modern laid paper, as differentiated from antique laid paper. Antique laid paper is heavier on each side of the chain line, where pulp accumulated around the wooden crossbeam. In modern laid paper the shadow of excess pulp is eliminated by inserting extra wire to lift the screen away from the crossbeam.

Lithography

A planographic printing process in which the image is printed from a level surface rather than from incised or raised areas, as in intaglio or relief printing. Lithography is based on the chemical incompatibility of grease and water. After an image is drawn on a slab of limestone or a zinc or aluminum plate with a grease-based medium in crayon or liquid form, the surface is chemically treated with gum arabic and acid to allow the image areas to accept printing ink and the nonimage areas to retain water. During printing the surface of the stone or plate is dampened so that the water-retentive nonimage areas will repel the stiff ink that is applied with a wide roller. A smooth paper is placed over the inked surface and passed through a scraper press. The scraper bar smooths the paper and pushes the ink into its fibers, giving the lithographic print a characteristic flat appearance. Lithography was invented by Alois Senefelder of Munich around 1798.

Mezzotint

An intaglio printing process that produces a velvety tone by directly pitting a copperplate with a tool known as a rocker. Traditionally the entire plate is systematically worked with the rocker's curved, serrated blade to produce a surface of tiny indentations and projections that hold ink like a drypoint burr, resulting in prints with previously unattainable rich, black tones. The artist works from dark to light by scraping and burnishing the roughened metal surface to achieve tonal gradations. The more burnished areas retain less ink and print as lighter tones; the less burnished, rougher areas as darker tones. Because mezzotint cannot produce a sharp line, it is often supplemented by engraving. The mezzotint was introduced in the mid-seventeenth century through the efforts of Ludwig von Siegen in Germany, and furthered by the development of the rocker by the German Prince Rupert in the same century.

Prepared Paper

Paper that has been coated to color the drawing surface and reduce the unevenness of the fiber texture. It may be covered with a solution known as a ground, which is composed of a pulverized filler such as bone dust, white lead, or chalk and an optional pigment mixed with gum or glue water. When dry the ground is burnished with an agate or boar's tooth. Paper may also be prepared by rubbing dry pigment into the fibers or applying a transparent wash of pigment in water or ink with a brush or sponge. The application of a ground to parchment, wooden tablets, and paper was common by the fifteenth century.

Relief Process

A printing process that transfers ink from the raised surfaces of a block, with the cut-away portions remaining blank. A stiff ink is applied to the raised areas with a dabber (a leather-covered pad) or roller. A piece of paper is laid over the inked surface and light pressure is applied by manually rubbing the paper's reverse with a pad or by placing the sheet in a vertical screw press. Woodcuts and wood engravings are among the most common relief prints.

Silkscreen

A printing process in which an image is transferred from a stencil applied to a gauze screen tautly stretched over a rigid frame. A viscous ink is poured into a margin on the top of the screen and forced through the mesh with a rubber-bladed squeegee. A film of ink is selectively deposited on the areas of the paper beneath the screen where there is no interference from the stencil. Silkscreen ink lies on the surface of the paper in a thick layer and often bears the textile impression of the screen. The silkscreen technique, also known as screen printing and serigraphy, was commercially used for packaging by the late nineteenth century and gained association with fine art printing in America through the Works Progress Administration in the early 1930s.

Soft-Ground Etching

An etching technique that produces the effect of a graphite drawing. Tallow is added to the standard etching ground to create a soft, tacky surface on the etching plate. A piece of paper is placed on the soft ground and the artist draws on the sheet with a pencil. The pressure of the pencil point forces the soft ground to adhere to the paper. As the paper is peeled from the plate, bare metal remains. The exposed metal then is bitten by acid, and when printed by the intaglio method produces a granular line reminiscent of the pencil's texture. Soft-ground etching came into general use during the last half of the eighteenth century.

Stipple Etching

An etching technique that produces a broad tonal effect by using a specialized tool to create densely packed, multiple dots on an etching ground. The ground may be perforated by the point of a stipple graver or an etching needle (sometimes bound together to make multiple points), or a roulette, a small, multitoothed wheel on a metal shaft attached to a handle. The small dots of bared metal are then etched in acid and printed by the intaglio method. The stipple process developed from the crayon manner, an etching technique that creates the effect of a crayon drawing, during the last quarter of the eighteenth century.

Watercolor

A liquid medium of pigment particles dispersed in a solution of water and gum arabic that is applied to paper in washes with fine-haired brushes. Transparent watercolors are often applied in thin glazes to utilize the brilliance of the paper to achieve pale hues; opaque watercolors, often called body colors or gouaches, are produced by mixing a white pigment such as Chinese white (zinc oxide) with colored pigments to produce opaque tints. Watercolor has been used since antiquity to decorate book illustrations, prints, and maps.

Woodcut

The oldest and most basic printing process, in which the plank side of a wood block is carved with knives and gouges to produce an image in raised relief against a cut-away background. A stiff ink is applied to the raised surfaces and transferred to paper by the relief process. Hardwood, such as fruitwood, sycamore, or beech, is traditionally preferred by the woodcut printer.

The earliest known woodcut on paper was produced during the Tang dynasty (A.D. 618–907) in China, where papermaking flourished. The European woodcut evolved from stamped textiles during the last years of the fourteenth century, when European-made paper became generally available. The woodcut print was used to illustrate the movable press type invented by Johann Gutenberg in Germany in the mid-fifteenth century because the wood block and type could be printed together by the relief process.

Wood Engraving

A relief printing process in which fine, V-shaped incisions are engraved on an end-grain block of boxwood with a tool known as a burin or graver similar to that used in engraving. The block is always cut across the grain of the wood, which provides a harder surface than the plank side used for a woodcut. As in the woodcut process, the ink is applied to the raised surfaces of the block and transferred to paper. The advantages of wood engraving over woodcut are the ability of the fine, engraved lines to produce minute detail and the greater durability of the end-grain boxwood. Wood engraving evolved from the woodcut process during the eighteenth century as a means of creating high-quality book illustrations.

Wove Paper

Paper distinguished by its smooth surface created by the wove wire screen mold cover used in sheet formation. A piece of paper is formed as a moist web of pulp cast onto a mold and deckle (see Laid Paper). The wove mold is a mesh of finely woven brass wires attached to a rigid frame; the deckle fits on top of the mold to contain the pulp slurry. Because of the physical arrangement of the moist fibers on the wove mold cover, wove paper, when dried, can exhibit an indistinct twill impression from the screen and appear slightly mottled through transmitted light. The development of wove paper is credited to the typographer John Baskerville, who encouraged its production at the Whatman-Balson Turkey papermill in England during the 1750s.

F.H.Z.

Selected Readings

Ackerknecht, Erwin H. *A Short History of Medicine*. New York, 1955.

Ackerknecht, Erwin H. *A Short History of Psychiatry*. Translated by Sulammith Wolff. 2d rev. ed. New York, 1969.

Amundsen, Darrel W. "Romanticizing the Ancient Medical Profession: The Characterization of the Physician in the Graeco-Roman Novel." *Bulletin of the History of Medicine*, vol. 48, no. 3 (Fall 1974), pp. 320–37.

Bell, E. Moberly. *Storming the Citadel: The Rise of the Woman Doctor*. London, 1953.

Binet, Léon, and Pierre Vallery-Radot. *Médecine et art de la Renaissance à nos jours: Prestige des sciences médicales*. Paris, 1968.

Block, Werner. *Der Arzt und der Tod in Bildern aus sechs Jahrhunderten*. Stuttgart, 1966.

Brockington, C. Fraser. "The History of Public Health." In W. Hobson, ed., *The Theory and Practice of Public Health*, pp. 1–7. 2d ed. London, 1965.

Bullough, Vern L. *The Development of Medicine as a Profession: The Contribution of the Medieval University to Modern Medicine*. New York, 1966.

Camac, C.N.B. *Imhotep to Harvey: Backgrounds of Medical History*. New York, 1931.

Carstens, Henry R. "The History of Hospitals, with Special Reference to Some of the World's Oldest Institutions." *Annals of Internal Medicine*, vol. 10, no. 5 (November 1936), pp. 670–82.

Castiglioni, Arturo. *A History of Medicine*. Edited and translated by E. B. Krumbhaar. 2d ed., rev. and enl. New York, 1947.

Cavendish, Richard, ed. *Man, Myth, and Magic*. 2 pts. New York, 1974.

Charcot, J.-M., and Paul Richer. *Les Difformes et les malades dans l'art*. Amsterdam, 1972.

Choulant, Ludwig. *History and Bibliography of Anatomic Illustration*. Edited and translated by Mortimer Frank. Rev. ed. 1945. Reprint. New York, 1962.

Draper, John W. *The Historical Influence of the Medical Profession*. 1863. Reprint. New York, 1977.

Dubos, René. *Man, Medicine, and Environment*. New York, 1968.

Duffy, John. *The Healers: The Rise of the Medical Establishment*. New York, 1976.

Dumesnil, René. *Histoire illustrée de la médecine*. Paris, 1935.

Faculté de Médecine, Pitié-Salpêtrière, Paris. *Anatomie monde insolite: Europe—Extreme-Orient*. September 29–October 8, 1972.

Fishbein, Morris. *Fads and Quackery in Healing: An Analysis of the Foibles of the Healing Cults, with Essays on Various Other Peculiar Notions in the Health Field*. New York, 1932.

Friends of the University of Iowa Libraries. *Heirs to Hippocrates: The Development of Medicine in a Catalogue of Historic Books in the Health Sciences Library, the University of Iowa*. Iowa City, 1980.

Futcher, Thomas B. "Association between Famous Artists and Anatomists." *Bulletin of the Johns Hopkins Hospital*, vol. 17, no. 178 (January 1906), pp. 38–39.

Garrison, Fielding H. *Contributions to the History of Medicine*. New York, 1966.

Garrison, Fielding H. *An Introduction to the History of Medicine*. 4th ed. Philadelphia, 1929.

Guerini, Vincenzo. *A History of Dentistry from the Most Ancient Times until the End of the Eighteenth Century*. Philadelphia, 1909.

Haggard, Howard W. *Devils, Drugs, and Doctors: The Story of the Science of Healing from Medicine-Man to Doctor*. New York, 1929.

Herrlinger, Robert. *History of Medical Illustration from Antiquity to A.D. 1600*. Nijkerk, The Netherlands, 1970.

Holländer, Eugen. *Anekdoten aus der medizinischen Weltgeschichte*. Stuttgart, 1931.

Holländer, Eugen. *Die Karikatur und Satire in der Medizin: Mediko-kunsthistorische Studie*. 2d ed. Stuttgart, 1921.

Holländer, Eugen. *Die Medizin in der klassischen Malerei*. 2 vols. Stuttgart, 1903.

Holländer, Eugen. *Plastik und Medizin*. Stuttgart, 1912.

Holländer, Eugen. *Wunder, Wundergeburt, und Wundergestalt*. Stuttgart, 1921.

Leake, Chauncey D. *An Historical Account of Pharmacology to the 20th Century*. Springfield, Ill., 1975.

Lyons, Albert S., and R. Joseph Petrucelli. *Medicine: An Illustrated History*. New York, 1978.

MacKinney, Loren. *Medical Illustrations in Medieval Manuscripts*. 2 pts. in 1. Berkeley, 1965.

Majno, Guido. *The Healing Hand: Man and Wound in the Ancient World*. Cambridge, Mass., 1975.

Martí-Ibáñez, Félix. *Ariel: Essays on the Arts and the History and Philosophy of Medicine*. New York, 1962.

Mayor, A. Hyatt. *Artists & Anatomists*. New York, 1984.

McClellan, George. *Anatomy in Its Relation to Art: An Exposition of the Bones and Muscles of the Human Body with Especial Reference to Their Influence upon Its Actions and External Form*. Philadelphia, 1901.

Meyer-Steineg, Th., and K. Sudhoff. *Illustrierte Geschichte der Medizin*. Edited by Robert Herrlinger and Fridolf Kudlien. Stuttgart, 1965.

Onians, Richard Broxton. *The Origins of European Thought: About the Body, the Mind, the Soul, the World, Time and Fate. . . .* 2d ed. Cambridge, 1954.

Osler, William. *The Evolution of Modern Medicine: A Series of Lectures Delivered at Yale University on the Silliman Foundation in April, 1913*. 1921. Reprint. New York, 1972.

Philadelphia Museum of Art. *The Art of Philadelphia Medicine*. September 15–December 7, 1965.

Poynter, F.N.L., ed. *Medicine and Culture: Proceedings of a Historical Symposium Organized Jointly by the Wellcome Institute of the History of Medicine, London, and The Wenner-Gren Foundation for Anthropological Research, New York*. London, 1969.

Richer, Paul. *L'Art et la médecine*. Paris, n.d.

Rousselot, Jean, ed. *Medicine in Art: A Cultural History*. New York, 1967.

Saunders, J. B. deC. M., and Charles D. O'Malley. *The Illustrations from the Works of Andreas Vesalius of Brussels*. 1950. Reprint. New York, 1973.

Schadewaldt, Hans, et al. *Kunst und Medizin*. Cologne, 1967.

Sigerist, Henry E. *Civilization and Disease*. Chicago, 1962.

Sigerist, Henry E. *The Great Doctors: A Biographical History of Medicine*. Translated by Eden Paul and Ceda Paul. 1933. Reprint. New York, 1971.

Sigerist, Henry E. "The Historical Aspect of Art and Medicine." *Bulletin of the Institute of the History of Medicine*, vol. 4, no. 4 (April 1936), pp. 271–97.

Singer, Charles. *From Magic to Science: Essays on the Scientific Twilight*. 1928. Reprint. New York, 1958.

Singer, Charles. *A Short History of Anatomy from the Greeks to Harvey (The Evolution of Anatomy)*. 2d ed. New York, 1957.

Singer, Charles. *A Short History of Medicine: Introducing Medical Principles to Students and Non-Medical Readers*. New York, 1928.

Steinbart, Hiltrud. *Arzt und Patient in der Geschichte, in der Anekdote, im Volksmund*. Stuttgart, 1970.

The Trent Collection, Duke University Medical Center Library, and the Duke University Museum of Art, Durham. *Reflections of Medicine: The Graphic Art*. November 17, 1972–January 7, 1973.

Underwood, E. Ashworth, ed. *Science, Medicine and History: Essays on the Evolution of Scientific Thought and Medical Practice Written in Honour of Charles Singer*. 2 vols. London, 1953.

Veth, Cornelis, ed. *Der Arzt in der Karikatur*. Berlin, n.d.

Wagner, Gustav, and Wolfgang J. Müller. *Dermatologie in der Kunst*. Biberach an der Riss, 1970.

Weber, A. *Tableau de la caricature médicale depuis les origines jusqu'à nos jours*. Paris, 1936.

Weinberger, Bernhard Wolf. *An Introduction to the History of Dentistry*. 2 vols. Saint Louis, 1948.

Wittkower, Rudolf, and Margot Wittkower. *Born under Saturn: The Character and Conduct of Artists. A Documented History from Antiquity to the French Revolution*. London, 1963.

Young, James Harvey. *The Medical Messiahs: A Social History of Health Quackery in Twentieth-Century America*. Princeton, 1967.

Zigrosser, Carl. *Ars Medica: A Collection of Medical Prints by Great Artists of the Past Presented to the Art Museum by Smith, Kline, & French Laboratories*. Philadelphia, 1955.

Zigrosser, Carl. *Medicine and the Artist*. 3d ed., rev. and enl. New York, 1970.

Zimmerman, Leo M., and Ilza Veith. *Great Ideas in the History of Surgery*. 2d rev. ed. New York, 1967.

Index of Artists and Authors

Photographic Credits

Joan M. Broderick: 1–4, 5b–12, 15–17, 18d, 19, 23–31a, 32–34, 36–39, 41b, 43–45, 46b, 48–51, 53, 56–61, 63–72a,c,d, 74, 75, 77, 79–81, 83, 85, 86, 90–105, 108b–12, 115

Will Brown: 35, 113

Eric Mitchell: cover, 14, 18a–c, 20–22, 40, 41a, 46a, 47, 52, 54, 55, 72b, 78, 87, 107, 114, 116

Acknowledgments

It is the nature of a project such as this, which covers a broad swath of the history of art as well as the history of medicine, that many people, each with a special talent, need to be deeply involved to create the final product. The many insights and energies that have been drawn from various perspectives have conjoined to make of this exhibition and catalogue a marvelously rich cloth composed of variegated threads. When properly woven together the diversity of the textures and colors of these threads gives the fabric its vitality, its strength, and ultimately its enduring value. I therefore wish to acknowledge not only those who served as contributing authors but also the many others without whom the project would never have succeeded. I would like also to acknowledge my debt to the late Carl Zigrosser and A. Hyatt Mayor as well as the other scholars and curators who laid the foundation for the interdisciplinary study of Ars Medica. Most importantly, I want to thank my husband, Joel, and my children, Danny and Ellie, who shared the pleasures and the problems, offering sage advice as well as humor, and my parents, who provided wisdom and support as well as perspective.

Kathleen P. Gibbs served as administrative assistant for the project, and it is through her patience and marvelous organizational and secretarial skills that the catalogue reached the light of day. Anne E. Havinga and Jan Howard contributed hours of research and other assistance in the final stages of the exhibition and catalogue as well as support and insights throughout their gestation. I am also grateful to William L. Grala and Peter P. Quinn of SmithKline Beckman Corporation, whose enthusiasm and continuous support made the project possible. It was Jean Sutherland Boggs, former Director of the Philadelphia Museum of Art, who offered me the opportunity to tackle such a new adventure, and David Pease and Philip Betancourt who granted me the leave of absence from teaching at Temple University to pursue it. Martha Chahroudi, Faith H. Zieske, and Denise Thomas listened calmly to the wildest ideas and contributed valuable insights into the organization and management of the project. My special thanks to Sherry Babbitt for providing both sound judgment and excellent editorial advice.

A vast number of people both at the Museum and other institutions also must be properly thanked for their valuable assistance in all phases of the endeavor: Clifford Ackley, Elizabeth A. Anderson, Christine Armstrong, Sheryl Bar, Robert M. Barfield, Jacob Bean, Julie S. Berkowitz, Sarah Bertalan, Nancy Bialler, Natalie Borisovets, Judith Ebbert Boust, Nancy T. Bove, Joan M. Broderick, Janet Byrne, Clarisse Carnell, Jean P. Carr, Gail Casterline, Riva Castleman, Janet M. Chase, Conna Clark, Bernice Connolly, Cynthia Cortenhorst, John Costello, Alan Cristea, Elizabeth Cropper, Marie Culver, Diane DeGrazia, Thomas S. Donio, Elizabeth Drazen, Teri Edelstein, Maria Esposito, Felice Fischer, Beatrice B. Garvan, Lawrence Gowing, Diana Long Hall, Sylvia M. Hamerman, William H. Helfand, Marjorie Lee Hendrix, Gary Hiatt, Shari E. Hiatt, Megan Higgins, Carol Homan, Sandra Horrocks, Thomas A. Horrocks, Joanna Starr Hynes, Christine Hyres, Donald Kaiser, Margaret Kaiser, Constance S. Lehman, Patricia Likos, Edward W. Lind, Louise W. Lippincott, Deborah Marrow, Martha Masiello, Russell Maulitz, Cheryl McClenney, John W. McCoubrey, Dennis McGinty, Sarah Anne McNear, Eric Mitchell, Charlotte Moulton, The Museum Guides, Ruth Muthmann, Otto Naumann, J. Paschetto, Maureen Pelta, Socrates Perakis, Joan Pierpoline, Lois Puglionesi, Robert Rainwater, H. Kathryn Ratner, Joseph J. Rishel, Tara G. Robinson, Charles Rosenberg, Mark Rosenthal, David Rubin, Christine A. Ruggere, Stuart Sammis, D. Lee Savary, Gina Scala, Ella Schaap, William Schupbach, Anne E. Schuster, John Beldon Scott, Barbara S. Sevy, Stuart Shapiro, Thomas Southall, Felice Stamfle, Patricia A. Steele, Allison Stewart, Sara Jane Stone, Yoonjoo Strumfels, Paula Suransky, Beatrice Sussman, Peter C. Sutton, Marion Stroud Swingle, Sarah E. Thompson, Gail E. Tomlinson, Phillip H. Unetic, Jane Iandola Watkins, Suzanne F. Wells, Susan Wheeler, Suzanne Wheeling, Jean Woodley, Elizabeth P. Woods, and my many other associates and friends.

D.K.